Insurgencies and Counterinsurg

This book is a major new study of the extent to which national mentalities, or 'ways of war', are responsible for 'national styles' of insurgency and counterinsurgency. Leading scholars examine the ways of war of particular insurgent movements and the standard operational procedures of states and occupation forces to suppress them. Through case studies ranging from British, American and French counterinsurgency to the IRA and the Taliban, they show how 'national styles' evolve, influenced by transnational trends, ideas and practices. They examine whether we can identify a tendency to resort to a particular pattern of fighting and, if so, whether this is dictated by constants such as geography and climate, or by the available options, or else whether there exists a particular 'strategic culture' or 'national style'. Their findings show that 'national style' is not eternal but can undergo fundamental transformations.

BEATRICE HEUSER occupies a Chair in International Relations at the University of Reading, and holds degrees from the Universities of London (BA, MA) and Oxford (D.Phil), and a Habilitation from the University of Marburg. She has previously taught at universities in London, France and Germany, and briefly worked at NATO headquarters. Publications include *The Evolution of strategy* (2010), *Reading Clausewitz* (2002) and many works on nuclear strategy, NATO, and Transatlantic Relations.

EITAN SHAMIR is a senior research fellow with the Begin Sadat Center for Strategic Studies (BESA) in Bar Ilan University Israel. He was formerly head of the National Security Doctrine Department at the Prime Minister Office, Israel, and served in the IDF General Headquarters. Recent works include *Transforming Command* (2011), as well as many other articles in leading academic journals, and book chapters.

Insurgencies and Counterinsurgencies

National Styles and Strategic Cultures

Edited by

Beatrice Heuser and
Eitan Shamir

CAMBRIDGE
UNIVERSITY PRESS

CAMBRIDGE
UNIVERSITY PRESS

University Printing House, Cambridge CB2 8BS, United Kingdom

Cambridge University Press is part of the University of Cambridge.

It furthers the University's mission by disseminating knowledge in the pursuit of education, learning and research at the highest international levels of excellence.

www.cambridge.org
Information on this title: www.cambridge.org/9781107135048

© Cambridge University Press 2016

This publication is in copyright. Subject to statutory exception and to the provisions of relevant collective licensing agreements, no reproduction of any part may take place without the written permission of Cambridge University Press.

First published 2016

Printed in the United Kingdom by Clays, St Ives plc

A catalogue record for this publication is available from the British Library

Library of Congress Cataloging-in-Publication Data
Names: Heuser, Beatrice, 1961- editor of compilation. | Shamir, Eitan, 1964- editor of compilation.
Title: Insurgencies and counterinsurgencies : national styles and strategic cultures / edited by Beatrice Heuser & Eitan Shamir.
Description: New York : Cambridge University Press, [2016] | Includes index.
Identifiers: LCCN 2016011211 | ISBN 9781107135048 (Hardback)
Subjects: LCSH: Counterinsurgency–History. | Insurgency–History. | Strategic culture.
Classification: LCC U241 .I55 2016 | DDC 355.02/18–dc23 LC record available at http://lccn.loc.gov/2016011211

ISBN 978-1-107-13504-8 Hardback
ISBN 978-1-316-50100-9 Paperback

Cambridge University Press has no responsibility for the persistence or accuracy of URLs for external or third-party internet websites referred to in this publication, and does not guarantee that any content on such websites is, or will remain, accurate or appropriate.

Contents

Contributors

Stephen Blank, Senior Fellow, American Foreign Policy Council, Washington DC, USA

Robert Egnell, Swedish National Defence College, and Georgetown University, USA

Jacques Frémeaux, Collège de France and University of Paris IV Sorbonne, France

Beatrice Heuser, University of Reading, UK

Efraim Inbar, Director, Begin Sadat Centre, University of Bar Ilan, Israel

David E. Johnson, RAND Corporation, USA

Jeannie Johnson, University of Utah, USA

Rob Johnson, Director, Changing Character of War Programme, University of Oxford, UK

Henning Pieper, University of Sheffield, UK

Spyros Plakoudas, Greece

Bruno C. Reis, Institute of Social Sciences–University of Lisbon, Portugal

Eitan Shamir, Begin Sadat Centre, University of Bar Ilan, Israel

Yitzhak Shichor, Hebrew University of Jerusalem, Israel

Jim Storr, Norwegian Military Academy, and Defence College of Management and Technology, Cranfield University, UK

Élie Tenenbaum, Institut des Sciences Politiques, Paris, France

David H. Ucko, National Defence University, USA

Carmit Valensi, Israeli National Security Studies (INSS), Israeli Defense
  Forces Military Intelligence Directorate, Israel

Eyal Zisser, Tel Aviv University, Israel

Acknowledgements

This volume had its origins in a conference that took place at the University of Bar Ilan in February 2012. It was made possible by a generous grant from the Academic Study Group, for which we want to thank Mr John Levy in particular, and by additional funding from the BESA Centre of the University of Bar Ilan, for which our thanks are due for the support of its Director, Professor Efraim Inbar. At the time, Beatrice Heuser was a visiting professor (on the Chaire Dupront) of the University of Paris IV Sorbonne, with some additional funding from the British Academy. Both institutions also deserve our personal thanks, and at the University of Paris IV, especially Professor Jacques Frémeaux. This visiting professorship made it possible for Beatrice Heuser to stay on in Paris for some months after the Chaire Dupront professorship had come to an end and made it possible to take a first stab at co-ordinating this volume.

We want to express our special thanks to Ariel Vishne and Elad Erlich from the BESA Center and to Dr Spyros Plakoudas for their assistance in editing this volume. Elad Erlich has also constructed the Index for this book. Many friends contributed Important advice; among them we must mention Dr. Eado Hecht.

1 Introduction
National Styles and Strategic Culture

Beatrice Heuser and Jeannie Johnson

This book examines a number of insurgency movements on the one hand and on the other hand polities repeatedly engaged in counterinsurgency (COIN) operations. The aim is to ascertain whether, in each case, one can identify a proclivity to resort to a particular pattern of fighting. We will ask whether a pattern exists and, if so, whether this is quite simply dictated by constants such as geography and climate or by the basic options available (a general, not a culture-specific 'tool kit' or instrumentarium for insurgents or COIN operations), or else whether one can speak of a cultural preference, a particular 'strategic culture' or 'national style'. These terms need explanations, and the following section will trace the origins of the notion that there are national or cultural peculiarities in 'ways of waging war' and survey its application in more recent times.

To simplify, our volume asks: Do national mentalities, martial preferences or strictures born of climate and geography compel a level of persistence in national style despite acknowledgement of lessons learned from others' experience in countering insurgents? An interesting aspect of national style and resultant strategic culture is examining the lessons each polity chooses to learn from its own and others' counterinsurgency experiences. Why are some lessons selected and not others? Were erroneous lessons drawn in order to serve a more comfortable fit within national narratives of war? Have counterinsurgency experiences been interpreted in a relatively consistent way?

These and many related questions will be surfacing intermittently throughout the book. But first things first, so let us begin by looking at the genealogy of the terms 'national style', 'Way of War' and 'strategic culture'.

Ways of War and 'National' Style

National Peculiarities

The idea that warring groups behave according to distinctive practices, with different traditions, with different styles, is not a new one. The

1

earliest example of comments on different styles of warfare can be found in the *Iliad*, which contrasts three times the chaotic, noisy Trojan army with the silent, cohesive Achaean Greek forces.[1] Classical writers took note of particular 'ways of war' practiced by Scythians, Persians, Huns, Saracens and Turks among others. In Aeschylus' *Persians* (dated 472 BCE, and thus very soon after the actual Graeco-Persian Wars), the contrast between the way of fighting of the Persians – relying heavily on their archers – and Greeks – who 'arm themselves with shields/and fight in close with spears' – is highlighted repeatedly.[2] Herodotus in his *Histories* had a Greek dismissively caricature the Persian, saying 'These foreigners have little taste for war, and [the Greeks] are the finest soldiers of the world. The Persians' weapons are bows and short spears; they fight in trousers and turbans – that will show you how easy they are to beat!' Elsewhere, he had a Persian concede that while the Greeks were 'pugnacious enough, and start fights on the spur of the moment without sense or judgement to justify them', they were easy for the Persians to vanquish.[3]

The notion that the peculiar fighting styles of a people were something eternal is an enduring characteristic, and linked with the climate, was made in the fourth century BCE by Aristotle, who unsurprisingly came to the conclusion that 'the Hellenic race' had the best balance of courage, passion and brain power, while other peoples had an excess of one and a deficit of the other.[4] Medieval students of Aristotle eagerly snatched up this notion of an inborn difference between races, turning it in a similar fashion to their own people's advantage. We need hardly be surprised that the French, at the latest since the early twelfth century pioneers in the development of medieval proto-nationalism, were also pioneers in appropriating this argument for themselves.[5] Italian-born Christine de Pizan, writing around 1400 for the French monarchy, pleased her countrymen by adoption when she wrote that

Ancient chronicles and a long experience show that the French . . . are courageous and valiant in the use of arms . . . First, this [is] because of the long-standing glory

[1] Homer, *The Iliad*, III.2–8 and IV.428–38, and implicitly at XVII.356–65; see H. van Wees, 'Heroes, Knights and Nutters. Warrior Mentality in Homer', in A. B. Lloyd (ed.), *Battle in Antiquity* (London: Duckworth, 1996), 60.

[2] Aeschylus, *The Persians*, lines 239–40.

[3] Herodotus, *Histories*, V.49.3–4 and VII.9b, here in the translation of Aubrey de Sélincourt (Harmondsworth: Penguin, 1954), 358, 445; see also Hans van Wees, *Greek Warfare: Myths and Realities* (London: Duckworth, 2004), 116.

[4] Aristotle, *Politics* VII.7, here in the translation of T. A. Sinclair (Harmondsworth: Penguin, 1962), 269.

[5] See Guibert of Nogent, *Gesta Dei per Francos* (c. 1107/1108).

and renown of this kingdom ... The second reason is the eventual influence of the planets and the French climate. One sees effectively ... that two qualities are necessary for the good fighter: intelligence and courage ... [I]n hot countries men are not very brave, as they are close to the sun, and the great heat weakens their blood; if they lack courage, they nevertheless do show extreme agility in all they undertake. Those who live in cold regions are by contrast sanguine, as they are far from the sun. They are courageous, but lack judgement. Those, however, who live in temperate regions, are at once courageous, audacious and prudent, as the climes are temperate.[6]

This conviction that the French were superior warriors to other nations became a commonplace in France. By the eighteenth century, French writers on strategy would claim that 'audacity, valour, impetuousness in [armed] clashes, the fury of the first moment are what particularly characterises the French nation' in the conduct of its wars.[7] By then, the French had even convinced their enemies of their particular national peculiarities. A Prussian officer wrote that the French were 'fiery, with a predisposition to be incited to become [extremely] enthusiastic'.[8] By the late nineteenth century, the French had even convinced themselves that they were incapable of a defensive strategy and that only the offensive was appropriate to their military genius, a genius that had been personified by Napoleon.[9]

More neutral notions of different styles in warfare were articulated in modern times by authors who had been struck by them in their own experience. The Welsh mercenary Henry Humphrey Evans Lloyd leaned on the, by then, usual examples from classical antiquity as well as his own experience in the service of three different sovereigns, one French, one Austrian and one Russian, and in the fight against the Ottoman Turks to make claims about marked differences in warfare between one polity type and another.[10] Clausewitz himself in a famous passage emphasised that

[6] Christine de Pizan, *Le Livre des faits et bonnes mœurs du roi Charles V le Sage*, II.xxii, Eric Hicks and Thérèse Moreau (trans. and ed.) (Paris: Stock, 1997), 159f.

[7] F.-J. de Mesnil-Durand, *Fragment de tactique ou six mémoires*, 2 vols. (Paris: Jombert, 1776) quoted in J. A. H. Count de Guibert, *Défense du système de guerre moderne* (1779), reprinted in Comte de Guibert, *Stratégiques* (Paris: l'Herne, 1977), 496.

[8] Anonymous (a Prussian officer), *Abhandlung über den kleinen Krieg und über den Gebrauch der leichten Truppen, mit Rücksicht auf den französischen Krieg* (Berlin: Christian Friedrich Himburg: 1799), 46f.

[9] G. G[ilbert], *Essais critiques et militaires* (Paris: Librairie de la Nouvelle Revue, 1890); G. G[ilbert], *Sept études militaires* (Paris: Librairie de la Nouvelle Revue, 1892).

[10] General H. H. E. Lloyd, *Continuation of the History of the Late War in Germany, between the King of Prussia, and the Empress of Germany and Her Allies*, Part II (1781), in J. Speelman (ed.), *War, Society and Enlightenment: The Works of General Lloyd* (Leiden and Boston: Brill, 2005), 375–478.

the conduct of war differed depending on the period of history and the character of the polity concerned:

> The semibarbarous Tartars, the republics of antiquity, the feudal lords and trading cities of the Middle Ages, eighteenth-century kinds and the rulers and peoples of the nineteenth century – all conducted war in their own particular way, using different methods and pursuing different aims.

Clausewitz then devoted several pages to the particularities in warfare and war aims of successive cultures and specific countries.[11]

In the late nineteenth century, the concept of a 'national Way of War' assumed biological-Darwinist dimensions. For the French, given their '*génie*' and their perception of what suited their particular *mentalité*, this meant embracing the offensive, nothing but the offensive, which contemporary strategists argued conformed best to the inherent French national Way of War, and led to what has been called a 'cult of the offensive'.[12] Oddly, all the other armies of Europe equally embraced the offensive, each for their own supposedly 'national' reasons, as in fact this desire to 'get their retaliation in first' (as one could say sarcastically), to be the most 'virile' and pugnacious in this battle for the survival of the fittest, had infected all of them. The result was the First World War, where the offensive strategies of all sides clashed in a bloody struggle which produced more victims in absolute terms than any previous war.

Writing after the great cataclysm, and building on the works of the naval historians Sir Herbert Richmond and Sir Julian Corbett, it was Captain Basil Liddell Hart who invented the term 'English/British Way of War'. Emerging from the First World War with its unprecedented numbers of casualties in its mass warfare, Liddell Hart like many others was driven by the commitment 'never again' to let this happen. It seemed to him on reflection that this war had been an aberration in English and British warfare. The result of his reflections, published in 1932, postulated that the 'historic Strategy of Britain' had been to keep away from conscription, from mass warfare, and above all, from any Continental commitment. Since the Elizabethan Age, he claimed, the proven successful strategy for Britain had been to keep off Europe's continental landmass and to offset land power by 'sea pressure on the enemy' and 'financial support to all possible allies'. And he concluded, 'I can see no convincing reason why we should have abandoned that practice, proved

[11] Carl von Clausewitz, *On War* (1832) M. Howard and Paret (trans. and ed.) (Princeton, NJ: Princeton University Press, 1984[2]), VIII.3, 586–93.
[12] S. Van Evera, 'The Cult of the Offensive and the Origins of the First World War' and J. Snyder, 'Civil-Military Relations and the Cult of the Offensive, 1914 and 1984' *International Security*, 9/1 (Summer 1984), 58–107, 108–46.

by three centuries' experience of warfare'.[13] He contrasted this with the 'fallacious' strategy of the French, which had led them to the stalemate of the trenches of Flanders.[14]

The formula of the 'Way of War' proved catching. An 'American Way of War' achieved particular fame with the magisterial 1973 study by Russell Weigley. Weigley made the claim that the truly American way, crystallising with the Civil War and so very different from any European aims to limit war, was to go for big battles with overwhelming firepower and massive casualties, which increasingly would affect the enemy rather than the Americans, as technology came in to replace manpower. He even interpreted the Cold War emphasis on nuclear weapons as a strategy of betting on massive firepower.[15] Weigley was inspired by Hans Delbrück's dual interpretation of the history of warfare as oscillating between the two extremes of a war aiming to defeat the enemy armed forces in a decisive battle (the *Niederwerfungsstrategie*, best translated as 'knock-out strategy') and a battle aiming to whittle away the enemy's strength in a long drawn-out war to exhaust his willpower (*Ermattungsstrategie* or 'exhaustion strategy'). Weigley used two translations of these terms, which would lend themselves to endless confusion. For *Niederwerfung* or knock-out blow, he used 'annihilation', not unreasonably, as this was a Clausewitzian expression that permeated German strategy literature in the nineteenth and early twentieth centuries. Only, by it, Clausewitz meant the infliction of a decisive defeat, not the slaughtering of entire armies. For *Ermattung*, the moral and physical exhaustion of the enemy, Weigley chose 'attrition', again not unreasonably so. For Hans Delbrück had created a scandal by criticising General Falkenhayn's strategy of attrition vis-à-vis the French, in which Falkenhayn tried to win by causing more French than German casualties, while seeing soldiers on both sides as dispensable cannon fodder or *matériel* in this gigantic *Materialschlacht*. Delbrück's dualism was too reductionist, however, and it was difficult to classify both Frederick the Great's many short battles in his drawn-out, multi-year wars as 'attrition' (admittedly with comparable casualty figures in total) in just the same way as Falkenhayn's brutal, almost year-long assaults on Verdun resulting in more than 700,000 casualties. The latter seemed like both attrition and annihilation in the sense of mass killing, which was increasingly the connotation of this word in the genocidal context of the two world wars. Weigley, too,

[13] B. H. Liddell Hart, *The British Way of Warfare* (London: Faber and Faber, 1932), 13–41.
[14] Ibid.
[15] R. F. Weigley, *The American Way of War: A History of United States Military Strategy and Policy* (Bloomington: Indiana University Press, 1973).

found it difficult to keep up the clear distinction between the two terms with which he began his narrative,[16] and other authors since have demonstrated their confusion about the terms.[17]

Nevertheless, many authors have taken up the 'American Way of War' formula for their own works.[18] The expression 'Way of War' has since also been applied many times over to other states and entities, talking about a British,[19] a Soviet or Russian,[20] a Canadian, an Arab, a European, a German, a Portuguese, an Afghan or a new Iraqi 'Way of War'.[21] Distinct differences from country to country in approaches to waging war do seem to exist at any one point, as open-eyed foreign observers will find

---

[16] B. M. Linn, 'The American Way of War Revisited', *Journal of Military History*, 66 (April 2002), 501–33.

[17] For example, M. Boot, 'The New American Way of War', *Foreign Affairs*, 41 (2003), 41–58.

[18] To cite just some titles, see E. Luttwak, 'The American Style of Warfare and the Military Balance', *Survival* , (March–April 1979), 57–60; W. K. Maynard, 'The New American Way of War', *Military Review*, 73/11 (1993), 5–10; F. G. Hoffman, *'Decisive Force': The New American Way of War* (Westport, CT: Praeger, 1996); R. B. Myers, 'The New American Way of War', *Military Technology*, 27/6 (2003), 64–75; A. K. Cebrowski and T. M. Barnett, 'The American Way of War', *British Army Review*, 131 (2003), 42–3; J. Laiq, 'High Explosive Hysteria: American Way of War', *Economic and Political Weekly*, 38/18 (2003), 1763–70; see also A. Echevarria, *Toward an American Way of War* (Carlisle, PA: US Army War College, 2004); T. Mahnken, *Technology and the American Way of War since 1945* (New York: Columbia University Press, 2008); M. B. Maitre, 'Echoes and Origins of a American Way of War', *Comparative Strategy*, 27/3 (2008), 248–66; Eugene Jarecki, *The American Way of War* (New York: Free Press, 2008); B. M. Linn, 'The American Way of War', *Magazine of History*, 224 (2008), 19–24; D. Tierney, *How We Fight: Crusades, Quagmires, and the American Way of War* (Boston: Little Brown, 2010); S. F. Kime, 'Return to the American Way of War', *Proceedings of the US Naval Institute*, 137/5 (2011), 40–3; F. G. Hoffman, 'Reassessing the American Way of War', *Orbis*, 55/3 (2011), 524–36; J. Kurlantzki, *The Ideal Man: The Tragedy of Jim Thompson and the American Way of War* (Hoboken, NJ.: Wiley, 2011); H. Rockoff, *America's Economic Way of War: War and the US Economy from the Spanish-American War to the First Gulf War* (Cambridge: Cambridge University Press, 2012).

[19] K. Nelson and G. Kennedy, *The British Way of Warfare: Power and the International System, 1856–1956* (Farnham: Ashgate, 2010).

[20] N. Leites, 'The Soviet Style of War', in Derek Leebaert (ed.), *Soviet Military Thinking* (London: George Allen and Unwin, 1981), 185–224; R. Harrison, *The Russian Way of War: Operational Art, 1904–1940* (Lawrence: University Press of Kansas, 2001).

[21] J. Cann, *Counterinsurgency in Africa: The Portuguese Way of War, 1961–1974* (Westport, CT: Greenwood, 1997); R. Gimblett, R. H. Edwards and A. L. Griffiths, 'The Canadian Way of War: Experience and Principles', in *Intervention and Engagement: A Maritime Perspective* (Halifax: Centre for Foreign Policy Studies, Dalhousie University, 2002); Layton, 'The New Arab Way of War', *Proceedings of the US Naval Institute*, 129/3 (2003), 62–63; S. Everts, *A European Way of War* (London: Centre for European Reform, 2004); M. Shaw, *The New Western Way of War: Risk-Transfer War and Its Crisis in Iraq* (Cambridge: Polity, 2005); R. Citino, *The German Way of War: From the Thirty Years' War to the Third Reich* (Lawrence: University Press of Kansas, 2005); S. J. Freedberg, 'The New Iraqi Way of War', *National Journal*, 39/23 (2007), 36–43; R. Johnson, *The Afghan Way of War: Culture and Pragmatism, a Critical History* (London: Hurst, 2011).

out quickly when comparing attitudes in their own countries to those of another when moving there for any length of time. Stanley Hoffmann, a French intellectual with Austrian parents who held a chair at Harvard, devoted many works to an 'American Style' of foreign policy making which he contrasted with that of France or other European countries with which he was familiar. Yet unlike some of the earlier authors, he did not claim that these were perennial and unchangeable features of the political cultures he knew.[22]

If there are distinctions between countries, are some of them, nevertheless, united by a more general albeit emphatically not universally human pattern? The concept of a 'Western Way of War' encapsulates this notion. It can be traced to the British historian Geoffrey Parker, who spoke about 'the Western Way of War, which ... boasts great antiquity'. He described it as resting upon several principles. 'First, the armed forces of the West have placed heavy reliance on superior technology, usually to compensate for inferior numbers.' Secondly, 'Western military practice has always exalted discipline ... in the twin forms of drill and long-term service'. Discipline was again required to compensate for numeric inferiority. Discipline was so important because Western 'wars were normally won by infantry'. Thirdly, Parker postulated that there was a great continuity in Western military tradition. This, Parker claimed, included the war aim of annihilating the enemy army – retro-projecting Clausewitz's views onto previous centuries: '[T]he overall aim of western strategy, whether in battle, siege, or attrition, almost always remained the total defeat and destruction of the enemy. And this contrasted starkly with the military practice of many other societies'. He thought that, in contrast to this, tribal warfare tended to produce far fewer casualties. To Parker, the fourth constant was a willingness to innovate, adapt and learn.[23]

It is in the nature of the basic configuration within which insurgencies occur, namely the predominance of a hated regime which controls most of a polity's resources (normally the state apparatus including, crucially, the armed forces). A Western 'Way of War,' as sketched by Parker, usually fits that of the (in the past, mostly, but not exclusively, 'Western') colonial power. Of these four factors, in the context of insurgency, the first

---

[22] S. Hoffmann, *Gulliver's Troubles: On the Setting of American Foreign Policy* (New York: McGraw-Hill, 1968); and see J.-B. Duroselle, 'Les changements dans la politique étrangère de la France depuis 1945', in S. Hoffmann et al. (eds.), *A la recherche de la France* (Paris: Eds. du Seuil, 1963).

[23] G. Parker, 'Introduction', in G. Parker (ed.), *The Cambridge Illustrated History of Warfare: The Triumph of the West* (Cambridge: Cambridge University Press, 1995, rev. ed. 2008), 2–9.

three rarely obtain, because insurgents tend to be confronted with *superior* government forces. In the context of insurgencies but also counterinsurgency, the principle of destruction can only apply to the 'enemy' narrowly defined, the leaders and militants of any insurgency, because what is being fought over tends to be the land, its resources and above all its (productive) population. To do these great harm would mean 'destroying the village to defend it' – admittedly something at least one Western power has been accused of in the past.

A similar interpretational pattern that can be found on the higher level of interstate relations is postulated by Thucydides fans among the International Relations theorists of the 'Realist' school, a name based on the claim that their own understanding of the world is 'realistic' as opposed to that of ideologically driven scholars supposedly describing interstate relations as they should be, not as they are.[24] Intrigued by what they perceive as the great 'modernity' of Thucydides' interpretations of the Peloponnesian War, these scholars have tended to connect the dots between him, then – completely omitting the millennium of medieval history – on to Machiavelli, then leapfrogging the intervening centuries straight on to nineteenth- and twentieth-century interstate relations and finally to twentieth-century international relations theory to illustrate a supposed continuity.[25] They tend to dispense with any requirements for a special understanding of the Hellenic world of Thucydides' times let alone its language, not to mention the centuries in between which this picture almost invariably leaves out.[26] One of them, Victor Davis

[24] H. J. Morgenthau, 'Six Principles of Political Realism', in R. J. Art and R. Jervis (eds.), *International Politics: Enduring Concepts and Contemporary Issues*, 8th ed. (New York: Pearson, 2007), 7–14.

[25] See the contributions by K. Hoekstra, 'Thucydides and the Bellicose Beginnings of Early Modern Political Theory'; S. Forde, 'Thucydides and 'Realism' among the Classics of International Relations', and R. N. Lebow, 'International Relations and Thucydides', in Katherine Harloe and Ned Morley (eds.), *Thucydides and the Modern World* (Cambridge: Cambridge University Press, 2012).

[26] See, for example, D. Garst, 'Thucydides and Neorealism', *International Studies Quarterly*, 33/1 (March 1989), 3–27; S. Forde, 'Varieties of Realism: Thucydides and Machiavelli', *Journal of Politics*, 54/2 (May, 1992), 372–93; L. J. Bagby, 'The Use and Abuse of Thucydides in International Relations', *International Organization*, 48/1 (Winter 1994), 131–53; S. Forde, 'International Realism and the Science of Politics: Thucydides, Machiavelli and Neorealism', *International Studies Quarterly*, 39/2 (June 1995), 141–60; Ahrensdorf, 'Thucydides' Realistic Critique of Realism', *Polity*, 30/2 (Winter 1997), 231–65; D. Kagan, *The Origins of War and the Preservation of Peace* (London: Pimlico, 1997); A. Eckstein, 'Thucydides, the Outbreak of the Peloponnesian War, and the Foundations of International Systems Theory', *International History Review*, 25/4 (Dec. 2003), 757–74; J. Monten, 'Thucydides and Modern Realism', *International Studies Quarterly*, 50/1 (Mar. 2006), 3–25. For a transposition of the Western Way of War to the United States, see R. Kagan, *Dangerous Nation: America and the World, 1600–1898* (New York: Knopf, 2006).

Hanson, has claimed this great continuity for a 'Western Way of War' in the sense of Geoffrey Parker and has postulated such continuity not just since early modern times, but all the way back from Hellenic times to the present. He starts with Herodotus, who has a Persian mocking the Greeks for going off together with their adversaries

to the smoothest and levellest bit of ground they can find, and hav[ing] their battle on it – with the result that even the victors never get off without heavy losses, and for the losers – well, the're wiped out. Now surely, as they all talk the same language, they ought to be able to find a better way of settling their differences: by negotiation, for instance or an interchange of views – indeed anything rather than fighting.[27]

This type of frontal confrontation in an all-out battle with high casualty figures is at the centre of what Hanson defines as a 'Western Way of War'. It is contrasted with a 'barbarian' (or Eastern) Way of War, for which Thucydides gives a summary, expressed by the Spartan general Brasidas in 423 BCE:

These opponents of ours ... fight in no sort of order, they have no sense of shame about giving up a position under pressure. To run forwards and to run backwards are equally honourable in their eyes, and so their courage can never really be tested, since, when every man is fighting on his own, there is always a good excuse for everyone saving his own skin. Otherwise they would join battle, instead of simply making a noise.[28]

These two passages not only seem to illustrate a 'Western' versus an 'Eastern' Way of War, but they also fit into a pattern of regular versus irregular warfare in an asymmetric conflict, portraying the respective preferences in fighting of counterinsurgency and insurgent forces, the former drawing on their conventional superiority, the latter generally on the avoidance of frontal clashes.[29]

Patrick Porter has noted that such a portrayal of cowardly barbarians – soon to become 'Orientals' in the definition of Edward Said – would be used as a cliché and anti-template for a self-portrayal of Westerners as brave, honest, straight-forward fighters – and proud of being so – in keeping with the Herodotus passage above,[30] culminating in Hanson's

---

[27] Herodotus, *The Histories*, VII.9b, here in the translation of A. de Sélincourt (Harmondsworth: Penguin, 1954), 445.

[28] Thucydides, *History of the Peloponnesian War*, IV.126, here in R. Warner's translation (London: Penguin, 1972), 341f.

[29] Exceptions, like Boudicca's Iceni's confrontation with the Romans in battle in 69 BCE, tend to end badly for the insurgents.

[30] Porter, *Military Orientalism: Eastern War through Western Eyes* (London: Hurst and Co, 2009).

narrative and resultant interpretations. Hanson, in turn, has been criti-
cised by many authors, from classical scholars to specialists on more
recent periods. Hanson either chose to ignore for his study (like the
Middle Ages) or which he arguably misinterpreted (like the 'Age of
Battles').[31]

Strategic Culture, National Style and Mentality

A more flexible concept was developed in the late 1970s in the term
'strategic culture', coined by Columbia University scholar Jack Snyder
and defined by him as '[T]he sum total of ideas, conditioned emotional
responses and patterns of habitual behavior that members of a national
strategic community have acquired through instruction or imitation with
each other with regard to nuclear strategy'. This, not other forms of war
such as small wars, was at the time the preoccupation of most leading
writers on strategy.[32]

Snyder was part of the first generation of strategic culture theorists who
devised this concept as a supplement, or amelioration, to the explanatory
shortcomings of the International Relations theories of 'Realism' and
'Neorealism'.[33] In Britain, Aberystwyth's professor Ken Booth propa-
gated Snyder's concept of strategic culture further.[34] Snyder, Booth and
the Anglo-American Colin S. Gray rejected the 'black box' theory
espoused by Realism and Neorealism, that is, the assumption that the
behaviour of states on the world stage is universally rational and could be
predicted according to commonly understood survival patterns in a fight-
for-survival world of anarchy.[35]

Moreover, Snyder claimed that 'once a distinctive approach to strategy
takes hold of members of a strategy-making elite and those writing about
strategy (jointly often referred to as the strategic community), it tends to
persist despite changes in the circumstances that gave rise to it, through
processes of socialization and institutionalization and through the role of

---

[31] Wees, *Greek Warfare*, 131–50; H. Sidebottom, *Ancient Warfare: A Very Short Introduction* (Oxford: Oxford University Press, 2004), passim; J. A. Lynn, *Battle: A History of Combat and Culture* (Boulder: Westview, 2003), 12–20 and passim.

[32] J. Snyder, *The Soviet Strategic Culture: Implications for Limited Nuclear Operations* (Santa Monica, CA: RAND Corporation, 1977), 8.

[33] J. Katzenstein (ed.), *The Culture of National Security: Norms and Identity in World Politics* (New York: Columbia University Press, 1996); and J. Glenn, D. Howlett and S. Poore (eds.), *Neorealism versus Strategic Culture* (Burlington, VT: Ashgate, 2004).

[34] K. Booth, 'The Concept of Strategic Culture Affirmed', in C. G. Jacobsen (ed.), *Strategic Power: The United States of America and the USSR* (London: Macmillan, 1990), 123.

[35] See K. N. Waltz, 'The Anarchic Structure of World Politics', in Art and Jervis (eds.), *International Politics*, 29–49.

strategic concepts in legitimating these social arrangements.'[36] This 'cultural inertia' is perhaps most striking when the evidence suggests that organizational beliefs or habits are out of step with new realities. This is demonstrated by Douglas Porch and Elizabeth Kier in their studies of the French defence posture before and after the First World War. Whereas Porch and others diagnosed a French obsession with the offensive à outrance,[37] Kier found that the French military leadership's distrust of conscript forces led them to dismiss the possibility of Germany attacking France and making great advances with their own conscript armies.[38] Despite being proved wrong, the French maintained their attitudes towards conscripts during the interwar years, when the political left won France's internal debate on the structure of the military, restricting its ranks to one-year conscriptions. Given this restriction, the French military elite resigned themselves to a defensive posture. Kier explained the establishment of this defensive posture as a result of the continuing organizational mind-set concerning the capabilities of conscript.[39] Traditions, tied to preferred ways of war, are difficult to give up.[40]

A further refinement of the interpretational tools was proposed by Valerie Hudson, who argued that cultural habits in the form of 'foreign policy action templates' are a far better potential predictor of state action than variables as elusive as beliefs or values: 'What culture provides its members is a repertoire or palette of adaptive responses from which members build off-the-shelf strategies of action. What matters for an analysis of behaviour is not the whole of culture, but rather "chunks" of pre-fabricated cultural response'.[41] Even if habitual solutions are somewhat suboptimal, they may be less 'expensive' in terms of time and energy than pausing before each

---

[36] J. Snyder, 'The Concept of Strategic Culture: Caveat Emptor', in C. G. Jacobsen (ed.), *Strategic Power: The United States of America and the USSR* (London: Macmillan, 1990), 4.

[37] D. Porch, *The March to the Marne: The French Army 1871–1914* (Cambridge: Cambridge University Press, 1981); C. W. Sanders: 'No Other Law: The French Army and the Doctrine of the Offensive', RAND Corporation P-7331 (March 1987); J. C. Cairns, 'International Politics and the Military Mind: The Case of the French Republic, 1911–1914', *Journal of Modern History*, 25 (March–Dec. 1953), 273–85.

[38] E. Kier, 'Culture and Military Doctrine: France between the Wars', *International Security*, 19/4 (Spring 1995), 82.

[39] Ibid., 68.

[40] K. Avruch, *Culture and Conflict Resolution* (Washington, DC: United States Institute of Peace Press, 2006), 20.

[41] V. Hudson, 'Cultural Expectations of One's Own and Other Nations' Foreign Policy Action Templates', *Political Psychology*, 20/4 (Dec. 1999), 768.

decision to weigh options carefully. This approach to rationality goes some distance in explaining 'cultural inertia' or bureaucratic practices that seem to have little fit with external context. Alastair Iain Johnston approaches the subject of historical inertia from a slightly different angle. His explanation focuses on the durability of heuristics. Early, formative experiences craft interpretive lenses that are slow to change, 'lagging behind changes in "objective" conditions'.[42]

The emphasis on long-lasting mind-sets, however, is not tantamount to claiming that they are immutable. This is very well explained in the complex approach taken by Colin Gray to the subject of strategic culture and Stanley Hoffmann's 'national style'. Gray in a book and a polemic article written during the last peak of the Cold War squared the circle by at once identifying fairly long-term characteristics of American defence strategy while emphasising their mutability and the big discontinuities in their evolution over a century or more (with a particular weight accorded to 1945 as the turning point). In a seminal essay, he showed himself to be particularly concerned not about the views of the American population as a whole, nor of the military in particular; instead, he admitted that his interest lay with the 'American defence community', all those writing and debating about (mainly nuclear) strategy.[43] In later works (see below), he focused particularly on the distinct strategic cultures of the US armed forces, a term he had previously used as a synonym of 'national style', but which he later found to be a useful label for strategy preferences of different sub-groups within a nation, in particular the different branches of the armed forces, the 'defence' or 'strategic community' of intellectuals writing on the subject, who in the United States would move in and out of government and out of and into academia with the revolving door of federal elections.

A thread that thus runs through recent scholarship is a renewed emphasis on the dynamism and complexity of culture, a topic which naturally prompts questions about the causes of cultural shift over time. Positions on this topic range the spectrum from Patrick Porter's portrayal of culture as menus of choice – undergoing constant morphing on the battlefield[44] – to Colin Gray's insistence that 'a community does not choose its strategic culture ... When attitudes, assumptions, habits of mind, and behaviours are sufficiently established and

---

[42] A. I. Johnston, *Cultural Realism: Strategic Culture and Grand Strategy in Chinese History* (Princeton, NJ: Princeton University Press, 1995), 1.

[43] C. S. Gray, *Nuclear Strategy and National Style* (New York: Hudson Institute, 1981); C. S. Gray, 'National Style in Strategy: The American Example', *International Security*, 6/2 (Autumn 1981), 21–47.

[44] Porter, *Military Orientalism*.

enduring to merit description as cultural, they are not easily amended, let alone overturned, by acts of will'.[45]

A similar attempt at identifying a national mentality, mind-set or at least framework of beliefs and reference, in constant flux with both important elements of continuity between important events and watersheds introducing significant shifts in attitude, was made by Beatrice Heuser. Her approach comes from the French *Annales* school of historiography of mentalities, the more recent offspring of which is now referred to as 'cultural history'.[46] Inspired by anthropological approach[47] the *Annales* school's members had set out to research the *mentalités* or collective mentalities and world views of peoples living in previous centuries, to uncover peculiar assumptions about the world, themselves, their adversaries and so on, sometimes assumptions that were not openly articulated because taken for granted at the time and thus difficult for later generations to reconstruct. A comparison of Britain, France and West Germany throughout the Cold War demonstrated that it was not any geographic differences or available manpower or hardware which determined their beliefs and preferences in the context of nuclear deterrence, as these arguably did not matter much in an age of air power and missiles. Instead, it was above all different historical experiences interpreted in ways that formed a framework of reference known to anybody living in these three countries, and their interpretations combined with particular sets of values, that determined strategic outlooks and debates.[48]

This did not and does not mean that everybody in a country thinks the same about subjects such as nuclear deterrence, defence in general, particular wars or a particular insurgency or counterinsurgency campaign – far from it. Within a polity, opposing groups favour different options. 'Strategic culture' can rarely be referenced in the singular for any particular regime. There is not, typically, one internal variety. Thus for Britain and West Germany, Heuser sketched various strategic

---

[45] C. S. Gray, 'British and American Strategic Cultures', paper prepared for Jamestown Symposium 2007: 'Democracies in Partnership: 400 Years of Transatlantic Engagement' (18–19 April 2007), 37. See also Gray's 'Irregular Enemies and the Essence of Strategy: Can the American Way of War Adapt?', Strategic Studies Institute monograph, March 2006, available at www.strategicstudiesinstitute.army.mil/pubs/display.cfm?pubID=650, accessed on 13 February 2015.

[46] See the works edited by R. Madrou and Ariès in the series *Civilisations et Mentalités* of the Parisian academic publisher Plon.

[47] See especially the path-breaking works of 'historical anthropology' of French medievalists, especially J. Le Goff and E. Leroy Ladurie.

[48] B. Heuser, *NATO, Britain, France and the FRG: Nuclear Strategies and Forces for Europe, 1949–2000* (London: Macmillan 1997); B. Heuser, *Nuclear Mentalities? Strategies and Belief Systems in Britain, France and the FRG* (London: Macmillan, 1998).

sub-cultures, each with their own take on nuclear strategy. Sometimes sub-cultures can converge in consensus: since the 1970s, the French have a consensus on nuclear deterrence.[49] Referring much the same thing, Walter Russell Mead identifies what he calls four distinct 'narratives' within US strategic culture and posits that its various foreign policies are formed from the 'collisions and debates' they inspire.[50] The idea of composite cultures is not restricted to analysis of the United States: authors writing on the United Kingdom, France and Germany,[51] China,[52] India,[53] and Iran,[54] to name a few countries, all note the internal conflict of competing views of security based on different narratives and world views within these cultures.

Strategic culture will also diverge in different branches of government and among different branches of the armed forces, as Jeannie Johnson's book on the particular culture of the US Marine Corps demonstrates.[55] Yet there again, they are subject to change. While Larry Cable noted that in the first half of the twentieth century marine doctrine was 'less hairy-chested' than US army doctrine,[56] by the early twenty-first century, the opposite seems to be the case. Oliver M Lee points out that that this does not render strategic cultures irrational or dysfunctional. Lee argues, rather, that a 'nation's political culture is the sum of many major subcultures ... [which] makes possible the formation of coalitions of subcultures, coalitions competing with each other to become and/or remain the dominant one'.[57]

What different sub-cultures within a polity have in common, however, is a repertoire of historical and value references, references to particular

---

[49] Heuser, *Nuclear Mentalities?*, chapters 2, 3. This was also articulated later by J. Black, *War and the Cultural Turn* (Cambridge: Polity, 2012), 3–5.

[50] W. Russell Mead, *Special Providence: American Foreign Policy and How It Changed the World* (New York: Century Foundation, 2001), xvii.

[51] Heuser, *Nuclear Mentalities?*, chapter 4; Anja Dalgarrd-Nielsen, 'The Test of Strategic Culture: Germany, Pacifism and Pre-emptive Strikes', *Security Dialogue*, 36 (2005), 339–45.

[52] H. Feng, 'A Dragon on Defence: Explaining China's Strategic Culture', in Johnson, Kartchner and Larsen (eds.), *Strategic Culture and Weapons of Mass Destruction*, 171–88.

[53] R. W. Jones, 'India's Strategic Culture and the Origins of Omniscient Paternalism', in Johnson, Kartchner and Larsen (eds.), *Strategic Culture and Weapons of Mass Destruction*, 117–36.

[54] A. Molavi, *The Soul of Iran: A Nation's Journey to Freedom* (New York: W. W. Norton, 2002).

[55] J. Johnson, *The US Marine Corps and the Problem of American Counterinsurgency* (Georgetown University Press, forthcoming). See also C. H. Builder, *The Masks of War* (Baltimore: Johns Hopkins University Press, 1989).

[56] L. E. Cable, *Conflict of Myths: Development of Counterinsurgency Doctrine and the Vietnam War* (New York: State University of New York Press, 1986), 281.

[57] O. M. Lee, 'The Geopolitics of American's Strategic Culture', *Comparative Strategy*, 27/3 (2008), 269.

debates or sayings, which are particular to that polity, united by its state, its election campaigns and their debates, its parliament and, very importantly, its press and public discourse.[58] One might say that it is with this repertoire of references as arguments or building blocks that debates are conducted within each polity about what policy or strategy to adopt. Closer study reveals that they are not logically coherent belief systems but rather clusters of beliefs, clusters of narratives each with their own particular moral (which can contradict each other), which are evoked for political purposes.

The Limits of Strategic Culture

No serious scholar of international relations would argue that the strategic culture component of security policy is the only variable influencing outcome. Readily acknowledged in the field is that strategy is a heavily contested enterprise in which a number of weighty players collide.[59] Strategy, and security policy generally, is the negotiated result of elite (usually civilian) agendas processed through national culture, the national policy process and security-related organizational cultures, constrained by material capabilities and inhibited or advanced by external actors. The 'strategic culture' portion of this formula is simply the influence of organizational and other cultures on strategy.

David Haglund in a critical essay compares the concept of strategic culture to equally amorphous and contested concepts such as 'power' and 'wealth'. Despite eluding precise definition, these remain essential components of understanding security policy. Wrangling over a definition appears to be a rather normal part of a concept's growth in any discipline. 'Thus, if strategic culture is to follow the normal trajectory of political concepts ... we can expect not only that debates about its meaning will be ceaseless, but that it will be prone, as are all concepts, to expansion'.[60] Haglund is right on both accounts. Snyder's original, narrow focus on the 'national strategic community' as the keeper of strategic culture and 'nuclear strategy' as its aim has since been widened considerably by scholars. Today some definitions stretch the entire spectrum of actors and issues relevant to security policy. By way of example, a group of scholars (including Jeannie Johnson) tasked by the Defence

---

[58] Heuser, *Nuclear Mentalities?*, chapter 5.
[59] Lawrence Freedman emphasises the importance of coalition building in this game; see *Strategy: A History* (Oxford: Oxford University Press, 2013).
[60] D. Haglund, 'What Good Is Strategic Culture?', in Johnson, Kartchner and Larsen (eds.), *Strategic Culture and Weapons of Mass Destruction*, 16.

Threat Reduction Agency to create a comprehensive strategic culture curriculum did so employing the following definition:

Strategic culture is that set of shared beliefs, assumptions, and modes of behavior, derived from common experiences and accepted narratives (both oral and written), that shape collective identity and relationships to other groups, and which determine appropriate ends and means for achieving security objectives.[61]

Reflecting on that definition and the scholarship that has since emerged, it is clear that the utility of the strategic culture approach has weakened in nearly direct proportion to its definitional expansion.[62] As has been effectively argued by Christopher Twomey, security studies that attempt to draw predictive power from the amorphous and often internally contradictory substance we call 'culture' often suffer follies of overgeneralization and static analysis and as a consequence reach questionable conclusions about the sources of security policy.[63] Colin Gray, as one of the first propagators of the concept, does not disagree. His recent work on strategy and culture argues that scholarship which attempts grand profiles often dispenses with complexity in the interest of an elegant simplicity that usually distorts reality.[64]

To summarise: states generally tend to contain several strategic cultures, but they co-exist with a common framework of reference, often in fierce debate with one another. Several caveats and limitations of the concept should be noted. For one, not all strategic (sub-)cultures are of great importance to policy making, so that the analyst might be advised to focus on those most likely to have most impact: organizational, national, tribal, ethnic or regional subcultures may shift considerably depending on the particular policy issue in question.

Most work, to date, privileges elite culture (usually at the organizational level), arguing with Dalgarrd-Nielsen that although public opinion may influence which of the various narratives within a policy compete for prominence, 'it is arguably the elite – owing to its role as gatekeeper, its expert knowledge and its privileged access to means of communication – that ultimately decides which way security policy goes.'[65] This logic

---

[61] Johnson, Kartchner and Larsen (eds.), *Strategic Culture and Weapons of Mass Destruction*.

[62] For a thorough review of strategic culture's theoretical history, see A. I. Johnston, *Cultural Realism: Strategic Culture and Grand Strategy in Chinese History* (Princeton, NJ: Princeton University Press, 1995), 4–31; J. S. Lantis, 'Strategic Culture: From Clausewitz to Constructivism', in Johnson, Kartchner and Larsen (eds.), *Strategic Culture and Weapons of Mass Destruction*, 33–52.

[63] C. Twomey, 'Lacunae in the Study of Culture in International Security', *Contemporary Security Policy*, 29/2 (August 2008), 338–57.

[64] C. S. Gray, *Perspectives in Strategy* (Oxford: Oxford University Press, 2013), 191–200.

[65] Dalgarrd-Nielsen, 'The Test of Strategic Culture', 342.

breaks down when one is assessing strategic culture within the context of counterinsurgency and stability operations. Given the pivotal role of local popular opinion and reaction to policy in this type of military engagement, understanding public culture, the cultures of the distinctive services, of the insurgent group(s) and significant sub-state groups becomes very important. The level of culture studied, and specific actor selected, must therefore be made explicit, and the main focus should depend on the policy issue in question and the fora in which debated, decided upon and implemented.

Secondly, as we have noted, strategic cultures, like their national counterparts, are periodically reinvented human constructs. They are subject to change, at times very profound change. Therefore, any tool devised to track strategic culture must employ questions that assume culture as somewhat moving target and look for areas where we might expect the next round of change. It is this core of assumptions that form the bedrock of this collective project.

Is There a Toolbox for Insurgents and Counterinsurgents?

Let us turn, then, to the set of tools or the instrumentarium of measures that have been resorted to in attempts to stage or counter insurgencies. Below we will list and briefly discuss measures that we have identified on one or both sides in such struggles. We will owe our readers the evidence to prove the recurrence of such measures until the final chapter, where we will consolidate such evidence so as to avoid duplication – but the method we have applied was, first, to identify such tools employed throughout history, and then to look out for them in the case studies presented in this book.[66]

There is no need here to list the obvious tactical measures in the context of clashes with the enemy's armed forces taken by weaker forces against stronger forces or of analogous measures by stronger forces against rebels, such as the resort to ambushes, surprise attacks especially at night or other stratagems of all sorts. Our interest here lies more in strategic approaches, or military measures with pronounced political, social and economic dimensions, which fall into a number of sub-categories:

- Brutal large-scale repression, indiscriminate killing or mutilation of civilians
- Burning towns and villages and/or 'scorched earth' tactics

---

[66] We may not have come across the earliest historically documented examples, but we are furnishing some such examples in our conclusions to show that these measures and tools are not recent inventions, let alone features of 'new wars'.

- Rounding up and executing leaders and/or targeted assassinations, and for this purpose creating 'bandit-hunter' units largely resembling the irregular units that are being fought
- Mutilations and rape
- Hostage taking and executions
- Forced populations transfers ('ethnic cleansing')
- *Quadrillage* – the control of territory by the COIN forces
- Sanctuary for insurgents outside the state's boundary
- Destruction of symbolic buildings and sites.

Benign Tools

The toolbox of insurgents and counterinsurgency forces also contains benign instruments, which are often subsumed under what is called a 'hearts and minds' approach.[67] Articulated since the sixteenth century by theoreticians and practitioners from several European countries – most notably, Spain, France and Italy and more recently the United States and the United Kingdom – these have included

- Deposing a (bad) government against which insurgents had risen up on the assumption that they had at least some good reason for their uprising, installing a new, better government
- Setting up different (often more participatory) government structures, holding elections, ultimately handing over the government to the local population (this, of all the tools listed, is the most recent one)
- Social welfare programmes and economic aid
- Building schools, hospitals, roads and other infrastructure
- Ensuring freedom of worship and cultural autonomy
- Building new, better, protected villages, patrolling and defending them ('strategic hamlets')
- Reforming/retraining the police and the judiciary system
- Issuing amnesties for all but the most extreme rebel leaders
- Propaganda and 'psychological warfare' measures which, it was generally admitted, had to be backed by concrete measures such as those listed above
- Spreading (usually republican, democratic, or communist) values by applying the above tools in the best interest of the populations.

---

[67] For the classical origins and theories of 'hearts and minds' approaches, see Beatrice Heuser, 'Atrocities in Insurgencies and Counterinsurgencies', in *Atrocities in Insurgencies and Counterinsurgencies*, special issue of peer-reviewed journal *Civil Wars*, 14/1 (March 2012), 2–28.

These values and ideals were supposed to spread, on top of these beneficial measures, like an oil slick – the *'tache d'huile'* of French theoreticians, but this is a concept that long predates the French term.[68]

It is debatable whether these tools existed in theory more than in practice, as successful instances of pacification and good governance have always left a weaker trace in the history books than tyranny and oppression leading to violent resistance. The following chapters will, however, give examples of all of these.

The Approach Taken in This Volume

Our approach of looking for national peculiarities or 'styles' has been applied previously to individual countries. Some very good collections of essays have compared the approaches of different countries to strategy (usually concerning major war) or war aims. There have also been a handful of collections on insurgencies and COIN strategies. Ronald Haycock's concise and impressive early volume *Regular Armies and Insurgencies* contains fairly narrow historical case studies mainly covering single episodes (such as British dealings with the Irish Insurgency 1918–1921, the French in the Algerian War, the Americans in Vietnam). Haycock's aim was not to draw comparative conclusions on national style but rather to offer a range of historical experience for consideration by future COIN strategists.[69] Ian Beckett's and John Pimlott's comparable edited volume, written in the last decade of the Cold War, contains excellent contributions which focus primarily on the 1960s and 1970s and consequently could not draw much (if at all) on archival sources, so that some of the chapters are in need of updating. They include the case studies of the British Dhofar Campaign 1970–1975, French experiences since the Second World War, the United States in Vietnam, Uruguay's 1963–1973 campaign against the Tupamaros, the Portuguese campaign in Mozambique 1964–1974 and the South African campaign in the border area to Namibia in the 1960s and 1970s.[70] Beckett's second edited volume, published a few years later, examined the period 1900–1945, arguing that this era represents a particularly critical period for the formation of modern

---

[68] For a history of these concepts, see B. Heuser, *The Evolution of Strategy: Thinking War from Antiquity to the Present* (Cambridge: Cambridge University Press, 2010), 427–36.

[69] R. Haycock (ed.), *Regular Armies and Insurgency* (London: Croom Helm, 1979).

[70] I. Beckett and J. Pimlott (eds.), *Armed Forces and Modern Counter-Insurgency* (London: Croom Helm, 1985).

counterinsurgency doctrine and style. Counterinsurgency innovations and practices typical of this period are examined within British, French, German, American and Soviet experiences towards understanding the roots of commonly accrued notions about how counterinsurgencies are to be fought.[71] Daniel Marston and Carter Malkasian's volume has the broadest scope in terms of time, including counterinsurgency episodes stretching from the Philippine Insurrection of 1898 to ongoing operations in Iraq, Afghanistan and Colombia, combining some much debated case studies of counterinsurgency (the British in Ireland and in Malaya, the French in Indochina and Algeria, the United States in the Philippines and Vietnam) with some understudied offerings (the Rhodesian campaign of 1962–1980, Israel and the al-Aqsa Intifada and Colombia versus the FARC). Theirs, again, is not a volume about persistent national tendencies in small war but rather a test of efficacy – scrutinising individual strategies for sound fit within a particular counterinsurgency context and potential as a general tool to be applied across counterinsurgent episodes.[72]

Particularly close to our own interests is the volume edited by David Charters and Maurice Tugwell in 1989 which compares the armed forces of Britain, France, the United States, Israel and Canada (but no insurgency movements). The chapters on Britain, the United States and Israel in particular are now sorely in need of updating. Charters's own chapter, for example, covers the British COIN record only from 1954 until the end of the Cold War, a period during which Britain in almost all instances itself furnished the recognised government, while since the publication of that volume, Britain, like the United States, was mainly an outside force intervening in a conflict.[73] It will be interesting here in particular to see whether the picture has changed (if there are enduring national styles, it should not have).

Much of the work on counterinsurgency to date, including volumes examining episodes in a comparative context, does so with an eye towards isolating lessons learned from the experiences of diverse nations with the intent to draw upon practised operational art to improve one's own. Our own approach is somewhat different, seeking to understand more about what is peculiar about individual insurgencies or COIN campaigns and what is generalisable. Rather than assume that lessons

[71] I. F. W. Beckett (ed.), *The Roots of Counterinsurgency: Armies and Guerrilla Warfare, 1900–1945* (London: Blanford Press, 1988).

[72] D. Marston and C. Malkasian (eds.), *Counterinsurgency in Modern Warfare* (Westminister, MD: Osprey, 2010).

[73] D. A. Charters and M. Tugwell (eds.), *Armies in Low-Intensity Conflict: A Comparative Analysis* (London: Brassey's Defence, 1989).

learned may be transported from one polity to the next we ask if there are cultural and geographic bounds on the degree to which national war-making institutions may learn from one another.

National styles, concentrated in sometimes overtly discernable strategic cultures, may manifest themselves through distinctive practices, like exceptional brutality, but also through subtler mechanisms like the consistent prioritisation of one task – for example, intelligence collection – over another – for example, winning public support through infrastructure development. Common understandings of the mechanics of counterinsurgent warfare mean that nations may engage in what appears to be a similar set of operational tasks but arrange and prioritise these in ways that take on a distinctive national flavour and yield dissimilar operational effect. Additionally, national style may be found not in a distinct practice but rather in pursuing a common counterinsurgency practice with distinctions in quality of execution.

Domestic perceptions of honourable warfare or, conversely, perceptions that distasteful tactics are a necessary evil may influence the choice of tools from a general toolbox made by any national military. One possibility considered here is that these sorts of pressures, such as keeping up popular support at home and seeking a comfortable fit within existing military norms, may weigh heavily in considerations of operational approach. In this sense, national motives also matter. The particular mentality of a particular society and its military, and views on why the conflict is being pursued and what defines a victorious end may have a consistent impact on the way the conflict is waged.

Our volume does not restrict an examination of national style to counterinsurgent forces. An equally interesting question is the extent to which insurgent forces operating within a particular national context are constrained by the distinctive social, political and geographic environs endemic to that polity. And last not least, both sides learn from each other; the hunters may emulate the fox, mutual brutalisation may be part of the picture or alternatively moves on both sides towards de-escalation.

In this volume, then, we present analyses of a selection of prominent 'players' in insurgencies and counterinsurgency campaigns. These 'players' tend to be states or insurgent movements. In emphasising the role of particular historical experiences in their even more particular culture-dependent narratives, our chapters first sketch this historical background and point to events and experiences that have had a particular impact on the state or movement in question. Secondly, against this background, we shall take snapshots of the current strategic cultures and how these are influenced by past experiences: Do they see themselves as standing in a tradition? Are there important ruptures that are marked and referred to? Are they strongly influenced by watershed events, by trends in other countries? Do they show strong features of continuity, are they monolithic over long periods of time, or do different 'schools' or approaches exist simultaneously? Are past experiences explicitly alluded to, as negative or positive points of reference ('never again Amritsar', 'no more My Lai', or, with approval, the approach of Hoche, as opposed to Bugeaud and Callwell, etc.)?

The choice of case studies here is dictated by the main actors that have confronted insurgencies in the past couple of centuries and a selection of widely known insurgency movements, where we could find competent experts able to comment on them. There are, in some societies, rivalling schools of thought (and sometimes also of practice) in dealing with insurgents or in what is allowed to insurgents when staging an uprising (e.g., targeting civilians, terror acts with or without warning). And, quite crucially, as the contribution of Elie Tennenbaum suggests, there are supremely important trans-boundary transfers of ideas, tactics, strategies and other approaches.

This, then, is the setting and the task we have undertaken. Let us turn now to the case studies, starting with select states that have histories of mounting COIN campaigns, moving then to insurgent movements and their campaigns and to some mixed cases examined from both sides. Then, to illustrate the movement of ideas and practices, we include a case study of international influences and learning among COIN practitioners. (No doubt a similar study could be made of knowledge transfer among insurgent movements.) We will attempt to draw together some conclusions in a final chapter.

Part I

COIN Strategies

2 True to Form?

Questioning the British Counterinsurgency Tradition

Robert Egnell and David H. Ucko

By virtue of its twentieth-century history and tradition the British military has long been considered master of counterinsurgency. During the recent wars in Iraq and Afghanistan, British experiences with counterinsurgency greatly informed the rediscovery of this operational approach and, accordingly, the principles and theory that fill today's counterinsurgency manuals. Within the United Kingdom, the reencounter with counterinsurgency also had particular significance. Both within and outside the British military, it was argued that it was uniquely equipped, by dint of its experiences of imperial conquest, policing and withdrawal, as well as the Troubles in Northern Ireland, to understand and manage political violence and defeat insurgency. The common narrative spoke of a certain British style based on the pillars of minimum force, close civil-military cooperation, intelligence-led operations and adaptability.[1]

This chapter provides a more complex image. The principles and theory derived from British experiences are generally still relevant, but the notion of an enduring British approach to counterinsurgency that reflects such theory must be challenged. As should be expected, there has been great variation in the conduct of operations both between and (critically) within specific campaigns. The more successful campaigns can be said to share certain unsurprising characteristics – such as operational adaption and the tailoring of armed force to political ends – but the track record as a whole is too inconsistent to speak of a particular style or institutional ethos. Instead, the British experience – while replete with lessons, both negative and positive – must be approached via specific cases rather than as a reified whole. Glossing over important discontinuities in the search for an approach encourages the construction of myths, which while identity-furnishing and flattering produces not only bad history, but a poor basis for operations to come.

---

[1] A. Alderson, 'Britain' in T. Rid and T. A. Keaney (eds.), *Counterinsurgency: Doctrine, Operations, Challenges* (London: Routledge, 2010), 28.

Indeed, from the discussion of a British approach to counterinsurgency cannot be excluded Britain's most recent experiences in Afghanistan and Iraq. In the aftermath of Saddam Hussein's toppling in 2003, it was expected that Britain would adapt more readily to the challenges of insurgency that soon enveloped the country. Yet, contrary to many hasty and largely decontextualised comparisons between British and American styles of combat, it was ultimately Britain that struggled to adapt, stumbling as it did over its own institutional complacence and its related misreading of the situation. The British campaign in Afghanistan reveals that the experience in Basra was no aberration and that something fundamental has changed in Britain's ability to conduct counterinsurgency as it often did. The question, then, for Britain and its allies is whether the notion of a British approach to counterinsurgency was ever helpful or can still be made relevant for operations today and tomorrow.

Untangling the Narrative

As Basra fell on 6 April 2003, the British Army quickly adjusted from a combat mind-set to one of peace-support operations. Leaning on their experiences with peacekeeping in the Balkans, troops marked the end of 'major combat operations' and the onset of 'post-conflict operations' by removing their flak-jackets and replacing their helmets for berets, so as to convey a more benign posture.[2] Despite the contextual differences between Iraq's Shia-dominated south, where British troops were operating, and the Sunni-dominated American area of responsibility, many attributed the relative stability in Basra following the invasion to the British Army's approach: its appreciation of the campaign's political and economic dimensions and its firm but friendly manner of conducting operations.[3] The House of Commons, in its 'Initial Assessment' of the campaign, suggested that British historical experience and the many lessons learned – most recently in Northern Ireland, but also half a century ago in Malaya and Aden – had made the difference.[4]

Back then, before the bruising experiences that were to come, this narrative was often accepted at face value. Claims of an innate talent

---

[2] W. Murray and R. H. Scales, *The Iraq War: A Military History* (London: Belknap Press, 2003), 152.

[3] House of Commons Defence Committee [hereafter HCDC], *Iraq: An Initial Assessment of Post Conflict Operations* (London: The Stationery Office, 2005), Q 361; W. Chin, 'Examining the Application of British Counterinsurgency Doctrine', *Small Wars and Insurgencies*, 18/1 (2007), 8; Murray and Scales, *The Iraq War*, 152; J. Keegan, *The Iraq War* (New York: Vintage Books, 2004) 178.

[4] HCDC, *Iraq: An Initial Assessment of Post Conflict Operations*, 34–5.

were rarely put to writing – much like any urban legend, the narrative builds on an oral rather than written tradition – yet there is sufficient evidence in the literature to indicate its prevalence.[5] Witness, for example, the prominent British historian who in 1986 alluded to the 'characteristic British mode of response to public security challenges, one which may well be labelled the "British way", a pragmatic, limited application of traditional legal doctrines'.[6] Similarly, an eminent British academic, counterinsurgency scholar and former soldier wrote in 1998 of the 'intuitive professional character' of the British Army that 'has for some time reflected the needs of smaller operations', also known as 'small wars'.[7] In 2001 the same authority explicated on the 'British institutional wisdom' in counterinsurgency, presented as deriving 'from Robert Thompson's classic articulation of doctrine in the 1960s'.[8] Also in 2001, the Army issued doctrine for counterinsurgency in which it suggested that 'the experience of numerous "small wars" ha[d] provided the British Army with a unique insight into this demanding form of conflict'.[9] The earlier 1995 manual on 'Operations Other than War' had similarly claimed that the 'long experience of dealing with civil populations, both benign and hostile' had contributed to the Army's 'current military policies' towards similar challenges.[10] This narrative survived into the initial phase of the Iraq War. Even as late as 2004, one former soldier and well-placed academic spoke of the British Army as 'a counterinsurgency army', while two years later, another leading British academic and retired officer wrote of a 'British approach to counterinsurgency' that 'allow[s] for a much easier transition to these from high intensity, as was witnessed in Basra in 2003'.[11]

---

[5] This observation of an oral tradition is based on extensive interviews with serving British military personnel and academics, dated for the most, but not exclusively, in the late 1990s and early 2000s.

[6] See C. Townshend, *Britain's Civil Wars: Counterinsurgency in the Twentieth Century* (London & Boston: Faber and Faber, 1986), 18.

[7] J. Mackinlay, 'War Lords,' *RUSI Journal*, 143/2 (1998), 24.

[8] J. Mackinlay, 'NATO and Bin Laden,' *RUSI Journal*, 146/6 (2001), 38.

[9] British Army, *Army Field Manual Volume 1 Combined Arms, Part X Counter Insurgency Operations*, Army Code 71749 (London: Ministry of Defence, 2009), 1–2.

[10] British Army, *British Army Field Manual Volume 1 Part X Countering Insurgency*, Army Code 71876 (London: Ministry of Defence, 2001). For other sources making similar points, see D. French, *The British Way in Counterinsurgency, 1945–1967* (Oxford: Oxford University Press, 2011), 4.

[11] R. Thornton, 'Historical Origins of the British Army's Counterinsurgency and Counter-Terrorist Techniques' in T. Winkler, A. Ebnöther, and M. Hansson (eds.), *Combating Terrorism and Its Implications for the Security Sector* (Stockholm: Swedish National Defence College, 2005), 26. See also R. Thornton, 'The British Army and the Origins of Its Minimum Force Philosophy', *Small Wars & Insurgencies*, 15/1 (2004), 83. D. Benest, 'Aden to Northern Ireland 1966–1976', in H. Strachan (ed.), *Big Wars and*

Where did this narrative come from? One of its most obvious foundations is the sheer frequency of British Army experience with imperial policing and counterinsurgency. As noted by General Sir Mike Jackson, former Chief of the British General Staff, there 'is a sense of a real historical thread in this type of operation for the British Armed Forces'. The thread, he adds, 'most certainly did not begin with Malaya, or even the period after World War II ... we can go back at least a couple of centuries to Ireland, to India a century and a half ago, to Africa at about the same time and, indeed, to Iraq almost a century ago'.[12]

These repeated engagements are said to have engendered a certain genetic predisposition towards the attendant tasks of counterinsurgency. During the days of Empire, the British military faced the challenge of managing a global realm with limited resources. The dilemma forced the British military to emphasise small-scale instead of large-scale operations, indirect control versus direct and some degree of consent rather than pure coercion.[13] As an example, the Army of British India operated with a relatively small number of British officers and soldiers over truly vast areas, including present-day India, Pakistan and Bangladesh.[14] Critical counterinsurgency practices – co-opting local elites, raising local forces and administrations and achieving sufficient legitimacy – reduced the scope for ruinous conflicts, allowed for indirect rule and thereby doubly mitigated the problem of limited resources.[15] This historical context explains the general proclivity within the British military for a type of counterinsurgency geared towards accommodation, local partnerships and the maintenance of 'normalcy' – as far as possible.

Indeed, these principles are present in the several British texts on counterinsurgency, which advocate 'police primacy', 'minimum force', 'operating within the law', not to mention the political need to co-opt local leaders and their armies. In themselves, these texts represent yet another pillar in Britain's counterinsurgency tradition: though few in numbers, the works authored by British soldiers and practitioners have

Small Wars: The British Army and the Lessons of War in the 20th Century (Abingdon: Routledge, 2006), 117–18, 141.

[12] M. Jackson, 'British Counter-insurgency', *Journal of Strategic Studies*, 32/3 (2009), 347.

[13] R. M. Cassidy, 'The British Army and Counterinsurgency: The Salience of Military Culture', *Military Review*, 85/3 (2005).

[14] See T. A. Heathcote, 'The Army of British India' in D. Chandler and I. Beckett (eds.), *Oxford History of the British Army* (Oxford: Oxford University Press, 2003), 362–84.

[15] I. A. Rigden, 'The British Approach to Counter-Insurgency: Myths, Realities and Strategic Challenges', in *US Army War College Strategy Research Report* (Carlisle, PA: US Army War College, 2008), 15–16. See also T. Mockaitis, *British Counter-Insurgency, 1919–1960* (Basingstoke: Macmillan, 1990), 64.

assumed proto-doctrinal status and had a remarkable influence on coun-terinsurgency theory both in Britain and beyond. Alexander Alderson has in a useful analysis of British counterinsurgency doctrine highlighted the key works, beginning with Colonel Charles Callwell's *Small Wars*, first published in 1896, and Charles Gwynn's *Imperial Policing* from 1934. Following the Malayan Emergency, we find *Defeating Communist Insurgency*, Sir Robert Thompson's classic account of British activities there, which was in 1972 complemented by *Low Intensity Operations* by Frank Kitson, another leading counterinsurgency practitioner. Beyond the principles listed above, these books also converge on such notions as 'civil-military cooperation', 'intelligence-led operations' and the need to 'learn and adapt' – principles that feature, often *verbatim*, in today's doctrine, including the British Army's latest field manual, *Counter Insurgency Operations*, released in 2009.[16]

Other tenets of the narrative obtain. The thirty-year-long conflict in Northern Ireland is often framed as a counterinsurgency training ground to which virtually all British soldiers were exposed, often through multiple tours. The 'quasi-tribal' regimental system of the British Army is also held up as enabling informal learning within close-knit and 'flat' community-based structures, where the wisdom of past and ongoing campaigns can be passed on and discussed infor-mally.[17] It is such factors that have led to the perception of a particular proclivity and, at times, the semblance of an unparalleled track-record, with one analyst suggesting that 'only the British have enjoyed notable success in counterinsurgency'.[18]

Deconstructing the British Tradition

The frequent engagements and doctrinal basis have made counter-insurgency part of the British Army's history. Contrary to the US Army, whose experiences with counterinsurgency have not historically been a source of institutional pride or generated high-profile accounts and theorisation, the British Army has a higher regard for such engage-ments, which it sees as reflecting a proud tradition. Yet the effects of this enculturation on the British military – institutionally and

---

[16] Alderson, 'Britain', 28; British Army, *Counter Insurgency Operations*.

[17] E. A. Cohen, 'Constraints on America's Conduct of Small Wars', *International Security*, 9/2 (1984), 172. See also A. Garfield, *Succeeding in Phase IV: British Perspectives on the U.S. to Stabilize and Reconstruct Iraq* (Philadelphia: Foreign Policy Research Institute, 2006), 32.

[18] R. M. Cassidy, *Peacekeeping in the Abyss: British and American Peacekeeping Doctrine and Practice after the Cold War* (Westport, CT: Greenwood Publishing Group, 2004), 62.

operationally – are far from linear, or entirely positive. The problem arises when an expectation of excellence is allowed to substitute for preparation, when mythologised history breeds complacence, or when the contextual enablers behind key past successes are neglected and repeat performances are demanded in their absence. Such a tradition misinterprets the history from which it borrows and provides poor guidance for practice.

An Inconsistent Approach

Scratching below the surface of the British counterinsurgency tradition, it soon becomes clear that the 'British approach' was far less consistent or uniform than the narrative would suggest. Indeed, it would be highly inaccurate to suggest that Britain has a stellar or uncontested record of fighting insurgencies, even during the colonial era. Among the handful of comparatively successful cases lie a number of far less notable campaigns, in which British policy faltered or can even be said to have failed. One informal tally carried out in 2008, on the basis of operations from 1945, arrived at seventeen British counterinsurgencies, whereof seven can be seen as successes (Malaya, Kenya, Brunei, Malaysia, Radfan, Dhofar and Northern Ireland), one is 'generally regarded as a draw' (Cyprus), five are failures (Palestine [1945–8], Egypt [1946–56], Aden [1955], Aden [1956–8], Aden [1965–7]), three are difficult to quantify (Greece [1945–6], Eritrea [1949], Togoland [1957]) and two (Iraq and Afghanistan) were, then, still in progress but today tend increasingly to be included among the seven failures.[19] Whether the assessment is entirely accurate is for our purposes irrelevant; the point is the lack of consistency in outcome, or even of gradual learning over time, which should force a serious questioning of what the British counterinsurgency tradition is all about.

From a more historical perspective, it is equally true that the *longue durée* of British (or English) 'counterinsurgency' goes back far beyond the cases alluded to above and provides a very different picture indeed. The English campaigns in Ireland, Wales or Scotland, not to mention India and the Boer Wars, were particularly nasty and reflect few of the principles of later doctrine. Indeed, talk of a British approach can quickly appear ahistorical, considering a different type of track record, one that harkens way back to the Harrying of the North by the Normans when

---

[19] Rigden, 'The British Approach to Counter-Insurgency', 1, 32. For the qualification of recent efforts as 'failed', see F. Ledwidge, *Losing Small Wars: British Military Failure in Iraq and Afghanistan* (New Haven: Yale University Press, 2011).

they first imposed themselves after 1066, the suppression of Welsh uprisings in the twelfth–fifteenth centuries and the attempts to impose overlord-ship on Scotland. To this list, one may also add the repression of Irish independence movements since Henry II appointed himself ruler of Ireland, the siege of Drogheda, the massacre of Glencoe, the punitive aftermath of the Battle of Culloden and in India, the repression of the Indian Mutiny, and – of course – Amritsar. Finally, what of the various early struggles against the indigenous populations encountered in many of Britain's colonial conquests, which tended to pit an organised and unrestrained British military against what Charles Callwell called the 'uncivilised or semi-civilised races' or those 'lowest in the human scale'?[20] Suffice to say that when references are made to British counter-insurgency prowess or a particular style, what is meant is only its post–World War II experiences, and even then, many of those campaigns are still excluded from consideration.

Indeed, even among these more recent campaigns, the 'British approach' has been rather mixed. On the one hand, variation in practice is to be expected: there is no template for counterinsurgency operations – each campaign must be tailored to the context in which it unfolds and responds to the *sui generis* drivers of violence, meaning of legitimacy and politics at hand. Accordingly, any determination about what constitutes the 'minimum' use of force, for example, is inherently subjective and a decision forced upon the commander (or his or her superior), often at short notice. For better and for worse, the systematic interpretive pro-cess – incorporating both structural and agency-related factors – explains why despite frequent engagements and consistency in doctrine, British counterinsurgency practice has varied greatly across time and space.

But there is a more fundamental issue at stake, beyond context. The British Army is not a doctrine-driven organisation and has historically preferred to adapt on the ground. Such an approach can be defended. As Brigadier Gavin Bulloch argued in 1996, 'despite long experience in counterinsurgency, the British have not developed any set methods of dealing with the problem of insurgency; indeed it is probably unwise to attempt this because every situation is different'.[21] Similarly Brian Holden-Reid notes 'a widespread reluctance to formulate scientific, doctrinal statements' within the Army and a preference 'to review and resolve each problem as it occurs on its own terms free from any

[20] C. E. Callwell, *Small Wars: Their Principles and Practice, 1906*, 3rd ed. (London: Her Majesty's Stationary Office, 1914), 50.

[21] G. Bulloch, 'Military Doctrine and Counterinsurgency: A British Perspective', *Parameters*, 26/2 (1996), 4.

system'.[22] The problem arises when flexibility is achieved at the cost of forgetfulness – not of step-by-step guides and templates, but of the basic considerations and principles unearthed through past experience.

Indeed, while the main British texts on counterinsurgency form the backbone of counterinsurgency theory as we know it, their effect on the British Army as an institution was less notable. Many of the works were not formal doctrine, or they were manuals written for a specific campaign; regardless, their long-term influence institutionally has been weak. It has therefore been difficult for the British Army to build counterinsurgency capabilities or internalise best practices, forcing a renewed process of adaptation with each new campaign. During the days of empire, sufficiently frequent engagement in notionally similar operations would produce individual (vice institutional) memory of relevant precedents, which would accelerate the necessary learning.[23] Even then, the tendency was to start on the back-foot and adapt, with greater or lesser success.

For long, the gap between narrative and practice was glossed over due to a misreading of the British counterinsurgency texts. At some point, through a process that warrants further examination, the *prescriptive* terms and notions elaborated in these texts were confused with actual *descriptions* of how British forces had and would perform in theatre. As David French perceptively notes, Robert Thompson's seminal work, *Defeating Communist Insurgency*, was never intended to be read as a 'historical treatise' on British operations but as a 'didactic book in which he tried to emphasise what future counterinsurgent operators should do if they wanted success'.[24] Fatefully, it is a misreading with significant impact on the general perception of Britain's counterinsurgency style. 'The effect', as Hew Strachan has noted, 'was to suggest that the British army conducted its minor conflicts with greater consistency than was actually the case'.[25] In so doing, it also encouraged complacence about a 'British approach' adopted instinctively by its military.

In practice, by contrast, the approach – even among post-1945 campaigns – is too broad to be codified and often differed substantively from

---

[22] B. Holden-Reid, 'A Doctrinal Perspective, 1988–98', *SCSI Occasional Paper*, 33 (1998), 12.

[23] See H. Eaton and G. Boehmer et al., *The British Approach to Low-Intensity Operations*, Network-Centric Operations (NCO) Case Study (Washington DC: Office of Force Transformation, 2007).

[24] D. French, *The British Way in Counter-Insurgency 1945–1967* (Oxford: Oxford University Press, 2011), 247.

[25] See H. Strachan, 'Introduction,' in Strachan (ed.), *Big Wars and Small Wars: The British Army and the Lessons of War in the 20th Century* (Abdingdon and New York: Routledge, 2006), 8.

the ideals stipulated in counterinsurgency theory. French argues that the hallmark of British counterinsurgency from 1945 to 1967 was the use of a 'wide range of coercive techniques to intimidate the civilian population into throwing their support behind the government rather than behind the insurgents'.[26] Similarly, Paul Dixon and Andrew Mumford argue that the operations of colonial withdrawal were actually far more violent than the literature would imply.[27] The same line has been taken in more recent accounts of British operations in Kenya, in Cyprus and in the Boer Wars, leading one analyst to conclude that 'the British never employed minimum force in their imperial policing and counterinsurgency campaigns'.[28]

These critical accounts of British counterinsurgency can be helpful in correcting the view of past campaigns as benign, enlightened acts of altruism in which the British forces unerringly implemented their trade-craft approach to good effect. Yet it is also possible to overstate the case and deduce that British counterinsurgency, *as a whole*, was therefore uniformly brutal.[29] Wars always involve violence and harm, and counter-insurgency is no exception, but beyond this simplistic point it is difficult to find a consistent pattern that characterises the many centuries of British counterinsurgency experience. Instead, it is important to move beyond these totalising notions in favour of a richer understanding that is sensitive to specific cases and also to variation within each. The British approach, *in toto*, was neither consistently brutal nor benign, and most if not all of the instruments and approaches highlighted in this volume have been used at different times and in different contexts. This particularised understanding would also provide the best chance of learning from past campaigns, by first of all understanding their context, their evolution and the political interests at hand.

Learning from Successes

If useful deductions are difficult to draw from the British counterinsurgency experience as a whole, what of the specific few campaigns that

[26] French, *The British Way*, 247.

[27] Dixon, '"Hearts and Minds"? British Counter-Insurgency from Malaya to Iraq', *Journal of Strategic Studies*, 32/3 (2009), 366; A. Mumford, *The Counter-Insurgency Myth: The British Experience of Irregular Warfare* (London: Routledge, 2011).

[28] See the special issue on British counterinsurgency in *Small Wars and Insurgencies* 23(4–5) (2012), wherefrom the quotation is also drawn (see M. Hughes, 'Introduction: British Ways of Counter-Insurgency', 583).

[29] See, for example, D. Porch, *Counterinsurgency: Exposing the Myths of the New Way of War* (New York: Cambridge University Press, 2013).

form the basis of its tradition? Among Britain's various engagements throughout history, the Malaya Emergency and the 'troubles' in Northern Ireland have received by far the most coverage and are those that most immediately spring to mind whenever British counterinsurgency excellence is discussed. They are also the campaigns which are thought to correspond most closely to Britain's own counterinsurgency theory and doctrine.

Both campaigns are rich in lessons. Malaya, in this context, provides us with an example of how counterinsurgency principles can be successfully applied and serves as the original blueprint for doctrine and theory. It seems beyond doubt that the outcome of the Emergency was successful: through British actions, the Malayan National Liberation Army (MNLA) was defeated, democratic elections were held, a multi-ethnic Malayan government was formed and by mid-1960, the Emergency was declared over, with many former guerrillas becoming valued members of the newly independent state. The campaign also showcases the British military's ability to adapt quickly on the ground and to develop an approach marked by tactical, operational and strategic congruence. In broad terms, it saw the gradual strengthening of the security forces; an operational shift towards intelligence-led small-unit operations; the establishment of a sophisticated intelligence-gathering infrastructure; and the creation of a network of executive committees, enabling inter-agency information-sharing, decentralised decision-making down to the district level and a coordinated counterinsurgency effort.[30]

Northern Ireland is where these principles were refined to suit a more constrained political and legal environment.[31] Again, the campaign as a whole was a success. Following three decades of conflict, in July 2005 the Irish Republican Army Council announced an end to its armed campaign. Since then, the Provisional IRA (PIRA) has ceased to exist in any meaningful sense. Northern Ireland remains part of the United Kingdom but is in many respects self-governed, while also being tied in some policy areas to the Republic of Ireland. Accounts of the British role in bringing about this outcome tend to underline the Army's effective gathering and use of intelligence, its conduct of patrols and other covert operations and its application of counterinsurgency methods as part of a broader political strategy.

---

[30] This draws on D. Ucko, 'The Malayan Emergency: The Legacy and Relevance of a Counter-Insurgency Success Story,' *Defence Studies*, 10/1 (2010), 29. See also K. Hack, 'The Malayan Emergency as Counter-Insurgency Paradigm', *Journal of Strategic Studies*, 32/3 (2009), 383.

[31] Alderson, 'Britain', 38.

For all this, the lessons gleaned from these two campaigns are too often uncritical of the circumstances and enabling factors unique to each case. The Malayan Emergency, for example, did not involve the challenges of urban operations, external support or sanctuary for the insurgents, or a more sophisticated guerrilla group capable of adapting to and circumventing British counterinsurgency practices. While the achievements in Malaya are not to be belittled, the transfer of lessons from this particular case to other essentially different, and perhaps more complex contexts, requires great caution – something not always apparent in treatments of this case.

In Northern Ireland, the three decades required to bring a political solution to the conflict may simply reflect the frustratingly long timelines of irregular conflicts, but it could also be argued that in this campaign there were as many mistakes and lost opportunities as successes. Certainly, the initial period of Army operations, until the introduction of police primacy, echoes many of the errors committed in the initial phase of the Malayan campaign: the lack of intelligence, excesses in the use of force and the uncertain or altogether absent political guidance from the home government in London.[32] Britain was also afforded key advantages in this campaign: the geographical proximity, lack of linguistic or cultural barriers and the familiarity of the troops with the urban terrain; certainly these advantages facilitated the intelligence collection for which the campaign is now known.[33] Is a thirty-year timeline nonetheless an adequate standard for success, and, if so, what precedent does this set for achieving 'success' in campaigns further afield?

Because discussion of British counterinsurgency is so dominated by Malaya and Northern Ireland, the variety of experiences alluded to above is often missed, to a point where even other success-stories, such as the Dhofar campaign, are crowded out.[34] This disproportionate focus on just two campaigns also encourages a view of British counterinsurgency experiences as on the whole successful – a gross and rarely stated generalisation of course, but one that has helped set the British record apart from those of the French, the Portuguese and also the Americans.[35] As such, the narrative of

---

[32] See R. Thornton, 'Getting It Wrong: The Crucial Mistakes Made in the Early Stages of the British Army's Deployment to Northern Ireland (August 1969 to March 1972)', *Journal of Strategic Studies*, 30/1 (2007), 104–5.
[33] See J. Storr's contribution to this volume.
[34] Dhofar has recently began to receive more attention but was tellingly included as part of the 'unknown wars' in older books on British counterinsurgency. See J. Newsinger, *British Counter-Insurgency: From Palestine to Northern Ireland* (New York: Palgrave, 2002), Chapter 6.
[35] Ibid., 1.

British counterinsurgency depends at once on the sheer frequency of experiences yet also on excluding many of them from consideration.

Going further, the memory of these campaigns, in particular Malaya, has also been dangerously distorted, providing a very two-dimensional nature to the lessons derived. The initial motive in resurrecting this campaign has typically been to underline its more exceptional facets, at least when compared to other wars. The notion of addressing the causes of violence, of building legitimacy and of integrating social, economic and political concerns into war planning and execution are so alien to the mind-set of most militaries that these aspects of the campaign have been lifted, underlined and emphasised, sometimes to the extent of skewing the overall understanding of what took place. Indeed, in giving special focus to the notion of 'winning hearts and minds', a phrase closely associated with the Malayan campaign, analysts tended also to misinterpret this very phrase. Presented as the 'soft', altruistic and humanitarian aspects of operations, winning hearts and minds was, historically, about combining coercion with co-option in such a way that a local population is secure, wants to side with the counterinsurgents and anyway sees resistance as futile.[36] This shrewder understanding is far from apparent in the popular telling of the campaign, yet it informed the use of coercion – and of co-option – seen in Malaya, particularly from 1950 onward.

Problematically, the experience in Northern Ireland would reinforce this interpretation, because of the tendencies alluded to above. For many years, the campaign helped the Army sustain its post-colonial self-understanding as a counterinsurgency force, not least as so many service members repeatedly rotated through the province. Yet, over time, the campaign evolved from outright conflict to a contested peace, in which the Army adopted a lesser role.[37] Certainly by the early 1990s, the conflict had reached a certain stability, and Army units were no longer engaged in countering insurgency as much as terrorism, along with discrete acts of violence. Whereas the frequency of engagement and the individual memories of service members from previous nominally similar campaigns had always been the best guarantee of adaptation in follow-on wars, the transmutation of its Northern Ireland deployments into something far removed from counterinsurgency, and the simultaneous shrinking of Britain's colonial duties elsewhere, meant that the soldiers of the British Army gradually found themselves missing

---

[36] This draws on R. Egnell, 'Winning Hearts and Minds?: Legitimacy and the Challenge of Counterinsurgency Operations in Afghanistan', *Civil Wars*, 12/3 (2010), 282–303.

[37] Mansoor, 'The British Army and the Lessons of the Iraq War', *British Army Review*, 147 (2009), 11–12.

their counterinsurgency 'instruction', such as it was. In the place of the counterinsurgency practices typical of the earlier phases of the campaign, what British soldiers learned during their later tours in Northern Ireland would more resemble the practices on show in the peacekeeping operations of the same decade, in Bosnia and Kosovo. Thus, counterinsurgency 'as we know it' came to subsume such principles as 'doing no harm', maintaining 'neutrality' and applying force only in self-defence. Along with the 'hearts and minds' historiography of the Malayan campaign, the Northern Ireland experience could easily encourage the misleading notion that 'nice guys finish first'.

A Military Approach?

Beyond the level of violence, methods employed and cases relied upon, another dangerous difficulty with the narrated tradition's accuracy is that it tends to exaggerate the role of the British Army. Most accounts are authored by officers or academics with a specific interest in military history, and, accordingly, they tend to give more space to the role of the armed forces. Within the British military and perhaps even more so within the political leadership, this reading of past campaigns led to over-confidence about what the Army can achieve on its own. Counterinsurgency then comes to be seen as a primarily military activity, obscuring the need for civilian partners and a political strategy to inform all military and civilian efforts.

A deeper understanding of past counterinsurgency successes reveals that, rather than involving just the Army, the prosecution of such mission relied on a broad array of actors. Even within the security domain, these would include locally recruited security forces like the Iban Scouts in Malaya, and perhaps most importantly national police forces, home guards and other paramilitary outfits trained and controlled by the British.[38] In Malaya, for example, a total of 250,000 men had by 1953 been recruited into various constabulary, police and self-defence units.[39] In Northern Ireland too, following the declaration of police primacy in the mid-1970s, responsibility for the campaign's day-to-day prosecution lay with the police, not with the Army, requiring the expansion of the Royal Ulster Constabulary (RUC) from 3,000 to more than 8,300 full-time officers and 4,500 reservists, and its development

---

[38] A. Jackson, 'British Counterinsurgency in History: A Useful Precedent?', *British Army Review*, 139 (2006), 12.

[39] Rigden, 'The British Approach to Counter-Insurgency', 13; F. Kitson, *Low Intensity Operations: Subversion, Insurgency, Peace-keeping* (London: Frank Cass, 1971).

of intelligence, surveillance and direct action capabilities.[40] In contrast, in the contemporary context, raising the standard, number and accountability of local police forces is a consistent challenge, not just in counterinsurgencies but in other efforts to stabilise war-torn lands.

Going further, the historiography of British counterinsurgency tends to underplay, in favour of the military aspects, the role of civilian infrastructure and partners to carry out what are typically lumped together as the 'non-military' lines of effort – reconstruction activities, the provision of basic services and the establishment of governance. Historically, these would be carried out by host-nation structures working together with colonial administrations that would commonly have years, if not decades, of experience within the particular political and cultural context. Their diminutive role in the historiography underplays the significance of their absence in today's counterinsurgency campaigns.

Finally, the focus on a military approach can easily obscure the fact that it required, to be meaningful, a political strategy. Whereas there is no shortage of books and articles on the conduct of jungle operations in Malaya, one tellingly under-researched element of the campaign is the way in which the British leadership in the country coaxed and convinced the Malayan elite to accept the inclusion of the ethnic-Chinese population as part of the new nation. As the ethnic tension between these two minorities lay at the root of the conflict, this was a political and social hurdle that had to be overcome and without whose resolution no amount of tactical and operational skill on the part of the British military would have sufficed. Similarly, the British *political* intent to work towards Malayan independence was the *sine qua non* of the outcome remembered today: 'had the British simply refused to leave, we would most likely be talking about a misguided British defeat—yet another Aden'.[41]

For these reasons, it is misleading and even harmful to focus on the 'British approach' in isolation, if by this we mean a *military* approach, without considering its placement within a political context and broader strategy. This point has significant implications also for military history as an area of study; as Jeremy Black puts it, where issues of co-option, of winning over or of fostering legitimacy are concerned, it is critical that 'military history becomes an aspect of total history; not to "demilitarise" it, but because the operational aspect of war is best

---

[40] B. Hoffman and J. Morrison Taw, *A Strategic Framework for Countering Terrorism* (Santa Monica, CA: RAND, 1992), 22. See also W. Chin, 'Northern Ireland (1976–1994): Police Primacy' in H. Eaton and G. Boehmer et al. (eds.), *The British Approach to Low-Intensity Operations* (Washington, DC: Office of Force Transformation, 2007).

[41] Interview with Thomas A. Marks, a leading authority on counterinsurgency and people's war, by David H. Ucko, Washington, DC, March 30, 2006.

studied in terms of the multiple political, social and cultural context that gave, and give, it meaning'.[42]

An Eye to Context

This question of context introduces this critique's final point on the British tradition. Key changes have occurred since the supposed heyday of British counterinsurgency in the mid-twentieth century. Not only has the strategic context and Britain's international role evolved dramatically since the campaigns in defence of the British colonies, but so has the British domestic political and military context, which provided the foundation for earlier successes. Invocations of the British counterinsurgency tradition are too neglectful of these shifts, which have compromised the British capabilities, latitude and strategic rationale to conduct counterinsurgency. This raises questions about the salience of its legacy for operations that, in many ways, are not actually comparable to those seen in recent years.

First, counterinsurgency is not situated with the same strategic context as before, and the character of insurgency has changed. Colonial counterinsurgency operations took place as 'internal' challenges within the realms of empire; today, operations are typically conducted by coalitions, in support of legally sovereign states. In the place of the leverage that comes with imperial control, we are left with weak yet entirely independent host-nation governments that are either unable or unwilling to follow Whitehall writ.[43]

The countries engaged in these struggles are also in a vastly different position than before. For Britain, its political and military capabilities for sustained expeditionary campaigns have subsided significantly since the days of empire. The colonial resources and structures are no more: instead of colonial administrators, most notably the Colonial Office, we are left with the 'Comprehensive Approach' – a mere rhetorical device that purports to link a massive inter-departmental bureaucracy, much of which domestically focused, for the purpose of coordinated campaigns abroad. Beyond the jargon, few Western states have invested in civilian expeditionary capabilities, which leaves the military perilously isolated whenever it deploys.

---

[42] J. Black, *Rethinking Military History* (Abindgon: Psychology Press, 2004), 19.
[43] John Mackinlay made this very point in 1998. See J. Mackinlay, 'War Lords', *RUSI Journal* 143/2 (1998). Still, the discontinuity, while extant, must not be exaggerated. See French, *The British Way*, 252–3.

The military, too, has changed. Given the nature of the colonial system, the British Army had long-standing experience of the countries in which it was operating, was used to protracted conflicts far from home and deployed its troops on two-year tours that provided some familiarity with local institutions. With the end of empire, the opportunity to sustain and develop these skills vanished. British troops now tend to deploy for six months – scarcely enough time to have a concerted effect in the field. Long-term exposure to foreign cultures, languages and politics is also far more difficult to acquire. While changes such as these should have forced a serious reconsideration of what British forces would be able to accomplish abroad, there is little evidence of such a reevaluation.

Instead, throughout the Cold War and into the 1990s, the British military's main institutional preoccupation remained conventional or state-on-state warfare, at the expense of counterinsurgency or irregular warfare as a whole. This prioritisation could be defended during the Cold War, given the prospect of a conventional, armoured and possibly nuclear confrontation across the Central Front, but its logic contravened the growing engagement (and expectation for) expeditionary peacekeeping, crisis management and interventions during the 1990s. To the extent that the decade's experience with peace support operations in the Balkans made a mark, these challenges were still considered 'containable and potentially resolvable within a state-centric framework and the national and international security arrangements developed during the Cold War'.[44] As an institution, therefore, the British Army that made its way to Iraq in 2003 had 'changed little in terms of structure, training focus and ethos from that which had stood ready to face the 3rd Shock Army on the plains of Westphalia during the Cold War'.[45]

This institutional neglect of counterinsurgency stemmed from the overarching premise that the British 'train for major war while constantly staying ready for different forms of peace operations'.[46] The apparent flexibility required for this system to work is a source of institutional pride, but it has never received the investment needed

---

[44] E. Krahmann, 'United Kingdom: Punching above Its Weight' in E. J. Kirchner and J. Sperling (eds.), *Global Security Governance: Competing Perceptions of Security in the 21st Century* (London: Routledge, 2007), 93.

[45] R. Dannatt, 'Address by Chief of General Staff at the Institute for Public Policy Research (IPPR)', London, 19 January 2009. Retrieved from: www.mod.uk/DefenceInternet/ AboutDefence/People/Speeches/ChiefStaff/20090119AddressToTheInstituteForPublic PolicyResearch.htm.

[46] Brig. Simon Mayall, interviewed by Robert Egnell, Ministry of Defence, London, November 2004.

for it to work. Instead, what dismissively used to be called 'Operations Other Than War' were marginalised or lumped together, despite their disparate requirements. In education, the focus on counterinsurgency in the British Army's Advanced Command and Staff Course decreased substantially in 1997.[47] Also in doctrine, counterinsurgency came to be subsumed as part of 'peace operations', which while overlapping in some respects differ critically in others.[48] While the British Army did publish updated counterinsurgency doctrine in 1995, as Alex Alderson explains, it was neither studied nor taught, and the subject fell into decline.[49]

This neglect could not be balanced out by the Army's regimental system, which some commentators see as the key to its purported adaptability. Whatever its merits, it has not protected these units from the overriding institutional focus on conventional warfare. Indeed, due precisely to its informality, this system of learning is dangerously dependent on an ad hoc practice of information sharing.[50] For this system to have any bearing on a unit's counterinsurgency capabilities, the latter must either have continuous experience in such operations, to keep the familiarity alive, or view such engagements as important and prepare accordingly. In the British case, since its withdrawal from empire, neither condition has obtained. Meanwhile, claims of a 'British approach' persisted, in spite of the sea-change in context.

Myths Come Home to Roost: Basra, Helmand and the Demise of a Tradition

Let us return to the British experience in Basra and Helmand. Specifically, an assessment of British actions and assumptions in these two wars brings out the dangers of the counterinsurgency myths and legacies that have dominated the British military at least since the 1980s. In neither Iraq nor Afghanistan did the outcome stem directly from the British counterinsurgency tradition. In Iraq, Britain failed to articulate or resource a clear strategy and was furthermore a junior coalition partner with limited say, and in Afghanistan there was little that British troops could by themselves do to address the central government's lack of legitimacy, NATO's shortage of deployable troops and Pakistan's

---

[47] Alderson, *The Validity of British Army Counterinsurgency Doctrine*, PhD dissertation (Shrivenham: Cranfield University, 2009), 94.

[48] On this latter point, see D. H. Ucko, 'Peace-building after Afghanistan: Between Promise and Peril', *Contemporary Security Policy*, 31/3 (2010).

[49] Alderson, *The Validity of British Army Counterinsurgency Doctrine*, 94.

[50] A point discussed previously in Ucko, 'The Malayan Emergency', 33.

reluctance to support fully the counterinsurgency effort.[51] Even so, in critical ways the constructed tradition undermined the type of adaptation needed to mitigate misperceptions and mistakes made at the political level.

First, in both campaigns, *a misplaced complacence* with counterinsurgency among British political and military leaders impeded an accurate reading of the situation. In Basra, during at least the first year of operations, many observers within the British government and armed services perceived the army's prior operational experience as compensating for the critical dearth of a strategy or formal planning.[52] To the UK Ministry of Defence (MoD), Britain's 'counterinsurgency experience from Northern Ireland and the Balkans [had] enabled the British Army to make a positive start in Iraq'.[53] Indeed, during this first year of the campaign, complacence developed around the notion of British soldiers in berets engaging with local community leaders, conducting reconstruction and operating in a manner that US forces, with their harsher methods and cultural resistance to peace operations, struggled to understand. That the British forces formulated this approach on the hoof and without strategic guidance also lent credence to the notion of a 'British approach' passed down and refined over time.[54] Problematically, the initial calm in Basra related more to the local population's opposition to the Saddam Hussein regime than to British inputs, and, more forcefully, it was also largely illusory or at least superficial, given the mass looting, crime and gradual takeover of Basra by sectarian militias and criminal networks. The failure to identify or react appropriately to these developments sowed the seeds for eventual British failure.

By the time British troops deployed to Helmand in spring 2006, there should have been plenty of opportunities to transfer lessons from the ever-worsening security situation in Basra. It is therefore remarkable that the seriousness and volatility of the security situation were once again severely underestimated. The units that initially deployed to Helmand Province were not prepared, manned or equipped for what turned out to be a hornet's nest of Taliban fighters and drug lords, all of whom viewed the arrival of British troops as a threat to their interests. The first

---

[51] For a broader assessment of these two campaigns, see D. H. Ucko and R. Egnell, *Counterinsurgency in Crisis: Britain and the Challenges of Modern Warfare* (New York: Columbia University Press, 2013), 45–108.

[52] UK MoD, *Operations in Iraq: An Analysis from a Land Perspective* (London: Ministry of Defence) 2005), 2–6.

[53] MoD, *Stability Operations in Iraq (Op Telic 2–5): An Analysis from a Land Perspective* (London: Director General Corporate Communication, 2006), 14.

[54] Ledwidge, *Losing Small Wars*, 24.

deployment comprised just one brigade (3,200 troops) for this largest of Afghan provinces (similar in size to Croatia). Despite meeting fierce resistance that put British and civilian lives – along with the mission – at risk, it took two years to increase that number to 8,500.[55]

Secondly, once counterinsurgency was under-way, British forces and commanders were *unfamiliar with the term's meaning and principles*. By the time the Army reached Iraq in 2003, it was not uncommon for British officers to be unable to 'list the British COIN principles, define their meaning, or discuss past British successes in a meaningful way'. There was also little familiarity with the canonical texts on counterinsurgency, given the limited focus on this topic from basic British officer education at the Royal Military Academy in Sandhurst through to the Staff College.[56] The lack of preparation for this type of engagement meant that the British military adapted on the basis of past experience, which by this point consisted of largely permissive deployments to Northern Ireland and peacekeeping in the Balkans. On this basis, the British military adopted a people-friendly, community-oriented approach that for some time was seen as a strategy in its own right. Altogether absent, despite their critical role in past counterinsurgency campaigns, was consideration of area control, population security and political reform.[57] Instead, British troops adopted a low profile and assumed that doing so would lead to greater support for the occupation. Intended to 'normalise' postwar Basra, this reflexive adherence to the principles of peace operations instead ceded the initiative.

In Helmand, the military failed repeatedly to make the most of the admittedly minimal resources provided for the task at hand. The decision to disperse the small number of troops available throughout the province, for example, was an operational-level decision and interpretation of political intent, but one that contravened key counterinsurgency principles of progressive occupation. As to adaptation to the context, as Anthony King has noted, the role of regimental culture was a far greater determinant of operational conduct than the environment, context, political aims or counterinsurgency best practices.[58] Consequently, each of the first three brigades deployed fell back to what they knew best, based

[55] T. Farrell, 'Improving in War: Military Adaptation and the British in Helmand Province, Afghanistan, 2006–2009', *Journal of Strategic Studies*, 33/4 (2010), 587.

[56] D. Marston, 'Adaptation in the Field: The British Army's Difficult Campaign in Iraq', *Security Challenges*, 6/1 (2010), 72; Alderson, *The Validity of British Army Counterinsurgency Doctrine*, 198.

[57] This draws on Ucko and Egnell, *Counterinsurgency in Crisis*, 52–7.

[58] A. King, 'Understanding the Helmand Campaign: British Military Operations in Afghanistan', *International Affairs*, 86/2 (2010), 325.

on their respective regimental core competences.[59] Counterinsurgency doctrine and principles were hardly in play.

Thirdly, the militarised recollection of past campaigns informed the overall *neglect of the political and developmental effort* necessary for counterinsurgency to succeed. Infrastructure in Basra required immediate redress, given the neglect under Saddam, damage during the war and further devastation during postwar looting. But, in contrast with Britain's colonial experiences, the civilian presence in Basra was too small and ill-resourced to carry out the interim functions of an occupying power. The Army-administered quick-impact projects attempted to compensate for this capability gap, yet as a later Ministry of Defence review would note, the armed forces lacked 'the resources and expertise to play more than a limited role in other campaign strands—political, economic, social, legal and cultural'.[60] As a result, while the transfer of political control floundered, garbage piled up, electricity outages were frequent and problems with sewage and water caused an outbreak of cholera. These problems turned the population against the occupying forces, and as instability soared, the few civilians remaining in theatre disappeared.

Similarly, in Helmand, the failure to provide stability or to hold more than very limited terrain not only impeded, but virtually precluded, any progress in the areas of economic development and governance – both essential aspects of the British strategy there. Regardless, the British-led Provincial Reconstruction Team (PRT) in Helmand – its civilian presence – was also understaffed, and it would take three full years for its civilian staff to increase, from twenty-five in 2007 to eighty in 2009.

Finally, it became increasingly clear in both Basra and Helmand that the strategic rationale that had underpinned and informed previous British counterinsurgencies – during its colonial era or in managing its demise – no longer obtained. Instead, Britain has acted with a sense of *strategic drift*, badly undermining its operations in the field. In Basra, the Blair government set out several grand strategic objectives to be met, but it was also painfully aware of the rancour back home over the war, resulting in an untenable balancing act. As early as May 2003, the British government began reducing its forces, and within three months of the fall of Basra, force levels had shrunk from a maximum of 46,000 to some 10,500.[61] For all their domestic appeal, these swift withdrawals made it impossible for deployed forces to provide any form of security or control the local population, whose

---

[59] Ibid.; see also Farrell, 'Improving in War,' 573.
[60] MoD, *Stability Operations in Iraq (Op Telic 2–5)*, 45.
[61] MoD, *Operations in Iraq: Lessons for the Future* (London: Director General Corporate Communication, 2003), 70.

safety was now in the hands of hastily formed local security forces. Indeed, by late 2003, only a little more than 9,000 coalition soldiers remained for the approximately 4.6 million inhabitants of Multinational Division–Southeast (MND-SE) – a far cry from the tentative force ratios found to apply in previous counterinsurgencies. Yet in contrast with the iconic campaigns of its past, Britain entered Iraq as a junior coalition member and was always less interested in seeing the operation through or responding robustly to new challenges. This strategic underpinning, such as it was, had crippling effects on the troops in theatre.

In Helmand things were, if possible, even worse. Occurring against the backdrop of NATO's expansion beyond Kabul, the deployment to Helmand was mired in confusion as to the purpose of the mission there. The British government's initial aim, in the wake of the 9/11 attacks, was to support the United States in countering international terrorism and to maintain the 'special relationship'. Both of these objectives pointed to the need to defeat Al-Qaeda and topple the Taliban regime that had given it sanctuary. The notion of state-building, on the other hand, was secondary and framed foremost as an indirect means of ensuring Al-Qaeda's permanent exile from the country. However, over time the aims morphed to include 'counterinsurgency, counter-narcotics, protection of human rights and state-building'.[62] At any time, the political leadership talked of a peace support operation to support counter-narcotics while the brigade personnel worked under the assumption of a major counterinsurgency campaign.[63] The confusion of trying to do so many (difficult) tasks at once raised questions that were never adequately answered: why were British forces being sent to Helmand, and where were the resources that would be commensurate with the complexity of their mission, however defined? Indeed, it was not until 20,000 US Marines reinforced the British effort in Helmand that the coalition came close to having a positive impact in the province, but by this time the strategic intent had shifted again, this time to emphasise withdrawal.

Conclusion: The Dangers of Myths

What is left of the 'British approach' after this deconstruction? The positive statements that can be made are modest in scope: some of

---

[62] House of Commons Foreign Affairs Committee, *Global Security: Afghanistan and Pakistan*, Eighth Report of Session 2008–2009, (London: HMSO, 2009), 9.

[63] D. Marston, 'Lessons in 21st-Century Counterinsurgency: Afghanistan 2001–2007' in D. Marston and C. Malkasian (eds.), *Counterinsurgency in Modern Warfare* (Oxford: Osprey, 2008), 237.

Britain's many engagements with counterinsurgency have yielded successful outcomes, and, on average, in so far as averages are in this context meaningful, its counterinsurgency experience post-1945 has been less brutal and less violent than it could have been. Such findings do not say much and certainly confer no innate ability or genetic predisposition towards counterinsurgency. The implicit belief in such a superiority was not just inaccurate and ahistorical, but dangerous, in that it left forces ill-prepared for the challenges they were to face both in Iraq and Afghanistan.

So of what relevance is the British counterinsurgency tradition today? Despite the contextual discontinuities between then and now, the past is not dead (in some ways it is not even the past). However, in learning from history, it must be treated with caution and care. The historical cases are rich in lessons but must be approached not as part of a reified whole but on their own merits. Counterinsurgency must also be seen as a function of the political context in which it unfolds – this is not purely, or even mainly, a military effort.

As to the theory derived from such experiences, the principles of British counterinsurgency are still largely relevant: indeed, it is difficult to argue against the importance of achieving a nuanced political understanding of the campaign, of operating under unified civil-military command, of using intelligence to distinguish civilians from insurgents, of isolating insurgents from the population, of using the minimum amount of force necessary to achieve set objectives and of assuring and maintaining the perceived legitimacy of the counterinsurgency effort in the eyes of the populace. Most valuable, perhaps, is the exhortation to 'adapt and learn' and to arrive at a tailored response rather than fall back on template solutions.

Somewhat unsurprisingly, these principles – when applied – have often met with success. And yet the critical distinction must be made: these principles are guideposts, some of them more obvious than others, not descriptions of what British armed forces have historically done or can in the future be expected to do. While valuable for military organisations beholden to more traditional and apolitical understandings of warfare, they are nevertheless insufficient in the absence of a viable strategy, adequate resources and the skills and capabilities to apply them in the field. In all of these respects, Britain, and Western states in general, are disconcertingly ill-prepared.

3 French Counterinsurgency in the Era of the Algerian Wars, 1830–1962

Jacques Frémeaux and Bruno C. Reis

France, like all major imperial powers, fought many colonial small wars against insurgents, not to mention some previous campaigns in Europe and in France itself like the crushing of the revolts in Corsica and Vendée by the *Ancien Régime* and the French Revolution respectively in the eighteenth century, or the fight against the Spanish uprising in the Peninsular War at the beginning of the nineteenth.[1] But two protracted counterinsurgency (COIN) campaigns in Algeria, separated by a century, stand out, marking the beginning and the end of French colonial COIN campaigns of the type that Michel Martin has called after them the type *guerres algériennes*.[2] Not only did they require an unusually high military effort overseas, but they also had an undeniably major impact on the French approach to this type of conflict. The campaign to consolidate and extend the initial French occupation in Algeria, from 1830 onwards, launched the second French colonial empire, ushering in the so-called 'New Imperialism' that in 1899 led to Kipling's coining the expression 'savage wars of peace' to describe the expansion of the European empires, mainly in Africa and Asia. A century later, from 1954 onwards, another massive COIN campaign in Algeria marked the end of

---

[1] A point already underlined in the pioneering study by Peter Paret, *French Revolutionary Warfare from Indochina to Algeria: The Analysis of a Political and Military Doctrine* (Princeton: Princeton University Press, 1964); for recent analysis that address both local insurgency and French counterinsurgency in the Peninsular War see, e.g., Charles J. Esdaile, *Fighting Napoleon: Bandits, Guerrillas, and Adventurers in Spain 1808–1814* (New Haven: Yale University Press, 2004); Miguel Artola, *La Guerra de Guerrillas, La Guerra de la Independencia* (Madrid: Espasa, 2007), 189–211; Emilio de Diego, *La Guerrilla y la Contrainsurgencia, España, el Infierno de Napoleón, 1808–1814. Historia de la Guerra de la Independencia* (Madrid: Esfera de los Libros, 2008), 119–37; Hugh Gough, Genocide and the Bicentenary: The French Revolution and the revence of the Vendée, *Historical Journal*, 30/4 (1987), 977–88; and the main doctrinal guidelines are translated by Jonathan North, General Hoche and Counterinsurgency, *Journal of Military History*, 67/2 (2003), 529–40.

[2] Michel Martin, 'From Algiers to N'Djamena: France's Adaptation to Low-Intensity Wars, 1830–1987', in David Charters and Maurice Tugwell (eds.), *Armies in Low-Intensity Conflict: A Comparative Analysis* (Washington, DC: Brassey's Defence Publishers, 1989), 77–138.

France as a major colonial power. Focusing on the period bracketed by these two conflicts, our key question here is whether or not there was a relatively consistent and specific French way of COIN.

Conflict Typology: Comparing Two French COIN Campaigns in Algeria

In 1830, France embarked on the conquest of Algeria. Its conventional side ended in 1857 with the occupation of the Kabylie. The French military faced recurrent insurgencies in the region, however, as the local population, formally subjected to French rule, violently resisted the new colonial order. These insurrections gained increasing significance from 1845 onwards, when religious leaders like Sharif Bou Maza started preaching rebellion. Insurgencies were frequent until the 1880s, the most important being the ones led by Ouled Sidi Sheikh in South Oran (from 1864 onwards) and in Kabylie (from 1871 onwards).

Such insurgencies were dangerous for France, even when militarily of low intensity, because they paralysed communications, harmed European businesses, cut off supplies and suspended mandatory labour and taxation. The French also worried because the insurgencies presented a challenge to their sovereignty that might prove dangerously contagious. While clearly anti-colonial and anti-French, these uprisings had no discernible political programme, at least not one that easily fitted Western political criteria. The slogans used by the insurgents were mostly religious with millenarian overtones. Their leaders do not seem to have had, or even sought, a nationalist following across the whole of Algeria. This first wave of insurgencies therefore lacked unity; they were often barely known and not supported outside Algeria, two key weaknesses in this type of conflict.

The irregulars whom the French fought in the nineteenth century were above all tribal warriors using their traditional weapons and ancient tactics –Arab horsemen attacking the French in the plains and Kabyl infantry in the mountains. They were excellent fighters at the individual level, but they were poorly armed with locally manufactured long rifles (*mokhala*s), accurate and easy to transport, but with weak penetration power. They were excellent soldiers when it came to ambushes or hot pursuit, but they could not resist a frontal assault by regular forces. The peasants, the main source of recruitment for these revolts, needed to tend their crops and livestock and consequently could not sustain a protracted war of the kind required for successful insurgencies.

By contrast, the second major French COIN campaign in Algeria that started on 1 November 1954 confronted an explicitly formulated modern political aim of national independence. This aim was espoused by the

National Liberation Front (FLN). Armed attacks, even if they were rarely fully coordinated, affected the entire territory of Algeria and were combined with political action aimed at organising and controlling the local population (through the Political-Administrative Organization [OPA]). Unlike the previous period, this time the insurgency also affected urban areas, was well-organized and had important international dimensions.[3]

The FLN fighters were no longer simple tribal warriors, but became professionals of guerrilla warfare, and their military value was recognised by French officers. They retained the frugality, endurance and ability to move quickly on foot of the Algerian fighters of previous periods. But now modern weaponry, small arms (rifles, automatic weapons) as well as grenades, mines and other explosives posed a major challenge to a massive French conventional force that peaked after 1959 at about 470,000 supplemented with close to 200,000 local forces, even if FLN insurgents probably never exceeded 55,000, many of whom from 1958 to 1961 were in Tunisia or Morocco, unable to infiltrate into Algeria.[4] They used unconventional tactics like raids and ambushes as well as surprise attacks when the enemy was in a position of relative weakness, while studiously avoiding any frontal and prolonged engagement with the conventional forces. The soldiers of the Algerian National Liberation Army (ALN) were adept at exploiting the local terrain, and their force structure was organized around territorial sectors (*wilayas*), but they were permanently on the move in vast remote areas, without being tied down, as in the past, by the defence of their families and their property. They needed some popular support but were not dependent upon the support of a specific village. Moreover, their legitimacy no longer stemmed from their tribal affiliation but from claims made in the name of the Algerian nation.

The words used by the French military to classify these two conflicts emphasise these differences. Officially, military operations in Algeria during the nineteenth century aimed to subdue the local population. In contrast, between 1954 and 1962 the official label used was 'operations to maintain public [colonial] order' in aid of the civil power by putting an end to the illegal activity of the insurgents or 'rebels' as they were called officially. During the nineteenth century the French military referred to the campaigns in Algeria as '*petite guerre*' or '*guérilla*', both meaning a small war, usually overseas, by contrast with the '*grande*

---

[3] See the corresponding chapter on the FLN in this volume.
[4] For a detailed analysis of these numbers cf. Guy Pervillé: *Atlas de la guerre d'Algérie* (Paris: Autrement, 2003), 50–1.

guerre' or major war between great states in Europe. The campaign in Algeria in the mid-twentieth century, by contrast, was labelled a *'guerre révolutionnaire'* or *'guerre subversive'*, that is, a revolutionary or subversive war. The ideological dimension, therefore, became paramount and was seen as inseparable from the broader strategic context of the global Cold War as well as from the methods of mass political mobilization that were then perceived by the French military as being vital in COIN.

The French Colonial Approach to COIN in the Nineteenth and Early Twentieth Centuries

During the conquest of Algeria, French military operations were conducted without any significant external intervention. On the eastern border of Algeria, the French government had secured the friendly posture of the Tunisian government by becoming an indispensable guarantor of Tunisia's de facto independence. On Algeria's western border, the battle of Isly, combined with gunboat diplomacy, had coerced the Moroccan government into neutrality with the Treaty of Tangier of September 1844. Similar French attempts to coerce Arab countries a century later to stop their support for the FLN, by contrast, caused major international crises. These included the Suez crisis caused by the Anglo-French intervention in 1956 against Nasser's Egypt or the 1958 crisis caused by the French aerial bombardment of Sakiet Sidi Yousef, a village inside Tunisia sheltering Algerian insurgents.

In the nineteenth century the French military command could count on well-trained professional troops, serving for periods of seven years, who could be used without hesitation to subdue an essentially rural Algerian population, an estimated three million inhabitants dispersed over an area of 300,000 square kilometres. French troop levels varied between eighty thousand and one hundred thousand men. The French military were divided into three provinces, subdivided in *'cercles'*, that is, districts or sectors that were the basic unit of the French military organization. Each officer in command of a *cercle* or a subdivision of it enjoyed a very large degree of autonomy and authority, concentrating all civil and military powers.

The French strategic aim was to force the populations into total submission by an operational concept based upon targeting local economic interests, which were primarily agricultural. The French war of conquest was primarily a form of economic warfare. It is in this context that the word *'razzia'* became common. *'Dégât'* – destruction – was the most common word to designate any kind of punitive military action before that time, and we certainly have examples of it in conventional warfare as well as in campaigns against insurgents in the Vendée or the Iberian Peninsula. But *razzias* marked a new and more systematic use of economic warfare against perceived insurgents and their supporters. The aim of the *razzia* was to keep insurgents constantly on the move, preventing them from cultivating or harvesting their fields or caring for their livestock. The French columns confiscated livestock, harvested crops for their own benefit or burned them, and emptied and destroyed silos, orchards and villages.

The choice of the term *razzia* for this approach to COIN points to lessons learned from the Ottoman Turks and other foreign rulers of the Maghreb. Often unable to occupy and administer vast dependent territories directly and permanently, the Ottoman Turks had frequently opted to send in – at more or less regular intervals – armed columns or *'mehalla'* primarily in charge of levying taxes. This probably had deeper roots in Bedouin raiding (*ghazwiya* in Arabic). In the case of resistance, they would impose retaliatory measures that would not stop until the local notables would come to offer their submission. It seems that the first French leading officer to resort to these methods was General Juchault de Lamoricière (1806–1865), one of the oldest Africa hands in the military and a younger rival to Marshal Thomas-Robert Bugeaud (1784–1849), even if the latter would be the one to conduct it most successfully in Algeria.

The *razzia* points to an interesting process of military diffusion in strategic culture coming not from Europe to the colonies, but the reverse, from the colony to the imperial power. It became an enduring characteristic of French colonial campaigns. More than a half-century afterwards, just before the First World War, a French military manual still stated: 'any operation that does not culminate in a *razzia* will have no more than short-lived results'.[5]

The indispensable tools for this French approach to COIN were joint groups of different army specialities, so-called columns. These could vary greatly in size. But during occupation campaigns or against major insurgencies they could reach thousands of men. Columns were made up of several infantry battalions and detachments of cavalry, artillery and military engineers of variable size, supported by a convoy of ammunitions, rations and medical support.[6] The essential quality of these French columns in Algeria was mobility. They therefore had to be self-reliant and live partly off the land – this was another rationale for the *razzia*.

---

[5] Lieutenant-colonel René-Jules Frisch: *Guerre d'Afrique, guide annexe des règlements sur le service en campagne et les manoeuvres* (Paris: Berger-Levrault, 1912), 61.
[6] Victor Almand and E. Hoc: *Le service du Génie en Algérie* (Paris: Berger-Levrault, 1894), 4.

The expression '*faire colonne*' – to organise a column – summed up the essence of French colonial campaigns. To be effective, columns had to be capable of attacking rapidly whenever and wherever an insurgent threat might arise, as well as act in support of other troops facing difficulties. This high level of responsiveness was of course relative and was limited by the technology and communications available at the time.

To remain fully operational a column still needed to be able regularly to get fresh food and munitions, be relieved of the sick and wounded, and ideally replace them and get some rest for its men. This was the basic function of so-called '*postes*', a network of support outposts. Between 1840 and 1844, there were about thirty *postes* in Algeria, organised in three parallel lines: along the coast, in the central mountainous area (*tell*) and, farther south, on the edge of the high plateaus. Bugeaud always insisted that the number of these fixed positions should be as small as possible, so as to minimise dispersal and the number of troops tied to the defence of static positions. Twenty years later, Napoleon III issued the guideline that '[military] outposts that are not demonstrably an absolute necessity become a source of trouble'.[7]

This military strategy was complemented in Algeria by a more political or civilian affairs dimension represented by the *bureaux arabes* or Arab Offices. The first one was created in 1833, but only in 1844 did Bugeaud organise them into a proper standing service. Each *bureau* was responsible for a territorial sector, province, subdivision or circle, with a total of about forty *bureaux* controlled by a directorate-general. The service employed close to two hundred officers, lieutenants or captains. The criteria for recruitment was a good education, military and otherwise, including a knowledge of Arabic (or Berber), and an interest for the culture of the country. Young promising officers were preferred for this line of work. Their responsibilities were wide-ranging: supervising local chiefs (*caïds*), Muslim judges (*cadis*), Koranic schools, taxation and certain public works (roads, bridges, dikes).

The *bureaux arabes* had two main objectives. Firstly, they were to prevent new insurgencies. In order to do that, they managed a vast intelligence network that relied on local notables and a number of informers. Secondly, they were to make the colonial authority more acceptable, for instance, by introducing innovations in agriculture, modern medicine (including vaccination) and increase in trade. They should, in sum, be able to ensure French authority over the local

---

[7] Lettre sur la Politique de la France en Algérie adressée par l'Empereur au maréchal de Mac-Mahon, duc de Magenta, gouverneur général de l'Algérie (Paris: Imprimerie Impériale, 1865), 59.

population by a mix of carrots and sticks. Typically they advocated the slow and controlled modernisation of local society – to enhance the security of the French, but also because they had only limited means for development aid to which the French national budget would not contribute until the final years of colonial rule. They often argued against mass colonisation by white settlers in the interests both of the locals and of the maintenance of peace. This advocacy of local interests had its limits. Yet this period saw the *bureaux arabes* tendentially siding with the locals against new settlers' interests. This was the period of the *Royaume arabe* or Arab Kingdom under the Napoleon III's Second Empire (1852–1870).[8]

An important element of this strategy of local co-option was the growing participation of Muslim contingents in COIN operations of the French Army in Algeria. Initially, the French military included a small proportion of native regular troops (about 10 percent of the total in 1850). The number, however, grew steadily. Furthermore, the army enrolled numerous local auxiliary forces. '*Goums*' was the name given to tribal fighters requisitioned for a specific mission under the command of their own leaders (*caïds* or *sheikhs*), who were in turn under commanded by officers of the *bureaux arabes*. Primarily used for scouting, their level of combativeness tended to be low. Regardless, their mobilisation on the side of the French forces was seen as having at least the important positive effect of preventing these locals from joining any anti-French insurgency. They could also participate in the *razzias*. The use of local troops – much cheaper to pay and maintain, less prone to disease – helped France manage the enduring problems of COIN: its inherently long-term nature and heavy requirement of manpower. Thus, it is easy to understand why France, starting in Algeria but then across its growing empire, used large numbers of locals or other colonials to deal with insurgencies, as well as relying on a significant edge in military organization and technology over local populations in most of Africa and even parts of Asia.

From the 1880s onwards, Algeria was generally pacified, which was still not the case for most of the French empire. From the 1890s to the 1920s, there were numerous military campaigns from Morocco to Madagascar frequently involving irregular forces during the initial stages of French occupation, later often followed by protracted insurgencies. Important French military thinkers on colonial COIN included Joseph Gallieni, who saw action primarily along the Niger River in the

---

[8] Jacques Frémeaux, *Les Bureaux arabes dans l'Algérie de la conquête* (Paris: Denoël, 1993).

1870s–1880s, in the Tonkin region of French Indochina during 1892–1896, and in Madagascar during 1896–1905, as well as Hubert Lyautey, a member of Gallieni's staff during the latter two campaigns. Lyautey would later write books about this shared experience as well as applying the lessons learned as the supreme French military commander in Morocco at the beginning of the twentieth century.[9]

Gallieni and Lyautey were perfectly willing to use force to coerce locals into submission to what they perceived as a legitimate French rule and superior civilisation. They were, after all, military commanders voluntarily contributing to French colonial expansion. Nevertheless, they also strongly advocated colonial COIN conceived as pacification, requiring a more comprehensive approach than mere reliance on military force.

There were evident tensions in the Gallieni/Lyautey approach to empire-building by securing a territory militarily, while also seeking the cooperation of locals through the careful management of local elites, local development and local customs. As always in military strategy, balancing these contradictions was more easily said than done. Yet even in Algeria, it cannot be maintained that the French approach offered nothing more than brutal repression. There was a very real concern, institutionalised in the *bureaux arabes*, to give the local population more than just the sword. Gallieni and Lyautey took the core mission of pacification seriously by advocating that the entire French military, not just a few civil servants, should be involved in a more comprehensive approach of winning over the local population by providing economic incentives, and not just fighting off armed insurgents. This approach required not just securing territory, but also a concern for what today would be called the economic security of the indigenous population. Managing local elites and respecting some local customs was also part of this approach. This was often hard to achieve given both local resistance and the centralizing trend of French colonialism, as illustrated by Lyautey's not altogether successful efforts to consolidate French control of Morocco through close engagement with the Sharifian monarchy. He correctly predicted but could not prevent an insurgency in Morocco in the 1920s. That the implications of this generic approach are not linear is illustrated by the fact that Gallieni had previously opted for abolishing the monarchy in Madagascar, not just because he saw it as anti-French, but also as an effort to gain support from other local groups whom he saw as disadvantaged by the existing local distribution of wealth and power.

[9] See, e.g., André Le Révérend, *Lyautey* (Paris: Fayard, 1983); Marc Michel, *Gallieni* (Paris: Fayard, 1989).

In any case, Gallieni and Lyautey represented a shift in the emphasis within the French approach to COIN, away from that first developed by Bugeaud, who had claimed that the only effective way a conventional force could defeat highly mobile insurgents was by adopting their *razzia* tactics, often involving brutal retaliation. Gallieni and Lyautey in their writings and, to certain degree, in their actions represented an attempt at a more systematic, multilevel and less militarised approach to COIN, as even some of the more critical analysis of their approach acknowledge.[10] Their approach is paradigmatically reflected in Gallieni's idea of '*tache d'huile*'. The rationale for this ink-spot approach to irregular warfare was the need to create a frontline in a war without frontlines and the conviction that to pacify an area, clearing it militarily was not enough. It was also crucial to hold the new territory, not just by garrisoning it, but also by creating positive incentives for locals to adhere to the new colonial order, including, for example, safe market-places, roads, bridges, hospitals, wells and schools. This required a planned occupation and administration through gradual expansion, instead of spectacular military actions by ambitious men on the spot without proper follow-up that could degenerate into chaos and failure. As advocates of this approach (to some extent a reinvention of the ideas of the eighteenth-century Spanish soldier-diplomat Santa Cruz de Marcenado, whose works had been translated into French and had stood in high esteem in France and elsewhere in Europe before the French Revolution),[11] Gallieni, and following him, Lyautey, may have exaggerated its benefits. But it would be wrong to read into their views the notion that purely peaceful means would always be enough. In fact, they were arguing quite strongly for a single command of a soldier-administrator over military and civilian means precisely because they believed pacification would require both carrots and sticks.[12] Some of the criticism levelled at these French military thinkers reflects an enduring problem in the analysis of COIN: it makes no sense to expect from better theories a guarantee of victory in all circumstances. How successful

---

[10] Douglas Porch, 'Bugeaud, Gallieni, Lyautey: The Development of French Colonial Warfare', in Paret (ed.), *Makers of Modern Strategy* (Oxford: Oxford University Press, 1986), 395–8.

[11] Santa Cruz de Marcenado: *Reflexiones militares*, excerpts in Beatrice Heuser (ed. and trans.), *The Strategy Makers* (Santa Barbara, CA: ABC Clio, 2010), 128–46.

[12] The most accessible presentation of this thesis by Lyautey as a staff officer under Gallieni, is his famous influential text, Louis H. G. Lyautey: *Durôle colonial de l'armée* (Paris: Armand Colin, 1900), 3 passim.

and how truly influential this less violent approach really was in the expansion and consolidation of the French empire is open to debate.[13]

From a Failure to Develop a Doctrine to Defeat in Indochina

Overseas insurgencies were often labelled a *'guerre d'Afrique'* (African war) or *'petite guerre'* (small war). This points to their relatively limited impact and marginal importance for the French military. They never resulted in claims of a generic theory of wider significance about a fundamentally different and important type of warfare. Even Bugeaud, who was the first to articulate lessons drawn from it, regarded it ultimately as a preliminary preparation (and an incomplete one) for a major war.

Thus, while France had a long experience of colonial COIN, this expertise took time to translate into official guidelines. When it did, it was mostly in guidelines focused on specific practical matters like logistics or engineering or manoeuvres, not on a comprehensive integrated doctrine for COIN. And insofar as it had a significant influence, it was on the French Army in (North) Africa or the Colonial Marine forces, not on the all French military.[14] In the context of the French Army as a whole small colonial wars tended to be seen as a minor matter or even a dangerous distraction from conventional war; this reflected the dominant bias among officers, institutionalised in their education at Saint-Cyr or the École Militaire, where the main emphasis was on conventional warfare (major war). To be fair, this also reflected the strategic priority in France, which during most of this period faced very real conventional threats to its survival in Europe. Colonial warfare was even blamed for lowering of military standards. But while there were good strategic reasons for this prevalence of conventional warfare in French military culture in the late nineteenth and the first half of the twentieth centuries, this became problematic after 1945.

Rather than speaking of a failure of the French approach to COIN, however, we should point to a failure to consolidate it into a formal doctrine, which might then be periodically revised and updated and widely spread across the French military. Colonel Lacheroy, a major

---

[13] Jacques Frémeaux: *De quoi fut fait l'Empire. Les guerres coloniales au XIXe siècle* (Paris: CNRS Éditions, 2010), 361–2.
[14] Pervillé, *Atlas de la guerre d'Algérie.*

figure in French COIN theory, includes a telling anecdote in his memoirs. When he was about to be sent to Indochina after the Second World War, a senior metropolitan officer told him: 'with your rank' and 'with your education, you have nothing to learn down there ... it is completely out-dated in relation to modern warfare'. Even in terms of testing new weapons Indochina was seen as useless because they were 'used quite inappropriately'.[15] Many officers who served in Indochina encountered similar attitudes.[16]

The French war in Indochina (1945–1955) derives its importance for France from its traumatic effect on the French military with the surrender of Dien Bien Phu. This greatly influenced key officers who went on to play an important role in Algeria, including the French military thinkers Colonels Lacheroy and Trinquier and Captain Galula.[17] The war is paradigmatic for how these unconventional small wars were becoming a major challenge for conventional armies after 1945. This war in particular provided a cautionary tale regarding the difficulties of fighting an insurgency without a proper doctrine. A well-armed, well-organised massive insurgency with significant popular support, such as the one carried out by the Viet-Minh with their own mix of nationalism and Maoist doctrine, is a formidable foe.[18]

The preliminary stage of the French War in Indochina, already with an element of counter-guerrilla activity, was the French reoccupation of Indochina from October 1945. Despite huge difficulties, the makeshift French expeditionary force under General Leclerc de Hauteclocque managed to recover control of the main cities and roads of South Vietnam and Cambodia in just four months using the traditional French approach of offensive columns. Colonel Massu, who as a general would play a major role in Algeria, was in charge of one of these columns and identified problems: tanks 'were of limited effectiveness' except 'as a display of French superiority', and therefore he recommended resorting

---

[15] Lacheroy, 'La Guerre Révolutionnaire', 308.
[16] Paul-Marie de la Gorce: *The French Army: A Military-Political History* (London: Weidenfeld and Nicolson, 1963), 394–5.
[17] Charles Lacheroy, 'La Guerre Révolutionnaire' in R. Trotabas et al. (eds.), *La Défense Nationale* (Paris: PUF, 1958); Roger Trinquier: *La Guerre moderne* (Paris: La Table Ronde, 1961), trans. as *Modern Warfare: A French View of Counterinsurgency* (Westport, CT: Praeger, 2006); David Galula, *Counterinsurgency Warfare, Theory and Practice*, 3rd ed. (New York: Praeger, 2005).
[18] See, e.g., Peter Dunn, *The First Vietnam War* (London: C. Hurst and Comp, 1985); Jacques Dalloz, *La Guerre d'Indochine 1945–1954* (Paris: Seuil, 1987); Lucien Bodard, *La Guerre d'Indochine* (Paris: Grasset, 2003); Michel Bodi, *Dictionnaire de la Guerre d'Indochine* (Paris: Economica, 2004); Martin Windrow, *The Last Valley: Dien Bien Phu and the French Defeat in Indochina* (London: Weidenfeld and Nicolson, 2004).

to local forces for a number of reasons, including propaganda.[19] General Leclerc defended the need to reach a political accommodation with the Viet-Minh quickly, seeing a purely kinetic approach as inadequate. Not only Leclerc but also General Gracey, who commanded the brief British occupation of South Vietnam in 1945, feared that if a political accommodation could not be reached, there would be 'guerrilla warfare'.[20] Others saw no need for change, holding on to a disparaging view of Vietnamese insurgents.[21] A more traditional colonial show of force may well have seemed like the only option for a weakened colonial power, particularly after the great violence of the Second World War.

This brutally violent traditionalist approach, after all, had been successful against the isolated and poorly organised uprisings in Sétif, Algeria, earlier in 1945 and would succeed again in Madagascar in 1947.[22] In Indochina, however, the insurgents were much better organised and armed thanks to Communist cells and captured weapons from the world war. They could rely on a porous border with China to find sanctuary out of the reach of the French army. The French display of force in Indochina resulted not in triumph but in uncontrollable escalation.

The guerrilla stage of the conflict really started after the Viet-Minh uprising of December 1946. The French military never fully recovered, especially in North Vietnam. By 1948, the Viet-Minh were already on the offensive, for the first time bringing on the near-collapse of a French military outpost. One of the key problems of the French approach in Indochina was that too few troops attempted to control too much territory with too many fixed positions, tasked to secure roads, bridges, dams, etc.

The real turning point came in 1949 with Mao's victory in China, making it the arsenal of the Viet-Minh, who were increasingly well-trained, well-organised, and well-armed as well as experienced. The fall of Dien-Bien-Phu in 1954 was the culmination of this trend towards what we might call hybrid warfare.[23] This was what future General André Beaufre, who also fought in Indochina, was getting at by referring to it as '*grande guerrilla*' in which the insurgents reached a very high level of

---

[19] Note on Pacification (17.11.1945), from Massu's personal archive, cit. official biography by Pierre Pellissier, *Massu* (Paris: Perrin, 2003), 119–20.

[20] Letter from General Gracey to General Slim (5 November 1945) cit. Peter M. Dunn, *The First Vietnam War* (London: C. Hurst and Comp, 1985), 293.

[21] Jean Planchais, *Le Malaise de l'Armée* (Paris, Plon, 1958), 73.

[22] Clayton, *The Wars of French Decolonization*, 30–3, 79–87.

[23] Williamson Murray and Peter Mansoor (eds.), *Hybrid Warfare* (Cambridge: Cambridge University Press, 2012).

organization, manpower and firepower while retaining key characteristics of irregular warfare like high mobility and stealth.[24]

The difficulties facing French COIN in Indochina were made worse by lack of support in France for a significant reinforcement of the expeditionary force and a divided French high command. Some insisted upon the need to secure the border with communist China, others pressed for a retreat from exposed border outposts, which they saw as inevitable. Eventually, a decision was taken, but its implementation was delayed; it was carried out only after one outpost had already fallen, leading to major losses. This in turn generated a panic that threatened to provoke a collapse of the French military in North Vietnam. A direr situation was avoided by the appointment of the charismatic figure of General de Lattre de Tassigny, who rushed to Hanoi to control the damage in person. He drew on signals intelligence – any other kind was very difficult to get by the disciplined and ruthless Viet-Minh – to order air attacks against the most threatening Viet-Minh units.

De Lattre's new approach can be summarised in two words: '*vietnamisation*' and '*béton*'.[25] Vietnamisation meant not only expanding but upgrading local forces. There were already pro-French militias of ethnic minorities or religious sects. But the aim now was to build up a national army that would be the military leg of a political strategy of greater devolution of power to anti-Communist and, it was hoped, pro-French elites. French units were paired with new 'sister' Vietnamese units for training and joint operations. The Vietnamese would initially take over more static duties, releasing French troops to become part of mobile groups integrated into a strategic reserve that gave de Lattre the offensive capability that he felt was lacking, with paratroopers playing an increasingly important role.

Béton, that is, concrete, was used to build a barrier to protect core French positions in Tonkin (North Vietnam). This 'de Lattre Line' was presented by the French command as necessary preparation against the new Viet-Minh divisions being equipped and trained in China – these would prove so effective at Dien-Bien-Phu – or even to stop or delay direct military intervention by Communist China as was the case in Korea. They were a concrete measure of French desperation with the growing intensity of the Viet-Minh insurgency. French intelligence estimated that even within this core area of Tonkin, five thousand out of seven thousand villages were under Viet-Minh control. This fortified line

---

[24] General André Beaufre, *La Guerre Révolutionnaire: Les Nouvelles Formes de la Guerre* (Paris: Fayard, 1972), 227–9.

[25] Raoul Salan, *Mémoires: Fin d'un Empire* (Paris: Presses de la Cité, 1970), vol. 2, 195, 208.

was evidently unable to stop small-scale infiltration or deal with a clan-destine insurgent organization. *'Pourrissment'* or rotting was the graphic word used by the French military to describe this dangerous loss of effective control over areas.[26]

Terminally ill, de Lattre was replaced by General Henri Navarre, an ambitious 'European' officer. The epithet says it all: this was someone with no experience of small colonial wars and little inclination to learn about them, as the disastrous decisions that led to Dien-Bien-Phu would confirm.[27] Even so, Navarre argued in his defence that this was of a completely different kind of conflict, one 'never seriously studied, to my knowledge, in any military school'![28]

Still, some tentative efforts were being made in Indochina by French officers to respond more effectively to insurgencies. For instance, to engage with the local population, the Groupes Administratif Mobile Opérationnel (GAMO), small teams of civilian affairs officers, were created by General Salan, a veteran of Indochina and later com-mander-in-chief in Algeria.[29] An embryonic and reactive Morale and Information Service grew into a more proactive Propaganda Service in 1951 and a Psychological Warfare Section in April 1953.[30] According to the official lessons learned of the campaign, these efforts were, however, 'hampered by a lack of adequate personnel'.[31]

The last French supreme commander in Indochina (later Chief of the General Staff during most of the war in Algeria), General Ély, commis-sioned three volumes of lessons learned to be 'very widely distributed' across the French military, which proved important as part of a wider trend to openly debate what should be done to revise the French approach to COIN – in part by revisiting past examples of pacification, but also very much having in mind their problems in Indochina.[32]

Indeed, concerns reflected in efforts to revise the French approach to COIN in Indochina after 1950 would again be central in Algeria after 1954: how to recruit and use local forces effectively; how to use both a territorial grid and a highly mobile and robust offensive reserve; how to deal effectively with cross-border infiltrations; and how to regain and

---

[26] Cf. Hugues Tertrais, *Atlas des Guerres d'Indochine 1940–1990...* (Paris: Autrement, 2004), 27.
[27] Salan, *Mémoires*, vol. 2, 402.
[28] Henri Navarre, *Agonie d'Indochine 1953–1954* (Paris: Plon, 1956), 38.
[29] Salan, *Mémoires*, vol. 2, 306–9.
[30] SHD 10H 346EMIFT, Note de service 800 (4 April 1953).
[31] SHD 10H 983 EMAT, *Enseignements de la Guerre d'Indochine*, vol. 2, 16–17.
[32] SHAT 10 H 983, France – EMAT, *Enseignements de la guerre d'Indochine*, (s.l., s.n., 1955), 3 vols. For the quoted reference to the first volume see General Ely, [untitled presentation], idem, vol. 2, 1–2.

maintain control of the local population. Some of the officers most involved in efforts to reform the French approach in Indochina – General Salan or Colonels Trinquier and Lacheroy – would play an even bigger role in revising the French approach in Algeria, pleading in writing for a new French way in COIN.

Significantly, it was not just French officers and paratroopers or legionnaires who experienced this type of warfare in Indochina. Algerian soldiers who had fought on the French side in Indochina were also very impressed by the success of the Viet-Minh insurgency, and some returned to Algeria to engage in an insurgency of their own against French colonialism. This is an interesting example of the risks of contagion of insurgency and potential blowback resulting from recruiting foreigners to fight one's wars on one's behalf.

The French Approach to the War of Decolonization in Algeria

France's long colonial experience and lessons learned in Indochina would have led us to expect the French army to have adopted a less conventional approach, a pacification approach. An eye-witness of great future influence, the then Captain David Galula, recorded that 'in Algeria the order was to pacify. But how exactly? The sad truth was that, in spite of all our past experience, we had no single official doctrine for COIN'.[33] Of course, the writings of the great military figures of French colonialism did exist for those willing to dig them out in the libraries, but they were not fused into a coherent doctrine in a single manual. Also some important aspects had changed compared with previous campaigns.

When facing the anti-colonial uprising in Algeria from 1954 onwards, the French military was clearly more vulnerable than in the past. The insurgents had bases for training, arsenals and support bases relatively safe from French attacks in now independent Morocco and Tunisia. With an active parallel diplomacy, the FLN also exploited an international public opinion increasingly favourable to decolonisation.[34] A central predicament that needs to be underlined in analysing French COIN in Algeria from 1954 to 1962 is that the more effective the military became, the more damaging this was in terms of France's international political standing.[35]

---

[33] David Galula, *Pacification in Algeria 1956–1958* (Santa Monica, CA: RAND, 2006), 64.
[34] Matthew Connelly, *A Diplomatic Revolution: Algeria's Fight for Independence and the Origins of the Post-Cold War Era* (Oxford: Oxford University Press, 2002), 279.
[35] Benjamin Stora, *Le Mystère de Gaulle: Son Choix pour l'Algérie* (Paris: Robert Laffont, 82 ff.

Algeria had also changed significantly. The population of Algeria had grown from three to ten million people, a growing proportion of whom lived in urban areas. Development at the level of infrastructure – roads, railways, bridges, communications, dams, electricity lines – multiplied the points vulnerable to sabotage. There were also now numerous European settlers, close to a million people, dispersed in five hundred towns and numerous isolated farms. The French military could not contemplate completely abandoning the villages and other settlements occupied by the local Muslim populations, for this would clash with the main political justification of the campaign – that Algeria was part of France – as well as the lessons of Indochina about the vital importance of controlling the population.

To respond to these multiple threats and tasks, the French military in turn was expanded massively to fill in a tightly-knit territorial grid of regions, zones, sectors and subsectors. The resultant static force structure was a major drain on manpower but was seen as necessary. The rationale was one of creating a '*quadrillage*' covering the country with a network of military outposts, saturating the whole territory with troops, so as to allow life to carry on as usual as much as possible, and deter surprise attacks. Another crucial element of the French approach consisted of sophisticated multi-layered barriers (including the 'Morice Line'), successfully sealing the Moroccan and Tunisian borders, while the Navy would keep a tight control of the coastline, so as to cut off the insurgents from outside help.

Colonel Lacheroy expressed the principle that 'to win a revolutionary war it is necessary to establish a core area, and within that area, to control it fully.'[36] This seemed to point to a return to the Gallieni-Lyautey approach of the '*tache d'huile*'. The problem was that, initially, it seemed few parts of Algeria could be excluded from this core area. One solution for this was massive resettlement.

The more vulnerable regions were turned into forbidden zones for locals, and their entire population was sent into about two thousand resettlement centres under military control. These forced resettlements affected between 20 and 25 percent of the Algerian population, that is, between two and three million people, but with significant variations from region to region.[37] This was perhaps a lesson learnt from Greece.[38] In Algeria, the creation of areas where the military was free

---

[36] Lacheroy: 'La guerre révolutionnaire', 328.
[37] Rapport du 14 novembre 1959, SHAT 1 H 3090.
[38] The French officer and theoretician David Galula, for example, had served on a UN mission to Greece during the Civil War and was later a captain in the Algerian War.

to operate was seen as indispensable for the effective fight against the insurgents. Lessons learned in Indochina and again in the initial stages in Algeria led to the conclusion that '*ratissages*' or massive sweeps that attempted to cover vast areas vaguely suspected of sheltering groups of insurgents were of limited efficacy, or even detrimental, because, going along with random destruction and lacking results, they alienated the civilian population and demoralised the troops. Eventually the most effective type of operation seemed to be the '*bouclage*', aimed at closing in on a more precisely located ALN unit, trapping it and forcing it into a battle for survival. Conducted in limited areas – usually a few dozen square kilometres – these *bouclages* involved, first, light mobile units that systematically sought engagement with the insurgents. Only after contact was made were the offensive reserves brought in, often in the shape of paratroopers. For operations such as this to be successful, they had to be well-targeted, based upon recent actionable intelligence, ideally not older than twenty-four hours so as to ensure surprise, lest the insurgents simply melted away.

The French were, moreover, fighting in Algeria an intelligence-centric conflict increasingly driven by the urgency in obtaining such intelligence. This meant first and foremost using torture in interrogation, but also reorganising intelligence into a systemic structure and using structures to control the population – DPOs (Dispositifs Opérationnels de Protection) in urban areas and *sections administrative specialisés* (special administrative units, or SAS) officers in rural areas. This was in blatant contradiction with the rhetoric of equality between metropolitan French and local Algerians, a contradiction glossed over by the argument that the French officers were preparing locals to become more fully French, and ensuring their support in the war.

This variety of missions explains the massive number of French troops that rose relatively rapidly from 1955 in a succession of surges. They were made possible only by sending French conscripts to Algeria from 1956 onwards. Conscripts made up 70 percent of the European troops in the Army at the beginning of 1961, professional soldiers the rest. This resulted in the not always easy coexistence of two very different types of troops. There were, on the one hand, the so-called sector troops, used in *quadrillage* and routine patrol missions. On the other hand, the professional troops were part of the general reserve of paratroopers and Foreign Legion used in offensive operations. The latter can be estimated at thirty thousand men in 1960 and were difficult to replace. The majority of the French military was again tied to very large numbers of fixed outposts – which peaked at close to five thousand in 1961, many in difficult conditions of isolation and manned by demoralised young conscripts. These were plentiful, and the insurgents were less numerous than in Indochina, but it meant heavy reliance on ordinary young Frenchmen.

The results in terms of erosion of support in the polls for the French government's posture in Indochina and Algeria were not a result of the use of conscripts alone. A crucial difference was that the Indochina war always seemed very distant. Algeria was not only the overseas territory closest to France, it was treated formally as a part of France – although, evidently, with a special status for most of its native population. There was consequently always a low degree of interest in the fate of Indochina among the public, and the mostly professional French expeditionary forces in Indochina numbered only about forty thousand. In a February 1954 poll about the war in Indochina, 42 percent of the French favoured a negotiated exit, 18 percent any kind of exit and only 7 percent favoured fighting on.[39] In the case of Algeria the interest peaked in 1956 with 63 percent stating they saw this as the most important problem facing France; then there was a drop, but in 1958 40 percent still believed that this was the supreme problem for France. Only with de Gaulle's careful handling of the issue did withdrawal from Algeria become thinkable for most French.[40]

Recruiting Algerians to fight on the French side would have been the obvious answer to a slow but real erosion of French interest in Algeria. It was increasingly tried but never on a scale able to solve the problem, probably because there was not enough time or political will – especially because of the very vocal French settler lobby – for that to happen. Alongside a relatively small number of sixty-five thousand Algerian soldiers (including forty thousand conscripts) serving in the regular Army, there was a recruitment of '*supplétifs*' or auxiliaries. These were volunteers for shorter contracts of active service (six to twelve months), renewable. In 1960 there were more than eighty thousand local men enlisted. To this number can be added, in certain villages, small militias, the so-called '*groups d'autodéfense*' or self-defence groups (GADs), provided with less sophisticated weapons. Alongside their military value, the enlisting of locals had propaganda value and was presented as proof – however questionable – that the majority of the Algerian population wanted to stay with France.

For a long time, COIN operations were reactive, dominated by the idea that the essential thing was to avoid even minor defeats which the active FLN propaganda, especially via radio from Cairo, could exploit.

---

[39] Michel Bodin, *Dictionnaire de la Guerra d'Indochine 1945–1954* (Paris: Economica, 2004), 198.

[40] Gil Merom, *How Democracies Lose Small Wars* (Cambridge: Cambridge University Press, 2003), 102. See also Stora, *Le Mystère de Gaulle*.

A systematic overall proactive plan, in line with the *tache d'huile* approach, was elaborated only under the direction of General Maurice Challe, Commander-in-Chief of all French forces in Algeria from December 1958 to April 1960. This Challe Plan, pursued from February 1959 to April 1961, consisted of applying the troops of the general reserve to maximum effect by deploying them systematically and con-centring their efforts in a selected area, then another, so as to weaken and disorganise the insurgency. The troops of the *quadrillage* system would then be strong enough to confront on their own the remnants of armed groups through offensive commandos. Also, thanks to increasingly effective border barriers, by 1958 the insurgents inside Algeria could not expect to receive any significant external help.[41]

The success of the plan required intelligence and mobility. Intelligence was the responsibility of the *Centre de Coordination Interarmées* (CCI) represented, at the regional level, by teams of DOPs, working in liaison with the intelligence officers of each unit, who were in charge of, notably, the interrogation of prisoners. The DOPs had represented the institu-tionalisation of the mercilessly intelligence-centric approach developed during the Battle of Algiers in 1957 with its strict control of the popula-tion based on a ID system and, often, torture and even summary execu-tions of suspected insurgents. Operations, planned after a careful study of the areas of transit and refuge of ALN units, relied primarily for high mobility on intervention troops closing in as quickly as possible on insurgent areas, notably by helicopter. *'Commandos de chasse'* (hunter commandos) made up of *'harkis'*, native Algerians, were meant to scout and detect the insurgents even in the most difficult terrains.

As part of the Challe Plan, operations started in the western part of the country, in Oran, from February to April 1959. From there the French effort concentrated on the adjoining western part of the department of Algiers and the eastern part of Ouarsenis (Operation Courroie from April to June 1959), followed by the mountainous areas of Hodna (Operation Étincelle, in July 1959), the greater Kabylie (Operation Jumelles, from July 1959 onwards), then the smaller Kabylie (Operation Pierresprécieuses, from November 1959 onwards). In April 1960, Challe's aims seem to have been achieved in the Kabylie area. The final efforts were on the mountainous areas of Aurès (Operation Trident, September 1960 to April 1961).

The Challe plan was militarily effective. Challe made sure the French military regained and kept the operational initiative. The estimated losses

[41] Jacques Frémeaux, 'Le plan Challe', *Science et Vie*, 'Algérie, 1954–62, la dernière guerre des Français', hors-série (2004), 78–85.

of the ALN amounted to half its total strength – about twenty-five thousand men of a total of about fifty thousand. Furthermore, to survive this steamroller, the remnants of the ALN were forced to disperse and hide, losing most of their operational capability. They were also greatly demoralised, all the more so because they felt inadequately supported by their senior leaders based in the safety of Tunisia and Morocco. This led some insurgent leaders inside Algeria to engage in secret talks with the French authorities towards a negotiated cease-fire. Most famously, Si Salah, head of *wilaya* IV, secretly went to a meeting at the Élysée Presidential Palace on 10 June 1960.

The French military had also developed a brutally effective approach to deal with urban COIN during the so-called Battle of Algiers (January–October 1957) that resulted in the almost complete elimination of the FLN network of bomb-makers and organisers of terrorist attacks in the main city of Algeria. The response was based on systematic arrests quickly followed by interrogation, often including torture, and organisation of a '*dispositif de protection urbaine*' (DPU) for close control of the population and collection intelligence.[42] This mix was primarily developed and implemented by Colonel Trinquier and ensured a rapid and dramatic fall in the number of terrorist attacks – probably never has a terrorist network been so quickly neutralised – even if at a high human and political cost.

And yet the political dimension was recognised in the French approach as vitally important in contemporary Maoist-inspired insurgency. It was made clear that a core aim of the French approach was 'to regain control of the populations that provide support [for the insurgents] in this type of war and amongst whom it takes place'. The key problem was not simply to destroy armed insurgents but to wean the population away from supporting the insurgency and to delegitimise the latter. This was the core mission of '*action psychologique*', or psychological operations, under the control of the 5^e *Bureaux*, the newly created Fifth Section of the military HQs, destined to be, according to General Allard, commander of the Army corps in Algiers, '*bureaux pilotes*', that is, pioneering offices in developing a new and more effective approach to countering revolutionary war (that is, the insurgency).[43] The rationale for this as put forward by Colonel Lacheroy, the main advocate of this type of struggle and the

---

[42] Jacques Frémeaux, 'La Bataille d'Alger', *Guerre d'Algérie-Magazine*, no. 7 (March–May 2007), 4–55.

[43] 'Les missions de l'Armée dans la guerre révolutionnaire d'Algérie' (15 novembre 1957), SHAT 1 H 1943.

founding figure of these Fifth Sections, was that all aspects of this type of warfare had a psychological dimension that should be duly exploited.[44]

This new emphasis on psychological warfare was controversial and dangerous; it was from this experience of psychological warfare that the rationale for the unsuccessful putsch of the triumphant military on 13 May 1958 emerged: a seizure of power in Algiers and across the rest of Algeria by '*Comités de Salut Public*', or National Salvation Committees (a term borrowed from the French Revolution of 1789), led by French military officers who wanted to keep hold of Algeria. This putsch was seen by many officers committed to psychological warfare as the 'necessary response to the insurgent OPA structure'.[45]

In order to pursue systematically this effort by the military to deal with the political problems that they believed were being exploited by the insurgents – the lack of proper civilian administration of large rural areas of Algeria – SAS units were created in September 1955, with a specific manual to guide them.[46] They were heirs to the *bureaux arabes*, which no longer existed in Algeria but had survived in Morocco. It was among these French officers with some Arabic language skills that the first SAS officers were recruited. They set up a communications network aimed at providing an effective response to the most immediate needs of locals, gathering information, controlling and administering, preferably by co-opting local elites. In 1959, there were still only seven hundred SAS officers, but their presence was significant.[47] In carrying this widespread militarization of the French comprehensive approach to COIN further, military officers took over important roles in all branches of the administration, not only in policing and justice (military courts), but also in education, health care or public works.[48]

This action by the French military was part of a wider programme in fighting poverty and other sources of grievances that according to French leaders were the main cause of the insurgency. The Plan Constantine was the culmination of this approach, as formally adopted by President de Gaulle in October 1958, with aim of raising the living standards of

---

[44] Charles Lacheroy, *De Saint-Cyr à la Guerre Psychologique : Mémoires d'un Siècle* (Panazol: Lavauzelle, 2003); see also Paul and Marie Villatoux, *La Republique et son armée face au peril subversif: guerre et action psychologiques en france, 1945–1960* (Paris: Les Indes Savantes, 2005).

[45] Georges Robin, *Commandant rebelle* (Paris : J.-C. Lattès, 1998), 142.

[46] Ministère de l'Algérie – Service des Affaires Algériennes, *Guide de l'officier des affaires algériennes* (Paris : SAA, 1959).

[47] Gregor Mathias, *Les SAS en Algérie* (Paris: L'Harmattan, 1999).

[48] *Rapport sur l'activité de l'administration en Algérie au cours de l'année 1960* (Alger, Baconnier, mai 1961), 107.

ordinary Algerians by 6 percent a year.[49] Already from 1954 to 1960, the number of Muslim children in primary school had risen from 317,000 to 725,000. There was a development of welfare services and of free health care (more than twenty-three million medical interventions in 1960). All this was meant to show that Algerians were indeed becoming ordinary Frenchmen, but that such a massive investment was needed was in itself telling of the gap in living standards and the difficulty in making French propaganda work.

Highs and Lows of Two Victories: Normative Dimension

Already early in the nineteenth century, the human cost of *razzias* became the object of some criticism. Particularly hard to accept was the fact that it affected women, children and old men, and that it sometimes led to mass killing and raping of civilians. Analyses of *razzias* have emphasised that such blind brutal subjection of the civilian population was not the rule, while civilians were indeed often imprisoned and used as hostages to coerce the insurgents to submit. But French public opinion at the time was particularly shocked by the massacres labelled '*enfumades*', in which local populations taking refuge in caves and refusing to surrender were 'smoked out', most dying as a result of the toxic fumes produced by fires at the entrance of the caves.[50] Also controversial were the frequent beatings with batons and other forms of torture to extract confessions. This did not, however, lead to a generalised French rejection of wars of colonial conquest in Algeria and elsewhere. The great majority of the French population had limited access to this information, especially in earlier periods. Moreover, it seemed to many, probably a majority of Frenchmen, that very violent means were justified in dealing with a violent uprising or insurgency against the State, and this was practised even in France itself, for example, after the Revolution of 1848 or against the Commune of Paris in 1871.

COIN methods developed during the war of decolonization in Algeria from 1954 to 1962 at the time faced much stronger French criticism. Some focused on the recurrent problem of the so-called collateral damage in warfare, of civilian casualties during military operations in general and bombings in particular, and on how proportional and

---

[49] Jean Morin, *De Gaulle et l'Algérie. Mon témoignage* (Paris: A. Michel, 1999), 52f.
[50] Thomas Rid, 'Razzia. A Turning Point in Modern Strategy', *Terrorism and Political Violence*, 21/4 (2009), 617–35.

avoidable they were. Others focused on the difficult living conditions in the resettlement camps in Algeria.[51] But it was above all the certainly frequent, even systematic, recourse to torture that was condemned, not least because of the repulsive parallels this had with the methods used during the Nazi occupation against the French Resistance during the Second World War and its evident contradiction with the stated ideals of the French Republic.[52] And yet to the frustration of many of these critics, officers and decision-makers had no problem defending the need to resort to all means necessary to win such a vital struggle in the name of the *raison d'état* and the greater good of national security. Nevertheless, the opposition to torture united a significant number of public intellectuals and a growing networks of activists – a strong French tradition since at least the time of Dreyfus – with different agendas but sharing a desire to put an end to the conflict that they saw as a menace to French values as well as France's standing in the world. The political as well as strategic implications of reaction against the violence of late colonialism in Algeria were therefore significantly different from that faced by the violence of earlier campaigns in Algeria because of the different normative standing of colonialism in the nineteenth and early twentieth centuries, not to mention the second half of the twentieth century.

This heated debate points to an objective tension at the core of French efforts to develop an effective approach to COIN in Algeria from 1954 onwards, building on but also vastly expanding the ambitions of previous campaigns. The new approach was actually trying to be more targeted, but this was predicated on an intelligence-centric approach to COIN that required a massive gathering of actionable information as quickly as possible by all means necessary. Still, brutal or not, French COIN was always population-centric. Especially in its more recent incarnation derived from a close reading of Mao after the trauma of Indochina, the local population was the centre of gravity in this type of conflict. However, the ability to win over the local population – to which many in the French military seemed truly committed, with integration to replace colonisation in their psychological campaign against the FLN and the latter's aim of national independence – was inevitably undermined by the negative impact of forced resettlement and torture. It would in fact create a major divide not

---

[51] Michel Rocard, *Rapport sur les camps de regroupement et autres textes sur la guerre d'Algérie* (Paris: Mille et une nuits, 2003).
[52] E.g., Pierre Vidal-Naquet, *La Raison d'État* (Paris : La Découverte, 2002).

only between France and newly independent Algeria, but also between Algerians fighting on the two sides, and in France itself, where it contributed significantly to undermining support at home, eventually leading President de Gaulle to abandon the struggle.

Resilience at What Cost and for How Long?

During both the occupation campaigns of the nineteenth century and the anti-decolonization campaigns of the twentieth century, the key question was how far and for how long could such a massive protracted effort be maintained successfully. Despite successive insurgencies that occasionally shook French control over Algeria until 1871, the liberal July Monarchy and the other French regimes that followed – the brief Second Republic and the Second Empire – always accepted that the costs of maintaining large forces in North Africa were preferable to the costs of losing Algeria. They all followed the rationale best formulated by François Guizot, head of government during most of the reign of Louis-Philippe I: 'in response to each crisis, we have too often ... proclaimed a final triumph, complete control, the accomplishment of a pacification mission. Let us get rid of those illusions, this will be the only way [for us] to continue to make the efforts needed to ensure those [claims] do become a reality'.[53] These continuous efforts of three decades – telling evidence of how long successful COIN takes – did eventually deter the Algerian tribes from rising up again, for some decades.

In the second half of the twentieth century the same degree of French determination to hold on to Algeria by protracted COIN warfare, if and for as long as necessary, was no longer realistic. French policy towards Algeria evolved rapidly, in no more than seven years. It began with the dogma of French sovereignty over it (1954–1959), followed by the recognition by de Gaulle of the principle of self-determination of the Algerians (September 1959), and then (June 1961 and March 1962) by negotiations with the FLN for independence according to terms ultimately dictated by the latter, and the new international norm of decolonization. The COIN effort was sustained during no more than eight years, clearly a period too short for it to be possible to deal with a well-organised insurgency with significant external support.

---

[53] Letter from Guizot to Bugeaud, 24 April 1846, in François Guizot (ed.), *Mémoires pour servir à l'histoire de mon temps*, vol. 7 (Paris : Michel Lévy, 1865).

Conclusion

What can we conclude regarding a French approach to COIN? Did it conform to the usual portrayal of French COIN? Did it show a certain specificity and continuity? And was it effective?

It has been customary to contrast British and French approaches to COIN, with the Algerian campaign as a paradigmatic example of the 'bankruptcy of French methods'.[54] Twentieth-century British small wars of decolonization are often portrayed as exemplary cases of success 'in contrast to the French tendency to resort to general punishment and intimidation'.[55] This stark contrast is not reflected in reality as we know from the growing revisionist archive-based literature on British COIN during the wars of decolonization.[56] The same reappraisal can be made for French COIN in the era of the *guerres algériennes*. The new literature does not deny that the French approach was often violent and coercive, or that it used torture, but it shows that France's was not an exceptional approach to this type of conflict. Nor did it necessarily equate with a lack of military effectiveness or of well-developed military thinking.[57]

One salient feature the French approach to COIN was the initial polarisation, lasting for more than a century, between colonial and metropolitan forces, and then in Algeria from 1954 increasingly between territorial conscripts and offensive professional reserve forces. A second was the total militarization of a French understanding of COIN as a total war – probably its most specific aspect. How specific these aspects were to France may require further comparative study, but that these features were central in the French approach seems very clear.

It is wrong to claim that France did not have a population-centric approach to COIN. The French approach to COIN was not population-friendly, but even at its most brutally coercive, it was very much population-centric.[58] The institutionalised expression of this

---

[54] Thomas Mockaitis, *British Counterinsurgency 1919–1960* (London: Macmillan, 1990), 56 passim.

[55] Anthony Joes, *Resisting Rebellion: The History and Politics of Counterinsurgency* (Lexington: University of Kentucky Press, 2006), 221–2. Even if the author exempts the more mature stage of the Algerian campaign from this.

[56] See the contribution of Robert Egnell and David Ucko in this volume.

[57] Among the contributions in English that demonstrate the greater complexity and sophistication of French counterinsurgency and the importance of the external dimension see, e.g., M. Alexander and J. F. V. Keiger (eds.), *France and the Algerian War, 1954–1962: Strategy, Operations and Diplomacy* (London: Routledge, 2013).

[58] This argument is further developed in a comparison with Britain in Bruno C. Reis, 'The Myth of British Minimum Force in Counterinsurgency during the Campaigns of Decolonization', *Journal of Strategic Studies*, 34/2 (2011), 245–79.

population-centric, comprehensive, integrated, but also highly militarised French approach to COIN was in the nineteenth century the
existence of *bureaux arabes* and the role of soldier-administrator advocated by Lyautey and Gallieni, that in the twentieth century resulted in
the setting up of GAMO in Indochina and SAS civilian affairs officers
as well as the growing apparatus of officers in charge of psychological
warfare.

But how effective were French methods? An answer to this question requires placing these campaigns and their aims in a global
strategic context. France in 1840 was a great power, strong economically and militarily. It was also then possible at an acceptable cost
militarily, economically and politically, even if only after a protracted
campaign, to overcome native resistance, in Algeria and elsewhere
overseas, just as the British dealt with the so-called Great Mutiny in
India from 1857 onwards, and the Russians with insurgents in the
Caucasus at more or less the same time. The wars of colonial conquest and occupation led to success defined in terms of a French
imperial peace that, as was usually case with an imperial *pax*,
resorted, at least in the initial stage, as a matter of course, to collective punishment, hostage taking and scorched earth tactics – the
razzia – and even to occasional massacres, to coerce local communities into obedience. This caused some misgivings in France, but
not a fundamental questioning of the righteousness of these wars for
spreading civilization in line with the dominant international norms
of the time.

Nevertheless, French colonial COIN was not based on more violence
than was current in other colonial campaigns at the time, and it was not
lacking in carrots as opposed to sticks, in both its wars of colonial expansion and decolonization.[59] This combination of coercion and attraction
was, in fact, central in the classic writings of the great colonial military
thinkers – Gallieni and Lyautey. In Algeria, it was against the advice of
some military officers that French expansion opened the way for massive
migration of European settlers that created a system based on the expro-
priation of land, forced resettlement and legal inequality between French
settlers and Muslim natives that was at the heart of the insurgency that
started in 1954.

---

[59] To cite but one example of another democracy using torture in its colonial COIN,
the British tortured Kenyans in their fight against the Mau Mau uprising in the
1950s, in recognition of which the UK government from 2013 made compensation
payments to surviving victims. See www.bbc.co.uk/news/uk-22790037, accessed 18
June 2014.

The international political context and the availability of modern weaponry, after 1945, significantly changed the odds against strategic success in late colonial COIN as conducted by any colonial power. In 1954, moreover, France, although richer than in the past, was relatively weaker military than the superpowers – the predominantly anti-colonial USSR and USA. France had been weakened politically and military by two world wars, like most other colonial powers. French efforts were made to think hard about how to develop a better approach to late colonial COIN. Confronting the French, the Vietnamese guerrillas were probably the best-armed and best-organised of all insurgencies that emerged between 1945 and 1975, reaching in Dien-Bien-Phu the level of high-intensity hybrid warfare and then going on to defeat the US military – arguably the most powerful in the world. In Algeria the Battle of Algiers, the Battle of the Borders and the Challe Plan achieved impressive operational results in terms of counterterrorism and COIN. They involved methods of strict control of the population, massive arrests and brutal interrogations, as well as forced resettlement into new villages in which conditions were often poor (especially at the beginning). Efforts were made to improve the living conditions of Algerian Muslims, and the Constantine Plan for massive development was also announced. All the French military propaganda and coercion was, however, clearly not enough in strategic terms to achieve the ultimate political aims of defeating the anti-colonial insurgency and integrating Algerians fully and willingly into France instead of opting for independence. This is evidently part of the world-wide drive towards decolonization. But it also raises the issue of the potentially very high human and political cost of military effectiveness in COIN, despite all the efforts that were made to provide carrots as well as sticks. The latter were simply too controversial in the light of new human rights norms and anti-colonial prejudices.

The fundamental problem with French late colonial COIN was therefore political and strategic, not military in the tactical or operational sense. This was the case *not* because the French military COIN doctrine ignored the political dimension of an insurgency or lacked a population-centric dimension. It was mainly the case because the basis of France's political strategy – the dogma that Algeria was 'French forever' and that all Algerians were French – was increasingly seen as factually false, and politically and even economically too costly to maintain in the context of the growing international crisis of the European empires. When French COIN reemerged later in the twentieth century, it was in a very different shape, in the context of the close security cooperation between France and its former colonies, primarily in Africa.

Epilogue Post-Algeria: COIN-Type *'guerres africaines'*, or the New 'OPEX'

More recent times have seen what Michel Martin has called a new era of French COIN of the type of the *guerres africaines*. They tend to be short, sharp, high-tech military interventions carried out by French professional forces and the Foreign Legion, mostly in support of governments, mainly in sub-Saharan states (occasionally also in the Indian Ocean – Mayotta – or the Middle East – Lebanon), mainly against insurgencies, more rarely acting in alliances. The scale of interventions has differed, from selective air strikes against the Polisario in the Western Sahara in the late 1970s, and internal police actions in Gabon in 1978, to airborne rescue operations such as that in Zaire in 1978, to larger operations including mechanised infantry with air support such as that in Chad in 1983–1984. Operations tend to rely on advanced weapons systems such as fighter aircraft, helicopters and precision-guided munitions, but also mobile ground forces, prepared and accompanied by intensive intelligence operations.[60] The French officers and units who were involved in these operations, and of course the Foreign Legion, drew prestige from this. Their standing within the French armed forces has become particularly important since the end of the Cold War, which marked a shift away from the main emphasis of the French military on the defence of central Europe. Together with the success of most of these 'exterior operations' (*opérations extérieures* [OPEX]), this prepared the revolutionary switch from conscript army to a purely professional army at the turn of the century.

Further distinctive characteristics of the OPEX include the emotional detachment of the French population from these operations, which involve no French conscripts and no French colonial ties and affect the majority of the French at best marginally. With the exception of the Yugoslav successor states and Afghanistan, they have not led to long-term engagement in the local conflict or to a more complex long-term strategy of pacification involving political and economic engagement in addition to military action. For the most part, they are the foreign intervention campaign that militaries dream of – short and effective, without the responsibilities of post-conflict reconstruction and state building. That chapter of French COIN operations is far from over. Most recently, France's operations in Libya, Mali and the Central African Republic follow this tradition.

---

[60] Martin, 'From Algiers to N'Djamena', 100–28.

4 Russian Counterinsurgency in Perspective

Stephen Blank

Introduction

Russia has always been an empire and has fought and is still fighting protracted insurgencies, generally, though not always, successfully. Yet this history remains virtually unknown abroad despite the flood of writings about counterinsurgency (COIN). Linguistic issues and a widespread distaste for the habitual brutality with which Russia and its enemies have fought these wars contribute to this neglect. But fastidiousness does not cure ethnocentrism, and the West's uninspiring COIN record suggests we might actually learn something from Russia's experience.

Moreover, Russia has learned from its past while conducting COIN in the North Caucasus since 1994. This conflict comprises discrete but linked, spreading and deepening insurgencies in Dagestan, Ingushetia, Kabardino-Balkaria and Cherkessia and represents a continuation or the latest stage of the war ignited in 1994 by Chechnya's struggle for independence. Despite their strategic importance for Russia and overt connection to global Jihadi movements, these wars and Russia's counterinsurgency campaign remain largely unknown abroad.[1] Therefore this essay aims to redress this lacuna in our thinking regarding insurgency and counterinsurgency. Our conclusions are hardly definitive, rather they are opening arguments that attempt to uncover at least some of the elements of this centuries-old tradition. We argue that while Russia has accepted several Western if not universal principles of war in its COIN operations, its history displays the development of an

The views expressed here do not represent those of the US Army, Defense Department or the US Government.

[1] G. Hahn, 'The Caucasus Emirate Jihadists: The Security and Strategic Implications' in S. J. Blank (ed.), *Russia's Homegrown Insurgency* (Carlisle Barracks, PA: Strategic Studies Institute, US Army War College, 2012), 1–98; A. Cohen, *Russia's Counterinsurgency in North Caucasus: Performance and Consequences* (Carlisle Barracks, PA: Strategic Studies Institute, US Army War College, 2014).

autochthonous approach (or approaches) towards insurgencies that has generally been successful even if at a high cost and protracted campaigns. Nevertheless, Russia is failing to meet its current challenge in the North Caucasus. Indeed, recently it had to dispatch the regular army to conduct missions rather than relying, as it previously did, on the armed forces of the Ministry of the Interior (VVMVD).[2]

Elements of the Russian Tradition

Russian history offers a rich palette of strategies, policies and courses of action available to rulers in conducting counterinsurgencies. There are clear 'constant operating factors' in Russian COIN which began with Ivan III's takeover of Novgorod in 1478 after which he promptly deported the entire population. As subsequent history has shown, mass deportations have remained part of Russia's 'instrumentarium' of approaches to COIN through Stalin's time, and some may cite the huge decline in Chechnya's population as either an intended example or unforeseen by-product of the Chechen wars after 1994. Meanwhile Russia's history reveals similarities in tactics and strategies with later practices, for example, mass deportations to Siberia, or into serfdom, as in the case of the Circassians to Turkey in 1863, up through Stalin's genocidal campaigns to the present Chechen war. Another apparent constant is an apparent lack of accounts and almost certainly a discouragement of small-unit tactical initiative. Russia's traditionally strong hierarchical and tightly controlled military heritage may encourage operational level or strategic independence to some degree, but there are few if any signs in the Chechen, North Caucasus or earlier Afghan campaigns of officers being trained or taught, as are US officers, to seize the tactical initiative. The 'Strategic Corporal'" does not exist in Russia's military.[3] But we also find alternative approaches where deportation was not feasible and where there are varying tactics and strategies.

Indeed, despite enduring constant features and even though we are simplifying drastically for reasons of space, two broad paradigms are discernible in Russia's counterinsurgency history. Tsarist, Soviet and post-Soviet authorities have frequently, though not always, successfully employed these paradigms. To some degree these paradigms are

[2] E. Souleimanov, 'Russia Redeploys Army to Dagestan', *Central Asia Caucasus Analyst*, 14 November 2012. Also available at old.cacianalyst.org/?q=node/5878 (last retrieved 20 February 2015).

[3] General C. C. Krulak (USMC), 'The Strategic Corporal: Leadership in the Three Block War', *Marines Corps Gazette*, 83/1(1999) Also available at www.au.af.mil/au/awc/awcgate/usmc/strategic_corporal.htm (last retrieved 20 February 2015).

alternative strategies and not usable simultaneously. Often where the first direct approach fails the second, more indirect, and socio-politically sophisticated paradigm replaces it. This does not preclude an overlap in the tactics employed in either or both of these paradigms, for example, deportations and great brutality. Nonetheless we can analytically distinguish between these two paradigms, especially in the North Caucasus.

The first strategic paradigm is one of brutal suppression entailing a comprehensive direct assault on the enemy and his society. Examples of this approach abound: General Alexei Ermolov's brutal assaults on the people and mores of the North Caucasus in 1816–1825 and his successors' similar assaults in the 1830s–1850s.[4] The direct approach utilised many of the classic scorched earth tactics cited in the introduction, burning of forests and villages, etc. Other examples include the suppression of the Tambov peasant insurgency in 1920–1921 that General Mikhail Tukhachevsky brutally suppressed, even using gas attacks on unarmed civilians and insurgents.[5] Subsequent examples are the collectivisation struggle of 1929–1833 in which whole communities and peoples were deported or, as in Ukraine and Kazakhstan, subjected to famine, and Stalin's deportations of many nationalities, particularly in the North Caucasus in 1943–1944.[6] Of course, even in some of these dramas, such as collectivisation, there were retreats and periods of concessions to the 'insurgents'. But in these wars the crushing direct attack on people and their way of life is quite visible and the primary approach. And an ongoing characteristic of this approach is its disdain, contempt for and ignorance of the native societies that resisted Russian attacks. That could explain why this approach often failed.

When this approach failed or was unavailable to Russian rulers they had to employ alternative strategies. Thus a second paradigm has been the attempt to combine relatively more tailored or measured force with political and cultural-religious-economic concessions to the insurgents, or the exploitation of indigenous values to achieve state objectives. In the early Soviet period this approach involved greater understanding of the

---

[4] M. Gammer, 'Russian Strategies in the Conquest of Chechniia and Daghestan, 1825–1859', in M. Bennigsen Broxup (ed.), *The North Caucasus Barrier: The Russian Advance towards the Muslim World* (New York: St. Martin's Press, 1992), 45–61; Cohen, *Russia's Counterinsurgency in North Caucasus: Performance and Consequences*, 6–7.

[5] forum.axishistory.com/viewtopic.php?t=127624; A. Statiev, *The Soviet Counterinsurgency in the Western Borderlands* (Cambridge: Cambridge University Press, 2010), 17; A. S. Bobkov, 'On the Issue of Using Asphyxiating Gas in the Suppression of the Tambov Uprising', *Journal of Slavic Military Studies*, 25/1 (2012), 65–104.

[6] For recent accounts see T. Snyder, *Bloodlands: Europe between Hitler and Snyder* (New York: Basic Books, 2010); N. M. Naimark, *Stalin's Genocides* (Princeton, NJ: Princeton University Press, 2010).

insurgents' socio-cultural milieu and often employed experts who 'knew the terrain'.[7] But it dates back to the Tsarist period as well – indeed, many of the same people were often involved in both periods of Russian rule. This strategy generally emerges during a protracted campaign when the state is either relatively weak, distracted by other contingencies, unsuccessful in its direct approach or understands that the size of the problem precludes the direct brutal tactics of the previous strategy. This particular paradigm emerged in the 1850s and 1860s in the North Caucasus against the legendary Shamil, again during 1920–1921 when the Bolsheviks sought to consolidate their rule there in the face of another of the periodic ethno-religious uprisings against its authority, in the Second Chechen war of 1999–2007 and in Ramzan Kadyrov's rule since then.[8] It also appeared in the 1920s in Central Asia in the attempt to suppress the Basmachi uprising when the direct approach had failed.[9] Soviet authorities also used this approach in the early 1920s to quell uprisings in the North Caucasus.[10]

These cases reflect a more sophisticated understanding and employment of the measures needed to undermine the insurgents' cohesion by splitting the movement and balancing concessions and appeals to indigenous values with repression. This strategy did not only make concessions to the enemies' way of life, nationality and/or religion. It is quite consciously a strategy of imperial management, whose main component is to find those elites who would work with Moscow or St. Petersburg, install them in leadership positions, co-opt them and their followers into the cosmopolitan Russian ruling elite, make the requisite concessions to the people and over the long term integrate these elites into the Russian state to deprive the population of a leadership stratum that could head any future revolts. Alternatively Moscow would designate a favoured

---

[7] F. Hirsh, *Empire of Nations: Ethnographic Knowledge and the Making of the Soviet Union (Culture and Society after Socialism)* (Ithaca, NY: Cornell University Press, 2005).

[8] R. W. Schaefer, *The Insurgency in Chechnya and the North Caucasus: From Gazavat to Jihad* (Santa Barbara, CA: Praeger Security International, 2011); S. Blank, 'The Formation of the Soviet North Caucasus, 1917–19', *Central Asian Survey*, 12/1 (1993), 13–32; A. J. Rieber (ed.), *The Politics of Autocracy: Letters of Alexander II to Prince A I Bariatinskii 1857–1864* (Paris: Mouton, 1966).

[9] S. Blank, 'Soviet Russia and Low-Intensity Conflict in Central Asia: Three Case Studies' in L. B. Ware et al. (eds.), *Low-Intensity Conflict in the Third World* (Maxwell AFB, Montgomery, AL: Air University Press, 1988), 37–79; R. F. Baumann, *Russian-Soviet Unconventional Wars in the Caucasus, Central Asia, and Afghanistan*, Leavenworth Papers (Fort Leavenworth, KS: Combat Studies Institute, US Army Command General Staff College, 1993), No. XX.

[10] S. Blank, 'The Formation of the Soviet North Caucasus, 1917–1924', *Central Asian Survey*, 7/1 (1993), 13–32.

social category and support them at the expense of less privileged groups and thereby restructure the local society.

Throughout the history of successful imperial advances Russia could rely quite successfully on these elites who form a pro-Russian party amidst targeted territories, peoples and states.[11] Combined with overwhelming force and Moscow's ability – a common operational thread in all its ventures – to isolate the theatre from foreign support, this blending of force and co-optation generally succeeded, most recently in Chechnya.

The Indirect Approach in Historical Perspective

Space precludes a comprehensive historical investigation of Russian counterinsurgency campaigns. But we can examine the relatively recent record and note the resemblance between successful COIN campaigns in the western Soviet Union during 1944–1953 and the Chechen campaign of 1999–2007 to underscore Moscow's ability to learn from failure (as in 1994–1996) and update its traditional recipes for success. Because the first direct assault failed to prevail in Chechnya in 1994–1996, in the second war Moscow revised its strategy and tactics. The new strategy in Chechnya clearly resembled the 1944–1953 strategy in the West. Indeed, in 2004 Commander-in Chief of the Army, Col. General Vladimir Moltenskoi, openly invoked the Soviet and Tsarist traditions in such wars going up to the 1950s.[12] In turn, Soviet authorities in 1944–1953 invoked their earlier COIN campaigns in the Civil War of 1918–1921 and the collectivisation struggles of 1929–1934 and learned from those efforts.[13]

In 1944–1953 in the western borderlands Soviet authorities employed the following tactics to prosecute a victorious counterinsurgency strategy. Many of these tactics have an ancient lineage, as shown in the introduction. But while they are analogues to other 'national military cultures', they also are used or combined in ways that are unique to Russia, and there appears to have been little effort to learn from others' experience, a continuing problem for the Russian military.

---

[11] For example, John Le Donne, *The Grand Strategy of the Russian Empire 1650–1831* (Oxford: Oxford University Press, 2004).

[12] Colonel General V. I. Moltenskoi and Colonel Y. A. Martsenyuk, 'Conceptual Approaches to a Nationwide System of Measures to Settle Internal Armed Conflict', *Military Thought*, 2 (2004), 1–10.

[13] A. Statiev, *The Soviet Counterinsurgency in the Western Borderlands* (Cambridge: Cambridge University Press, 2010).

- The decisive and publicised application of superior, even brutal, force in a war conducted against and among the entire population.
- The incitement of class warfare and relentless ideological mobilisation to split the peasant community and undermine the foundations of any other conceivable form of socio-political life as in collectivisation. This meant the incitement of poor peasants against so-called 'middle' peasants (*Serednyaki*) or 'rich' peasants (*Kulaks*) even to the point of engendering mass starvation. For this tactic to succeed it was and is essential that the theatre(s) of operation be informationally and in all other ways sealed off from outsiders so that neither combatants nor residents of the area know what is happening abroad except through official media. Likewise, Russian (Soviet citizens) must be deprived of alternative sources of events in the theatre so that the authorities can wholly and exclusively control the dissemination of the 'narrative' of the war. This deprives the insurgents of either outside support or of the growing war weariness and support of the Russian/Soviet population and preserves the insurgents' isolation from all outside potential sources of support.
- Soviet authorities regularly deported thousands of citizens, especially 'class enemies' and potential alternative elites, to the gulags or else created conditions forcing thousands to migrate out of the theatre, thereby 'draining the swamp' and limiting bases of support among the indigenous population for the insurgents. There have similarly been huge migrations of Russians from the war zones if not comparable migrations by Chechens and other residents of the area due to the fighting.[14] Here migration on the basis of economic incentives to replaces a conscious deportation policy but its effects may be comparable. In many cases, particularly after regions have been pacified, we see a conscious process of state-sponsored colonisation of the newly occupied or acquired territories. This colonisation involved not only Russians but also foreigners whom the Russian government invited in to these territories to settle and develop them.[15] Subsequently in the nineteenth and twentieth centuries we see as well that economic development, either autonomous or state-directed, also directly contributed to this process of colonisation as did also the evacuation of much of the Soviet population to the East during World War II. As the 2014 crises in Moldova and Ukraine show, these settlers are reliable

---

[14] S. Cornell, 'The "Afghanization" of the North Caucasus: Causes and Implications of a Changing Conflict' in Blank, *Russia's Homegrown Insurgency*, 121–53.

[15] S. Sebag Montefiore, *Potemkin: Catherine the Great's Imperial Partner* (New York: Vintage Books, 2005).

bulwarks of imperial Russian state nationalism. Thus we see the lasting residual effects of this state-sponsored but also economically-induced colonization in Moldova and Ukraine.

- Because they perceived this war of 1944–1953 as a class war Soviet authorities were attuned to the population and believed that members of the enemy, especially rank and file but also potentially leadership cadres, could be persuaded to turn by judiciously using amnesties. Then the authorities would use those amnestied former enemies as a symbol of the positive benefits of siding with Moscow.

- Moscow concurrently created local militias to conduct police and combat operations against the insurgents and using local people to show local support for Moscow.

- The total impact of all these tactics also facilitated deep intelligence penetration of the insurgents.

- The civil war and collectivisation taught Moscow the importance peasants attached to the Church, and in 1943 Stalin made peace with it. This allowed Soviet authorities in 1944–1953 to exploit opportunities to win churchmen and churches to their side through unrelenting ideological mobilisation and terror. This, in turn, persuaded some peasants to stay on the Soviet side and again undercut the mass and ideological bases of revolt.[16]

Learning in Chechnya

Chechnya during the 1999–2007 represented the latest adaptation to this well-established history of COIN. In virtually every insurgency Russia has succeeded in insulating the theatre(s) at risk from foreign support. Afghanistan after 1979 stands as the great exception that proves the rule that foreign support goes far to ensure insurgent victory, a lesson that US forces have signally failed to implement. For the West, too, Vietnam, Iraq and now Afghanistan show what happens when the theatre cannot be isolated.[17] This political, diplomatic and we would now say informational isolation of the theatre has been crucial and a constant tactic to preserve the integrity of the state against insurgent and potential foreign threats. Moscow, by isolating the theatre, also showed that it did not regard the insurgents' hearts and minds as necessarily representing the war's centre of gravity. Instead the Russian population was the centre of

---

[16] Statiev, *Soviet Counterinsurgency*, passim.

[17] A. Mumford, *Puncturing the Counterinsurgency Myth: Britain and Irregular Warfare in the Past, Present and Future* (Carlisle Barracks, PA: Strategic Studies Institute, US Army War College, 2011), 19–20, 22.

gravity also in Russia, and it too was informationally isolated from the war zone and from foreign opinion.

This operation displays Moscow's understanding of Information Warfare and Information Operations (IW and IO). Rather than appeal to Chechens' 'hearts and minds', it waged a systematic campaign to capture Russian hearts and minds recognising that target as the true centre of gravity and to make public support the lubricant of the armed forces. Using the media campaign to seize that public support, Moscow isolated the insurgents from domestic and foreign support, and framed the war as a terrorist campaign or as fundamentalists bent on destroying Russia rather than a war to 'control the narrative'.[18] This operation demonstrates just how important to any war control of the media and of the 'narrative' or 'framing' of the war have become in formulating and conducting a victorious strategy. And Russia's subsequent operations in Estonia, Georgia and Ukraine show how assiduously Moscow is implementing its own version of information warfare, which greatly differs from Western concepts. Here Russia has learned from and arguably innovated upon Western concepts.[19]

In 1999–2007 Moscow sealed off the area from virtually all journalists and seized control of the 'narrative' to portray the Chechen rebels as foreign Wahhabi terrorists who were aiming to seize Russian territory:

As far as the military was concerned, the goal of the robust state-controlled media campaign served three inter-related purposes. First, it helped to isolate the region politically as a precondition for military operations; second, it rendered the public at home deaf to the suffering of the Chechen state and its inhabitants; and finally it prepared the Russian families to accept war casualties.[20]

This 'information preparation of the battlefield' allowed Moscow to use the unrestricted and overwhelming force that media criticism had precluded during the first Chechen war.[21] Thus we see the sophisticated integration of an unrelenting deep intelligence penetration, subversion (of the Chechen regime in 1996–1999) and media portrayal of the area as run by Muslim terrorists.[22] And we see this again in the Crimean operation of February 2014 that from Moscow's standpoint may in some

---

[18] Ibid., 648–9.
[19] S. Blank, *Information Warfare à la Russe Forthcoming, 2016 Strategic Studies Institute US Army War College*, (this is an expanded, revised, and updated version of an earlier article, 'Russian Information Warfare as Domestic Counterinsurgency', to be published in the journal *American Foreign Policy Interests* and derives from a paper presented at GSPIA-SSI conference on Information Warfare, University of Pittsburgh, Pittsburgh, PA, 1–2 November 2012).
[20] Mumford, *Puncturing the Counterinsurgency Myth*, 666–7.   [21] Ibid.
[22] Schaefer, *Insurgency in Chechnya*, 199–200, 221–32.

ways resemble a COIN operation against the Ukrainian revolution. And beyond the benefits this suppression of the media provided to the armed forces it also greatly contributed to habituating the Russian population to accept overall media censorship and acknowledge that they were living in a state of siege, and induced them therefore to provide unlimited support for the government, which used this media policy as a major source of its overall campaign to impose an authoritarian state. This strategy investing Putin with virtually unlimited and even dictatorial powers at least as prescribed by law and custom accords with at least some theorists' view of the necessity for strong centralised leadership in an emergency situation and certainly facilitated and justified Putin's accumulation of powers even after the emergency.[23] Thus this strategy of securitisation of the media – invoking security as a pre-eminent criterion for defining the purview of state activity – was materially boosted by the Chechen attacks of 1999 and also served a major 'state-building' purpose.

This understanding also suggests that at least some elements of Russia's approach are not so unique as to bear no resemblances to or lessons for Western practices. For example, like Israel, Russia has systematically targeted Chechen leaders with considerable success.[24] Second, much of Russian strategy in 1999–2007 either corresponds to Western writing or should at least inform it, for example, to resort to more effective unity of command. Thus a 2004 article by the Deputy Chief of the Army, General V. I. Moltenskoi, openly argued for an integrated state system to prevent any manifestation of secessionism as in Chechnya. Moltenskoi argued that the national leadership should be so structured as to pre-emptively react to 'negative trends' in areas that are at risk, contending that the state must have a far-reaching capacity to monitor developments in these zones and guide socio-economic trends, and that this system should be subordinated to one-man control.[25] These precepts, though of long provenance in Russian military writing, clearly resemble the Western insistence on unity of command.

Indeed, Robert Schaefer analyses Russia's winning strategy in Chechnya in terms of its points of congruence to Western theory, implicitly dismissing the argument that Russia created something unique.[26]

---

[23] Ibid., 215.   [24] Ibid, 217–21.

[25] General V. I. Moltenskoi, Col. Y. A. Martsenyuk, 'Conceptual Approaches to a Nationwide System of Measures to Settle Internal Armed Conflicts', *Military Thought*, 12/2 (2004), 1–9.

[26] D. Cheng, 'Chinese Lesson from the Gulf Wars' in A. Scobell, D. Lai and R. Kamphausen (eds.), *Chinese Lessons from Other People's Wars* (Carlisle Barracks, PA: Strategic Studies Institute, US Army War College, 2011), 195–232; E. Miakinov, 'The

Russia's experience here and earlier may also possess considerable utility in the overall study of contemporary war, not just insurgency and counterinsurgency campaigns, even if many argue that these represent 'the medium-term future of warfare'.[27] But Schaefer's contention that Moscow's strategy can wholly be captured through Western categories may not be completely valid.

Third, Russia's experience in the Second Chechen War may have indirectly contributed ultimately to the improved understanding of the new requirements of contemporary war that finally prevailed in Russia's overall defence policy after 2008. Certainly the wars in Chechnya demonstrated the need to ensure genuine unity of command but also to provide a command structure that integrated not just the Army but also the forces of the Ministry of Interior (*Vnutrennye Voiska Ministertsvo Vnutrennykh Del* – Internal Forces of the Mnistry of Interior) and conducted a comprehensive socio-economic, political, administrative, ideological and 'reasonable' use of military force.[28] This flexible yet centralised and united operational command operating under Putin's highly centralised leadership from Moscow may also have been the germ of the idea to install joint and interdepartmental regional/strategic commands that fully flowered after 2008.[29]

However, it is also entirely arguable that Moscow in 1999–2007 learned and employed vital lessons from Tsarist and Soviet counterinsurgencies, applied them creatively and thus triumphed, at least operationally, in Chechnya. Indeed, after the initial debacle of the 1994–1996 phase of the Chechen war the Russian military came to study past experiences in Chechnya to see what had worked and outlined the following principles that had ensured past success and that should do so again if properly executed:

Agency of Force in Asymmetrical Warfare and Counterinsurgency: The Case of Chechnya', *Journal of Strategic Studies*, 34/5 (2011), 647–80.

[27] Mumford, *Puncturing the Counterinsurgency Myth*, 22.

[28] Moltenskoi and Martsenyuk, 'Conceptual Approaches', 1–3.

[29] M. De Haas, *Russia's Military Reforms: Victory after Twenty Years of Failure*, Clingendael Paper No. 5 (Clingendael, the Netherlands: Institute of International Affairs, 2011), 17; R. N. McDermott, *The Reform of Russia's Conventional Armed Forces: Problems, Challenges, and Policy Implementation* (Washington, DC: Jamestown Foundation, 2011) David M. Glantz, Foreword; I. Isakova, *Russian Governance in the Twenty-First Century: Geo-Strategy, Geopolitics and Governance* (London: Frank Cass Publishers, 2004); I. Isakova, *Russian Defense Reform: Current Trends* (Carlisle Barracks, PA: Strategic Studies Institute, US Army War College, 2006); C. Vendil Pallin, *Defense Decision Making and Russian Military Reform: The Oblomov Approach* (Stockholm: Swedish Defense Research Establishment (FOI), 2006), 174–9; D. Trifonov, 'Russian Defence Reform: Reversing Decline', *Jane's Defence Weekly*, June 8, 2005, Also available at www.4janes.com/subscribe/jdw/doc.

- Interdicting foreign intervention, that is, sealing off the theatre from foreign help of any kind to include informational assistance and media coverage.
- Creating a legal-political regime so tightly integrated to the state that it precluded any hope of secession and entails constant reforms and improvement of the state's governing mechanism to increase its capabilities.
- Enhancing the theatre's socio-economic dependence upon the Russian state and precluding outside economic assistance so that the rebels and local residents had nowhere else to go but Russia, while the regime isolated the rebels and took effective steps to dry up their economic basis of insurgency, or as the Soviets did, collectivise the villages to deprive peasants of means of resistance.
- In every way showing respect for the religious sensibilities and authorities of the people and their moral code.
- Establishing an integrated system of state measures to prevent an insurgency and settle the area so as to prevent or pre-empt internal armed conflict. This entails subsystems for the monitoring of internal political situation and for unified direction (control) of military and non-military measures and includes, and presumes, a deep surveillance and intelligence penetration of the society living in the theatre.
- Under central direction establish the equivalent of a plenipotentiary agent of the centre to oversee these measures in the North Caucasus.[30]

In practice during 1999–2007 many of these guidelines and lesser included precepts were adopted and used successfully by the Russian Army.

In Chechnya after 1999 we find a striking resemblance at the strategic level to this strategy and the key points of the paradigm of a more indirect approach. Even though class war rhetoric and ideology had long since been discredited, the idea of finding elites from within the insurgent community or utilising amnestied or other such elites who had recanted their past allegiance was essential. Moscow exploited the willingness of Akhmad Kadyrov and after his death his son Ramzan's willingness to support Moscow in return for power as Moscow's satraps in Chechnya. Since Akhmad Kadyrov was the Mufti of Chechnya, not only did his support exemplify the fracturing of elites that has been a common strategy for imperial success since the 1460s, it also divided the Muslim religious community and deprived the insurgents of the argument that they alone represented the true Islam. Not only have the Kadyrovs

---

[30] Moltenskoi, and Martsenyuk, 'Conceptual Approaches', 1–9.

validated Moscow's belief in their loyalty (admittedly well lubricated by massive subsidies), they also have applied the tactic of creating a seemingly loyal pro-Moscow armed force or militia, as in the 1944–1953 period to conduct operations not only to secure themselves but also to root out the insurgents and terrorise the remaining inhabitants of Chechnya. And in so doing they have undoubtedly attracted veterans of the first war and induced great divisions among the Chechen insurgents.[31]

Moreover, Moscow devised a genuine system of integrating both regular and VVMVD as well as other forces, Border Troops, FSB (*Federativnaya Sluzhba Bezopasnosti* – Federal Security Service), etc., under a truly unified command structure.[32] The Russian Army proved itself to be in some respects a learning organisation. There was a decided tactical adaptation even under most inauspicious conditions. In the Second Chechen War Russia avoided casualties and instead more effectively integrated artillery, land forces and aerial capabilities – both helicopter and fixed wing aircraft – to lay down overwhelming fire. This systematic application of firepower greatly reduced the insurgents' asymmetrical advantages, such as their mobility, while saving Russian lives. Overwhelming firepower also greatly reduced domestic support for the insurgents and undoubtedly functioned in many ways as an equivalent for inducing deportation or migration away from Chechnya.[33] This use of firepower was also connected to a strategy to reduce casualties and thus public unhappiness and to the reorganisation of command and control in ways that distinctly improved upon Russia's performance in 1994–1996.[34]

Another benefit of this reliance on firepower was that Moscow could use it indiscriminately in ways that proved successful in suppressing Chechen movement and tie down the rebels, and crucially, it did not lead to new attacks by insurgents or peasants caught in that net. While this finding may outrage the moral and academic values of many Western writers on counterinsurgency who find it a morally repugnant policy and argue that it breeds more opposition, in Chechnya at least, the facts prove otherwise. This counter-intuitive conclusion represents another way in which Russian practice diverges from Western teaching.[35] While we certainly cannot espouse such a policy, for those practising COIN it may turn out to be successful, and for them that is sufficient justification.

---

[31] Miakinov, 'Agency of Force', 664.   [32] De Haas, *Russia's Military Reforms*, 17, 28.

[33] Miakinov, 'Agency of Force', 674

[34] MG R. H. Scales Jr., 'Russia's Clash in Chechnya: Implications for Future War', *National Security Studies Quarterly*, 7/2 (2000), 49–58.

[35] J. Lyall, 'Does indiscriminate Violence Incite Insurgent Attacks?', *Journal of Conflict Resolution*, 3/3 (2009), 331–62.

We also see Moscow employing tactics akin to the ability to win over at least some of the indigenous religious authorities in 1944–1953. Using the Kadyrovs and the growing war weariness of those left in Chechnya, Moscow was able to craft an appeal to Chechens that claimed that the insurgents, who had in fact succumbed to a Salafist, Saudi-inspired version of Islam, not unlike that espoused by Osama Bin Laden and Aymen Zawahiri, were interlopers, outsiders who sought to hijack an indigenous Islamic theology for their own political purposes. Whether this development and promotion of religious schisms among the Chechens was a conscious FSB strategy or a serendipitous exploitation of an opportunity that presented itself is irrelevant because the exploitation of this tactic fits so well with the evolving Russian strategy after the shameful defeat of 1996.[36]

Finally as the insurgency weakened, Moscow was able to rely increasingly on the Kadyrovs and its policy of 'Chechenisation' buttressed by the Kadyrovtsys' loyal troops and a massive infusion of capital for reinvestment or redevelopment of Chechnya, and the grant of enormous autonomous powers to Kadyrov, who has said he is Putin's man.[37] Here again we see the dividends that accrue to Moscow from its ability to split the elite, namely the ability to play what amounts to the amnesty card as many insurgents think either revolt is hopeless or that Ramzan Kadyrov is achieving as much of their former dream as is possible. Likewise, the Kadyrov forces are the functional analogy to the militias of the 1944–1953 and collectivisation periods. In effect the increasing resort to this militia imparted the aspect of a civil war among Chechcens rather than an anti-Russian insurgency to the conflict, a development that clearly redounded to Moscow's benefit.[38]

The North Caucasus Quagmire

Consequently Moscow's failure to replicate its relative success in Chechnya is difficult to explain, although the continuing corruption, brutality and misrule that characterise its rule in the North Caucasus is the fuel igniting the fire.[39] Indeed, Moscow was slow to recognise that an insurgency had even begun there. Meanwhile as of this writing, no end is in sight, while Chechnya has meanwhile paradoxically achieved relative autonomy within the Russian Federation under the Kadyrovs' leadership; Ramzan Kadyrov

---

[36] Schaefer, *Insurgency in Chechnya*, 170–2.   [37] Cornell, 'Afghanization'.
[38] J. Lyall, '"Are Coethnics More Effective Counterinsurgents?" Evidence from the Second Chechen War', *American Political Science Review*. 4/4 (2010), 1–20.
[39] Both available at www.jamestown.org.

is clearly Moscow's and Vladimir Putin's chosen overlord there. But this seeming stability has been purchased at the cost of the spread of the war throughout the North Caucasus. While the war began as Chechnya's quest for national independence, the war in the North Caucasus has long since become a religious war conducted by the Caucasus Emirate, which is clearly affiliated ideologically, materially and politically with Al-Qaeda.[40] Paradoxically a war whose proximate cause was Chechnya's quest for national independence has morphed into a religious war largely motivated by the enduring pathologies of Russian governance.

To be sure, at least some of the army's recent exercises involve training for operations consonant with anti-terrorist or COIN operations. In 2009 a motorised brigade stationed in Buynaksk in Dagestan practised sealing off insurgents, and a battalion-level tactical exercise there witnessed motorised rifle subunits rehearsing the destruction of insurgents in tandem with artillery, tank and army aviation helicopter support.[41] Russian Airborne (*Vozdusnaya Desantskaya Voiska*) forces also conducted landings that were advertised as being against insurgents during the Kavkaz-2009 exercises.[42] Nevertheless most exercises are apparently directed against NATO/US or the Chinese PLA, not insurgents even when listed as anti-terrorist operations.[43] Moreover, most operations in the North Caucasus have been undertaken by the VVMVD, a force notorious for its corruption, venality and brutality.

Professional Russian military writings seldom discuss operational or strategic problems of either the Chechen or the current phase of the war, similarly to the absence of such writing during the Soviet war in Afghanistan. That absence suggested a disinclination to learn lessons from these wars, and that still may be the case in the current reform of the Russian military that apparently has in mind optimising the military to fight network-centric wars, which hardly resembles what is needed in the North Caucasus.[44] As Roger McDermott recently warned, there is a danger that the Russian army's strategic doctrine, tactical and

---

[40] G. M. Hahn, *Russia's Islamic Threat* (New Haven, CT: Yale University Press, 2007) and subsequent writings cited below; Z. M. Peck, *Insurgency in the North Caucasus: From Islamic Nationalism to Islamist Jihad* (Carlisle Barracks, PA: Strategic Studies Institute, US Army War College, 2012).

[41] McDermott, Reform of Russia's Conventional Armed Forces, 233.   [42] Ibid.

[43] For example, J. Kucera, 'Russian, Central Asian Militaries to Practice Counterinsurgency, Naval Warfare', Eurasia Insight, 13 September (2011), available at www.eurasianet.org; T. Ivlentyevna, 'Kapsiyets: Continuing Grand Strategy', Astrakhan, *Kaspiyets*, in Russian, 18 November 2011, *Open Source Center, Foreign Broadcast Information Service, Central Eurasia* (henceforth, *FBIS SOV*), 30 November 2011.

[44] McDermott, *Reform of Russia's Conventional Armed Forces*, passim.

operational training and procurement priorities reflect mainly a pre-occupation with large-scale conventional theatre war that could escalate to nuclear war. Therefore it might find itself fighting the war for which it is not prepared in the North Caucasus or Central Asia.[45] Should that happen, Russia would then, to some degree, replicate the Afghan war, where this silence also reflected the Russian military's inability to formulate a strategy adequate to the challenges of insurgency and counterinsurgency.

Current procurement policy openly emphasizes new nuclear weapons and then advanced conventional technologies that pertain more to a theatre conventional war in Europe against the US and NATO or against China. The huge Western debate over counterinsurgency does not appear in professional military literature, which reflects this preoccupation with major theatre war. We may explain this strange lacuna to some degree by the VVMVD's prominence in this theatre. Nonetheless a war that by 2006 had tied up 250,000 Russian forces, from both the regular army and the VVMVD in the North Caucasus Military District, should logically generate more professional commentary than we have seen to date.[46]

Meanwhile the consequences of this war for Russia are already serious, if not dire. Apart from the war's serious financial costs, Moscow's visible failure to terminate it has led the leading American analyst of that war, Gordon Hahn, to call Russia a failing state.[47] Ethnic Russians are visibly emigrating from the war zone, reversing the historic pattern of migration that accompanied and abetted the creation of the Russian empire, thus continuing trends seen a generation earlier in Central Asia. Public disaffection has taken the form of riots in Moscow against the Caucasus' overall financial burden, and some have even raised the possibility of simply letting the North Caucasus go, a recommendation that is still unthinkable to most elites.

Paradoxically the causes for this failure lie in the motives that drove Moscow's successful COIN campaign in Chechnya. That campaign's ultimate goal was not just the salvation of the state but rather its total reconstruction on the basis of an ever more centralised autocratic and authoritarian regime run from Moscow and increasingly driven by the

[45] Ibid., 400.
[46] J. B. Dunlop and R. Menon, 'Chaos in the North Caucasus and Russia's Future', *Survival*, 48/2 (2006), 110.
[47] G. M. Hahn, *Russia's Islamic Threat* (New Haven, CT: Yale University Press, 2007), 1; for close and up-to-date analyses of the North Caucasus see the Jamestown Foundation's *North Caucasus Weekly*, at www.jamestown.org for weekly coverage and its sister publication *Eurasia Daily* Monitor for frequent reporting from the war zone.

personal acquisitiveness and greed of its ranking officials to the point where today corruption is the system and brutality, misrule and harsh, violent repression are the norm. The two principal causes of the ensuing resurgence of violence in an already troubled environment are thus the destruction of local mechanisms of local self-governance in favour of corrupt, self-seeking toadies of Moscow, and Russian leaders' brutal anti-Islamic policies that aggravated tensions in an area adjoining an insurgency and experiencing difficult economic conditions.[48]

By 2006 if not earlier it was clear that these trends were directly responsible for the upsurge of violence. Gordon Hahn observed then that Putin's policies to create 'a power vertical' and dismantle the residual traces of genuine federalism established by Boris Yeltsin lay at the heart of the causes for this insurgency. These measures included the following steps:

- Creation of new, extra-constitutional districts to facilitate federal inter-ference in regional politics.
- New legal requirements rendering federal law supreme in all spheres of life that it addresses.
- A 'federal intervention' mechanism allowing the president to remove a regional governor or republic president and call elections to a regional parliament should it refuse to follow court findings in cases of conflict between federal and regional law.
- Termination of power-sharing treaties between the federal government and individual Russian regions, effectively ending regional autonomy.
- Reorganization of the Federation Council, the upper chamber of the Russian parliament, into a legislative body appointed by regional offi-cials, half of whom are appointed by the Russian president.
- Re-centralisation of budget revenues.
- Presidential appointment, rather than popular election, of regional governors and republic presidents (and possibly even city mayors and district heads).

Not surprisingly, these steps galvanised greater nationalism in several Muslim republics. Absent democratic federalism, Russia's complex ethno-geography and administrative structure are likely to produce out-liers. In Russia's Muslim republics, those outliers tend to be Muslim ethnic groups, creating a pool of potential allies and recruits for radical Islamists. In Dagestan, Putin's harmonising of regional and federal laws

---

[48] Apart from the evidence brought below see R. B. Ware and E. Kisriev, *Dagestan: Russian Hegemony and Islamic Resistance in the North Caucasus* (Armonk, NY: M. E. Sharpe & Co., 2009).

and (re)interpretation of the Russian constitution rigged the dismantling of Dagestan's 'consociational' political system that had previously preserved inter-ethnic harmony among Dagestan's many small ethnic groups through pluralistic representation in the executive and legislative branches. Consequently by 2003, Dagestan's two largest Muslim ethnic groups, Avars and Dargins, were on the brink of a major inter-ethnic conflict due to disputes over power sharing within the region's ruling State Council.[49]

Simultaneously the newly empowered Power Structures (*Silovye Struktury*), freed from any accountability to either local or central parliamentary or even quasi-democratic officials and organisations, and having no standing other than their loyalty to Moscow – because Moscow had ousted any truly popular and locally authoritative figures from power – conducted a veritable orgy of corruption and brutal anti-Islamic repression. In the wake of the Beslan tragedy, a COIN or counterterrorist operation that went horribly badly in September 2004:

Putin has called for – and the Russian Duma has prepared – new legislation granting the Kremlin vastly greater police and security powers in the name of 'counterterrorism'. Given the inherently anti-democratic instincts of Russia's security services, this new leeway has inevitably reinforced heavy-handed law enforcement practices. In mid-September 2004, for example, Moscow police conducted a series of 'counterterrorism' sweeps that resulted in the detention of more than 11,000 suspects. Authorities in the Moscow Oblast rounded up about 2,500 unregistered people during similar sweeps. Such tactics have been particularly aggressive in Russia's Muslim republics, exacerbating the alienation of Muslims from the Russian state. Meanwhile, Vladimir Ustinov, Russia's Prosecutor-General, has publicly proposed the detention of the families of hostage-takers, noting the policy could be broadened to families of all 'terrorists', however that might be defined. And, according to Ustinov, the round-up of family members of terrorists should be 'accompanied by a demonstration to these terrorists of what might happen to (their families)'. This proposal has met with widespread approval in the Russian Duma. Russian authorities have also undertaken several assimilationist policies, including bans on ethnic and religious parties and on non-Cyrillic alphabets as well as an attempt to establish mandatory courses on Russian Orthodox Christian culture in schools. In this political climate, grassroots targeting of Muslims has predictably expanded, with cases of assault and harassment rising exponentially.[50]

The reaction came quickly. By 2005 the entire region was on the brink of a massive outbreak of violence on top of what had already begun as

---

[49] Ibid.; G. Hahn, 'The Perils of Putin's Policies', *Journal of International Security Affairs*, 10/1 (2006), 67–8, Also available at at:www.securityaffairs.org/issues/2006/10/hahn.php.
[50] Ibid., 65–6.

Putin's policies made their impact after 2002–2003.[51] Yet Moscow still cannot grasp the problem that it has created for itself. Similarly this author has repeatedly argued that Russia's failure to subject defence policy and the institutions responsible for it to authentic civilian democratic control creates a constant temptation for war either in Russia or around it. The record of five wars in and around Russia since 1991, the coups of 1991 and 1993, two Chechen wars in 1994–1996 and since 1999, plus the war with Georgia in 2008 that Russia instigated, not to mention Yeltsin's projected coups against elections in 1996, 1998 and 1999 and the ongoing insurgency – all highlight the danger of this trend.[52] Absent such control, uncontrolled brutality becomes a normal feature of military life that is only further augmented by the stresses of COIN and makes victory more unlikely.

Conclusion

Russia's success in 1999–2007 and its previous and subsequent failures suggest that much of the current Western writing and practice on counterinsurgency, even when valid and/or successful, is culture-specific and does not always contain universally valid prescriptions. At the very least it should be broadened and amended to account for Russia's successes and failures.

As regards learning from foreign wars, national, state and strategic culture still decisively influences the belligerents' strategic and operational choices. States and militaries learn those lessons that seem most relevant to or in harmony with their traditional or entrenched ways of thinking about war in general and about operations, and not only COIN operations.[53] One recent analysis of the Russian campaign argues strongly that Moscow reshaped many of the variables called for in Western counterinsurgency theory and practice and devised its own 'autochtonous formula'.[54] This formula reflects the outlook and needs of an authoritarian regime convinced that the very integrity of the state itself is under attack and determined to use this insurgency as a pretext

[51] Ibid., 66–7.
[52] S. Blank, 'The 18th Brumaire of Vladimir Putin' in U. Ra'anan (ed.), *Flawed Succession: Russia's Power Transfer Crises*, foreword by Robert Conquest (Lanham, MD: Lexington Books for Rowman and Littlefield, 2006), 133–70.
[53] For an example of how China, e.g., learns from other wars and does so in idiosyncratic ways see A. Scobell, D. Lai and R. Kamphausen (eds.), *Chinese Lessons from Other People's Wars* (Carlisle Barracks, PA: Strategic Studies Institute, US Army War College, 2011).
[54] Miakinov, 'Agency of Force', 647–80.

or justification for constructing a centralised and authoritarian 'power vertical'. But he missed the fact that Russia's adjustments comported with Russian traditions of adaptation to the requirements of counterinsurgency, not a wholly new formulation. Indeed, the punitive and exceptionally brutal nature of Russia's COIN tradition suggests that its practitioners have always believed that the state along with their power was at risk from these insurgencies and proceeded accordingly, another sign of the inherent brittleness of autocratic power as perceived by its possessors.

To conclude, we can analyse Russian counterinsurgency practice in terms of Western categories. In Chechnya, the government understood that the responsibility for eradicating terrorism and insurgency rests with it, but failed to assimilate that lesson in the North Caucasus just as it failed to learn that in ethnically and religiously divided societies good governance is an essential prerequisite or precondition for preventing uprisings. Many other lessons can be gleaned from Western experience. For example, it is possible for armed force applied overwhelmingly and intelligently to virtually eliminate the military component of insurgencies.[55] Other, similar universal principles and lessons may also apply. But we would do well to take careful heed of those points where Russian practice and thinking have diverged from our own approaches and understand how and why they succeeded or failed in these cases since in many respects Russian practice and thinking diverge from our own thinking, and Russia has frequently succeeded at imperial management even when acting brutally.

Meanwhile operational and some strategic success in Chechnya bred later strategic failure in a typical example of strategy's paradoxical logic.[56] These wars in the North Caucasus have always been and remain generated by Russian brutality, misrule, corruption and attacks on Islam and the local inhabitants' way of life. While the Russian army and government showed themselves capable of learning from their mistakes in the first Chechen war, in a broader sense they have shown themselves utterly incapable of overcoming the past and learning from this miserable history. Tactical, operational and even strategic adjustments allowing Moscow to prevail may yet be forthcoming. But in that case they will only put a lid on the problem, for the fundamental issue here is the nature of the Russian state. And that nature, despite everything, still remains

---

[55] R. Giles, 'The Essential Soldier: Case Studies of Some British Military Responses to Terrorism & Insurgency', *Journal of International Security Affairs*, no. 5 (2003), 11–30.

[56] E. Luttwak, *Strategy: The Logic of War and Peace*, revised and enlarged ed. (Cambridge, MA: Belknap Press of Harvard University, 2001).

that of a Hobbesian state of nature or, as Western diplomats, journalists and intelligence officers like to say, a Mafia state. For either or both of those typologies, violence is not an incidental feature of rule, but actually the essence of governance. And where that is the case, insurgency, even if driven underground, is never far from the surface.

5 Crackdown
Insurgency, Potential Insurgency and Counterinsurgency in Modern China

Yitzhak Shichor

Introduction

One of the most important keys for unlocking the mysteries of contemporary China has to do with using the right terminology. As rich as it is, Chinese traditional civilisation – and its vocabulary – had been unprepared for the encounter with the West in the nineteenth century. New words had to be borrowed from abroad, usually through Japan, to represent political and social values and institutions that had not existed before. To be sure, genuine Chinese terms have been used, yet with a different meaning. Many of these reflect its pre-modern experience related to internal disorder including *baoluan, baodong, panluan, zaofan, qiyi* and others that correspond to the variety of English terms: insurgency, insurrection, revolt, uprising, rising, rebellion, riots, mutiny, unrest, etc. It is sometimes difficult to distinguish between them and to define them precisely. For the sake of this chapter I shall deal with 'insurgency' as a major armed and organised attempt to undermine a legitimate central and/or local government's existence, policy or decisions. Insurgency should be carefully distinguished from sporadic and individual anti-state violence, representing terrorist acts. Applied equally to both pre-modern and modern China, this definition calls for different COIN, as well as preventive, measures.

China's pre-modern history, and especially during the nineteenth century, had been infected by numerous insurgencies – some of an extremely largescale. Many had been suppressed, occasionally after a long time, but had finally led to the collapse of the last ruling (Qing) dynasty and to the disintegration of China. It is not only the patterns of pre-modern counterinsurgency that later fed modern China's counterinsurgency policies but also the collective memories of traumatic historical failures and their consequences. Contemporary China's leadership is very much aware of both successes and failures of historical counterinsurgency which greatly affect their own. This chapter attempts to outline the essence of pre-modern and contemporary China's insurgencies and counterinsurgency policies and their relationship in an attempt to underline unique Chinese patterns, or 'national style'.

Insurgency and Counterinsurgency in Nineteenth-Century China

Spanning over twenty-one centuries, the Chinese Empire had witnessed several periods of deterioration and degeneration – some quite long and painful – but none as bad as the nineteenth century, which led to its final collapse. Unlike earlier declining dynasties, the Qing had been facing an external threat of a powerful civilisation unprecedented in Chinese history, with advanced military technology outranking China's. Like earlier declining dynasties, Qing had also to cope with an additional internal threat of organised disorder and unrest, yet on a scale unknown before. No other century in Chinese history had so many rebellions and insurgencies of such extensive dimensions.[1]

Two major rebellions that had originated in the late eighteenth century launched the nineteenth century in China. Triggered by the influx of Han Chinese settlers into minority populated regions mainly in southwest China, the Miao Rebellion started in 1795. This was one in a series of similar rebellions going back to the Ming Dynasty that exacerbated tension with local and central authorities. Regular troops were sent from other provinces and, together with local militia and self-defence units, finally crushed the rebellion, but not before 1806. Forced assimilation, the prohibition of cultural habits and separation by walls and watchtowers only aggravated the situation, ending in another severe Miao rebellion in 1854–1873. The transfer of troops to help suppress the Miao Rebellion at the turn of the eighteenth century had facilitated another rebellion in gathering momentum, the White Lotus.[2]

A messianic movement dating back to the fourteenth century, the White Lotus Rebellion broke out in 1794 on behalf of impoverished local Han settlers in central China who protested against tax collection and extortion. By 1796 the rebellion had reached its climax, and the government dispatched more forces to suppress it. Using local militias (*tuan*), a good deal of brutality, extermination of rebel leaders, offering amnesty

---

[1] P. A. Kuhn, *Rebellion and Its Enemies in Late Imperial China: Militarization and Social Structure, 1796–1864* (Cambridge, MA: Harvard University Press, 1970); J. Gray, *Rebellions and Revolutions: China from the 1800s to 2000* (Oxford: Oxford University Press, 2003); E. J. Perry, *Challenging the Mandate of Heaven: Social Protests and State Power in China* (Armonk, NY: M. E. Sharpe, 2002).

[2] D. S. Sutton, 'Ethnic Revolt in the Qing Empire: The "Miao Uprising" of 1795–1797 Reexamined', *Asia Major*, 3rd series, 16/2 (2003), 105–52.

for deserters and separating villages by walls, the rebellion was finally quelled in 1805.[3] The combined use of social and military means to suppress the White Lotus later became a model for putting out the major nineteenth-century rebellions, primarily the Taiping. In fact, the frequency of these large-scale rebellions may have been a direct outcome of the dynasty's difficulties in crushing the late eighteenth-century insurgencies. These started a chain reaction, igniting the next major insurgency, the Eight Trigrams Uprising of 1813.[4]

Triggered by droughts and floods and the consequent sharp increase in the price of wheat, the Eight Trigrams sect – a millenarian offshoot of the White Lotus Society – invaded the Forbidden City aiming to kill the Emperor, overthrow the Qing rulers and restore the Ming Dynasty. The rebels nearly succeeded in their aim, but were quickly suppressed, leaving more than 20,000 insurgents killed. Originally religious, the Eight Trigrams sect launched one of the more political rebellions in premodern China.

The dynasty survived but had to face a number of major insurgencies, the worst being the Taiping Rebellion. Led by Hong Xiuquan, of the Hakka minority, who in 1836 had failed in his last attempt to pass the imperial examinations – the key to a bureaucratic appointment – the rebellion began in Guangxi Province in late 1850 and early 1851. Fuelled by a mixture of popular religions as well as Buddhism and Christianity, the Taiping armies managed to withstand the government troops and even defeat them. Hong set up his own state within a state, the Heavenly Kingdom of the Supreme Peace (*Taiping Tianguo*), with its capital in Nanjing. It took fourteen years to suppress the Taiping Rebellion and restore imperial control by the Qing Dynasty armies, supported by European officers who trained the Chinese in the art of modern warfare. Nanjing fell to government forces in July 1864, signalling the end of the rebellion, but it was not before August 1871 that they finally managed to put down the Taiping surviving remnants. In addition to mass civilian murder, some six hundred cities were destroyed.[5] Dwarfing the casualty figures even of most major European *inter*-state wars, this *intra*-state war

---

[3] K. C. Liu, 'Religion and Politics in the White Lotus Rebellion of 1796 in Hubei' in K. C. Liu and R. Shek (eds.), *Heterodoxy in Late Imperial China* (Honolulu: University of Hawaii Press, 2004), 281–320; Y. C. Dai, 'Civilians Go into Battle: Hired Militias in the White Lotus War, 1796–1805', *Asia Major*, 3rd series, 22/2 (2009), 145–78.

[4] S. Naquinn, *Millenarian Rebellion in China, the Eight Trigrams Uprising of 1813* (New Haven, CT: Yale University Press, 1976).

[5] P. A. Kuhn, 'The Taiping Rebellion' in J. K. Fairbank (ed.), *The Cambridge History of China: Late Ch'ing, 1800–1911*, Vol. X, Part I (New York: Cambridge University Press, 1978), 264–317; M. C. Yu, 'The Taiping Rebellion: A Military Assessment of Revolution and Counterrevolution' in D. A. Graff and R. Higham (eds.), *A Military History of China*

is considered the bloodiest insurgency in Chinese history (and one of the bloodiest in world history). About twenty to thirty million people died (some claim as many as fifty million).

Around the same time of the Taiping Rebellion, the Qing had to cope with another revolt, the Nian Rebellion. It was triggered in 1851 when the Yellow River overflowed its banks, causing an immense loss of life and damage to agricultural land. The government's failure to provide assistance (among other things – because of its preoccupation with the Taiping Rebellion and the Western powers' belligerence) was underlined in 1855 when the Yellow River yet again flooded, leading to a large-scale disaster. Even more organised than earlier revolts, well-trained and better armed, the Nian troops (including cavalry) cut the dynasty's lines of communication, which were overstretched anyway, and forced the Qing armies to withdraw, leading to social and economic devastation. In 1856 the Qing began a counter-attack, but its infantry was no match for the rebels' cavalry. Former Taiping commanders now joined the Nian, a move that enabled the rebels to withstand the government's reprisals. By the mid-1860s it appeared that the Qing was losing, but in 1866 its newly-appointed generals managed to split the rebels into two fronts. In 1867 the Qing recaptured most Nian territories, and in early 1868 it finally crushed the insurgency.[6]

By that time, ethnic minority (usually Muslim) insurgencies were sweeping over China's southwestern and northwestern peripheries. These were essentially separatist insurgencies. Led by Du Wenxiu (who named himself Sulayman ibn 'Abd al-Rahmān), a Han who had converted to Islam, an uprising broke out in Yunnan Province in 1856 following conflicts between Han and Hui (ethnic Chinese who had adopted Islam). These conflicts reflected racial antagonism and class discrimination rather than religious persecution. Indeed, motivated by political rather than by religious incentives, the rebels included Muslims and non-Muslims alike who shared the goal of overthrowing the Manchu. Similarly, the Qing forces set to crush the rebellion incorporated loyalist Muslim troops. Captured by the rebels, the city of Dali became their headquarters and the capital of an 'independent' entity they called Pingnan Guo, the Peaceful Southern Country. Du, known in foreign sources as 'Sultan', chose the title Qā'id Jami' al-Muslimin

---

(Boulder, CO: Westview Press, 2002), 135–51; Y. W. Zhang, 'Problems of Strategy during the Late Stages of the Taiping War', *Social Sciences in China*, 2/2 (1981), 85–112 ; Y. W. Jian, *The Taiping Revolutionary Movement* (New Haven, CT: Yale University Press, 1973); J. Spence, *God's Chinese Son: The Taiping Heavenly Kingdom of Hong Xiuquan* (New York: Norton, 1996).

[6] E. J. Perry, *Chinese Perspectives on the Nien Rebellion* (Armonk, NY: M. E. Sharpe, 1981).

(Leader of All the Muslims) and asked Queen Victoria for official recognition and military assistance. His requests were turned down. By the late 1860s the dynasty's armies were making headway in suppressing the rebellion, and, after they captured and beheaded the Sultan in 1872, the insurgency was put down. Thousands of Hui rebels were brutally massacred, and many fled beyond the borders to Burma, Laos and Thailand. The annihilation of the rebels was facilitated by one of Du's generals, Ma Rulong (himself a Muslim), who defected to the Qing forces and then gained almost total control of Yunnan Province. Dali fell in January 1873. Up to one million people perished during the insurgency in southwest China.[7]

Meanwhile, another Muslim rebellion broke out in 1862 in northwest China. It may have begun by a misunderstanding. As the Taiping insurgents advanced to the north, local Han communities began to organise militias to face the rebels, an act interpreted by the Hui as directed against them. Indeed, some may have cooperated with the Taiping, but the revolt was triggered by marginal incidents over prices of bamboo poles that ended in a massacre of a number of Hui. This indiscriminate bloodshed led the Hui to attack Han communities, and before long the insurgency swept many regions. Initial successful operations by Qing forces pushed the rebels farther west in the direction of Xinjiang, a region reincorporated into China by the mid-eighteenth century. Before the end of the 1860s Xinjiang had been seized by another rebel, Yaqub Beg.[8]

Still preoccupied by other insurgencies, Qing generals tried new, less violent tactics such as a policy of reconciliation, promoting agriculture, especially cotton and grain, as well as Confucian values. They planned to finance the campaigns against the Muslims by loans from foreign banks to be repaid later by the richer southeastern provinces. Using troops from other parts of China armed with Western weapons, the Qing armies began to slowly overrun the rebels. Several Muslim generals defected, and resisting Hui communities were expelled (following a policy of 'wash away the Hui' or *Xihui*) and their leaders were brutally executed. By late 1873 the provinces of Shaanxi and Gansu had been recovered. Success was facilitated by divisions among the rebels, especially along religious lines: on the one hand the Old Teaching (*Khufiyya*), an officially legitimate Islamic doctrine; on the other hand the New Teaching (*Jahriyya*), an illegitimate doctrine considered heterodox. Those identified with the

---

[7] D. G. Atwill, *The Chinese Sultanate: Islam Ethnicity, and the Panthay Rebellion in Southwest China, 1853–1873* (Stanford, CA: Stanford University Press, 2006).

[8] H. D. Kim, *Holy War in China: The Muslim Rebellion and State in Chinese Central Asia, 1864–1877* (Stanford, CA: Stanford University Press, 2004).

New Teaching 'sect' were ruthlessly punished. This distinction, very much like treating Buddhism as a legitimate orthodox religion and the White Lotus as an illegitimate heterodox sect, reflected China's policy of *divide et impera*. This rebellion, however, had nothing to do with separatism or independence, something that cannot be said about the insurgency in Xinjiang.

The Xinjiang insurgency aimed at establishing an Islamic state and called for *Jihād* (Holy War). Its origins related to the Qing increase of its military presence to prevent incursions from abroad. Yet the costs of maintaining these armies were considerably higher than the region's taxes could provide. Coping with other insurgencies and Western encroachment, the Qing could not raise enough money from other sources. Growing expenses had to be met by raising taxes and selling official posts, ultimately paid by the people. Discontent was exacerbated by the Muslim insurgency of 1862 and the information, often distorted, about a forthcoming slaughter of Xinjiang's Hui. Thus, Hui were the first to revolt, soon to be joined by local Muslim-Turkic people – Uyghurs, Kyrgyz and Kazakhs.

In March 1863 an initial attempt to rebel was quickly suppressed, but the insurgencies that broke out in June 1864 were too frantic and widespread for local troops to withstand. Before long the rebels captured a number of government fortresses and garrisons all over Xinjiang, and both they and Beijing applied for Russian support – and were turned down. This complicated the rebels' situation in Kashgar, China's westernmost city, where they could not overcome the government forces. At their request, help arrived from Kokand – on the other side of the border – in early 1865, which included a small military outfit led by a young commander named Yaqub Beg. His soldiers quickly occupied Kashgar but also crushed the local rebel forces – thereby gaining control over the region and expanding further into Xinjiang. As he advanced, his Turkic-Muslim warriors (primarily Uyghurs, known then as *Taranchis*) assaulted the Hui (also Muslim, but of Chinese origins) and declared *Jihād*. A time-honored legacy, the breach between Turkic and Hui still persists in Xinjiang.

By the beginning of 1871 Yaqub Beg controlled most of Xinjiang's Tarim Basin and also managed to win Russian, British and Ottoman recognition, and some military assistance, despite their misgivings. Yet Qing forces – now joined by Hui troops – managed to crush the rebellion and regain Xinjiang. Qing adopted a relatively conciliatory attitude towards the Muslims who had failed to join the rebels. Many of the rebels defected or fled (many to Russian Central Asia), and the insurgency was falling apart. Han Chinese were settled instead. With the fall of Kashgar in December 1877 the insurgency was over, and Qing regained its control of Xinjiang. Yaqub Beg and one of his sons were burned alive, and his other son and grandsons were castrated and sent to the Imperial Palace in Beijing to serve as eunuchs, a punishment probably unique to China's COIN *instrumentarium*.

Before the turn of the century additional insurgencies took place. Although motivated by religious, yet violent, disagreements between two Sufi Muslim orders, the Hui rebellion that erupted in 1895 in Qinghai and Gansu in northwest China was ultimately directed at the Qing. By early August 1896 the insurgency had been brutally suppressed by Muslim loyalist troops, culminating in a large-scale massacre of the rebels and their collaborators. Finally, the nineteenth century closed with an insurgency that turned into a war: the Boxer Rebellion. Called by foreigners 'boxers' because they practiced martial arts and athletics, 'The Righteous and Harmonious Fists' (*Yihe Quan*) was a secret society that originated in Shandong Province (eastern China) in the late 1890s in protest of the suffering of the people caused by the dynasty's failure to deal with natural disasters and mainly with the Western and Christian encroachment.[9]

Soon, however, the rebels began to side with the dynasty. In October 1898 they attacked both Chinese and foreign Christians (who enjoyed special privileges) using, for the first time, the slogan 'Support the Qing, Extinguish the Foreigners'. Indeed, in January 1900, reversing its earlier policy of suppressing the Boxers, the court offered them protection. By the spring the Boxer Rebellion had spread from Shandong, reaching the outskirts of Beijing. On their way they burned churches, killed Christians and confronted hostile officials. In response, the Western powers sent troops to defend their diplomatic missions in Beijing. In June German soldiers executed a Boxer boy, which instigated a rebel assault on Beijing where several churches were burned down. Perhaps not protected by magic, as they claimed, the Boxers nevertheless enjoyed widespread popularity and support by the people.

[9] P. A. Cohen, 'The Boxer Uprising' in T. Buoye et al. (eds.), *China: Adapting the Past, Confronting the Future* (Ann Arbor, MI: Center for Chinese Studies, University of Michigan Press, 2002), 62–74; D. D. Buck (ed.), *Recent Studies of the Boxer Movement* (Armonk, NY: M. E. Sharpe, 1987); M. Elvin, 'Mandarins and Millenarians: Reflections on the Boxer Uprising of 1899–1900' in H. D. R. Baker and S. Feuchtwang (eds.), *An Old State in New Setting* (Oxford: JASO, 1991), 223–47; R. R. Thompson, 'The Lessons of Defeat: Transforming the Qing State after the Boxer War', *Modern Asian Studies*, 37/4 (2003), 769–73; J. N. Wasserstrom, 'Terror and War at the Turn of Two Centuries: The Boxer Crisis Revisited' in J. W. Esherick, W. H. Yeh and M. Zelin (eds.), *Empire, Nation, and Beyond: Chinese History in Late Imperial and Modern Times* (Berkeley: University of California Press, 2006), 192–210.

Following the foreign navies' bombardment of Chinese forts near Tianjin on 17 June, the court began to support the Boxers openly and, on 21 June declared war against all foreign powers. Thousands of Qing soldiers joined by Boxer rebels besieged Beijing's Legation Quarter from 20 June to 16 August 1900. They could have easily overcome the besieged foreigners, but did not, and for good reasons. An allied force of 20,000 men had landed in China prompting the court to declare an armistice on 17 July. Violated several times, though never seriously, it ended on 13 August when Chinese armies resumed their offensive. Within one day the foreign forces intervened, the Chinese armies fell apart and on August 16 the siege was over and so was the Boxer Rebellion. Precise data about the number of those involved in the rebellion are not available. It is estimated that some 100,000–300,000 Boxers along with some 100,000 soldiers fought on the Chinese side against 50,000–90,000 Western troops (including the Russians in Manchuria). About 20,000–30,000 Chinese Christians (mostly Catholics) as well as some 200 missionaries are believed to have been killed, along with some 2,000 Chinese soldiers and nearly 1,000 Western troops.

Taking place at the turn of the nineteenth century and the beginning of the twentieth century, the Boxer Rebellion symbolises the transition from tradition to modernity. More than any other nineteenth-century insurgency (and definitely earlier) the Boxers displayed both internal and external objectives and incorporated foreign as well as Chinese traits. It should be underlined that the insurgencies mentioned above are only the major ones; in addition, scores, perhaps hundreds, of smaller uprisings broke out in different parts of China throughout the nineteenth century. Even without offering all the comparative historical data, it is clear that the Chinese Empire experienced more insurgencies in the nineteenth century than any other country. In this respect, nineteenth-century China can be regarded as a huge laboratory for studying insurgencies. Based on the empirical evidence presented above, it is time now to sum up the principal features of China's pre-modern insurgencies and counterinsurgency policies and find out whether they reflect a 'national style'.[10]

Pre-modern Chinese insurgencies can be classified according to their motivations, targets and location. Most common among the reasons for uprisings were human disasters caused by the government's inefficiency in handling natural disasters, usually droughts or floods that left many – occasionally millions – homeless, starving, ill or dead. Their grievances

---

[10] See also H. Eckstein, 'On the Etiology of Internal Wars', *History and Theory*, 4/2 (1965), 133–63 and idem., *Internal War: Problems and Approaches* (New York: Praeger, 1980).

were usually exacerbated by religious millenarian and messianic beliefs associated with Buddhism, Daoism, Islam or (since the mid-nineteenth century) Christianity. Uprisings were sparked not just by religious persecution but also by ethnic discrimination. In general the Chinese Empire was tolerant (much more than Europe) towards ethnic groups or those with religious convictions – as long as they did not intervene in politics. With few exceptions (the Miao Rebellion mentioned above is one) attempts were hardly made to assimilate non-Chinese, certainly not by force (especially since there was no official and institutionalised Chinese 'religion' in the Western sense). Being of non-Chinese stock itself, the Qing Dynasty (as well as the Mongol Yuan Dynasty and even indigenous Chinese dynasties) did not reject the employment of non-Chinese, whatever their religion or ethnicity (including Muslims, Christians and Jews, Arabs, Persians and Turks) – yet within prescribed and well-defined political borders. When these borders were breached by uprisings – that targeted local tax collectors, district officials or provincial governors or, in major insurgencies, the dynasty itself – the Court reacted without mercy. Tolerance went hand in hand with intolerance.

Pre-modern Chinese counterinsurgency policies consisted, as in many other countries, of brutal use of force – but not only. Indeed, usually, and especially with regard to small and local insurgencies, the authorities used uncompromised brutality to suppress the rebellion and to punish the rebels, their leaders and collaborators, and occasionally innocent people and bystanders. Torture – promoted by the Chinese to an art form – was not uncommon. The Chinese also would isolate the rebels by erecting walls and stockades. While similar methods were applied also, and often even more intensively, to large-scale insurgencies, counterinsurgency policy also consisted of non-violent methods.

These included preventive measures like sharing authority with local autonomous semi-independent leaders who received official titles and, beyond assuming responsibility for transferring a fixed amount of taxes to the court, could do whatever they wanted. Another preventive measure was the migration of Han Chinese settlers into peripheral lands populated by ethnic groups. This may have prevented uprisings by changing the regional demographic balance but may have also exacerbated unrest among the original inhabitants now driven out of their lands and property or otherwise discriminated against. Once the confrontation ended, Han settlers also helped to pacify the region because unrest and riots were detrimental to their interests as well. The Qing used social and economic incentives that offered amnesty for deserters and rewards for turncoat rebels. While enforcing ethnic segregation policy the Qing also attempted to introduce Confucian education, to adopt a policy of reconciliation, promote agriculture, especially cotton and grain, and raise financial support from outside the insurgent regions. The architect of China's more benevolent policy towards rebels was Zuo Zongtang, who nevertheless managed to crush a number of insurgencies in the nineteenth century.[11] He pardoned people who did not rebel or surrendered or had been motivated by religious beliefs. He instructed the Qing troops to be benevolent and generous towards the local people who were not to blame for the rebellion and were not to be mistreated. Moreover, administrative measures were taken to improve the livelihood of the local population, in particular Muslim, by providing means of subsistence and seeds, constructing roads for facilitating trade and travel, and taking precautions to prevent the outbreak of epidemics or famine.

Applied mainly in Xinjiang and northwest China, these policies helped in suppressing rebel forces and restoring Qing rule. Yet this is only one side of the coin (or COIN). The other side is the use of clever military tactics as well as Western-made arms that most rebels did not have, and instruments of brutal force, punishments, torture and executions. Thus, if there is a 'national style' in China's counterinsurgency, it derives, perhaps, from the dualism that is typical of Chinese traditional values: *yin* and *yang*, both hard and soft responses to pre-modern insurgencies. In this perspective, insurgencies have played a positive role in history by providing a dynamic force of change, facilitating the collapse of old dynasties and the emergence of new ones. Historical progress required insurgencies and could not have done without it. There is no history without insurgencies; it is part of human nature. It is also part of the Chinese pragmatist worldview. The ideal history is not without insurgencies (an unrealistic possibility) but with the proper balance between insurgency and counterinsurgency. This is also the legacy transmitted to contemporary China that offered additional dimensions.

Counterinsurgency without Insurgency in Contemporary China

Following the collapse of the Qing Empire in 1911, China disintegrated into a number of political units governed by warlords, the Nationalist Party (*Guomindang*), the Communist Party and the Japanese occupation forces. The result was a civil war as well as an international war. Under these complex circumstances, it is difficult to isolate different insurgencies or to identify legitimate entities engaged in counterinsurgency. The

---

[11] L. B. Fields, *Tso Tsung-t'ang and the Muslims: Statecraft in Northwest China, 1868–1880* (Kingston, Ont.: Limestone Press, 1978).

Nationalists' control of China was not only partial but also fluid. In the 1920s and again from 1937 to 1945 it was shared with the Communists ('the insurgents') based on united fronts, primarily but not only against Japan, that made the borders between the insurgents and the government indistinct and, more significantly, legitimised the Chinese Communist Party and contributed to the consolidation of its power towards the final showdown.[12] This uncertainty has changed since October 1949 when China was again reunified, this time under Chinese communism.

Since the proclamation of the PRC in 1949, its history can be clearly divided into two distinct periods: Mao's China from the late 1940s to the late 1970s, and post-Mao China from the late 1970s. There are substantial, even dramatic, differences between the two periods, but there are also interesting continuities. Indeed, some argue – myself included – that it was Mao's China policies that, willingly or not, had laid the foundations for post-Mao China, as different as it is. Noteworthy among the differences (and the continuities) are the outbreak of insurgencies and the nature of the response to insurgencies.

China's COIN in the first decade reflected the experience of premodern China. Relative tolerance for different social, ethnic and religious groups by no means implied tolerance for political opposition. This was especially true in the early years of the CCP rule when China's new communist leaders were still uncertain about their control over the Chinese mainland and, therefore, responded by force to any sign of disobedience. Violence was needed not only for achieving political consolidation and safeguarding CCP rule but also, and not less importantly, as an educational lesson for deterring and preventing future cases of insurgency and uprising.

Soon after its establishment, the new regime had to face opposition and unrest instigated primarily by former Nationalist troops and ethnic minorities that could not reconcile with the communist rule of China. Beijing's new rulers had to take measures to overcome this domestic unrest and opposition. Indeed, sporadic incidents of armed resistance to Chinese communist rule had taken place mainly in the first decade (1949–59), by remnants of the Civil War. In the early 1950s Beijing had to suppress local and isolated riots, mainly in the periphery.[13] Once again, much of this unrest took place in northwest China, and notably in

---

[12] R. Mitter, *Forgotten Ally: China's World War II 1937–1945* (Boston and New York: Houghton Mifflin Harcourt, 2013).

[13] J. C. Strauss, 'Paternalistic Terror: The Campaign to Suppress Counter-Revolutionaries in the People's Republic of China, 1950–1953', *Comparative Studies in Society and History*, 44/1 (2002), 80–105; K. S. Yang, 'Reconsidering the Campaign to Suppress Counterrevolutionaries', *China Quarterly*, no. 193 (2008), 102–21.

Xinjiang, where the Chinese communist rule was perceived as relatively weak. Gardner Bovingdon provides details of thirty-four cases of unrest in Xinjiang between late 1949 and the mid-1970s.[14] Yet, although he terms some of them 'armed rebellions', 'revolts', 'armed uprisings' and 'insurgencies', none deserves these terms – certainly if compared to China's nineteenth-century insurgencies mentioned above. Further-more, given that Xinjiang is about one-sixth of China's total area and larger than that of France, Germany and Spain combined, thirty-four incidents, some admittedly small, over twenty-five years is rather modest. Unrest in Mao's China and – as we shall see below – in post-Mao China's as well was limited in time and space, lasting for a few days and up to five months at the most, and involving relatively few protesters, as well as troops. All, without exception, were put down by the military and disap-peared. None really threatened the regime.

In our mind, Mao's China is associated with upheavals, radicalisation, attempts to create a new revolutionary society and waves of unrest. In fact, despite the political upheavals, there have been no insurgencies in China since its establishment with *one* exception: the Tibetan Uprising of 1959, to be discussed below. This remarkable accomplishment is an outcome of a number of reasons, first and foremost the historical legacy, particularly that of the nineteenth century. China's communist leaders could have drawn two important lessons from China's history that are still valid today. One is that insurgencies should be crushed or, better, prevented at all costs since they might lead to the collapse of the PRC similarly to their responsibility for the collapse of most Chinese dynasties (e.g., Han, Tang, Yuan, Ming and Qing). The other lesson is that foreign intervention should be prevented at any cost since it exacerbated domes-tic tensions and occasionally facilitated insurgencies at home. These are two foundations of China's internal and external policy to this very day.

Faced with unrest in the late 1940s and early 1950s, Beijing responded with brutal use of force, mass arrests and large-scale executions. At the same time it offered 'autonomy' to minority areas and adopted social and economic policy to pacify the resisting opposition. These traditional counterinsurgency measures were taken although there was no real insurgency in China. There was no symmetry between the unrest and

---

[14] G. Bovingdon, *The Uyghurs: Strangers in Their Own Land* (New York: Columbia University Press, 2010), 174–90. See also Y.X. Zhang, 'Xinjiang jiefang yilai fandui minzu fenliezhuyi de douzheng ji qi lishi jingyan' [The Struggle against National Separatism since Xinjiang's Liberation and Its Historical Lessons] in F. R. Yang (ed.), *Fan Yisilanzhuyi, fan Tujuezhuyi yanjiu* [Research on Pan-Islamism and Pan-Turkism] (Urumqi: Xinjiang shehui kexue yuan [Xinjiang Institute of Social Sciences], 1994), 331–63.

the response, which, in many cases, has been out of proportion to the actual event. Beijing has adopted severe measures that were not really needed to quell the unrest. Yet this extra use of force (also evident during the 1989 Tiananmen demonstrations, not an insurgency either) should be related not to the *actual* unrest but to its *potential* outcome. Small-scale episodes of unrest, that I call *potential insurgencies* and Daniel Byman calls *proto-insurgencies*,[15] have not been allowed by Beijing leaders to develop, or deteriorate, into a full-fledged insurgency. There was one possible exception: Tibet.

The violent hostilities of the 1950s reached their climax in 1959 with the Tibetan Uprising – the first, and last, large-scale insurgency in contemporary China. Tibet, which had maintained a quasi-independent status since 1912, was reincorporated into China in October 1950, the last frontier to be occupied by the communists. It took China's People's Liberation Army another year to end its invasion, and, although collect-ivisation and socialisation processes were not enforced in Tibet itself, they were applied as in the rest of China, in the adjacent provinces of Sichuan and Qinghai where many Tibetans lived (in fact, more Tibetans live outside Tibet than in Tibet). Resistance to Beijing soon deteriorated into armed clashes in Tibet's periphery in 1956, aided by Taiwan and the CIA.[16] By early 1959 the insurgents had proceeded towards Lhasa while withstanding brutal Chinese punitive counterattacks. At the same time, rumours spread about China's plans to abduct and arrest the Dalai Lama. In Lhasa, enraged young Tibetans began organising armed opposition to China's forces, and in early March the insurgency broke out. Suppressed in Lhasa within a few days, the insurgency's guerrilla fighters spread to the countryside, and it was not before 1962 that Beijing managed to put an end to it. Casualties are estimated at 87,000, and a good deal of damage was inflicted to Tibetan monasteries and culture.[17]

Despite all the harsh measures taken by the Chinese in the early 1950s, they had failed to prevent the Tibetan Uprising. Tibet was too remote and too backward to run an effective campaign that could block the

[15] D. Byman, *Understanding Proto-Insurgencies* (Santa Monica, CA: RAND National Defense Institute, 2007).

[16] K. J. Conboy and J. Morrison, *The CIA's Secret War in Tibet* (Lawrence: University Press of Kansas, 2011); M. Dunham, *Buddha's Warriors: The Story of the CIA-Backed Tibetan Freedom Fighters, the Chinese Invasion and the Ultimate Fall of Tibet* (New York: Penguin, 2004); J. Kenneth Knaus, *Orphans of the Cold War: America and the Tibetan Struggle for Survival* (New York: Public Affairs, 2000); C. McGranahan: *Arrested Histories: Tibet, the CIA, and Memories of a Forgotten War* (Durham, NC: Duke University Press, 2010).

[17] T. Shakya, *The Dragon in the Land of Snows* (New York: Columbia University Press, 1999); W. W. Smith, Jr., *Tibetan Nation: A History of Tibetan Nationalism and Sino-Tibetan Relations* (Boulder, CO: Westview Press, 1997).

deterioration of unorganised and unarmed resistance into an organised and armed insurgency – all the more so as external intervention fuelled the unrest. All parties involved have learned the lesson. While articulating their resistance in the following years by staging demonstrations, riots, protests and even self-immolation, the Tibetans have never again launched an organised armed insurgency against Beijing. Likewise, those external players – Taiwan and the United States – that had tried to train and equip the Tibetan insurgents have been careful not to try it again. And, finally, Beijing has learned the lesson and has ever since prevented both domestic insurgencies and external intervention at all costs.

China's preemptive measures, especially since the beginning of reform in the late 1970s, reflected Zuo Zongtang's nineteenth-century policy of combining military, social and economic programs. By the mid-1980s, the People's Liberation Army had – willingly or not – given up its internal security duties, now assigned to a newly created People's Armed Police.[18] Deployed all over the country, its regiments were used to enforce law and order together with other organisations such as local militias, public security personnel, regular police, special forces and regional production-construction corps – a semi-military outfit. These organisations – relatively small compared to the population and territory[19] – responded to occasional unrest, often using disproportionate force. Brutal suppression procedures have ended in casualties, mass arrests, imprisonment, trials and executions. Restrictions have also been imposed on religious activities, cultural customs and the use of non-Chinese languages, thereby promoting assimilation policies, hardly adopted in pre-modern China and even in Mao's time. Essentially counterinsurgency measures, these campaigns, called 'Crackdown' and 'Strike Hard' (*Yanda*), have been applied even when there was no *real* insurgency, perhaps only a *potential* one.

In addition, other, 'non-violent' policies were adopted that include settlement of Han Chinese in less-populated minority areas, primarily in Xinjiang and Tibet. Thus, the share of Han Chinese in Xinjiang has increased from around 4 per cent in 1949 to more than 40 per cent today. Intended to promote regional stability, this measure has occasionally been counterproductive as – very much like in pre-modern China – it entailed competition with the local population over scarce resources,

---

[18] Y. Shichor, 'Worst Case Scenario: The Paradox of PLA Response to Major Ethnic Unrest', CAPS-RAND-CEIP-NDU PLA Conference on Contingency Planning, PLA Style, Arlington, VA, 30 November–1 December, 2012, unpublished paper.

[19] Y. Shichor, 'The Great Wall of Steel: Military and Strategy in Xinjiang' in F. A. Starr (ed.), *Xinjiang: China's Muslim Borderland* (Armonk, NY: M. E. Sharpe, 2004), 120–60, 408–15.

fuelling tension and ultimately conflicts. Also, Han Chinese have usually been given preferential treatment in terms of employment and education, thereby aggravating social unrest. Still, realising that economic development and modernisation might defuse regional tension, Beijing has invested in infrastructure, industry, agriculture and tourism in an attempt – usually quite successful – to spur gross domestic product, especially *per capita*. Based on the assumption that satiated people do not rebel but also on economic logic, these policies have converged since the early twenty-first century in China's Great Western Development Strategy (*Xibu Dakaifa*).[20] As in the past, significant financial investment has come from the richer southeastern provinces that, in fact, have subsidised western and northwestern development programs. Indeed, economic growth has been accompanied by *relative* stability. Since 1998, incidents of unrest in Xinjiang have declined considerably, and, needless to say, there has been no insurgency. Still, this appeared to be a short-term phenomenon: in recent years, incidents involving ethnicities have increased, implying that unrest is fed less by economic deprivation and considerably more by social, cultural and religious grievances.

Nevertheless, the issue of insurgency in China, now or in the future, is still on the agenda. Especially over the last few years, unrest in post-Mao China has become a popular topic for Western media and academics. Official Chinese data admit that tens of thousands of incidents have taken place all over China, related to ethnic, ecological, economic, social and religious grievances. These include demonstrations and riots, occasionally violent – but by no means can they be considered 'insurgencies'.[21] Since, objectively speaking, the prospects of a large-scale insurgency in China are rather low, how can we account for its prominence in the public discourse? The answer is that all parties concerned, Chinese and non-Chinese – while otherwise representing conflicting and even contradictory interests, each for its own different reasons – *share* the tendency to inflate unrest in China and exaggerate the instability of China's internal affairs.[22] On the one hand, China is interested in demonstrating the

---

[20] D. Lu and W. A. W. Neilson (eds.), *China's West Region Development: Domestic Strategies and Global Implications* (Singapore: World Scientific, 2004); Y. M. Yeung and J. F. Shen (eds.), *Developing China's West: A Critical Path to Balanced National Development* (Hong Kong: Chinese University Press, 2004); Q. J. Tian, 'China Develops Its West: Motivation, Strategy and Prospect', *Journal of Contemporary China*, 13/41 (2004), 611–36; D. S.G. Goodman (ed.), *China's Campaign to 'Open Up the West': National, Provincial and Local Perspectives* (Cambridge: Cambridge University Press, 2004).

[21] Cf. M. Scot Tanner, 'China Rethinks Unrest', *Washington Quarterly*, 27/3 (2004), 137–56.

[22] Y. Shichor, 'Blow Up: Internal and External Challenges of Uyghur Separatism and Islamic Radicalism to Chinese Rule in Xinjiang', *Asian Affairs*, 32/2 (2005), 119–35.

seriousness of the challenge it faces in order to justify the use of force and 'strike hard' policies. On the other, Uyghurs, Tibetans and others who challenge the Chinese authority and policies are interested in demonstrating that there is an organised and powerful anti-Chinese movement that cannot and should not be ignored. Finally, the media – while trying to be objective and avoid identification with either side – is not always familiar with the historical background and the details of the confrontation and is primarily interested in publishing a 'good story' – a bloody one if possible.[23] Also, some academics, who rely extensively on the media, occasionally share this tendency. These attitudes create an impression that at any moment China is about to fall apart, unable to cope with forthcoming demonstrations, riots, uprisings – or a major insurgency. It is such attitudes that in turn feed Beijing's anxieties, nervousness and sensitivities that propel the regime to respond to small-scale incidents with force out of all proportion as if it is faced by large-scale insurgencies. Irresponsible use of words legitimises Beijing's reprisals.[24]

Conclusion

As these words are being written, Beijing provided another example of its policy of using COIN measures against a potential or proto-insurgency. By 21 December 2012, Chinese security officials across the country had become concerned about the activities of a sect, called the Church of Almighty God (*Quanneng Shen*), that was blamed for 'sowing social panic' (related to the 'end of the world'), 'preaching heresies and breaking families'. An official notice underlined: 'It is a social cancer and a plague on humankind'. Also known as 'Eastern Lightening' (*Dongfang Shandian*), this clandestine sect has managed to attract a membership estimated at nearly one million[25] and its website starts with the words

See also S. Roberts, *Imaginary Terrorism: The Global War on Terror and the Narrative of the Uyghur Terrorist Threat*, PONRAS Eurasia Working Papers (Washington, DC: Elliott School of International Affairs, The George Washington University, March 2012).

[23] For example, J. Kurlantzick, 'Repression and Revolt in China's Wild West,' *Current History*, 103/674 (2004), 262–7; for a similar inflation of unrest in Xinjiang, see 'Uighur Insurgency,' available at www.globalsecurity.org/military/world/war/uighur.htm.

[24] For a misuse of the term 'insurgency' see C. Kwan Lee, 'From the Specter of Mao to the Spirit of the Law: Labor Insurgency in China', *Theory and Society*, 31 (2002), 189–228. There is no labor 'insurgency' in China. See also J. Zenn, 'Insurgency in Xinjiang Complicates Chinese-Pakistan Relations', *Terrorism Monitor*, 10/8 (2012), 6–7. There is no 'insurgency' in Xinjiang.

[25] A. Jacobs, 'Chatter of Doomsday Makes Beijing Nervous,' *New York Times*, 19 December 2012.

'China is the land where the great red dragon inhabits.' This 'Red Dragon' 'resists God and condemns God most severely throughout history'. It 'is like a fortress of demons and a prison controlled by the devil, impenetrable and watertight'.[26] Reflecting its alarm, Beijing arrested around one thousand worshippers all over China. There is no way this sect would threaten China, but Beijing, aware of its historical lessons, does not take chances.

An ongoing debate among scholars concerns the question to what extent contemporary China is a 'new' phenomenon or a continuation of its pre-modern history. The answer is typically 'Chinese': it is both. Some (myself included) claim that it is hard to understand contemporary China's behaviour without an awareness of China's traditional civilisation, political principles, military doctrine, social structure and past experience. This applies to insurgency and counterinsurgency patterns. China's traditional political culture regarded insurgency as an illness that undermined the 'harmonious' social and political structure. While some insurgencies were of local nature, fed by heavy taxes and bad weather, large-scale insurgencies – primarily those triggered by religion – were perceived as cracking the foundations of the empire. Insurgencies were brutally suppressed not only for security reasons but also for educational ones. At the same time, attempts were made to solve the problems that could have led to insurgencies by settling Han populations, improving the economic infrastructure, showing tolerance towards different ethnicities and religions, and offering local or regional autonomy. These essentially *preventive* measures, undertaken to pre-empt insurgencies (or other types of socio-political unrest), are typical of pre-modern as well as modern China. Furthermore, they reflect China's continued authoritarianism. There is no way to change the government except by force. A systemic political change, unanticipated in the near (or far) future, would probably lead to reduced unrest, modified COIN, and *real* autonomy. As of now, open debates on COIN hardly exist, and the society is tightly supervised by millions of cameras, through the Internet and by using informers.

Contemporary China, including the People's Republic, inherited and even expanded these legacies. Insurgencies have originated in a variety of political, ethnic, religious, economic and social as well as intellectual and even personal grievances. Beijing's armed response reflected the nature of the insurgency (the degree of threat to Party rule), its location (the closer to the capital – the more brutal the response), the intention to

[26] www.hidden-advent.org/en/about/html.

teach the insurgents (and future insurgents) a lesson and the degree of the government's self-confidence. This is why Beijing's counterinsurgency policies have been proportionate to *potential* threats rather than to *actual* threats. The scarcity of insurgencies in contemporary China has to do with the traditionally bureaucratic and centralist nature of its political system (unlike the federative and aristocratic nature of Russia and the Soviet Union). Many insurgencies in China have taken place in regions incorporated into China's borders (e.g., Xinjiang and Tibet) or have been fed by exogenous religious or political ideologies (e.g., Christianity, Islam, democracy, self-determination) that still affect China today. Given these 'foreign' elements, government forces (regular and irregular) find it difficult to deal with unrest of all kinds, insurgencies included.

6   You Go to COIN with the Military You Have

The United States and 250 Years of Irregular War

David E. Johnson

The United States was born of an insurgency against Great Britain. The principal reason for the success of the American Revolution is ironically similar to that identified by Andrew Mack in 1975 as to why insurgents have often prevailed since World War II: 'for the insurgents the war is "total", while for the external power it is necessarily "limited"'.[1]

Regular Even in Revolution—The Origins of American Conventionality in War

The American Revolution became a protracted conflict wherein the populace of the thirteen colonies presented a persistent challenge to pacification, because of rebel militia, guerrillas and a Continental Army that created a constant military problem that the British sought to solve conventionally through 'maneuver, battle, and pursuit'.[2]

General George Washington's imprint on the conduct of the Revolution is fundamental to the way the United States approached warfare—then and into the future. Washington, when others asked him to wage an irregular campaign against the British, refused this option, eschewing any notions that a war for revolutionary principals required guerilla warfare.[3] Indeed, Washington modelled the Continental Army along British lines, which he understood from his service during the Seven Years' War. By war's end, Washington had created a respectable army that was a mirror

This article reflects the author's views and not necessarily those of RAND or any of its clients. I thank Brad Carson, Dan Bolger, Tim Bonds, Gian Gentile, Bruce Hoffman and Morgan Plummer for reading this chapter and offering valuable suggestions to improve it. Finally, I appreciate the support provided by RAND to write this.

[1]   A. Mack, 'Why Big Nations Lose Small Wars: The Politics of Asymmetric Conflict', *World Politics*, 27/2 (1975), 181.

[2]   J. Shy, *A People Numerous and Armed: Reflections on the Military Struggle for American Independence*, revisited edition (Ann Arbor: University of Michigan Press, 1976), 233.

[3]   R. F. Weigley, 'American Strategy from Its Beginnings through the First World War' in P. Paret, G. A. Craig and F. Gilbert, *Makers of Modern Strategy: From Machiavelli to the Nuclear Age* (Princeton, NJ: Princeton University Press, 1986), 410.

image—but in buff and blue—of the British redcoat Army it had fought.[4]
Despite the mythology that the American Revolution was won by militia
fighting irregular warfare, at the end of the day what defeated England
was an American Army fighting by the rules of war of the day.[5]

The insurgencies the US government concerned itself with after the
Revolution were domestic. Shay's Rebellion (1786–1787), the Whiskey
Rebellion (1791–1794) and Fries's Rebellion (1799–1800) all had their
origins in responses to federal taxation and were early tests of the US
government's ability to enforce its laws. The Constitution of the United
States reflected the concerns of the drafters about domestic insurrection
by giving Congress the power 'To provide for calling forth the Militia to
execute the Laws of the Union, suppress Insurrections and repel
Invasions'.[6]

The defence establishment of the United States until World War I was
reflective of one needed to protect a nation guaranteed safety because of
its isolation and, after the War of 1812, the protection of *Pax Britannica*.
During times of peace, the Regular Army remained small and stationed
on the periphery of the nation to guard its frontiers and coastlines and,
after the Spanish American War, its overseas possessions. In the event of
any crisis, the small Regular Army would swell its ranks with volunteers
and militia or, as during the Civil War, turn to conscription. The Navy
'deployed its small squadrons around the world to protect the merchant-
men from piracy, to carry diplomatic representatives abroad, to explore
and chart unknown seas, to suppress the African slave trade, to persuade
hermit kingdoms like China and Japan that the American flag was to be
taken seriously in matters of personal safety and commerce'. The principal role of the Marine Corps served as a security force for the Navy and as
landing parties.[7]

The military establishment of the United States in the nineteenth
century faced similar challenges to that of today: preparing for the
worst case regular war, while simultaneously conducting irregular
campaigns. This approach worked against America's adversaries until
World War I. The military forces of the Unites States conquered the
continent, defeated Mexico and Spain, and adapted sufficiently in the

---

[4] C. Royster, *A Revolutionary People at War: The Continental Army and American Character,
1775–1783* (New York: Norton, 1981), 331–2.

[5] R. F. Weigley, *History of the United States Army*, enlarged edition (Bloomington: Indiana
University Press, 1984), 44–73.

[6] *Constitution of the United States*, Section 8: Powers of Congress, and R. W. Cokely, *The
Role of Federal Military Forces in Domestic Disorders, 1789–1878* (Washington, DC, 1988).

[7] A. R. Millett, *Semper Fidelis: The History of the United States Marine Corps*, revised edition
(New York: Free Press, 1991), 52, 128.

moment to prevail over irregular adversaries, be they Sioux warriors
or Filipino guerillas.

Adapting the Regular Army for the Irregular – the Indian Wars (1790–1891)

It was the Regular Army upon whom major responsibility fell for policing
America's frontiers before World War I. Regardless of adversary, the
Army clung to its conventional doctrines and organisations, constantly
adapting in the face of irregular opponents during the Indian Wars. This
was not always appropriate, as pointed out by historian Robert Utley:
'The frontier army was a conventional military force trying to control, by
conventional military methods, a people that did not behave like conventional enemies and, indeed, quite often were not enemies at all'.[8]

The conflict between Native Americans and Euro-Americans in North
America was continuous, at various levels of violence, from before the
Revolution until the end of the Indian Wars in 1891. And these were
wars of extraordinary brutality on all sides.

A journal entry by Major Robert Rogers, commander of the storied
Roger's Rangers fighting for the English during the French and Indian
War (1754–1763), shows the toolkit employed in that war, and it fore-
shadows the total war waged by General William Sherman in the Civil
War and in the campaigns against Native Americans in the west.
Rogers's commander instructed him 'to use my best endeavors to distress the French and allies, by sacking, burning, and destroying their
houses, barns, barracks, canoes, battoes, etc. and by killing their cattle of
every kind'.[9]

These methods are similar to those recorded by Army officer James
Parker about an encounter between the Army and a Native American
tribe a hundred years after Rogers: 'The Cohardie Comanches, the
scourge of Texas and the Southwest, were in 1874 attacked by
Mackenzie with the 4th Cavalry, at their camp ... Twelve Hundred
Indian ponies were captured and shot to prevent their recapture. Most
of the Indians then surrendered'.[10]

---

[8] R. M. Utley, 'The Contribution of the Frontier to the American Military Tradition' in
H. R. Borowski (ed.), *The Harmon Memorial Lectures in Military History, 1959–1987:
A Collection of the First Thirty Lectures Given at the United States Air Force Academy*
(Washington, DC: Office of Air Force History, 1988), 531.
[9] R. Rogers, *The Journals of Major Robert Rogers* (Albany, NY: Joel Munsell's Sons,
1883), 46.
[10] J. Parker, *The Old Army: Memories, 1872–1918* (Mechanicsburg: Stackpole Books), 33.

In the campaigns in the West, the advantage the Army had on the vast frontier was its ability to sustain itself on campaign as the campaign itself sought to deprive the adversary the capacity to subsist. Again, much like Roger's Rangers, the aim was to target nomadic Native American's means to subsist, destroying food, horses and shelter. This was particularly devastating on the Native Americans in the winter and often forced them to enter reservations for survival.[11]

This approach, however effective, caused problems for the US government that would reverberate in future COIN campaigns as deaths and deprivations among noncombatants – particularly women and children – were inevitable when Native American encampments were attacked. As a result, the tactics 'brought down upon the Army the wrath of Eastern newspapers and philanthropists who chastised it for waging barbaric campaigns of extermination'.[12]

Intelligence during the Indian Wars was a key issue – finding an elusive adversary in the broad expanses of the West was a huge challenge. Tactically, the essence of the Army's approach to campaigning was, in the words of another veteran campaigner, General Nelson Miles, to '"find, follow, and defeat" the enemy wherever he might be'. To this end, the Army mounted long-duration small unit reconnaissance patrols. Additionally, the Army employed Native American scouts who provided what is now known as cultural understanding and local knowledge.[13] Veteran Indian fighter George Crook employed scouts from the tribes he was fighting, recalling: 'To polish a diamond there is nothing like its own dust'.[14]

Despite the in-the-field adaptations of the Army in the irregular Indian Wars that extended from the founding of the United States until 1890, '[Army] commanders considered Indian affairs an unfortunate distraction ... a messy, morally ambiguous, and unpleasant task that offered few chances for distinction'.[15] What was learned was passed on in lore, not doctrine or policy.[16] What evolved over the course of the campaigns of the nineteenth-century Indian Wars was a pragmatic military approach of 'whatever it takes' in a succession of campaigns against

[11] M. Boot, *Invisible Armies: An Epic History of Guerrilla Warfare from Ancient Times to the Present* (New York: W. W. Norton, 2013), 147.
[12] A. J. Birtle, *U.S. Army Counterinsurgency and Contingency Operations Doctrine, 1860–1941* (Washington, DC: U.S. Army Center of Military History, 2006), 68.
[13] Ibid., 69.   [14] Utley, *Frontier Regulars*, 55.
[15] W. B. Skelton, *An American Profession of Arms: The Army Officer Corps, 1784-1761* (Lawrence: University of Kansas Press, 1992), 305.
[16] R. M. Utley, *Frontiersmen in Blue: The United States Army and the Indian, 1848–1865* (New York: Macmillan, 1967), 342.

individual tribes.[17] Consequently, there was little institutional learning about how to deal with the 'irregular'.

US government policy towards Native Americans was largely set in 1830, when President Andrew Jackson announced the Indian Removal Act, which focused on separating Native American populations from whites and concentrating them on reservations. Jackson noted that the purpose of the Removal Act was to 'place a dense and civilised population in large tracts of country now occupied by a few savage hunters'.[18] These relocations were frequently forced.[19]

The Indian Wars were brutal on both sides with mass killings, torture, mutilation, indiscriminate killing, rape and captive taking common throughout the hundred years of conflict. A particularly horrific episode that would shape US attitudes about how to prosecute the Indian Wars was the 1862 US-Dakota War that erupted when four Dakota killed five white settlers near Acton Township, Minnesota, on 17 August 1862. Over the next six weeks, the Dakota killed some six hundred whites (of which some 480 were unarmed civilians, 30 per cent of them children under ten) and took more than two hundred hostages; between seventy-four and one hundred Dakota died. A letter from Major General John Pope, the commander of the Department of the Northwest, shows the depth of the animus towards the Dakotas – a perspective that would typify that of many westward moving Euro-Americans in the coming decades: 'It is my purpose utterly to exterminate the Sioux ... Destroy everything belonging to them and force them out to the plains ... They are to be treated as maniacs or wild beasts, and by no means as people with whom treaties or compromises can be made'.[20]

On 23 September 1862, the war ended with Chief Little Crow's defeat at the Battle of Wood Lake. In the aftermath, 392 Dakota prisoners were tried for capital crimes, of whom 303 were sentenced to death. President Abraham Lincoln approved only thirty-eight for execution.[21] The sentence, death by hanging, was carried out on 26 December 1862 and still

---

[17] E. A. Cohen, *Conquered into Liberty: Two Centuries of Battles Along the Great Warpath That Made the American War of War* (New York: Free Press, 2011), 338.

[18] US National Archives and Records Administration, 'Transcript of President Andrew Jackson's Message to Congress "On Indian Removal"' (1830), also available at www .ourdocuments.gov/doc.php?doc=25&page=transcript (last accessed 5 October 2014).

[19] The Library of Congress, 'Primary Documents in American History: Indian Removal Act', also available at www.loc.gov/rr/program/bib/ourdocs/Indian.html (last accessed 7 December 2014).

[20] Minnesota Historical Society, *The U.S.-Dakota War of 1862*, also available at usdakotawar.org/history/aftermath (last accessed 7 December 2014).

[21] Minnesota Historical Society, *The U.S.-Dakota War of 1862*.

remains the largest mass execution in US history.[22] The majority of the surviving Dakota were exiled from Minnesota. In the face of continued Dakota raids, the Minnesota state Adjutant-General authorised in July 1863 bounties for Dakota scalps. Chief Little Crow was killed and scalped by settlers. The tribe was relocated to Crow Creek Reservation in South Dakota, following the abrogation or revocation of treaties between the US government and the Dakota.[23]

Crow Creek and other reservations created during and after the Indian Wars were not 'strategic hamlets', as suggested by one author.[24] Reservations were ways to contain Native Americans on lands deemed not of value to whites – at the time – and to force them into dependency on the Bureau of Indian affairs for sustenance, although some believed reservations a humane means to assimilate Native Americans.[25]

The actions of the Army were secondary in the demise of the Native Americans in the West.[26] The realisation of what was popularly called 'Manifest Destiny' with millions of white settlers moving west in the aftermath of the Mexican War and the acquisition by the United States of territory from the Mississippi River to the Pacific Ocean was responsible.[27] Indeed, the biggest cause of the demise of native populations was disease, malnutrition and murder: 'Next to disease', however, 'white civilians with guns were the most dangerous threat to Indian survival'.[28] Ultimately, with Native Americans confined to reservations, the US government approach became one advocated by Captain Richard Henry Pratt, founder of the Carlisle Industrial Training School in Carlisle, Pennsylvania. Pratt wrote: 'Kill the Indian in him, and save the man'.[29]

[22] R. K. Elder, 'Execution 150 Years Ago Spurs Calls for Pardon', *New York Times* (13 December 2010), also available at www.nytimes.com/2010/12/14/us/14dakota.html?pagewanted=all&_r=0, (last accessed 1 December 2012).

[23] Minnesota Historical Society, *The U.S.-Dakota War of 1862*, Bounties were common throughout the Indian Wars, but generally established by states or localities. See R. F. Heizer (ed.), *The Destruction of California Indians* (Lincoln: University of Nebraska Press, 1993) 268–9.

[24] P. B. Rich, 'A Historical Overview of US Counter-insurgency', *Small Wars and Insurgencies*, 25/1 (2014), 9.

[25] Minnesota Historical Society, *The U.S.-Dakota War of 1862*.

[26] G. F. Michno, *Encyclopedia of Indian Wars: Western Battles and Skirmishes, 1850–1890* (Missoula, MT: Mountain Press, 2003), 353.

[27] G. Lewy, *Essays on Genocide and Humanitarian Intervention* (Salt Lake City: University of Utah Press, 2012), 102.

[28] Michno, *Encyclopedia of Indian Wars*, 360.

[29] National Public Radio, 'American Indian Boarding Schools Haunt Many', 12 May 2012, www.npr.org/templates/story/story.php?storyId=16516865 (last accessed 4 December 2014), and University of Washington, 'Assimilation through Education: Indian Boarding Schools in the Northwest', also available at content.lib.washington.edu/aipnw/marr.html (last accessed 6 December 2014).

To this end, an expansive system of 'assimilation through education' evolved, with more than a hundred thousand Native American children attending some 460 boarding and day schools. These schools worked to erase tribal languages and cultures and replaced them with English and Christianity.[30]

The Indian Wars were existential for both Euro-Americans and Native Americans at their inception in the 1600s. At their conclusion, Euro-Americans had killed or forced remaining Native Americans onto reservations and conquered the continent from the Atlantic to the Pacific Oceans. In 1898 the United States looked outward with aspirations of world power. In so doing, it would become involved in an insurgency far from its shores in the Philippines.

Expeditionary COIN – The Philippine War (1899–1902)

In 1898 the United States defeated Spain in what future US Secretary of State John Hay described as a 'splendid little war'. The war served US strategic aspirations in the Pacific. After the war it acquired the Philippines from Spain for $20 million, annexed Guam and supported a coup against Queen Liliuokalani in Hawaii and annexed the islands in 1898.[31] The United States now had a firm foothold in the Pacific region and bases to provide military support to its Pacific strategy. In the process, it found itself with responsibilities to establish governance in its new possessions and confronted its first off-shore insurgency in the newly acquired Philippine Islands. Here the United States would endeavor to learn COIN and begin its first attempt to build a foreign nation.

The insurrection in the Philippines began when Filipino revolutionaries, led by Emilio Aguinaldo, who had been fighting the Spanish, refused to acknowledge US authority over the Philippines after the Spanish-American War.[32] Benjamin Foulois, a junior officer in the Philippine War and in the following Moro War that lingered until 1913, summed up the frustration of the Philippines for those who served there – a frustration that would recur in future US irregular wars: 'a few hundred

---

[30] Public Broadcasting System, 'Indian Boarding Schools', at www.pbs.org/indiancountry/history/boarding2.html (last accessed 3 December 2014). See also University of Washington, 'Assimilation through Education: Indian Boarding Schools in the Northwest', also available at content.lib.washington.edu/aipnw/marr.html (last accessed 6 December 2014).

[31] US Department of State, Office of the Historian, 'The Spanish-American War, 1898', at history.state.gov/milestones/1866–1898/spanish-american-war (last accessed 7 December 2014).

[32] Birtle, *U.S. Army Counterinsurgency and Contingency Operations Doctrine, 1860–1941*, 108.

natives ... could tie down thousands of American troops, have a serious impact on the economy of the United States, and provoke a segment of our population to take the view that what happens in the Far East is none of our business'.[33]

Aguinaldo fought a conventional war against US forces until he was defeated in November 1899 by Major General Elwell Otis. Aguinaldo then began a three-year-long insurgency that cost the United States more than seven thousand casualties and $400 million.[34] Aguinaldo did not hope to defeat the United States, rather he sought to exhaust the Americans, betting that President William McKinley would lose the election of 1900 and his successor would grant Philippine independence. McKinley won and was committed to defeating the insurgency.[35]

US methods during the Philippine War were reminiscent of the counter-guerrilla campaigns of the Civil War and the Indian Wars. Indeed, many of the commanders in the Philippines were veterans of one or both wars. Major General Adna R. Chaffee, commander of the Department of the Philippines in mid-1901, had been part of General Philip Sheridan's cavalry when it had torched much of Loudon Valley, Virginia, in the campaign to quell Confederate irregulars.[36] Chaffee had also served in the Indian Wars in Texas and Arizona.[37] Comments by Brigadier General Theodore Schwan, a brigade commander, showed the deep imprint the Indian Wars had on the perceptions and methods of senior commanders: 'they [Filipinos] are in identically the same positon as the Indians of our country have been for many years, and in my opinion must be subdued in much the same way ... and then win them by fair and just treatment'.[38]

The Philippines created enormous challenges of understanding for the US occupiers. As they would do in future insurgencies, US forces rotated in and out of the Philippines on tours of duty. They also came 'armed with the confidence, can-do attitude, racism, and cultural insensitivity of

---

[33] B. D. Foulois, *From the Wright Brothers to the Astronauts: The Memoirs of Major General Benjamin D. Foulois* (New York: McGraw-Hill, 1968), 41.

[34] Birtle, *U.S. Army Counterinsurgency and Contingency Operations Doctrine*, 108.

[35] R. D. Ramsey III, *Savage Wars of Peace: Case Studies of Pacification in the Philippines, 1900–1902*, Long War Series Occasional Paper (Fort Leavenworth, KS: Combat Studies Institute Press, 2007), 115.

[36] Birtle, *U.S. Army Counterinsurgency and Contingency Operations Doctrine*, 133.

[37] M. E. Gates (ed.), *Men of Mark in America* (Washington, DC: Men of Mark Publishing Company, 1905), 208–14, Also available at archive.org/stream/menofmarkinameri00 gate#page/n7/mode/2up (last accessed 8 December 2014).

[38] Letter, Theodore Schwan to Henry Corbin, 25 October 1899, cited in G. Anthony May, *Battle for Batangas: A Philippine Province at War* (New Haven, CT: Yale University Press, 1991), 95.

Americans of that time'. Additionally, as in future American interventions and insurgencies, there was little understanding of local languages or culture, and US forces relied heavily on translators of 'dubious loyalty'. The approach was 'to make over the Filipinos into little brown Americans' without realising the Filipinos' passion for independence.[39] Colonel Arthur L. Wagner testified in Congress about results of this lack of understanding: 'The natives were afraid to give us any information because if they did they were boloed [attacked with a machete-like weapon] ... It was a very embarrassing situation ... the island was practically in the possession of a blind giant; strong, but unable to see where to strike'.[40]

At the beginning of the insurgency, the American policy was that advocated by President McKinley of 'benevolent assimilation'. General Otis 'emphasised that the army's role was as much to restore order and protect the population as it was to suppress armed resistance'.[41] Otis also began dispersing his forces to counter Aguinaldo's insurgency, realising the need to control the population and isolate them from the insurgents. This evolved into what is now called a 'clear, hold, build' strategy, and within two years the number of outposts grew to 639.[42]

In May 1900, Major General Arthur MacArthur replaced Otis and dramatically shifted the emphasis from civic action to coercion. He also implemented the Civil War–era General Orders 100, which authorised the use of harsh measures by US forces to quell the insurgency, and aggressively went after the guerilla infrastructure[43]

The context within which the Philippine War took place is important to its eventual outcome. Because of the US Navy's presence, the insurgents were isolated on the various islands where they operated and received no external support from abroad and could not replace lost weapons. Indeed, the number of captured enemy weapons became a 'metric of success'.[44] Although US troop strength in the Philippines averaged forty thousand (with a peak of seventy thousand in December

[39] Ramsey, *Savage Wars of Peace*, 114, 116.

[40] Testimony of Colonel Arthur L. Wagner, US Congress, Senate, *Affairs in the Philippine Islands. Hearings before the Committee on the Philippines of the United States Senate* (Senate Document 331, part 3, 57th Congress, 1st Session, 1902), 2850–1, cited in Ramsey, *Savage Wars of Peace*, 118.

[41] B. McAllister Linn, *The Philippine War, 1899–1902* (Lawrence: University of Kansas Press, 2000), 326.

[42] Birtle, *U.S. Army Counterinsurgency and Contingency Operations Doctrine*, p. 113.

[43] Linn, *The Philippine War*, 326–7.

[44] Ramsey, *Savage Wars of Peace: Case Studies of Pacification in the Philippines, 1900–1902*, 118.

1900), and about 60 per cent of the number actually available in the field, the US forces were much more effective than the insurgents.[45]

The Philippine War had two major policy components: attraction and chastisement. Attraction combined benevolence, civic action and social reform, and, as recalled by one veteran officer, had specific tasks and desired outcomes: 'The formation of local governments including the establishment of educational, sanitary, fiscal and welfare systems'. The policy of attraction was not, however, sufficient to end the insurgency, because 'soldiers found they could neither offer sufficient rewards to win over their opponents nor sufficient protection to save their friends form guerilla retaliation'.[46]

As the war ground on, the US forces escalated the policy of chastisement. Their 'toolkit' included 'the imposition of fines and communal punishments, the destruction of private property, the exile of individuals and the relocation of populations, imprisonment and, in the case of guerrillas and their closest civilian allies, execution'. Eventually, the United States employed all of these measures against the insurgency. These types of measures would persist in the United States military until after World War II.[47]

Much like General William T. Sherman's realisation during his 'march to the sea' during the American Civil War, the US military in the Philippines believed it was fighting 'a hostile people, and must make old and young, rich and poor, feel the hard hand of war'.[48] And the hand of war was hard. Soon after announcing the implementation of General Orders 100, General MacArthur 'exiled a group of prominent Filipino leaders, terminated the policy of automatically releasing prisoners (although he still exchanged prisoners for guns), and authorised commanders to destroy towns harbouring guerrillas and confiscate the property of rebel sympathisers'. MacArthur also authorised arrests and detention without evidence. Arrests and executions increased, and the Army destroyed 'homes, villages, storehouses, orchards, crops, livestock, boats, and even fishing nets' to deny shelter and supplies to the insurgents and 'as an object lesson in American power'.[49] These measures, coupled with the US Navy's blockade of trade and fishing, resembled tactics employed by soldiers during the Indian Wars and were devastating to the population.[50]

---

[45] Linn, *The Philippine War*, 325.   [46] Ibid., 327.
[47] Birtle, *U.S. Army Counterinsurgency and Contingency Operations Doctrine*, pp. 126, 254.
[48] Letter, William T. Sherman to Henry W. Halleck, 24 December 1864, at www.civilwar.org/education/history/primarysources/william-t-sherman-to-henry.html (last accessed 10 December 2014).
[49] Birtle, *U.S. Army Counterinsurgency and Contingency Operations Doctrine*, pp. 128–9.
[50] Linn, *The Philippine War*, 309.

Perhaps the harshest campaign of the war was that conducted in Samar by the 6th Separate Brigade, commanded by Brigadier General Jacob H. Smith. Major Littleton Waller, commander of a US Marine battalion, recalled in his court martial General Smith's orders to him as he went into Samar: "'I wish you to kill and burn. The more you kill and the more you burn, the better you will please me" ... He said he wanted all persons killed who were capable of bearing arms; and I asked if he would define the age limit ... and ten years was given'. Furthermore, Smith instructed that 'the interior of Samar must be made a howling wilderness'.[51]

US forces also employed, on occasion, 'retaliatory executions' and torture, most notably the 'water cure' – a precursor to 'water-boarding' – to gain information from insurgents who were equally, if not more ruthless. Another method was 'a good hanging', where an insurgent was hung until he passed out and then was revived and the hanging repeated. Some Americans chose not to participate directly, but would instead give their prisoners to Filipino interrogators.[52] This is a practice that would be repeated in later US wars.

More benign methods were also employed. The Army used spies, informants and translators; issued identity cards and passes; conducted censuses; and maintained intelligence files.[53] Finally, the US military also used voluntary and forcible 'concentration' to separate insurgents from the populace, euphemistically calling them 'colonies' and 'zones of protection' to obscure their activities.[54]

The US military also began recruiting and equipping local forces, creating the Philippine Scouts and Philippine Constabulary. In this endeavour, a pattern began that would be repeated in the future: Filipinos were trained in the US image, based on Army organisation and drill regulations. Eventually, Philippine Constabulary forces assumed responsibility for public order. The Philippine Scouts prepared for conventional war to support US forces to defend against invasion, which came in 1941.[55]

On 4 July 1902, President Theodore Roosevelt declared the Philippine Insurrection ended and in a congratulatory letter to the Army lauded its

---

[51] Court Martial of Littleton Waller, Microfilm #30313, RG153, NAB, cited in C. T. Dean, 'Atrocity on Trial: The Court-Martial of Littleton Walker', Master of Arts Thesis (Tempe: Arizona State University, 2009), 89.

[52] Linn, *The Philippine War*, 222–3. Linn also notes that 'it appears that the use of torture steadily increased' during the insurgency.

[53] W. E. Kretchik, *U.S. Army Doctrine: From the American Revolution to the War on Terror* (Lawrence: University of Kansas Press, 2011), 100–101.

[54] Birtle, *U.S. Army Counterinsurgency and Contingency Operations Doctrine*, 131.

[55] J. R. Arnold, *The Moro War*, 259, and Birtle, *U.S. Army Counterinsurgency and Contingency Operations Doctrine*, 116, 155–6.

Indian war lore in this victory: 'In more than two thousand combats, great and small, within three years ... Utilising the lessons of the Indian wars, it has relentlessly followed the guerrilla bands to their fastnesses in mountain and jungle and crushed them'.[56]

Back to Conventionality: The Post–World War I US Military (1918–2006)

In the years following the Philippine War, the Armed Forces of the United States were involved in counterinsurgency and constabulary operations in China, Mexico, the Caribbean and the Philippines. The Marine Corps captured its lessons in its *Small Wars Manual*. However, both the Army and the Marine Corps shifted the focus of their institutions to conventional war following World War I.[57]

The Army turned to becoming the land force of a great power. Its 1923 *Field Service Regulations* highlighted the centrality of conventional operations and the importance of preparing for wars against other great powers, with other contingencies being 'lesser included', declaring: 'An army capable of waging successful war under these conditions will prove adequate to any less grave emergency with which it may be confronted'.[58]

The Pacific, and support of War Plan Orange, became the priority for the Marine Corps although it remained poised for service in the Atlantic and Caribbean contingencies. The Marine Corps turned to preparing for amphibious operations, and in 1920 the Joint Army and Navy Board approved its mission as an advanced base force.[59]

As one scholar put it, World War II, the Korean War and the early years of the Cold War would 'swamp the tiny boat of small wars doctrine and send it to oblivion'. In the 1960s, the United States would find itself in another large-sale conflict in Vietnam. Unlike the Philippines, where veterans of the Indian Wars passed on the lore of irregular wars, there were few veterans with relevant experiences.[60] The US military was the conventional force of a superpower – with little institutional memory of unconventional operations – that would find itself in a different kind of war in Vietnam.

---

[56] Extract of Message from President Theodore Roosevelt to the US Army, 4 July 1902, in Ramsey, *Savage Wars of Peace*, 163–4.
[57] A. Long, *Doctrine of Eternal Recurrence – The U.S. Military and Counterinsurgency Doctrine, 1960–1970 and 2003–2006* (Santa Monica, CA: RAND, 2008).
[58] US War Department, *Field Service Regulations* (Washington, DC: 1924), III.
[59] Millett, *Semper Fidelis*, 320–1.
[60] Birtle, *U.S. Army Counterinsurgency and Contingency Operations Doctrine*, 261.

America in Vietnam (1945–1975)[61]

US involvement in Vietnam began in 1945 during World War II with support of Ho Chi Minh's forces rescuing Allied airmen and fighting the Japanese. Direct military assistance to Vietnam began with the establishment of a Military Assistance Advisory Group (MAAG) in September 1950.[62] After the defeat of the French and the partition of Vietnam, the United States began increasing its advisery and training efforts for the South Vietnamese military. During the Eisenhower administration, this amounted to some seven hundred advisers. When President Kennedy was assassinated in November 1963, the United States had sixteen thousand troops in Vietnam.[63] US efforts sought to assist the South Vietnamese in their efforts to 'maintain a viable, effective, and anticommunist South Vietnamese government'.[64]

The push to confront unconventional 'sublimited or guerrilla warfare' began in the Kennedy administration. This, Kennedy believed, was 'the most active and constant threat to free world security'.[65] Kennedy's defence strategy required the DoD (Department of Defense) 'to fight two and a half wars simultaneously – major wars in both Europe and Asia and a brush-fire war elsewhere'.[66]

Kennedy attempted to force the Services, particularly the Army, to address unconventional challenges. It soon became clear to an increasingly frustrated Kennedy that the US military, particularly the Army, did not share his vision. Army Chief of Staff General George H. Decker had reportedly 'shrugged off preparation for counter-guerrilla warfare as something it [the Army] can take in stride', telling President Kennedy that 'any good soldier can handle guerrillas'. It was also obvious that Decker – and others in the US military – viewed counterinsurgency as a distraction from the real threat: Soviet conventional military power in Europe.[67]

---

[61] Much of this section on the Vietnam War is from a draft manuscript, 'The Path to Today's Army', written as part of a RAND Corporation study and D. E. Johnson, *Modern U.S. Civil-Military Relations: Wielding the Terrible Swift Sword*, McNair Paper 57 (Fort McNair, DC: Institute for National Strategic Studies, National Defense University, 1997).

[62] R. H. Spector, *Advice and Support: The Early Years, 1941–1960*, United States Army in Vietnam (Washington, DC: Center of Military History, United States Army, 1985), 39–40, 115–16.

[63] D. Kinnard, *The War Managers: American Generals Reflect on Vietnam* paperback edition (Boston: Da Capo Press, 1991), 5–6.

[64] G. Gentile, *Wrong Turn: America's Deadly Embrace of Counterinsurgency* (London: New Press, 2013), 65.

[65] L. Norman and J. B. Spore, 'Big Push in Guerrilla Warfare', *Army*, 12(1962), 32–3.

[66] Weigley, *The American Way of War*, 568.

[67] Norman and Spore, 'Big Push in Guerrilla Warfare', 32–5.

As the 1960s progressed, the US military worked to understand the implications of the insurgencies in the post–World War II context of decolonisation. Andrew Birtle details these extensive efforts in the realms of doctrine, organisation, education and interagency efforts: US policy held that the host nation was responsible for defeating the insurgency, and there was recognition that entrenched local elites would resist reform efforts to maintain their power.[68] The central tenet, however, was that 'The ultimate objective of operations against an irregular force is to eliminate the irregular force and prevent its resurgence'.[69]

The United States looked to foreign examples of successful COIN efforts, particularly in Malaya, Algeria and the Huk Rebellion in the Philippines.[70] The Army also used instructors from France, most notably Paul Aussaresses, a key figure in the France's war in Algeria. Algeria, in particular, held interest for the US military, and Aussaresses instructed students at the School of Special Warfare at Fort Bragg, North Carolina, where he later recalled that 'I taught about the conditions in which I did a job not normal in classical warfare, the techniques of the Battle of Algiers, arrests, intelligence, torture'. Years later Brigadier General John Johns and Colonel Carl Bernard, both retired Army officers who had studied with Aussaresses, recalled that they had read galley proofs of Colonel Roger Trinquier's monograph *Modern Warfare: A French View of Counterinsurgency*. Trinquier's work detailed how the French had fought in Algeria and how they had broken the insurgency, using the methods Aussaresses detailed in his classes. Johns and Bernard also recalled Trinquier's ideas had 'a considerable impact on all the green berets who left for Vietnam'. Bernard sent Trinquier's work to Robert Komer, whose 'Project Phoenix' replicated many of the approaches the French had taken in Algeria. Bernard later recalled: 'Starting with that book [Trinquier's *Modern War*] Project Phoenix was conceived'.[71]

By 1963 the situation in South Vietnam under the regime of President Ngo Dinh Diem had become dire. The Viet Cong were becoming increasingly aggressive and competent in the field and had inflicted defeats on South Vietnamese forces. Particularly alarming was the

---

[68] Birtle, *U.S. Army Counterinsurgency and Contingency Operations Doctrine*, 223–90.

[69] US Department of the Army, *FM 31-15: Operations against Irregular Forces* (Washington, DC: Headquarters, Department of the Army, 1961), 4.

[70] See S. T. Hosmer and S. O. Crane, *Counterinsurgency: A Symposium, April 16–20, 1962*, new edition (Santa Monica, CA: RAND, 1993).

[71] Transcript of M. M. Robin, *Escadrons de la Mort: L'école Française (The Death Squads: The French School*, (2003), at groups.google.com/forum/#!topic/misc.activism.progressive/ U4h-Yc_HQo4 (last accessed 1 December 2014). See also Élie Tenenbaum's chapter in this book.

23 January 1963 defeat of the ARVN (Army of the Republic of Vietnam) 7th Division at Ap Bac, which demonstrated the ARVN's poor training and lack of fighting effectiveness.[72] Furthermore, the VC terror campaign was very effective: six thousand government officials had been killed and thirty thousand civilians kidnapped to this point in the war.[73]

By late 1964, the North Vietnamese were sending regular army combat units into South Vietnam via the Ho Chi Minh Trail.[74] President Johnson, fearing the collapse of South Vietnam, escalated the war, declaring, 'I am not going to be the President who saw Southeast Asia go the way China went'.[75]

It is important to understand the context of the Vietnam War. Vietnam was significantly different than the other post–World War II insurgencies (Malaya, the Philippines, Indochina, Algeria and Kenya), the points of reference of much twentieth-century COIN theory. The war in Vietnam involved main force units, both VC and North Vietnamese, physical sanctuary in Laos and Cambodia, and strong external financial and material support from China and the Soviet Union.[76] Additionally, given Johnson's desire to limit the war so as not to conflict with his Great Society programs or risk Chinese or Soviet direct intervention, the ground war was limited to South Vietnam.[77]

Unlike previous counterinsurgencies or irregular wars, the United States had a new capability in its toolkit that enabled it to take the war to North Vietnam without ground forces: air power. The Johnson administration initially crafted a strategy 'based on the central assumption that if the Communists sustained enough military punishment they would finally relent, forsaking (at least temporarily) their war effort'.[78] Central to the strategy was the belief that the North Vietnamese had a breaking point towards which US bombing could push them. By contrast, if the Communists gave up in the South, they would be left in peace in the North.[79]

---

[72] R. Buzzanco, *Masters of War: Military Dissent and Politics in the Vietnam Era* (Cambridge: Cambridge University Press, 1996), 137.

[73] G. A. Daddis, *Westmoreland's War: Reassessing American Strategy in Vietnam* (Oxford: Oxford University Press, 2014), 59.

[74] Gentile, *Wrong Turn*, 65.

[75] H. Y. Schandler, 'America and Vietnam: The Failure of Strategy, 1965–67' in P. Braestrup, (ed.), *Vietnam as History* (Washington, DC: University Press of America, 1984), 23.

[76] Hosmer and Crane, *Counterinsurgency: A Symposium*.

[77] Johnson, *Modern U.S. Civil-Military Relations*, 28–9.

[78] J. E. Mueller, 'The Search for the "Breaking Point" in Vietnam: The Statistics of a Deadly Quarrel', *International Studies Quarterly*, 24 (1980), 499.

[79] Ibid..

Clark Clifford, Secretary of Defense from February 1968 to January 1969, recalled later, 'When the military was told that we were going in there and save South Vietnam, I ... felt that it was not going to be a particularly difficult task. Here were a lot of little people running around in black pajamas in North Vietnam, and here we came in, the greatest nation in the world, with the most enormous firepower and with bombing that could wipe them out'.[80]

Johnson began an air campaign, dubbed Operation Rolling Thunder, to persuade the North Vietnamese to stop their aggression in the South. In this air campaign of graduated escalation Johnson maintained tight control of the bombing effort. Rolling Thunder ended on 1 November 1968 after it failed to convince the North Vietnamese to quit the war.[81]

The situation in the South continued to deteriorate as Rolling Thunder was unable to force the North Vietnamese to capitulate and General Westmoreland believed he 'could not experiment with the time-consuming tasks of pacification and political reform, nor ... did the RVN possess the stability requisite for such measures'. President Johnson also wanted measurable results to demonstrate progress, 'soldiers killed, northern targets destroyed, reduced infiltration'.[82] In July 1965, President Johnson approved General Westmoreland's request for a thirty-five-battalion force of some 175,000 troops – 'a major threshold had been crossed'.[83] The president also noted ominously, 'Additional forces will be needed later, and they will be sent as requested'.[84]

The focus in South Vietnam shifted from advising the South Vietnamese to the destruction of enemy forces, and resources were organised to that end by General Westmoreland during his tenure as Commander, Military Assistance Command Vietnam (MACV).[85] Westmoreland began the big unit war in the South to close with and destroy the enemy, and US force levels increased until they peaked at almost 550,000 in the spring of 1969.[86] The United States took over

[80] Congress, House, Committee on Foreign Affairs, 'The Lessons of Vietnam: Hearing before the Subcommittee on Asian and Pacific Affairs', 99th Congress, 1st Session, 29 April 1985, 37.

[81] R. H. Kohn and J. P. Harahan (eds.), *Strategic Air Warfare: An Interview with Generals Curtis E. LeMay, Leon W. Johnson, David A. Burchinal, and Jack J. Catton*, (Washington: Office of Air Force History, 1988), 125.

[82] R. Buzzano, *Masters of War* (New York: Cambridge University Press, 1997), 247, 253.

[83] H. Y. Schandler, 'America and Vietnam: the Failure of Strategy' in R. Haycock (ed.), *Regular Armies and Insurgency* (London: Croom Helm, 1979), 90.

[84] Westmoreland, *A Soldier Reports*, 143.

[85] Johnson, *Modern U.S. Civil-Military Relations*, 32.   [86] Kinnard, *The War Managers*, 6.

the war, relegating the ARVN to a secondary role until the policy of Vietnamisation began under President Richard M. Nixon.[87]

All other efforts were increasingly displaced to contribute to the effort to destroy the enemy. This also included the reorientation of Special Forces units from their previous role of controlling and gaining the support of the indigenous minorities so that they would not fall to the Communists, to an offensive role of destroying the Viet Cong.[88] This is not to say advising or pacification was abandoned: these efforts just became clearly secondary in an effort to defeat VC and NVA (North Vietnamese) units in a war of attrition.

Not surprisingly, adviser duty, previously sought out as the only way to get combat experience in a peacetime Army, became less desirable as the best officers sought duty in combat units, knowing these jobs were career-enhancing. Advisers had little preparation for the 'acute culture shock from being dropped into a completely alien environment', a situation not helped by their preparation; they had only cursory culture and Vietnamese language training at the MATA (Military Assistance Training and Advisory) course at Fort Bragg.[89]

A constant issue throughout the US military (particularly the Army, which dominated Westmoreland's headquarters) was tour lengths. A normal tour of duty in Vietnam was one year, but Army officers generally served in their specific assignments for six months.[90] Thus, while the Vietnam War has been called a war fought for twelve years, one year at a time, in reality, it was a war whose officers fought six months at a time.

The toolkit employed in Vietnam included targeted assassinations, executions, forced population transfers, destruction of villages, scorched earth, controlling roads, the use of identification cards and searching people. Especially famous was Project Phoenix, the program to go after the VC shadow government, was in the words of its founder, Robert 'Blowtorch Bob' Komer (head of Civil Operations and Revolutionary Development Support [CORDS]), designed as a precision operation focused on 'Cutting off the heads of the infrastructure at local levels ... to degrade the whole structure'.[91] Mark Moyar, in his assessment of Phoenix, writes that the program was very effective, with the Allies arresting, killing or capturing a significant portion of the shadow

---

[87] Schandler, 'America and Vietnam', 92.
[88] F. J. Kelly, *U.S. Army Special Forces, 1961–1971*, Vietnam Studies, (Washington, DC: Department of the Army, 1973), 77.
[89] Clarke, *Advice and Support*, 510–11.   [90] Ibid., 510.
[91] M. Moyar, *Phoenix and the Birds of Prey: Counterinsurgency and Counterterrorism in Vietnam*, revised edition (Lincoln: University of Nebraska Press, 2007), 53.

government between 1967 and 1972, with many more neutralised during the 1968 Tet Offensive. He also provides a table that reflects the scope of Project Phoenix between 1968 and 1972: 22,013 rallied (defected), 33,358 captured, 26,369 killed for a total of 81,740 'neutralisations'.[92] An additional 200,000 VC defected by 1972 in the Chieu Hoi (Open Arms) program.[93] Moyar also notes that while the GVN tortured and killed prisoners, the US military and CIA wanted to prevent these practices. Nevertheless, US officers, much like in the Philippines, got information from their less inhibited South Vietnamese counterparts.[94]

CORDS also worked for the establishment of a national identification card fingerprinting system, with police issuing 'tamperproof' ID cards to all South Vietnamese over the age of fifteen. Such a system, in the view of Komer, was essential to identify VC infrastructure and enable the Phoenix program. Additionally, Vietnamese police ran checkpoints with searches on roads and canals to control movement, restrict supplies going to the communists and catch VC suspects. The system was only partially effective, given the corruption of the GVN. The police accepted bribes; captured VC often bought their release and would then retaliate against those involved in their capture.[95]

Throughout the Vietnam War the United States and the GVN forced the relocation of civilians and designated the cleared areas free-fire zones (after December 1965, specified strike zones), particularly between 1966 and 1970. The purpose of these relocations was threefold: '(1) deny the enemy manpower, food and revenue; (2) to clear the battlefield of innocent civilians, establish SSZs [specified strike zones] and make possible the freer use of firepower; (3) to score a political victory by making people vote with their feet for the GVN'.[96] Pacification programs continued, but Westmoreland's large-scale military operations and the population relocations worked at cross-purposes to them. The GVN lost authority in the countryside because of the way the war was conducted.[97] Eventually, military activity resulted in the displacement of some seven million South Vietnamese.[98]

From 1962 to 1970, the United States conducted a high-technology scorched earth effort with its defoliation and crop destruction programs

---

[92] Moyar, *Phoenix*, 236, 390.
[93] J. P. White, *Civil Affairs in Vietnam* (Washington, DC: Center for Strategic and International Studies, 2009), 10.
[94] Moyar, *Phoenix*, 93, 99, 396.
[95] R. A. Hunt, *Pacification: The American Struggle for Vietnam's Hearts and Minds* (Boulder, CO: Westview Press, 1998), 27, 117–18.
[96] Lewy, *America in Vietnam*, 226.   [97] Schandler, 'America and Vietnam', 93.
[98] Gentile, *America's Deadly Embrace of Counterinsurgency*, 76.

using herbicides, most famously the carcinogen Agent Orange. General W. B. Rosson (Commander, US Army Pacific) emphasised that 'Militarily, both defoliation and crop destruction programs in support of the counterinsurgency effort had demonstrated their values by: reducing the tactical advantage accruing to the enemy through the use of natural concealment; and by denying subsistence to the enemy, thus reducing his mobility and compounding his logistical problems'.[99]

US forces also destroyed villages (although not wantonly as portrayed in the press or movies like *Platoon*). The two most famous of these episodes occurred at Cam Ne in August 1965 and Ben Tre in February 1968. At Cam Ne, a CBS television crew filmed US Marines using cigarette lighters to light thatched huts on fire[100] At Ben Tre, Peter Arnett of the *New York Times* famously reported 'the decision by allied commanders to bomb and shell the town regardless of civilian casualties, to rout the Vietcong' during the Tet Offensive. Arnett's quote from a US major at the scene came to epitomise the war: 'It became necessary to destroy the town to save it'.[101]

The VC frequently used villages as bases and supply hubs, and civilians were used for labour. Nevertheless, American tactics virtually guaranteed civilian casualties and the damage to villages. As one officer wrote: 'More concern must be given to the safety of villages. Instances were noted where villages were severely damaged or destroyed by napalm or naval gunfire, wherein the military necessity of doing so was dubious'.[102]

US forces relied on massive firepower throughout the war. A report by the US Army Combat Developments Command – *Dynamics of Fire and Maneuver* – concluded that the goals of the strategy of attrition, coupled with an imperative to limit US casualties, resulted in tactics that employed 'fire in massive quantities and to give it primacy over maneuver, particularly in dense jungle and against strongly fortified positions'.[103]

The available firepower was massive, ranging from the weapons of individual soldiers to the use of B-52 bombers in close air support

---

[99] W. B. Rosson, *Assessment of Influence Exerted on Military Operations by Other than Military Considerations*, reprint (Washington, DC: US Army Center of Military History, 1993), 1–25.

[100] Lewy, *America in Vietnam*, 53.

[101] 'Major Describe Moves', *The New York Times* (8 February 1968), 14.

[102] 1st Battalion, 7th Marines, After Action Report #1, STARLIGHT, 27 August 1965, cited in Lewy, *America in Vietnam*, 55.

[103] United States Army Combat Developments Command, *Dynamics of Fire and Maneuver (FIRMA III) Final Report* (Fort Belvoir, VA: United States Army Combat Developments Command, 1969), 27.

missions and area bombings of 'suspected enemy locations' as large as eight square kilometres.[104] Even after the beginning of the Vietnamisation of the war, available air power was significant: tactical air sortie rates of twenty-one thousand per month and B-52 sortie rates of sixteen hundred per month."[105]

US forces pursued the enemy in search and destroy operations that were highly destructive and produced collateral damage and refugees. As one brigade commander recalled, 'The awesome firepower-artillery, air strikes, and ARA [Aerial Rocket Artillery from helicopter gunships] ... despite our best efforts, began taking a toll of innocent civilians killed and maimed, villages destroyed, and farm animals slain'.[106] Much of the firepower was expended in unobserved H&I (Harassment and Interdiction) fires against known or 'suspected' enemy locations and infiltration routes.[107] Again, these operations ran counter to the pacification efforts, but they were deemed necessary to the continued attrition of NVA conventional forces and VC main force units.

Firepower, particularly air power, kept the South Vietnamese in the war by preventing their defeat by the NVA during the 1972 Easter Offensive by North Vietnam.[108] Many former Vietnamese military and civilian leaders believed that air power could have saved the day again in 1975.[109]

The materiel used by American forces also made immense strides during the war. Helicopters provided lift for manoeuvre, medical evacuation and, with the advent of gunships, accompanying fire power. Unmanned aerial vehicles, wire-guided anti-tank missiles, unattended ground sensors, night vision equipment, precision-guided munitions, electronic and kinetic countermeasures against surface-to-air missiles systems, air-to-air-missiles, improved tactical radars, improved conventional munitions for artillery, fixed-wing gunships and a host of other technologies and weapons. Most, if not all of these technologies, were developed in the context of improved capabilities for the broader Cold War. Vietnam, however, offered a test-bed for in-combat innovation and the new technologies added to the

---

[104] R. M. Kipp, 'Counterinsurgency from 30,000 Feet – The B-52 in Vietnam', *Air University Review*, 19 (1967), 13.

[105] Rosson, 'Assessment of Influence Exerted on Military Operations', 54.

[106] H. G. Moore, *We Were Soldiers Once ... and Young – Ia Drang: The Battle That Changed the War in Vietnam* (New York: Random House, 1992), 342.

[107] Lewy, *America in Vietnam*, 99.   [108] Clodfelter, *The Limits of Air Power*, 153.

[109] S. T. Hosmer, K. Kellen and B. M. Jenkins, *The Fall of South Vietnam: Statements by Vietnamese Military and Civilian Leader* (New York: Crane, Russak, and Company, 1980), 257.

capabilities of the forces in that war.[110] Despite these US materiel advantages, the VC and NVA decided the tempo of fighting: 'until late 1969, roughly 85% of the ground contacts were initiated by the enemy'.[111]

As already noted, the United States did engage in 'Hearts and Minds' approaches. There were extensive pacification efforts – 'Reconstruction, Civic Action, Agrovilles, Strategic Hamlets, New Life Hamlets, Hoc Tap (Cooperation), Chien Thang (Victory), Rural Construction, Rural Reconstruction, and Revolutionary Development' – but they were secondary to dealing with security issues and episodic until the creation of CORDS.[112] Komer pushed the GVN on land reform, economic, health care and democratic institution development. By 1970, the Hamlet Evaluation System (HES) estimated that 93 per cent of the population of South Vietnam reported living in 'relatively secure' villages.[113] Nevertheless, as one former CORDS analyst pointed out: 'we collected lots of data indicating the security of the regions and provinces but nowhere did we find any evidence or indication of popular support of the [national-level] government'.[114]

The HES was emblematic of the insatiable demand for data on progress in the war by the US government. In the conventional war, progress was measured by body count; in pacification, the HES survey data from thousands of Vietnamese villages were supposed to determine whether the villages were under government or Communist control. The HES used quantifiable data – such as economic and social indicators and dubious attitudinal survey data – to assess what were fundamentally qualitative issues.[115]

The daily press briefings given by the military in Saigon at MACV headquarters, derisively known as the '5 O'clock Follies', relied on statistics in attempts to show progress and manage the message.

[110] T. G. Mahnken, *Technology and the American War of War since 1945* (New York: Columbia University Press, 2008), 89–117.

[111] BDM, *A Study of the Strategic Lessons Learned in Vietnam: Omnibus Executive Summary*, EX-11.

[112] Lewy, *America in Vietnam*, 1 89.

[113] J. P. White, 'Civil Affairs in Vietnam' (Washington, DC: Center for Strategic and International Studies, 2009), at csis.org/publication/civil-affairs-vietnam (last accessed 16 December 2014), 10.

[114] R. Coffey, 'Revisiting CORDS: The Need for Unity of Effort to Secure Victory in Iraq', *Military Review* (March-April 2006), 32.

[115] 'Afghan Metrics and Vietnam', *The Economist* (13 August 2009), at www.economist.com/blogs/democracyinamerica/2009/08/afghan_metrics_and_vietnam (last accessed 16 December 2014).

Reporters believed 'They seldom bore any resemblance whatever to the facts in the field'.[116]

Komer eventually recognised the limits of the pacification efforts, recalling: 'Perhaps the most important single reason why the United States achieved so little for so long was that it could not sufficiently revamp, or adequately substitute for, a South Vietnamese leadership, administration, and armed forces inadequate to the task'.[117]

Even if the United States had pacified South Vietnam, and even if that government had had the support of its people, the South still faced an existential threat from North. The United States had invested considerable resources in creating the South Vietnamese military in the image of the US military. During the 1972 North Vietnamese invasion the ARVN held – in no small part because of American airpower that the North could not counter. Absent this air power edge and other critical US capabilities, the South fell to the North in 1975.[118]

No More Vietnams (1975–2006)

President Nixon made two key decisions that shaped how the United States would approach the international security environment and Vietnam. First, he announced the Nixon Doctrine in July 1969, replacing Kennedy policies of confronting Communist expansion wherever it occurred. In essence, Nixon ended using American ground forces to stop wars of national liberation.[119] Second, Nixon adopted a 'one and one half war' strategy, dramatically reducing force requirements and resources. In this new strategic environment the United States focused on conventional threats and abandoned COIN as it riveted its focus on the Cold War and, beginning with the Carter Doctrine, East Asia and the Persian Gulf Region.[120]

The Services turned to demonstrating their relevance in the high-stakes Cold War with the Soviet Union. The Army, the Service most deeply committed in Vietnam, and the one most subject to resource cuts in its aftermath, almost immediately moved past the war. General William DePuy, the commander of TRADOC (US Army Training and Doctrine Command) after Vietnam, was one of the principal architects of the Army's refocus on NATO. He later recalled that 'The Vietnam

---

[116] 'The Press: Farewell to the Follies', *Time* (12 February 1973), at content.time.com/time/subscriber/article/0,33009,903831-1,00.html (last accessed 17 December 2014).
[117] Coffey, 'Revisiting CORDS', 32.
[118] Hosmer et al., *The Fall of South Vietnam*, 257–60.   [119] Millett, *Semper Fidelis*, 596.
[120] Johnson, *Modern U.S. Civil-Military Relations*, 51–4.

War – combat with light and elusive forces – was over' and that 'The defense of central Europe against large, modern, Soviet armored forces once again became the Army's main, almost exclusive, mission'.[121] General Donn Starry, Depuy's eventual successor at TRADOC commander and a key figure in developing the Army's new AirLand Battle, was equally clear: 'After getting out of Vietnam, the Army looked around and realised it should not try to fight that kind of war again elsewhere'.[122] He also believed the Army should avoid its tendency to dwell on understanding the 'last war [Vietnam]' and 'to look ahead, not back'.[123] This view prevailed, and as the 1980 BDM report presciently noted: 'It is doubtful if the US has yet learned how to defeat – in a reasonable time and an acceptable cost – a well-organised and led "People's War": the institutional knowledge gained in Indochina have been discarded or degraded, as have been the interest and incentives'.[124]

The 1976 *FM 100–5: Operations* that was the Army's first doctrinal expression of its post-Vietnam direction returned to the 'lesser included' model that had long undergirded its culture, noting: 'Battle in Central Europe against forces of the Warsaw Pact is the most demanding mission the US Army could be assigned'. Furthermore, *FM 100–5* emphasised that 'The principles set forth in this manual ... apply also to military operations anywhere in the world'. Nowhere was there any mention of Vietnam, the political dimensions of warfare or COIN. Thus, 'the fundamental lesson for the military that emerged from the Vietnam War was crystal clear – "no more Vietnams"'.[125]

History, although not repeating itself, would rhyme in the twenty-first century.

Twenty-first-Century US COIN (2006–?)

Relearning COIN after 'Winning' in Afghanistan and Iraq

Between the end of the Vietnam War and 2003 the United States built a formidable conventional military that seemingly prevailed in every use. Although there were discussions about 'MOOTW' (Military Operations

[121] W. E. DePuy, 'FM 100–5 Revisited', *Army* (November 1980), 12.

[122] D. B. Vought, 'Preparing for the Wrong War?', *Military Review* (May 1977), 32.

[123] D. A. Starry, 'A Tactical Evolution-FM 100-S', *Military Review* (August 1978), 3.

[124] BDM, *A Study of the Strategic Lessons Learned in Vietnam: Omnibus Executive Summary*, VI-7.

[125] D. Johnson, 'Failure to Learn: Reflections on a Career in the Post-Vietnam Army', *War on the Rocks* (January 24, 2014), at warontherocks.com/2014/01/failure-to-learn-reflections-on-a-career-in-the-post-vietnam-army/ (last accessed 17 December 2014).

Other Than War), 'Stability and Support Operations' and 'Low Intensity Conflict', the prevailing attitude was that espoused in the Army's 2001 version of *FM 100–5: Operations* – the doctrine it would take into Afghanistan and Iraq: 'The doctrine holds warfighting as the Army's primary focus and recognises that the ability of Army forces to dominate land warfare also provides the ability to dominate any situation in military operations other than war'.[126]

The growing insurgency in Afghanistan and the descent of Iraq into chaos within months of its liberation made both wars ground-centric from a military perspective. Ironically, the US invasions of Afghanistan and Iraq probably more closely resemble the Philippine War than the cases generally discussed in US COIN doctrine: Algeria, Malaya and Vietnam. After the defeat in battle and removal of the regime – the Taliban in Afghanistan, Saddam Hussein in Iraq – both wars descended into violent insurgencies and long-term occupations. As in the Philippines, a civil-military effort adapted to the changing conditions that the protracted insurgencies created and involved a broad range of nation-building and security efforts.

Iraq was the more violent of the two conflicts and had the highest strategic consequences for the administration of President George W. Bush. Although Secretary of Defense Donald Rumsfeld had famously corrected General Peter Pace, the vice chairman of the Joint Chiefs of Staff, for even using the word 'insurgency' to describe the situation in Iraq in 2005, there was growing realisation across the US government that wheels were coming off in Iraq. There was also an emerging consensus that the approach of General George W. Casey, Commander of the Multi-National Force-Iraq, of turning the war over to the Iraqis – 'standing down as they stand up' – was not working.[127]

President Bush, in an address to the nation on 10 January 2007, announced a new approach: 'Our troops will have a well-defined mission: to help Iraqis clear and secure neighborhoods, to help them protect the local population and to help ensure that the Iraqi forces left behind are capable of providing the security that Baghdad needs'. Securing would require more US troops, and the key to Bush's new approach was a dramatic increase in US troop strength – 'the Surge'.[128]

---

[126] US Department of the Army, *FM 3-0: Operations* (Washington, DC: Headquarters, Department of the Army, 2001), vii.

[127] T. E. Ricks, *The Gamble: General Petraeus and the American Military Adventure in Iraq* (New York: Penguin Press, 2009), 74–128; J. A. Nagl, *Knife Fights: A Memoir of Modern War in Theory and Practice* (New York: Penguin Press, 2014).

[128] The White House, Office of the Press Secretary, 'President's Address to the Nation' (10 January 2007).

President Bush had already made a change at the top of the Department of Defense, replacing Donald Rumsfeld with Robert Gates in December 2006. Gates replaced General Casey with General David Petraeus in January 2007. Even before Petraeus's confirmation, there had been significant adaptation on the ground in Iraq. Lieutenant General Raymond Odierno, commander of the Multi-National Corps–Iraq, was at odds with Casey over the strategy in Iraq and began planning on how to secure Iraqi cities, particularly Baghdad, rather than withdraw from them. Additionally, there was broad adaptation by commanders to the insurgency. What had been missing was an institutional response that forced a dramatic shift in the culture of the US Armed Forces, particularly the Army and Marine Corps, from 'close with and destroy the enemy' to 'protect the population' – along with the means (sufficient troops) to change conditions on the ground.[129]

The result was the 2006 Army/Marine Corps manual *FM 3–24/MCWP 3–33.5: Counterinsurgency* (hereafter referred to as *FM 3–24*), crafted under (then) Lieutenant General David Petraeus when he commanded the Combined Arms Center at Fort Leavenworth, Kansas.[130] This concept of 'population-centric' COIN became the 'way' in which the new 'means' of additional troops would be employed to reach policy 'ends' of stability in the wars in Iraq and then Afghanistan.

FM 3–24 was more a concept than doctrine, if 'a concept is a hypothesis – an inference that suggests that a proposed pattern of behavior *may possibly* lead to a desired result, a doctrine is a generalisation based on sufficient evidence to suggest that a given pattern of behavior *will probably* lead to the desired result' (I. B. Holley).[131] *FM 3–24* is a self-fulfilling prophecy and distinctively American in its engineering approach. The manual assumes that the desired end state for a COIN campaign can be designed using LLOs (Logical Lines of Operations), which, if successfully executed, ineluctably lead to the achievement of the desired end state. LLOs as described in FM 3–24 are not rigid, but the 'logic' behind the LLOs is inexorable progress over time through the execution of a synchronised, highly detailed plan: 'Progress along each LLO contributes to attaining a stable and secure environment for the host nation. Stability is reinforced by popular recognition of the HN government's legitimacy, improved governance, and progressive, substantive reduction of the root causes of the insurgency'.[132]

---

[129] Ricks, *The Gamble*, 122.   [130] Nagl, *Knife Fights*, 105–49.

[131] I. B. Holley, Jr., *Technology and Military Doctrine: Essays on a Challenging Relationship* (Maxwell Air Force Base, AL: Air University Press, 2004), 21.

[132] *FM 3–24* (2006), 5-3.

FM 3–24 offers the example of five LLOs to demonstrate how to achieve the end state of positively affecting a population's support for the host nation government: combat operations/civil security operations host nation security forces, essential services, governance and economic development, all supported by information operations. Information operations, like much of the discussion of LLOs, these proceed from a basic assumption that saying they must be done well means they will be done well. This is most evident in the statement that information operations must 'Discredit insurgent propaganda and provide a more compelling alternative to the insurgent ideology and narrative'.[133] There is no consideration of whether or not a western non-Muslim occupier on short tours of duty can 'provide a more compelling alternative to the insurgent ideology and narrative'. This point highlights a fundamental flaw in *FM 3–24:* what the concept says must be done is frequently conflated with what can be done – aspirations become capabilities.

FM 3–24 also specifies two necessary preconditions for a COIN campaign to succeed. First, there is a historically based force requirement: 'Twenty counterinsurgents per 1,000 residents is often considered the minimum troop density required for effective COIN operations; however as with any fixed ratio, such calculations remain very dependent upon the situation'.[134] Second, although there is an acknowledgement that successful COIN required a whole of US government approach, the manual recognises that 'Participants best qualified and able to accomplish nonmilitary tasks are not always available . . . In those cases, military forces perform those tasks. Sometimes forces have the skills required; other times they learn them during execution'. The manual did elaborate the skills needed – cultural understanding, 'Functional skills needed for interagency and HN coordination (for example, liaison, negotiation, and appropriate social or political relationships)', and 'Knowledge of basic civic functions such as governance, infrastructure, public works, economics, and emergency services' – but did not offer a source for these skills other than to enjoin commanders to 'identify people in their units with regional and interagency expertise, civil-military competence, and other critical skills needed to support a local populace and HN [Host Nation] government'.[135]

Satisfying these two imperatives – capacity and capability – would be a constant issue in both Iraq and Afghanistan. This was because the US military, although it expanded during the two wars, had a fixed capacity

[133] *FM 3-24* (2006), 5-3–5-4.   [134] *FM 3-24* (2006), 1–13.
[135] *FM 3-24* (2006), 2–9.

well below that necessary to provide the security force to resident levels specified in *FM 3–24*. Furthermore, military personnel would have to do jobs for which they were not prepared, because of a lack of civilian capacity.[136] In many cases, contractors were the recourse for shortages. Finally, complicating the capacity and capability issues were two other realities that the United States had faced in Vietnam: the insurgents had external sources of supply and sanctuary outside the country.

Efforts to better prepare American advisers for duty in Iraq and Afghanistan increased with the opening of a training program at Fort Riley, Kansas, to train Military Transition Teams. This sixty-day training program, reminiscent of the MATA course at Fort Bragg during the Vietnam War, was elementary at best, covering 'survival skills and tactics, individual- and crew-served weapons and equipment, communications, combat lifesaver skills and cultural awareness'.[137] Furthermore, as during the Vietnam War, advisory duty was seen a less career enhancing than service in a conventional unit.[138]

Finally, as in Vietnam, tour lengths in Afghanistan and Iraq worked against attaining deep understanding of the operational, much less cultural environments. US Army tour lengths began at twelve months, but extended to fifteen months to meet the capacity demands of the Iraq surge, and are now nine months. US Marine tours were seven months; many of the coalition partners had even shorter tours.[139] This constant turnover made it difficult, if not impossible, to sustain coherence in long-term security and development programs.

The Twenty-first-Century US COIN Toolkit

The toolkit of US COIN in Afghanistan and Iraq has emphasised hearts and minds approaches and the importance of creating legitimate governments with popular support. General Petraeus emphasised that the 'operative concept' was 'clear, hold and build', rather than just killing

---

[136] D. E. Johnson, 'What Are You Prepared to Do? NATO and the Strategic Mismatch Between Ends, Ways, and Means in Afghanistan – and in the Future', *Studies in Conflict and Terrorism* (May 2011), 394–5. Other departments within US Federal Government relied on, and incentivised, volunteers to fill positions in Afghanistan and Iraq; only the US military has mandatory deployments.

[137] S. Howard, 'Army Secretary Views MiTT Training at Fort Riley' (2 November 2006), at www.army.mil/article/501/Army_Secretary_views_MiTT_training_at_Fort_Riley/ (last accessed 20 December 2014).

[138] J. A. Nagl, 'In Era of Small Wars, U.S. Army Must Embrace Training Mission', *World Politics Review* (5 February 2015), at www.worldpoliticsreview.com/articles/print/12693 (last accessed 20 December 2014).

[139] Johnson, 'What Are You Prepared to Do?', 393.

or capturing insurgents.[140] This has proved difficult, given the deep ethnic divisions in Iraq and the highly dispersed tribal population in Afghanistan. Additionally, enormous funds have been invested in both countries by the United States and other donor nations in the form of aid, support to programs, construction, and forming and equipping Afghan and Iraqi armed forces.

There have also been population transfers in Iraq, mostly incidental to the conflict and brutal ethnic separations – particularly after the massive increase in sectarian violence subsequent to the 22 February 2006 bombing of the al-Askari shrine. The war has resulted in large numbers of refugees and internally displaced persons. For example, in 2009 Syria had some one and a half million Iraqi refugees.[141] The one instance of large-scale forced relocation by US Coalition forces was during the November 2004 battle in Fallujah. Civilians in Fallujah were told to leave or be treated as combatants. Some 70 to 90 per cent of the 300,000 residents fled[142] before the battle, which was a block-to-block fight employing massive amounts of firepower.[143]

Identity cards are used in Afghanistan and Iraq, with sophisticated technology, including biometric data in a chip in the card.[144] Checkpoints and searches are common. In Iraq, US forces used T-walls (large twelve-feet-tall and five-feet-wide wall sections made of reinforced concrete, each weighing between 12,000 and 14,000 pounds) to create what amounted to gated communities to protect against VBIEDs (Vehicle-Borne Improvised Explosive Devices). Walling off areas, particularly troubled neighbourhoods at places where large numbers of people congregated, such as mosques and markets, resulted in dramatic reductions in the deaths caused by these weapons.[145] These walls were not without

---

[140] P. Mansoor, *Surge: My Journey with General David Petraeus and the Remaking of the Iraq War* (New Haven, CT: Yale University Press), 107.

[141] US Department of Defense, *Measuring Stability and Security in Iraq: March 2009*, 7, at www.defense.gov/pubs/pdfs/Measuring_Stability_and_Security_in_Iraq_March_2009.pdf (last accessed 22 December 2014).

[142] D. Filkins and J. Glanz, 'With Airpower and Armor, Troops Enter Rebel-Held City', *New York Times* (8 November 2004), at www.nytimes.com/2004/11/08/international/08CND_IRAQ.html?_r=1&ex=1114401600&en=2bb5b33cda9ccdd9&ei=5070 (last accessed 22 December 2014).

[143] D. E. Johnson, M. Wade Markel and B. Shannon, *The 2008 Battle of Sadr City: Reimagining Urban Combat* (Santa Monica, CA: RAND, 2011), 110.

[144] J. E. Stern, 'Afghanistan's Growing Identity (Card) Crisis', *Foreign Policy* (21 January 2014), at foreignpolicy.com/2014/01/21/afghanistans-growing-identity-card-crisis/ (last accessed 22 December 2014), and 'Giesecke & Devrient Wins Another Major Contract from Iraq', at www.gi-de.com/en/about_g_d/press/press_releases/Giesecke-%26-Devrient-Wins-Another-Major-Contract-from-Iraq-g28224.jsp (last accessed 22 December 2014).

[145] Johnson et al., *The 2008 Battle of Sadr City*, 10, 14.

controversy. Some compared them to what the Israelis were doing; others charged they 'were dividing neighbor from neighbor and choking off normal communications'.[146] US and Iraqi forces also created fortified combat outposts and joint security stations throughout key city areas. Active patrolling further enhanced security and kept insurgents and death squads moving. Their communications enabled US forces to monitor and frequently intercept them.

Again, the situation in Afghanistan is different, because most of the population is not concentrated in large cities. Checkpoints and barriers are used in urban areas and on roads. Active patrolling and presence in rural areas is employed, although increasingly by Afghan forces, because of ever-decreasing ISAF (International Security Assistance Force) troop levels. Furthermore, in both Iraq and Afghanistan, local militias have been paid and armed to provide local, village-level security in programs that harken back to strategic hamlet programs in Vietnam. In Afghanistan, given tribal divisions and the paucity of ISAF soldiers, this approach may be the only one with even a marginal chance to clear, hold and build contested areas throughout Afghanistan.[147]

General Petraeus famously noted when he assumed command of the Multi-National Force-Iraq that 'we would not be able to kill or capture our way out of the industrial-strength insurgency that confronted us in Iraq', there was one big exception, in both Iraq and Afghanistan, for high-value targets. In Iraq in 2007, Petraeus 'encouraged' Lieutenant General Stanley A. McChrystal, commander of the US Joint Special Operations Command and the Counterterrorism Special Operations Task Force in Iraq, 'to be relentless in the pursuit of Al-Qaeda and other Sunni Arab extremist leaders, bomb makers, financiers and propaganda cells – and to do the same with key Iranian-supported Shi'a Arab extremists as well'.[148]

The hunting of high-value targets was not new to McChrystal; his Task Force 714 had been going after 'the deck of cards' high-value former Ba'athist leaders since the collapse of the Saddam Hussein regime and had been instrumental in capturing Saddam and killing his two sons, Uday and Qusay, and radical Islamist Abu Musab al-Zarqawi.[149]

---

[146] Ricks, *The Gamble*, 173.
[147] See S. G. Jones and Arturo Muñoz, *Afghanistan's Local War: Building Local Defense Forces* (Santa Monica, CA: RAND, 2010).
[148] Mansoor, *Surge*, xii, xiv.
[149] S. A. McChrystal, *My Share of the Task*, 101–11. See also S. Stewart, 'Why U.S. Bounties on Terrorists Often Fail', *STRATFOR Global Intelligence* (12 April 2012), at www.stratfor.com/weekly/why-us-bounties-terrorists-often-fail#axzz3MjR7KcMC (last accessed 22 December 2014).

Subsequently, McChrystal's special operators produced dramatic results: 'the targeted operations – as many as ten to fifteen per night – removed from the battlefield a significant proportion of the senior and midlevel extremist group leaders, explosives experts, planners, financiers and organisers in Iraq'. All was not killing. Petraeus later recalled: 'We preferred to capture insurgent and militia leaders, as their interrogation inevitably generated intelligence that led to improvements in our understanding of the enemy networks and generated actionable intelligence for follow-on targeted operations'.[150]

It is difficult to ascertain the specifics of the COIN and counterterrorism programs for finding and killing or capturing high-value targets in Iraq, Afghanistan and elsewhere given that they are classified. What is apparent, however, is that these programs are highly sophisticated and effective, using integrated intelligence from across multiple agencies, special operators and high technology, including unmanned aerial vehicles (drones).[151] When General Petraeus took command in Afghanistan after General McChrystal's resignation, he stepped up the killing or capturing of Taliban leaders, tripling the number of night raids.[152] These operations also tacitly acknowledge that killing or capturing insurgent leaders is viewed as a key means of degrading insurgencies through assaults on their cellular networks, particularly in Afghanistan as ISAF force levels recede. These operations are of a type that Roger Trinquier and Robert Komer would instantly recognise and likely envy.

Measuring Success

The Department of Defense has consistently used metrics to demonstrate progress in COIN, which share the issues from Vietnam of using quantitative data to assess qualitative progress. Congress requires reports on progress in Afghanistan, as it did on Iraq prior to the US departure. These reports are publicly available. The breadth of the efforts to obtain data is seen in the contents of areas measured in the section headings of the June 2010 Iraq report: political stability, economic activity, security environment, transferring security responsibility, assessed capabilities of the Iraqi forces, Ministry of Interior, Ministry of Defense and Iraqi National Counter-Terrorism Force. What is apparent in the majority of the reports is the attempt to use metrics to demonstrate progress – progress

[150] Mansoor, *Surge*, xv, 293.
[151] See McChrystal, *My Share of the Task* for his description of the kill or capture programs.
[152] P. Dixon, *The British Approach to Counterinsurgency from Malaya and Northern Ireland to Iraq and Afghanistan* (New York: Palgrave MacMillan, 2012), 260.

that is almost always assessed as proceeding, despite challenges. Two examples are the reporting of the state of readiness of Iraqi Security Forces and the metric of Enemy Initiated Attacks in Afghanistan.

The June 2010 quarterly report to Congress, *Measuring Stability and Security in Iraq*, gave an optimistic, if somewhat cautious, report on the state of the Iraqi Security Forces as the United States on the eve of departure that showed the results of US training, advising and assisting efforts:

The ISF have executed their security responsibilities extremely well, maintaining historically low levels of security incidents … USF-I [US Forces-Iraq] is on track to complete the transition to stability operations by September 1, 2010. The ongoing implementation of the SFA this reporting period sets the stage for long-term cooperative efforts as Iraq develops into a sovereign, stable, self-reliant partner.[153]

In reality, the Iraqi Security Forces suffered from many of the same deficiencies as those of South Vietnam after the US withdrawal. They were organised on a US model, and absent US support in the form of enablers, particularly air power, they collapsed in the face of ISIS.

Recently retired Lieutenant Dan Bolger raises troublesome connections to Vietnam in the way metrics have been used to 'exaggerate progress'. A key metric in Afghanistan was Enemy Initiated Attacks (EIAs). Bolger notes that in a 2013 report Anthony Cordesman 'shows how ISAF selectively claimed percentage decreases in hostile attacks from April 2008 to October 2012'.[154] In a section of the report headed 'Spin, Missing Data and a Return to the Follies', Cordesman wrote:

there has been a steady shrinking in the metrics and analysis provided on the full range of civil-military progress in the war over the last two years as the pressure for a rapid transition has risen. The end result has … been a return to the "good news" emphasis of the 'follies' in Vietnam … making EIAs the modern equivalent of the body count.[155]

Bolger wrote about the reporting in Afghanistan: 'You had the sick feeling in your stomach you were looking at the hamlet evaluations from outside Da Nang, circa 1967'.[156]

---

[153] US Department of Defense, *Measuring Stability and Security in Iraq: June 2010*, at www.defense.gov/pubs/pdfs/June_9204_Sec_Def_signed_20_Aug_2010.pdf (last accessed 20 December 2012), x.

[154] D. P. Bolger, *Why We Lost: A General's Inside Account of the Iraq and Afghanistan Wars* (Boston: Houghton, Mifflin, Harcourt, 2014), 390–1.

[155] A. H. Cordesman, *The War in Afghanistan at the End of 2012: The Uncertain Course of the War and Transition* (Washington, DC: Center for Strategic and International Studies, 2012), 24.

[156] Bolger, *Why We Lost*, 391.

Has US COIN Become More Humane?

On the question of humaneness in US COIN practices, the record is clear that there has been a considerable attempt by US forces and those of its partners in Iraq and Afghanistan to minimise harm to civilians and reduce collateral damage, particularly after the promulgation of *FM 3–24*. Unfavorable incidents – the Abu Ghraib prisoner abuse scandal, the Haditha killings in Iraq, the Blackwater killings of civilians and others – have all been widely reported in the press and legal action taken. These types of activities are impossible to hide in a world of instant information, and the policy of the US has been to act to curb them. The ongoing debate about 'enhanced interrogation techniques' and the recent US Senate Select Committee on Intelligence *Committee Study of the Central Intelligence Agency's Detention and Interrogation Program* shows that there is a debate over what measures are appropriate in COIN and counterterrorism. Whether or not the Iraqis and the Afghans (or contractors) follow the example of their Western partners is open to question.

Another perhaps ironic indicator of the more humane nature of US COIN practices is the use of what amounts to a reverse of the body count metric in Afghanistan. Reducing civilian casualties is a key objective for ISAF and the Afghan government. An April 2014 US government Report on Afghanistan highlighted that the insurgents caused the majority of CIVCAS (civilian casualties) – 5,482 casualties, or 88 per cent, compared to 3 per cent by Afghan security forces and 2 per cent by ISAF.[157] Nevertheless, the report also noted 'However unpopular, Taliban attacks, intimidation tactics, and propaganda enable the insurgency to project influence in rural areas'.[158]

Furthermore, the evolution of technology since the Vietnam War has made the precise application of force against targets more accurately located through sophisticated intelligence, surveillance and reconnaissance (ISR) much more feasible. Gone are the Vietnam days, for many reasons, of indiscriminate H&I fires. This is not to say that US forces will not use violence to protect people. In the Battle of Sadr City in Baghdad over a six-week period in March–April 2008, US Army forces killed more than seven hundred JAM (Jaish al-Mahdi) militia and fired 818 120-mm rounds from M1 tanks and 12,091 25-mm rounds from Bradley fighting vehicles. US forces also employed

---

[157] Department of Defense, *Report on Progress toward Security and Stability in Afghanistan* (April 2014), at www.defense.gov/pubs/April_1230_Report_Final.pdf 14 (last accessed 15 December 2014).

[158] DoD, *Report on Progress toward Security and Stability in Afghanistan*, 12.

Hellfire missiles against JAM rocket positions and 500-pound guided bombs to destroy buildings where JAM snipers sheltered.[159]

The US Style and Strategic Culture

The inability to *imagine* anything but success in any strategic environment, regardless of climate or geography, has been the essence of US style and strategic culture, particularly since World War II. This is not necessarily hubris, but a national sense of optimism and what some have termed 'American exceptionalism' and the conviction that 'inside everyone is an American yearning to be free'. There is little difference between Clark Clifford's recollection of the dismissal of the North Vietnamese by US policymakers as 'little people running around in black pajamas' who would not be able to long resist 'the greatest nation in the world, with the most enormous firepower and with bombing that could wipe them out', and Donald Rumsfeld's remark in November 2002 on the eve of the Operation Iraqi Freedom 'I can't tell you if the use of force in Iraq today would last five days, or five weeks, or five months, but it certainly isn't going to last any longer than that'.[160]

The seeming unpreparedness of the United States for COIN is the result of how the United States has designed its military and civilian agencies since the American Revolution: military forces designed to fight large-scale, high-technology wars and civilian departments with little, if any, excess capacity. As Conrad Crane not so jokingly wrote: 'When I describe the U.S. government to foreign officers at the Army War College, I tell them to envision a fiddler crab with one large claw labeled "Department of Defense" and a small claw labeled "the mythical interagency" ... the fact still remains that there are more musicians in the Department of Defense than foreign service officers in the State Department'.[161] As a result, the US military in every large-scale insurgency in its history has been forced to adapt to COIN with forces organised, trained and equipped for conventional warfighting. They have struggled to learn on the job, because only they have the capacity for the tasks. These challenges are only further complicated by the fact that US military forces, other than special forces, have rarely, if ever, had more

---

[159] Johnson et al., *The 2008 Battle of Sadr City* (Santa Monica, CA: RAND, 2011), 11–14.

[160] Committee on Foreign Affairs, 'The Lessons of Vietnam', 37, and 'Rumsfeld: No World War III in Iraq', *CNN.com/U.S.* (15 November 2002), at edition.cnn.com/2002/US/11/15/rumsfeld.iraq/ (last accessed 15 November 2014).

[161] Conrad Crane, 'Observations on the Long War', *War on the Rocks* (10 September 2014), at warontherocks.com/2014/09/observations-on-the-long-war/ (last accessed 20 October 2014).

than a cursory understanding of the cultures and languages of the places they are trying to execute COIN operations. Furthermore, rotational short-term assignments do not markedly increase this doctrinally required knowledge to an appreciable degree.

The future does not look much better. The capacity guidelines in the 2006 *FM 3–24: Counterinsurgency* have not been achievable because the size of the all-volunteer US military and the size of the populations in the countries where the United States has recently been engaged. James Quinlivan, the author of one of the seminal documents that provided the intellectual basis for the security force requirements in *FM 3–24*, presciently wrote in 1995: 'The populations of many countries are now large enough to strain the ability of the American military to provide stabilising forces unilaterally at even modest per capita force ratios ... And we must finally acknowledge that many countries are simply too big to be plausible candidates for stabilisation by external forces'.[162] Apparently indirectly admitting to this capacity dilemma, the 2014 revision of *FM3–24: Insurgencies and Countering Insurgencies* makes no mention of minimum troop densities required for effective COIN.[163]

While US conventional forces have been attempting to execute COIN doctrine without sufficient capability or capacity, a modern-day Project Phoenix is degrading the competence of insurgent and terrorist organisations by killing or capturing their leaders. Thus, while the conventional force is executing COIN based on the more humane theories of David Galula; the special operations force is going after leadership networks following the direct action methods of Roger Trinquier and Robert Komer.

Force size has other deleterious effects. Given the protracted nature of the wars in Afghanistan and Iraq, and the relatively fixed size of the militaries engaged, tour lengths have been a year or less, except during the Iraq Surge, and most militaries have used unit rotations, rather than individual replacements. Thus, these wars have been fought one year – or less – at a time with the resultant displacement of local knowledge as units come and go. Success in combat assignments – as during the Vietnam War, or any other war for that matter – is crucial for career advancement and there is pressure to show results. I have heard more than one mid-grade officer discuss their tours in Afghanistan and Iraq and cynically recall 'everything was broken in our area when we arrived;

[162] J. T. Quinlivan, 'Force Requirements in Stability Operations', *Parameters* (1995), 68.

[163] Headquarters, Department of the Army, *FM3-24/MCWP 3–33.5, C1: Insurgencies and Countering Insurgencies* (Washington, DC: Headquarters, Department of the Army, 2014).

we developed a plan, and over the course of the year our stoplight chart showed us going from red to green; we departed and got awards for our achievements; the next unit arrived and said everything was broken'.

Two final observations about the American way of COIN bear noting, because they will repeat themselves in the future. First, there is a pervasive American trait that demands continued, if not immediate, success for the support of non-existential conflicts. Thus, patience is politically not normal, and the American tendency is to treat 'not winning' as 'losing'. There is little tolerance for Clausewitz's admonition:

Wearing down the enemy in a conflict means using *the duration of the war to bring about a gradual exhaustion of his physical and moral resistance.* If we intend to hold out longer than our opponent we must be content with the smallest possible objects, for obviously a major object requires more effort than a minor one.[164]

Consequently, as Hew Strachan recently wrote, there is an inevitable strain on civil-military relations between a military committed to victory and a body politic making trade-offs with other priorities. Absent a threat to national survival, politicians are reluctant to escalate or stay 'as long as it takes'.[165] It is not politically feasible to follow Max Boot's recommendations, to 'make a long-term commitment' to see things through to the end, particularly if the costs in blood and treasure exceed the perceived political benefits.

What will the United States do to attempt to understand its experiences in Afghanistan and Iraq, particularly in assessing the efficacy of COIN to address irregular threats? This question is extremely important, given the state of the world and the proliferation of irregular threats – ISIS, Boko Haram, Al-Qaeda in the Islamic Maghreb, Hezbollah, to mention but a few – that are destabilising regions of strategic importance to the United States. If the US COIN approach has not worked as advertised by its advocates – and staying forever is not an option – then what approaches need to be developed? This question is particularly important for the US military, given that it has provided the majority of the capacity for these two wars and developed the COIN and other capabilities with which they were waged. Unfortunately, the US history with irregular warfare, as discussed in this essay, is not encouraging – and appears to be repeating itself.

The post-Vietnam US military returned to conventionality – its institutional preference – shifting its focus to NATO and deterring the Soviet

[164] C. von Clausewitz, *On War*, M. Howard and P. Paret (eds.) (Princeton, NJ: Princeton University Press, 1976), 93.

[165] H. Strachan, *The Direction of War: Contemporary Strategy in Historical Perspective* (Cambridge: Cambridge University Press, 2013).

Union. As discussed, there was no incentive to do otherwise, given the Nixon Doctrine. The same thing is happening now with the 'pivot' or 'rebalance' to Asia. COIN capacity is being consciously withdrawn from the military toolkit, as seen in this statement in the *Quadrennial Defense Review 2014*: 'our forces will no longer be sized to conduct large-scale prolonged stability operations'. Although this document promises to 'preserve the expertise gained during the past ten years of counterinsurgency and stability operations in Iraq and Afghanistan' and to 'protect the ability to regenerate capabilities that might be needed to meet future demands'[166]the message is clear to the US military services: 'no more Afghanistans or Iraqs'.

Absent any tangible bureaucratic incentive to preserve the capacity for prolonged-stability operations, currently captured in COIN doctrine, the capabilities and the tacit knowledge gained since 9/11 by the US Armed Forces will join that from the Philippines and Vietnam as a painfully earned, but fading, lore. Smaller forces will focus on tasks and capabilities rewarded in the defence budget. Future US leaders who attempt to regenerate the 'needed capabilities' to counter an insurgency will face the same challenge as their predecessors – that of refocusing a US military designed for regular wars into one capable of prosecuting irregular wars.

---

[166] US Department of Defense, *Quadrennial Defense Review 2014*, Pt. VIII. Also available online at www.defense.gov/pubs/2014_Quadrennial_Defense_Review.pdf (last accessed 23 December 2014).

7   From Fighting 'Francs-Tireurs' to Genocide
German Counterinsurgency in the Second World War

Henning Pieper

Strategies against guerrillas had been developed and applied by the German military leadership since the late nineteenth century, and resulted in war crimes and genocide during several conflicts before 1939. When the Second World War began, however, the political aims of National Socialism replaced other considerations in the field of counterinsurgency. In carrying out Adolf Hitler's intentions, the Wehrmacht was also supported by paramilitary formations of the SS *(Schutzstaffel)* and order police. The fighting at the front and against insurgents, the exploitation of the conquered territories, and the destruction of the European Jews became interconnected, and the radicalisation of the German approach in the form of a war of annihilation led to the formation of underground resistance movements throughout Europe. This chapter seeks to identify the key factors in defining German counterinsurgency policy by examining six operational areas (Poland, the Soviet Union, Yugoslavia, Greece, France and Italy) between 1939 and 1945.

Forging the 'Franc-Tireur Myth' – The Prehistory of German Responses to Insurgencies

The foundations for German approaches to counterinsurgency policy during the Second World War were laid in three conflicts that preceded it. Between 1870 and 1939, several key characteristics emerged which continued to have an effect on those officers and soldiers who were sent into battle by Adolf Hitler:

- Change of attitude towards the civilian population: due to the appearance of guerrillas in the Franco-Prussian war of 1870–1871, military necessity was newly defined as traditional respect for non-combatants was given up and French civilians fell victim to retaliation and destruction.
- Inexperience in battle: the German armies consisted largely of conscripts, and German command agencies failed to prevent their troops

149

from panicking in confusing situations and from resorting to overreactions towards innocents.

- Absence of specific preparation: the German High Command did not introduce any particular training on how to deal with insurgents, even after soldiers had experienced guerrilla warfare in 1870–1871.
- Racism: extreme brutality was shown towards people considered to belong to an inferior race, especially in Namibia in 1904–1908.
- Mentality: German military tradition, in this case an enduring conception of a treacherous enemy fighting a 'Franc-tireur war', led to an inability to adapt to new requirements and to a recurrence of behavioural patterns displayed in earlier conflicts.
- Refusal to accept international agreements: insurgents were denied the status of legitimate combatants, even after this possibility had been decreed by the Hague conventions.

Contempt for guerrillas and irregular warfare, as opposed to standing armies and traditional strategies, was already observed for German military circles by Otto August Rühle von Lilienstern, a military thinker and contemporary of Carl von Clausewitz, in the early nineteenth century.[1] It was not until the Franco-Prussian war of 1870–1871, however, that this sentiment found its way into the implementation of counterinsurgency, as German soldiers confronted guerrillas for the first time during this conflict. The driving forces of German political and military leadership, Prime Minister Otto von Bismarck and Helmuth von Moltke the Elder, the Prussian Chief of Staff, initiated a harsh response to attacks of so-called 'Francs-tireurs'. Some 120,000 men, about a quarter of the German forces, were deployed in areas where ambushes had occurred and along strategic supply and communication arteries. Troops untrained for asymmetric warfare carried out brutal countermeasures such as hostage-taking, collective reprisals and executions of irregular fighters as well as civilians. Moreover, villages were razed, and tributes were exacted from communities where raids had occurred. The 'Franc-tireur war' had a lasting effect on officer training and military doctrine and also influenced the German empire's contributions to the Hague conventions of 1899 and 1907. The German stance of persisting in the illegality of guerrilla warfare, in combination with an overstatement of the role played by the 'Francs-tireurs', led to the creation of a 'Franc-tireur myth'.

---

[1] B. Heuser, *The Strategy Makers: Thoughts on War and Society from Machiavelli to Clausewitz* (Santa Monica, CA: ABC-Clio, 2010), 4.

'Guerrillaphobia' constantly resurged in the following decades, and the extension of retaliatory measures to the civilian population was further ideologically charged during the Second World War.[2]

Other instances of insurrectionary warfare against Germans occurred in German South-West Africa, now Namibia, between 1904 and 1908. In this colonial theatre, the suppression of uprisings of the Herero and Nama nations went beyond the breaking of military resistance. After defeating the Herero in a short campaign, the occupying power pursued survivors into the Omaheke desert, where thousands were killed or died of thirst and starvation. Others were interned in concentration camps under poor living conditions. When the Nama nation rose against the Germans shortly afterwards, a brutal guerrilla war ensued, and mass internment was used as a means to bring entire ethnicities under control. It can be assumed that the conflict caused the death of eighty thousand Herero and Nama. This was the first genocide of the twentieth century and also the first genocide in modern German history.[3]

As far as atrocities in the African colonies are concerned, other European colonial powers resorted to brutal approaches to counter-insurgency around the turn of the century.[4] The Boer War (1899–1902) offers a particular possibility of comparison as British forces followed a combined strategy of internment and combat which was similar to that employed by the Germans in South-West Africa a few years later. In contrast to imperial Germany, however, the exercise of parliamentary control and the prevailing of more moderate voices

---

[2] J. N. Horne and A. Kramer, *German Atrocities, 1914: A History of Denial* (New Haven, CT: Yale University Press, 2001), 140–53; S. Förster, 'The Prussian Triangle of Leadership in the Face of a People's War: A Reassessment of the Conflict between Bismarck and Moltke, 1870–71', in S. Förster and J. Nagler (eds.), *On the Road to Total War: The American Civil War and the German Wars of Unification, 1861–1871* (Washington, DC and Cambridge: Cambridge University Press, 1997), 129; M. Messerschmidt, *The Prussian Army from Reform to War*, 277–81; M. Jones, 'Fighting "This Nation of Liars to the Very End": The German Army in the Franco-Prussian War, 1870–1871', in W. Murray and P. Mansoor (eds.), *Hybrid Warfare: Fighting Complex Opponents from the Ancient World to the Present* (New York and Cambridge: Cambridge University Press, 2012), 185–91.

[3] J. Zimmerer, 'Krieg, KZ und Völkermord in Südwestafrika. Der erste Deutsche Genozid', in J. Zimmerer and J. Zeller (eds.), *Völkermord in Deutsch-Südwestafrika: der Kolonialkrieg in Namibia (1904–1908) und seine Folgen* (Berlin: Links, 2003), 45–58; D. J. Schaller, 'Ich glaube, daß die Nation als solche vernichtet werden muß: Kolonialkrieg und Völkermord in "Deutsch-Südwestafrika" 1904–1907', *Journal of Genocide Research*, 6 (2004), 395; I. V. Hull, *Absolute Destruction: Military Culture and the Practices of War in Imperial Germany* (Ithaca, NY: Cornell University Press, 2005), 44–69.

[4] See the contributions on France and Britain in this volume.

within the military and the political leadership of the colony curtailed the use of violence and stopped the use of extreme methods in the second half of the conflict.[5]

The 'Franc-tireur myth' flared up again in Germany when the First World War broke out in 1914. Along the entire front, the armed forces responded to what they perceived as 'Franc-tireur' attacks by carrying out executions and the destruction of towns and villages, which resulted in the death of more than six thousand Belgian and French civilians between August and October 1914. During the first months of the war, German soldiers showed a behavioural pattern which stemmed from their lack of experience in combat and the impression that they were under attack from a hostile population. In reality, they fell victim to a mass delusion, as most war crimes and acts of violence were directly or indirectly connected with combat operations. This conduct was influenced by their mentality and ideology, most importantly the memory of the 'Franc-tireur war' during the conflict of 1870–1871.[6]

Poland

The beginning of the Second World War with the German attack on Poland on 1 September 1939 marked a turning point as Nazi ideology henceforth contributed to shaping counterinsurgency tactics. At this time, the German army did not have comprehensive service regulations on fighting guerrillas but viewed this aspect as combat under special conditions, similar to fighting in a forest. The largely inexperienced soldiers of the Wehrmacht were unprepared for this situation, as well as for operations in built-up areas. The SS and its agencies, however, used a 1933 police manual, part of which dealt with counterinsurgency.[7]

Preparation for conflict was fuelled by anti-Slavic, anti-Polish and anti-Semitic propaganda which led soldiers to believe that all parts of the Polish population could be expected to take up arms against them. During the campaign, these preconditions added to a combination of motivational and situational factors: National Socialist ideology was

---

[5] Hull, *Absolute Destruction*, 129, 182–93.
[6] Horne and Kramer, *German Atrocities*, 74–8, 166–7.
[7] On Wehrmacht doctrine, see *H.Dv. 300/1 Truppenführung (T.F.), Teil 1* (Berlin, 1933). For the 1933 guidelines, see C. Hammer, *The Gestapo and SS Manual* (Boulder, CO: Paladin Press, 1996). I would like to express my gratitude to Peter S. Randall for providing this information.

blended with traditional 'Guerrillaphobia', and the confusing circumstances of combat as well as the nervousness of German soldiers caused a situation that bore strong similarity to what had happened in Belgium and France twenty-five years earlier. Members of the Wehrmacht and the SS were unable to distinguish between civilians and combatants and reacted to this by committing mass killings of innocents.[8]

What began with the excessive conduct of combat operations soon became part of the genocidal intentions of the Nazi regime: until the end of 1939, about fifty thousand Poles fell victim to the German army, SS, police and other formations. The murder of Polish elites, prisoners of war and at least seven thousand Jews characterised an occupation policy which was intended to destroy both military and ideological enemies. From 1939 to 1941, the conduct of German forces in Poland lowered inhibitions, which later helped to implement a particularly brutal ideological campaign in the Soviet Union. Thus, some historians stated that these two years constituted the first phase of a 'war of annihilation' or the 'genesis of genocide'.[9] Significantly, the Germans did not even aim at winning the support of the Polish population, but rather at forcing the Poles into submission.

The result of this approach was not the elimination of real or suspected guerrillas but the emergence of 'arguably the most comprehensive civil and military resistance organisation in occupied Europe, which established an underground state'. The most important organisation in this context, the Home Army (*Armia Krajowa* – AK), was mainly concerned with gathering intelligence and preparing for a national uprising from 1939 to 1943.[10] Between 1943 and 1945, two large-scale operations were conducted by the Polish underground: the Warsaw ghetto uprising in 1943, a desperate attempt by the Jews to resist deportation into death camps, and the Warsaw Uprising in 1944, which aimed at overthrowing German rule in Poland. The SS managed to put down both revolts: whereas the former was a baptism of fire for security troops and recruits,

---

[8] J. Böhler, *Auftakt zum Vernichtungskrieg: Die Wehrmacht in Polen 1939* (Frankfurt: Fischer, 2006), 147–68; A. B. Rossino, *Hitler Strikes Poland. Blitzkrieg, Ideology, and Atrocity* (Lawrence: University Press of Kansas 2003), 153–85.

[9] J. Böhler et al., *Einsatzgruppen in Polen: Darstellung und Dokumentation* (Darmstadt: Wissenschaftliche Buchgesellschaft, 2008); Rossino, *Hitler Strikes Poland*, 234; Klaus. M. Mallmann and B. Musial (eds.), *Genesis des Genozids: Polen 1939–1941* (Darmstadt: Wissenschaftliche Buchgesellschaft, 2004).

[10] P. Latawski, foreword to Part II – Poland in J. Pattinson and B. Shepherd (eds.), *War in a Twilight World: Partisan and Anti-partisan Warfare in Eastern Europe, 1939 – 45* (Basingstoke: Palgrave Macmillan, 2010), 134.; P. Latawski, 'The Armia Krajowa and Polish Partisan Warfare, 1939–43', 137–55.

the latter was 'the zenith of *Bandenbekämpfung*' (=fight against banditry), as the Germans termed counterinsurgency. The key points to this operation were advanced urban warfare tactics, mass violence and the brutal leadership of SS General Erich von dem Bach-Zelewski. When the Warsaw Uprising was finally put down after two months, the Polish underground had lost its chance to defeat the Germans and define Poland's future.[11]

The Soviet Union

From the outset, German planning for invading the Soviet Union broke international law. As opposed to the preparation for the attack on Poland, German soldiers did not just receive vague warnings of threats posed to them by elements of the civilian population. In the spring and summer of 1941, the men of the Wehrmacht were also issued concrete directives which meant that operation 'Barbarossa' induced the next phase of a war of annihilation: the 'Martial Jurisdiction Decree' envisaged the killing of guerrillas without trial and the exoneration of German soldiers from punishment for crimes against the civilian population, and the 'Commissar Order' called for the immediate execution of all political commissars of the Red Army.[12]

The war in the east was further characterised by a close cooperation between the army and the SS: according to pre-invasion consultations between the quartermaster-general of the Wehrmacht, General Eduard Wagner, and SS-*Gruppenführer* Reinhard Heydrich, the head of the SS security police and security service, the army was to defeat the military enemy, and the SS was responsible for the 'pacification' of the newly conquered territories. This agreement was intended to define the respective tasks of both organisations; the Wehrmacht also needed additional manpower for securing the hinterland. The SS was thus given free rein for ethnic cleansing.[13] SS and Wehrmacht behaved with

[11] P. W. Blood, *Hitler's Bandit Hunters: The SS and the Nazi Occupation of Europe* (Washington, DC: Potomac Books, 2006), 219–22, 230–9; T. Snyder, *Bloodlands: Europe between Hitler and Stalin* (London: Vintage, 2010), 280–312.
[12] Böhler, *Auftakt zum Vernichtungskrieg*, 165–6; K. J. Arnold, *Die Wehrmacht und die Besatzungspolitik in den besetzten Gebieten der Sowjetunion. Kriegführung und Radikalisierung im 'Unternehmen Barbarossa* (Berlin: Duncker & Humblot, 2005), 124–46; J. Hürter, *Hitlers Heerführer. Die Deutschen Befehlshaber im Krieg gegen die Sowjetunion 1941/42* (Munich: Oldenbourg, 2006), 247–65; F. Römer, *Der Kommissarbefehl: Wehrmacht und NS-Verbrechen an der Ostfront 1941/42* (Paderborn: Ferdinand Schöningh, 2008).
[13] C. Hartmann, *Wehrmacht im Ostkrieg. Front und militärisches Hinterland 1941/42* (Munich: Oldenbourg, 2009), 643–6.

increasing brutality, as will be demonstrated using the example of Belorussia and the SS Cavalry Brigade.

Counterinsurgency formed one of the most important aims within the German military and occupation framework. General officers of the Wehrmacht shared Hitler's intention of eliminating 'Judaeo-Bolshevism' and made the army a willing accomplice in acts of mass violence directed at the Soviet population, as they held the opinion that resistance against the Germans was to be suppressed by all means. Formally, the supreme commanders of army groups and armies bore the main responsibility for the fight against insurgents as they not only commanded troops on the eastern front but also relayed Hitler's criminal orders to the security forces guarding the hinterland.[14]

In practice, however, guidelines for safeguarding the vast areas behind the frontline were defined by a small group of men: the Wehrmacht commanders in charge of the rear areas of Army Groups North, Centre and South, and Heinrich Himmler's direct representatives, the so-called Higher SS and Police Leaders. The close collaboration of the two institutions is best exemplified by General Max von Schenckendorff, who was commander of the rear area of Army Group Centre from 1941 to 1943 and became a specialist for partisan warfare in the Wehrmacht, and his SS counterpart, the aforementioned 'Higher SS and Police Leader Centr[al Area]' von dem Bach-Zelewski, who later assumed the same role in Himmler's organisation. The area of responsibility of these two men, Belorussia, was to become the partisan stronghold of Europe.[15] All National Socialist aims for the transformation of the East into living space or 'Lebensraum' overlapped in this territory: it was part of a theatre of operations where feeding the troops was to be achieved at the expense of the population, a strategy that explicitly envisaged the starvation and killing of up to thirty million people. The complex question of securing the hinterland led to major crimes against humanity as well. Von dem Bach-Zelewski became Himmler's executioner as he was

[14] Hürter, *Hitlers Heerführer*, 404–41.
[15] J. Hasenclever, *Wehrmacht und Besatzungspolitik in der Sowjetunion: die Befehlshaber der rückwärtigen Heeresgebiete 1941–1943* (Paderborn: Ferdinand Schöningh, 2010), 174–9, 344–67, 477–522; Blood, *Hitler's Bandit Hunters*, 53; M. Barelkowski, 'Vom "Schlagetot" zum "Kronzeugen" nationalsozialistischer Verbrechen. Die Karriere des Erich von dem Bach-Zelewski', in H. J. Bömelburg (ed.), *Der Warschauer Aufstand 1944: Ereignis und Wahrnehmung in Polen und Deutschland* (Paderborn: Ferdinand Schöningh, 2011), 129–70; C. Gerlach, *Kalkulierte Morde. Die deutsche Wirtschafts- und Vernichtungspolitik in Weißrußland 1941 bis 1944* (Hamburg: Hamburger Edition, 1999).

appointed to rid a major sector of European Russia of all possible enemies of the Reich.[16]

In the Soviet Union, most German troops were deployed in frontline service and only few formations actually guarded the rear areas, which meant that they bore the brunt of the fighting against guerrillas.[17] But before it even came to large-scale partisan warfare, the dynamics of the beginning Holocaust and the German approach to counterinsurgency through preemptive terror became inseparable. This development was epitomised and defined by the SS Cavalry Brigade, a Waffen-SS unit under the command of Hermann Fegelein, which had already carried out atrocities against Jews as well as anti-partisan operations and reprisal killings in Poland between 1939 and 1941. One such mission, which had resulted in the execution of 250 Polish villagers, was later viewed as a success by Fegelein: 'The set tasks of burning down guilty villages and executing sinister elements were completed in such a clean and decent SS-worthy way that every doubt about the troops' strength of character had to be eliminated'.[18] The proven ruthlessness of this particular unit led to its selection for the 'combing' and 'pacification' of the Pripet Marshes in southern Belorussia, a vast region previously largely untouched by German forces during the summer of 1941. Acting upon direct orders from Heinrich Himmler, the SS cavalry was placed at von dem Bach-Zelewski's disposal one month after the beginning of operation 'Barbarossa'.[19] Its main task, the execution of Jews, was only partly camouflaged by claiming security risks in the first mission order:

If the population, from a national viewpoint, is composed of hostile, racially and humanly inferior [inhabitants] ... everybody suspected of supporting the partisans is to be shot; women and children are to be deported, livestock and food to be seized. The villages are to be burned to the ground.[20]

---

[16] A. J. Kay, '"The Purpose of the Russian Campaign Is the Decimation of the Slavic Population by Thirty Million": The Radicalization of German Food Policy in Early 1941', in A. J. Kay, J. Rutherford, and D. Stahel (eds.), *Nazi Policy on the Eastern Front, 1941: Total War, Genocide, and Radicalization* (Rochester, NY: University of Rochester Press, 2012), 101–29; Snyder, *Bloodlands*, 234.

[17] C. Hartmann, 'Verbrecherischer Krieg – verbrecherische Wehrmacht? Überlegungen zur Struktur des deutschen Ostheeres 1941–1944', in C. Hartmann et al. (eds.), *Der deutsche Krieg im Osten 1941–1944: Facetten einer Grenzüberschreitung* (Munich: Oldenbourg, 2009), 3–71.

[18] Gefechtsbericht Kdr. 1. SS-T-RS v. 10.4. 1940 in Vojenský ústřední archiv Prague, 8th SS Cavalry Division *Florian Geyer*, box 3, file 22, quoted in M. Cüppers, '". . . auf eine so saubere und SS-mäßige Art". Die Waffen-SS in Polen 1939–1941', in Mallmann and B. Musial, *Genesis des Genozids*, 100.

[19] Kommandobefehl Nr. 19, 19 July, 1941, in Vojenský ústřední archiv Prague, Kommandostab RFSS, box 1, file 3.

[20] Kommandosonderbefehl. Richtlinien für die Durchkämmung und Durchstreifung von Sumpfgebieten durch Reitereinheiten, 28 July 1941, in Vojenský ústřední archiv Prague, Kommandostab RFSS, box 24, file 3.

On the same day, this order was further specified by the brigade commander:

Jews are to be treated as looters for the most part. Only skilled workers such as bakers etc. and especially doctors are exempt [from this directive]. Women and children are to be driven away from derelict villages, together with the cattle.[21]

As he was not satisfied with the progress of the killings, Himmler amended his orders again after just a few days. On 1 August 1941, he intervened directly and radioed the SS cavalry in the field: 'Explicit order from the R[eichs]F[ührer-] SS: All Jews must be shot, drive Jewish women into the swamps'.[22] Motivated by the ambition of 'working for the Führer', the dynamic inherent to the Nazi system, the commander of one of the brigade's two cavalry regiments radicalised this directive even further: 'No male Jew stays alive, no residual family in the villages'.[23] The execution of this order, cynically termed '*Entjudung*' ('dejewification') by Gustav Lombard, the SS officer responsible, resulted in the murder of tens of thousands of Soviet Jews within several weeks. This set the SS Cavalry Brigade apart as a precursor for the Holocaust, as it became the first German unit to annihilate entire Jewish communities, including women and children.[24]

What may seem like a sequence of radical orders that had more to do with genocide than anti-partisan operations was soon to have major implications. The German approach to counterinsurgency in the Soviet Union was now not only theoretically defined, but also practically implemented by a combination of military and ideological aims, which culminated in the equalisation of Jews and partisans just a few months into the campaign. A turning point in this context was the infamous 'anti-partisan course' hosted by General von Schenckendorff at Mogilev between 24 and 26 September 1941. At this conference, high-ranking officers of army, SS and police presented their experiences, amongst them Gustav Lombard, the commander of the 1st SS Cavalry

---

[21] Regimentsbefehl Nr. 42 für den Einsatz Pripec-Sümpfe, 27 July 1941, in Bundesarchiv-Außenstelle Ludwigsburg, Dokumenten-Sammlung, Ordner Verschiedenes 291-17, 2–5.

[22] Radio message, KavRgt. 2 an Reitende Abteilung, 1 August 1941 (10 a.m.), in Bundesarchiv-Militärarchiv Freiburg, RS 3–8/36.

[23] Abteilungsbefehl Nr. 28, Kommandeur Reitende Abteilung, 1 August 1941, in Bundesarchiv-Militärarchiv Freiburg, RS 4/441.

[24] On the SS Cavalry Brigade in the Holocaust, partisan warfare, and combat at the front, see H. Pieper, *Fegelein's Horsemen and Genocidal Warfare: The SS Cavalry Brigade in the Soviet Union* (Basingstoke: Palgrave Macmillan, forthcoming); on the precursor role of units under Himmler's direct command, see M. Cüppers, *Wegbereiter der Shoah: die Waffen-SS, der Kommandostab Reichsführer-SS und die Judenvernichtung 1939–1945* (Darmstadt: Wissenschaftliche Buchgesellschaft, 2005).

Regiment. His statement, 'The Jew is the partisan!', was viewed as the quintessence of the course, as part of which the participants also watched a village search that included an execution of Jews by police and SS personnel. Guidelines developed by von Schenckendorff after the course were accepted as new counterinsurgency doctrine by the High Command on 25 October 1941.[25] The directives issued to the SS Cavalry Brigade had by this time also become common practice in rear area units of the army and the order police. Whereas the efforts of the so-called 'security divisions' to 'pacify' their operational areas included a significant amount of activity that helped to facilitate the Holocaust, German policemen viewed the war against partisans as 'race war' as they appropriated the equalisation of Jews and partisans as a basic principle of their deployment in the east.[26]

Despite Hitler's announcement that Slavs should not be allowed to bear arms, large numbers of collaborators were recruited in the Soviet Union: throughout the occupation, 150,000 men joined the battalions of *Schutzmannschaften* (guard units, also referred to as *Schuma*), 158 of which were organised in the Baltic states, 23 in the central sector of the eastern front, and 65 in the Ukraine. Although *Schuma* and other collaborator formations, such as units consisting of Cossacks, were deployed as police forces, and took part in anti-partisan missions as 'bandit hunters', results were mixed: they could be successfully integrated into operations alongside German forces, but lacked discipline in many cases.[27]

Three different time periods of insurrectionary warfare and counter-measures in the Soviet Union can be distinguished: an initial phase that ended with the battle of Moscow in late 1941, the second phase during which the Wehrmacht lost the initiative to Soviet guerrillas in the summer of 1942, and the third phase from the battle of Kursk until the extensive liberation of Soviet territory in 1944.[28] The first phase was characterised by the absence of an organised partisan movement. Tens of thousands of Red Army stragglers (sometimes entire units) were trapped behind German lines and posed a greater threat to security than guerrillas. German commanders acted upon criminal orders and the

[25] Hasenclever, *Wehrmacht und Besatzungspolitik*, 363–6; Cüppers, *Wegbereiter der Shoah*, 221–2. The new doctrine was called Richtlinien für die Partisanenbekämpfung; see GenStdH/Ausb.Abt. 1900/41 v. 25.10.41, Federal Archive Dahlwitz-Hoppegarten, ZWM Ia.

[26] B. Shepherd, *War in the Wild East: The German Army and Soviet Partisans* (Cambridge, MA: Harvard University Press, 2004), 82–90, 106–7; E. B. Westermann, *Hitler's Police Battalions: Enforcing Racial War in the East* (Lawrence: University Press of Kansas, 2005), 16–18, 187–93, 237–9.

[27] Blood, *Hitler's Bandit Hunters*, 141–2, 147–8, 179–82.

[28] Hasenclever, *Wehrmacht und Besatzungspolitik*, 344.

presuppositions of an existing underground and a hostile population, to which belonged a large Jewish minority that was to be removed from their sphere of influence. Thus, the Holocaust and the mass death of Soviet prisoners of war were initiated to solve what was perceived as 'security problems'.[29]

In the second phase, the genocidal behaviour of German troops led to a quick radicalisation of insurrectionary warfare and countermeasures. The time period of 1942–1943 saw several 'large operations', during which the Germans used a strategy of killing Jews as well as civilians, most of whom were unarmed and not associated with guerrillas. Soviet partisans, on the other hand, were now able to disrupt German transport, communication and administration behind the front. In August 1942, the German Army High Command issued Directive 46, which placed guerrillas outside the law of war by labelling them as 'bandits'. In an attempt to combat them more effectively, von dem Bach-Zelewski was promoted to chief of anti-partisan warfare by Himmler, a role he later assumed for all of occupied Europe.[30]

After the battle of Stalingrad, guerrillas controlled the rear areas in large part and mounted major operations, which were coordinated with the Red Army and helped to prepare Soviet offensives, most notably in the summer of 1944. The Germans turned to a strategy of mass recruitment of forced labour, which was combined with executions. Attempts at establishing so-called *Wehrdörfer*, or fortified villages populated by armed locals, could not win back territory lost to the partisans, despite initial successes in Belorussia in 1943–1944. Finally, entire regions were left deserted, and the already existing contradiction between feeble attempts to win the support of the population on the one hand and counter-insurgency as well as genocide on the other could finally no longer be reconciled. In Belorussia alone, more than 500,000 Jews and 345,000 'partisans' – mostly innocents – were killed between 1941 and 1944.[31]

Yugoslavia

As an operational theatre for asymmetrical warfare and German countermeasures, Yugoslavia offers a possibility of comparison with the Soviet Union in general and Belorussia in particular as both territories saw

[29] Shepherd, *War in the Wild East*, 60–3; Arnold, *Wehrmacht und Besatzungspolitik*, 203–9, 425–33; C. Streit, *Keine Kameraden: Die Wehrmacht und die Sowjetischen Kriegsgefangenen, 1941–1945* (Bonn: Dietz, 1997), 128; Hartmann, *Wehrmacht im Ostkrieg*, 631.
[30] Snyder, *Bloodlands*, 235–43; Blood, *Hitler's Bandit Hunters*, 77–90.
[31] Hasenclever, *Wehrmacht und Besatzungspolitik*, 560–5; Snyder, *Bloodlands*, 277, 244–52; Gerlach, *Kalkulierte Morde*, 1036–52.

conventional fighting, the emergence of large underground movements and the destruction of the Jews. Moreover, different concepts of counter-insurgency were applied, and events in the two regions had a strong influence on other parts of occupied Europe. In Yugoslavia, Germany and Italy were involved as occupying powers and faced various forms of collaboration and insurgency. As the Germans split up the former kingdom in 1941, they found themselves in a very complicated situation: Serbia came under German occupation and Italy annexed Dalmatia, whereas Bulgaria now incorporated Macedonia, and Slovenia was divided between Germany and Italy. The Croat Ustaša state, an ally of Germany and Italy, also included Bosnia-Herzegovina during the war.[32]

The formation of this 'independent state of Croatia' (NDH) with its problematic ethnic diversity (especially the conflict between Catholic Croats and Orthodox Serbs) triggered 'two overlapping but distinct genocides with very different causes and serving different purposes: a Nazi-led genocide of Jews and Gypsies and an independent Ustaša genocide of the Serbs'.[33] In Serbia, low German troop strength after the attack on the Soviet Union and information about massacres of Serbs in Bosnia caused a rebellion to which the military administration responded with extremely harsh measures: Field Marshal Keitel issued the so-called 'hostage decree' on 16 September 1941, which envisaged the shooting of fifty hostages for every wounded German soldier and that of one hundred hostages for every deadly casualty. Although it was formulated and designed for Yugoslavia, it soon was applied in the rest of occupied Europe as well. Communists and male Jews became the preferred victims of reprisals; in Serbia, the execution of the decree initiated the destruction of the Jews. This practice paralleled the development in the Soviet Union, where the identification of Jews and insurgents was applied at the same time by the SS Cavalry Brigade and underlay the way they were treated by all armed forces until the end of 1941.[34]

Between 1941 and 1943 the occupants missed their chance to end resistance in Yugoslavia by military means, as they focused on a concept

[32] K. Schmider, *Partisanenkrieg in Jugoslawien 1941–1944* (Hamburg: Mittler, 2002), 11; K. Schmider, foreword to Part III – Yugoslavia, in Pattinson and B. Shepherd, *War in a Twilight World*, 181; M. A. Hoare, *Genocide and Resistance in Hitler's Bosnia. The Partisans and the Chetniks, 1941–1943* (London: Oxford University Press, 2006), 14–15.

[33] Hoare, *Genocide and Resistance in Hitler's Bosnia*, 19.

[34] C. Browning, 'Wehrmacht Reprisal Policy and the Mass Murder of Jews in Serbia', in *Militärgeschichtliche Mitteilungen* 33 (1983), 311–49; W. Manoschek, '"Serbien ist judenfrei": militärische Besatzungspolitik und Judenvernichtung in Serbien 1941/42' (Munich: Oldenbourg, 1995); B. Shepherd, 'Bloodier than Boehme: The 342nd Infantry Division in Serbia, 1941', in Pattinson and Shepherd, *War in a Twilight World*, 189–209; Blood, *Hitler's Bandit Hunters*, 63–5.

of brute force, even though the troops at their disposal were ill-equipped, insufficiently trained and not strong enough to combat insurgents in difficult terrain. Moreover, the cooperation with the Italian and Croat allies proved to be unsuccessful, and the Germans failed to reach out to those parts of the population that were willing to cooperate.[35] The genocidal measures against Serbs and Jews that were perpetrated by the Germans and the Croatian Ustaše gave rise to the formation of two resistance groups: the Serb-nationalist Četniks and the communist partisans under the command of Josip Broz (known as 'Tito'). For about two years, a power struggle between the two factions ensued in Bosnia, which became the principal theatre of partisan warfare in Yugoslavia. In 1943, the partisans prevailed as they had developed the strength and combat methods of a regular army and managed to integrate all parts of an ethnically diverse population. The Italian surrender in September further exacerbated the situation of the occupying powers. Although the Germans fought hard not to lose ground, Bosnia was conquered by the communist Partisans in 1944–1945.[36]

The failure of German military leadership in Yugoslavia mainly stemmed from their negligence in not suggesting a change of the incompetent and genocidal regime in Croatia to Hitler. Moreover, strategy and tactics proved to be ineffective as large encirclement operations were impossible with too few soldiers in rugged terrain, and other approaches such as the use of smaller, specialised anti-guerrilla units also failed due to a lack of manpower. Throughout the second half of the war, the Germans relied on a principle of terror and deployed few elite units to regain the initiative, such as the 1st Mountain Division.[37] Wehrmacht and SS formations, however, were characterised by misconduct, a lack of training and insufficient coordination with other formations, as is exemplified by an ill-fated attempt to eliminate Tito, his staff and his Allied advisers in late May 1944. The partisan leader escaped the overstretched German troops, and Allied air superiority helped to pin them down when they tried to pursue him.[38] It can be concluded that the Germans could not defeat a robust and determined enemy in the form of Tito's forces in the second half of the war as they lacked capable allies, troops and commanders who were able to pursue complex politics.[39]

[35] B. Shepherd, *Terror in the Balkans: German Armies and Partisan Warfare* (Cambridge, MA: Harvard University Press, 2012), 236–42.
[36] Hoare, *Genocide and Resistance in Hitler's Bosnia*, 239–352.
[37] Schmider, *Partisanenkrieg in Jugoslawien*, 532–5, 542–52; H. F. Meyer, *Blutiges Edelweiß. Die 1. Gebirgs-Division im Zweiten Weltkrieg* (Berlin: Links, 2010), 113–28, 557–62.
[38] Blood, *Hitler's Bandit Hunters*, 258–62.
[39] Schmider, *Partisanenkrieg in Jugoslawien*, 568–72.

The debate about how many Yugoslavs died in all in the Second World War, deaths due to Italian and German military actions, reprisals and executions and also to internecine feuds, but ultimately caused by the invasion of the Axis powers, is still ongoing. It seems clear, however, that more than a million Yugoslavs perished, which, in relation to the total population of Yugoslavia of perhaps fifteen million, makes Yugoslavian losses relatively the highest in the Second World War.[40]

Greece

Unlike in neighbouring Yugoslavia, neither genocide nor ethnic cleansing but dearth triggered civil unrest in Greece. From their invasion in April 1941, the Germans pursued a strategy of plundering the country's resources, which plunged the economy and currency into chaos and led to widespread hunger and starvation during the first year of occupation. In response to killings of German soldiers on the island of Crete during the summer of 1941, General Kurt Student issued an order for reprisals which led to the destruction of several villages and the execution of hundreds of Greek civilians. This retaliatory policy was soon extended to other parts of the country, and different resistance groupings took up arms against the Germans and their Bulgarian and Italian allies. Beginning in late 1941, the two most important groups took shape: the communist underground party EAM, with its armed wing, the ELAS, and the nationalist EDES. Throughout the following year, they consolidated their forces to an extent that denied full control of the countryside to the occupants; despite the Axis policy of terror, effective deterrence could be achieved only temporarily.[41]

The end of Italian occupation after the fall of Benito Mussolini in September 1943 marked a turning point, after which both insurrection and counterinsurgency policy in Greece escalated, a process that has been described by Mark Mazower as a 'logic of violence'.[42] On the German side, this 'logic' is again exemplified by the behaviour of the 1st Mountain Division, which operated in northwestern Greece between June and November 1943. Its soldiers destroyed dozens of villages and killed hundreds of innocent civilian victims; amongst other atrocities, they committed the massacre at Kommeno in September 1943.[43]

[40] J. Tomasevich, *War and Revolution in Yugoslavia,1941–1945: Occupation and Collaboration* (Stanford, CA: Stanford University Press, 2001), 735.
[41] M. Mazower, *Inside Hitler's Greece: the Experience of Occupation,1941–44* (New Haven, CT: Yale University Press, 1993), 23–75, 85–143; Meyer, *Blutiges Edelweiß*, 129–37.
[42] Mazower, *Inside Hitler's Greece*, 155–89.
[43] Meyer, *Blutiges Edelweiß*, 159–238, 557–646.

In Greece, cooperation and confrontation were not defined along ethnic lines. Instead, politics were more important in defining the motivation of the different underground organisations: whereas the communists resisted the Germans throughout the entire occupation, nationalists from late 1943 onwards began to seek agreements and sometimes even carried out 'cleansing operations' against their left-wing enemies.[44] The fight against guerrillas continued until late 1944, when the Germans retreated from Greece. But neither the infliction of sheer terror nor the deployment of battalions of Greek collaborators or the use of informers could prevent the growing power of the communist EAM and ELAS organisations and, ultimately, the emergence of self-governed 'Free Greece' in the uncontrollable hinterland. Between 1941 and 1944, more than sixty-five thousand Greeks lost their lives as a result of starvation, partisan warfare and retaliation.[45]

France

Unlike the brutal policies applied in Eastern Europe, the German conduct of war and occupation regime in northern and western Europe were long viewed as having been in accordance with the Hague Convention, apart from 'individual excesses'.[46] Regarding the occupation of France, this hypothesis has been disproved, as acts of mass violence occurred during military operations, and the French resistance movement was suppressed by means of a brutal strategy which not only led to an escalation of violence but was also linked to the genocide of the European Jews.

During the German advance in the spring of 1940, the 'Franc-tireur psychosis' reappeared and manifested itself in the form of killings of French prisoners of war from African colonial units.[47] After the end of hostilities, a duality of German military occupation and a French collaboration regime at Vichy was established. From late 1941, the security situation worsened as the communist underground began to spread after the invasion of the Soviet Union. The identification of Jews amongst the members of communist resistance groups gave the occupiers an

---

[44] Ibid., 537–56.   [45] Mazower, *Inside Hitler's Greece*, xiii, 265–96.
[46] H. E. Volkmann, 'Zur Verantwortlichkeit der Wehrmacht', in R. D. Müller and H. E. Volkmann (eds.), *Die Wehrmacht: Mythos und Realität* (Munich: Oldenbourg, 1999), 1202.
[47] About 1,500–3,000 black French soldiers were murdered during the German campaign against France in 1940; see R. Scheck, *Hitler's African Victims: The German Army Massacres of Black French Soldiers in 1940* (Cambridge: Cambridge University Press, 2006), 81–117, 165.

opportunity to initiate so-called security measures that were soon helping to facilitate the 'Final Solution': acts of resistance were answered with the taking of communist and Jewish hostages as well as reprisal killings and mass internment, and deportations of male Jews to extermination camps in Eastern Europe were also carried out as sanctions. Anti-Jewish and counterinsurgency measures were devised by the SS and police apparatus and coordinated with the Wehrmacht and French authorities. Through the introduction of a Higher SS and Police Leader (HSSPF) in late May 1942 the executive authority for security matters in France was transferred to the SS. In connection with radical orders from Berlin, this change marked a paradigm shift in counterinsurgency during the second half of the war.[48]

The development in France between 1943 and 1945 partly mirrored events in Italy and Greece as the hardships of occupation policy discredited the Germans and sparked resistance, which in turn was answered with reprisals and even genocidal measures. Mass recruitment of forced labour antagonised the population, especially the workers, many of whom fled to the countryside and joined the partisans. The French resistance movement was unable to conduct large operations against the Germans in the first years of occupation and confined itself to acts of sabotage until 1943. Allied support with weapons, however, changed the situation and led to an increase in attacks.

Three forms of counterinsurgency tactics were applied from late 1943 onwards: the use of specialised platoon-sized units (so-called '*Jagdkommandos*', hunter-commandos), large encirclement operations and 'forays' of battalions or regiments through partisan areas.[49] The Germans issued orders not to take prisoners and used terror against innocents, whereas the real guerrillas escaped the searches. Case studies of operations throughout 1944 indicate a close cooperation of army and SS and summary executions of hundreds of French civilians, including the inhabitants of Oradour-sur-Glane and villagers living on the Vercors plateau near the Swiss and Italian borders. Personal continuity also played a key role in anti-partisan operations: the massacre at Oradour

[48] A. Meyer, *Die deutsche Besatzung in Frankreich 1940–1944. Widerstandsbekämpfung und Judenverfolgung* (Darmstadt: Wissenschaftliche Buchgesellschaft, 2000), 47–77; T. J. Laub, *After the Fall: German Policy in Occupied France, 1940 – 1944* (Oxford: Oxford University Press, 2010), 112–36, 163–93; Lieb, *Konventioneller Krieg oder NS-Weltanschauungskrieg? Kriegführung und Partisanenbekämpfung in Frankreich 1943/44* (Munich: Oldenbourg, 2007), 20–7; B. Brunner, *Der Frankreich-Komplex: Die nationalsozialistischen Verbrechen in Frankreich und die Justiz der Bundesrepublik Deutschland* (Göttingen: Wallstein, 2004), 33–52.

[49] Laub, *After the Fall*, 249–64; Lieb, *Konventioneller Krieg oder NS-Weltanschauungskrieg*, 43–8, 284–309.

was ordered by the commander of the 2nd SS Panzer Division *'Das Reich'*, SS-Brigadeführer Heinz Lammerding, who had served as von dem Bach-Zelewski's chief of staff in the Soviet Union.[50]

Italy

Italy became a theatre of partisan warfare only from September 1943 onwards, when the armistice between the Italian kingdom and the Allies was announced. The country was now divided into a northern part ruled by a Fascist government supported by the Germans, the Repubblica Sociale Italiana (RSI), and a southern part, the so-called *'regno del sud'*, which was under Allied supervision. This division led to the interference of three different conflicts between 1943 and 1945: the war between German and Allied troops, the fight of German occupation forces against Italian partisans (the *Resistenza*) and the conflict between the Fascist government in northern Italy and left-wing underground groups.

Partisan warfare in Italy claimed a staggering loss of life: about seventy to eighty thousand Italians were killed, ten thousand of whom were civilians who were murdered during massacres and reprisals. Moreover, some thirty thousand partisans and as many Italians fighting for or standing on the side of the RSI lost their lives, as well as at least three thousand German soldiers and policemen.[51]

The conduct of German forces in the Italian theatre is characterised by diversified attitudes towards their opponents. In combat against the Allies, the Germans for the most part respected the rules of conduct set by international law. When fighting insurgents, however, they showed great ruthlessness and did not respect conventions.

In late 1943, civil unrest and military crisis increased the frustration of German troops, who again developed a 'partisan psychosis' and committed atrocities on their retreat through southern Italy. Under the impression of a steadily deteriorating security situation, Field Marshal Albert Kesselring, the supreme German commander in Italy, intervened in anti-guerrilla operations. He disregarded counterinsurgency guidelines issued by the Wehrmacht High Command (OKW) in May 1944, according to which partisans were to be granted prisoner of war status if captured. Instead, Kesselring exempted German soldiers from punishment for

---

[50] Meyer, *Deutsche Besatzung in Frankreich*, 128–70; Lieb, *Konventioneller Krieg*, 309–96; Blood, *Hitler's Bandit Hunters*, 265–9.

[51] C. Gentile, *Wehrmacht und Waffen-SS im Partisanenkrieg: Italien 1943–1945* (Paderborn: Ferdinand Schöningh, 2012), 13–15, 32; L. Klinkhammer et al. (eds.), *Die 'Achse' im Krieg. Politik, Ideologie und Kriegführung 1939–1945* (Paderborn: Ferdinand Schöningh, 2010).

infringement of military law and gave out criminal retaliation orders. Faced with a growing threat from partisans, the Germans lashed out against innocents on the base of these directives. Some units, especially those which combined ideological fanaticism with a perceived elite character, even went so far as to wage a war against the civilian population: the 16th SS infantry division 'Reichsführer-SS' killed more than two thousand people in northern Italy and became responsible for the massacres at Marzabotto and Sant' Anna di Stazzema, and the Luftwaffe armoured division 'Hermann Göring' carried out mass violence as well. On the other hand, other units of the Wehrmacht and the order police showed comparative moderation and professionalism. Thus, German anti-partisan warfare in Italy was defined by a particularly brutal command, but also by a variety of attitudes by the respective units deployed.[52]

Conclusion

Despite the formation of powerful underground movements all over Europe, the current state of research indicates that their contribution to the Allied victory in 1945 did not bring about strategic decisions. It was politically influential and of high morale value, but the Germans did not devote a major part of their war effort to counterinsurgency and were not pushed out of occupied countries by insurgents but rather by the conventional armed forces of their enemies.[53]

In the German approach to countering asymmetric warfare, a continuation of the characteristics developed between 1870 and 1914 could be observed throughout the Second World War, thus constituting a national pattern. As far as the instrumentarium of measures applied by the Germans is concerned, there was an exceptionally strong emphasis on the most brutal methods, such as large-scale repressions and mass executions. National Socialist ideology was a defining factor in this context, as Adolf Hitler and his military leaders combined a concept of the enemy based upon the spectre of 'Judaeo-Bolshevism' with the much older element of 'Guerrillaphobia' inherent to the German army since the Franco-Prussian war. This disposition proved to be utterly counterproductive, as is exemplified by the disastrous escalation in Yugoslavia and the Soviet Union. But failure was not predetermined by murderous

[52] Gentile, *Wehrmacht und Waffen-SS im Partisanenkrieg*, 32, 143–7, 404–14.
[53] E. Mawdsley, 'Fifth Column, Fourth Service, Third Task, Second Conflict? The Major Allied Powers and European Resistance', in P. Cooke and B. Shepherd (eds.), *European Resistance in the Second World War* (Barnsley: Pen & Sword, 2014), 29–30.

ideology: collaborationist regimes and forces supported German rule throughout occupied Europe, and the Wehrmacht as well as the SS sought to exploit new sources of manpower and raised divisions from different ethnicities. These instants show that other approaches were possible, as does the establishment of *Wehrdörfer*.

When viewing the German way of counterinsurgency, however, the combination of several factors rendered an effective consideration of more moderate ideas – and thus, successful occupation – impossible: with Nazi 'Weltanschauung' providing the background, a majority of German commanders relied on inflexible and brutal tactics such as large encirclements, and for the most part, insurgents were not offered the option to become prisoners of war. The incompetence of the German military leadership in anti-guerrilla warfare coincided with the over-stretch of troops and resources from the Atlantic to Russia. Harsh measures against real or imagined irregular fighters became an accepted means until the end of the war, and led not only to an escalation of violence but, ultimately, also to a failure in combating insurgents. More-over, they were inextricably linked to the genocide of the European Jews.

8   Israel's Counterinsurgency Experience

Efraim Inbar and Eitan Shamir

Israel's national experience with different forms of counterinsurgency and irregular warfare is very rich, reflecting its involvement in a prolonged intractable conflict. This conflict divides two communities along separate historical narratives, cultures and religions, leading to seemingly unbridgeable territorial claims. At the core of the more than a century-old conflict are Israeli Jews versus mostly Muslim Arabs in Palestine. The Arabs have rejected the legitimacy of the Jewish national aspiration to establish a separate political entity in Palestine and turned to various forms of irregular armed struggle against what they believed to be a foreign occupation of their homeland. The goal of the armed struggle remained constant through the years: to receive international attention and wear down Israel's national will, in the hope that it will eventually collapse.

As Israel has dealt with various non-state organisations and armed resistance outside its borders, it sees insurgency as a threat with an international dimension. The magnitude of the threat posed by irregular war varied through the years. In the early 1950s it was considered a strategic threat, while in the 1960s only a strategic nuisance in comparison to the challenge posed by Arab states' conventional armies. Its magnitude increased during the 2000s, primarily as a result of missile fire. The previous decade also witnessed a growing activism by non-Palestinian Muslim groups, such as the Shiite, Iranian proxy Hezbollah in Lebanon and the Sunni Salafist groups in the Sinai Peninsula.

This chapter reviews Israel's national experience with irregular wars and counterinsurgency. Israel's experience can be roughly divided into four main periods:

1) Intercommunal conflict, 1920–1948
2) Infiltration and retaliation, 1948–1967
3) Low-intensity conflict, 1967–2000
4) 'Mowing the Grass' of non-state armed entities, 2000–2013.

While there are continuities, each period has a distinct character. Despite certain constants in the strategic dimensions of the conflict, the operational and tactical dimensions evolve and acquire new forms and patterns.

Intercommunal Conflict (1920–1948)

The 1917 Balfour Declaration in favor of a 'national home' for the Jews in Palestine led to a wave of nationalist Arab violence against Jews in mixed communities and Jewish settlements in 1920–1921. The attacks were relatively small-scale and were parried by British military intervention and Jewish defenders.

Yet they were significant for the development of the Jewish attitudes towards the use of force. The Jewish community realised it could not rely solely on British defence and decided to establish the Hagana, an underground military organisation that served as the basis for the Israel Defence Forces (IDF). Moreover, the heroic defence of the Tel Hai settlement by Joseph Trumpeldor and his comrades in 1920 became a central element in the Zionist ethos of settling the Land of Israel and the need to defend the Zionist enterprise by force. These events led to the publication of a seminal article in 1923 by the Zionist leader Ze'ev Jabotinsky, titled 'The Iron Wall'. Jabotinsky argued that the Arabs would adamantly oppose Jewish immigration and settlement in Palestine. Therefore, the Zionists needed to create what he metaphorically termed, an 'Iron Wall', a protective force that would allow them to further develop the Zionist enterprise. The combination of such a defence force and a burgeoning Jewish community would eventually bring about Arab acceptance of the Jewish presence in Palestine as a *fait accompli*.[1] Jabotinsky's analysis laid the foundation for Israel's national security concept for the decades to come.[2]

A major violent eruption took place in August 1929, when Arab mobs instigated by Haj Mohammed Amin el-Husseini, the Grand Mufti of Jerusalem, attacked Jews in major mixed cities such as Jerusalem, Safed, Jaffa and Hebron. Over the course of several weeks, 133 Jews and 116 Arabs were killed. An additional 198 Jews and 232 Arabs were injured, mostly by the British police.[3] The riots led to further consolidation and expansion of the Hagana.

---

[1] V. Z. Jabotinsky, 'The Iron Wall' (original in Russian, Razsviet), *The Jewish Herald* (1937), 3.
[2] I. Ben-Israel, *Israel's Defence Doctrine* (in Hebrew) (Ben Shemen: Modan, 2013), 13.
[3] Great Britain, 'Report of the Commission on the disturbances of August 1929, Command paper 3530', *Shaw Commission Report* (1930), 65.

Despite British attempts to limit Jewish immigration and settlement, the Zionists' efforts were successful in expanding numerically, as well as in increasing the number of Jewish settlements in Palestine. These developments eventually led to the Arab revolt against the British rule, and to attacks on the Jewish community, in 1936–1939. The revolt started in the urban centres and spread to rural areas. The British tried to find a compromise, and an inquiry commission headed by Lord William Peel recommended a partition of Palestine into Jewish and Arab states. Yet the Arabs rejected the recommendations, and after a short break in October 1936 intensified their struggle. The year 1938 marked the high-point of the attacks on British installations, Jewish settlements and public transportation, threatening effective British control over Palestine.[4]

Short on manpower, the British were forced to arm and train Jewish policemen. In addition, the illegal Hagana gained some freedom of action, although it initially adopted restraint by adhering to a static defence. (In contrast, the Irgun[5] advocated 'tit for tat' operations.) As the Arab revolt intensified, the Hagana leadership realised that static defence was insufficient and that there was a need for mobility and initiative. To this end it established the 'Field Companies' in 1938. These units, under the command of Yitzhak Sadeh – a seasoned and decorated former Russian Army officer in the First World War and Russian Civil War – adopted an offensive approach, known as the 'beyond the fence' doctrine. The Companies operated in small groups concentrating on patrols and ambushes.[6]

The arrival of Charles Orde Wingate, a British Army officer, to train the Jewish forces in 1938 was a turning point. Wingate – a devout Christian – passionately supported Zionism and was experienced in counterinsurgency (primarily in Sudan). He founded the Special Night Squads (SNS), a unit that in its first month alone ambushed and killed sixty Arab attackers.[7] He taught the importance of night operations, retaliatory raids, the element of surprise and leading by example.[8] Two of his disciples, Yigal Alon and Moshe Dayan, later became famous

---

[4] B. Morris, *Righteous Victims: A History of the Zionist-Arab Conflict, 1881–1998* (New York: Vintage, 2011), 136, 144.

[5] The paramilitary organisation of the revisionist Zionist wing, commanded by Menachem Begin. Founded in 1931, the Irgun became famous for several operations against the British, most notably the King David Hotel bombing on July 1946. Along with the other militias, the Irgun was disbanded in May 1948 and incorporated into the newly-created IDF.

[6] M. van Creveld, *Moshe Dayan* (London: Weidenfeld and Nicholson, 2004), 44.

[7] Morris, *Righteous Victims*, 147.

[8] R. Gal, *A Portrait of the Israeli Soldier* (Westport, CT: Greenwood, 1986), 5.

commanders who were instrumental in shaping the IDF organisational culture.

The Arab revolt was slowly crushed in the beginning of 1939, but the British tried to appease the Arabs and further limited Jewish immigration. During the period of the Arab revolt the Jews acquired fighting expertise, created organised units developed leadership and commanders, founded their first intelligence units and weapon factories, and even established new settlements. This period allowed the Jews in Palestine to prepare better for the next large-scale round of violence in 1947–1948.[9] In contrast, Arab fighting was never elevated to more than the level of local war lords leading raiding parties who often fought also against each other.

In 1941, in response to Rommel's African Corps advances in North Africa, the British set up a Jewish guerrilla force, the Palmach, to fight the Germans in the event of a British withdrawal from Palestine. Trained as a commando force, the Palmach participated in the Allied invasion of Syria and Lebanon in 1941. After the Germans were stopped at El Alamein in November 1942, the British withdrew their support from the Palmach, which subsequently went underground. Its *modus operandi* stemmed from the ideas of Sadeh and Wingate, rather than the regular British Army doctrine, emphasizing individual initiative, independence of action and group cohesiveness. The Palmach became the training ground for many of Israel's future army leaders and a source for its military thinking.[10]

After the end of the Second World War, the Palmach joined other Jewish militias to fight the British, transforming itself into an insurgency force. It focused on sabotaging British installations and smuggling illegal Jewish immigrants into Palestine. Following the approval of the UN Partition Plan in November 1947, the UK decided to evacuate Palestine, gradually thinning its military presence. The resulting vacuum allowed for a war to commence between the two ethnic communities, one that included sniping, ambushes and terrorism. This small war lasted until the British mandate expired in May 1948; as long as the British were present, neither side could easily conquer territory, forcing them to focus on harassing each other. Eventually, the Arabs – who had less social cohesion and organisation – collapsed.[11]

---

[9] Y. Eyal, 'The Arab Revolt, 1936–1939: A Turning Point in the Struggle for Palestine', in M. Bar-On (ed.), *Never Ending Conflict* (Mechanicsburg: Stackpole Books, 2002), 39.

[10] E. Luttwak and D. Horowitz, *The Israeli Army* (London: Allen Lane, 1983), 19, 21.

[11] Y. Gelber, 'The Israeli Arab War of 1948: History versus Naratives', in M. Bar-On (ed.), *Never Ending Conflict* (Mechanicsburg: Stackpole Books, 2002), 50.

The British evacuation in May 1948 was immediately followed by an invasion of a coalition of regular Arab armies, which marked the beginning of the second phase of the war – regular conventional warfare, which became the main threat facing the State of Israel until the end of the twentieth century. In Israeli strategic parlance this type of existential threat was termed 'Basic Security'. In contrast, insurgency, terror and guerilla warfare were only secondary at the time and were labelled 'Current Security'.

Infiltration and Retaliation, 1948–1967

One of the main challenges the IDF faced after the conclusion of the War of Independence in March 1949 was securing Israel's borders from infiltrators. After the end of the 1948 war, Palestinians refugees tried to return to their former homes and fields. Similarly, Arab gangs infiltrated the newly born state to plunder and/or perpetrate terrorist attacks. In the 1950s the IDF lacked the means to close the border in a way that would provide security for the population and its property. At its peak in 1952 there were more than sixteen thousand infiltrations,[12] extracting a heavy toll on the young and vulnerable country with its mere 1.3 million residents. Each year, scores of Israelis were killed and hundreds injured.[13] The psychological damage was much worse; those living in the border areas felt insecure, and many families either left or refused to settle in these areas.

As defensive measures were ineffective, punitive actions were conducted. The chief architect of the retaliatory policy was Lt. Gen. Moshe Dayan, Israel's Chief of Staff (1953–1958). Dayan's early military experiences in the SNS and Palmach led him to prefer an offensive campaign to arrest infiltration. Dayan held Arab governments responsible for preventing infiltration; he was sceptical about the usefulness of diplomacy to calm the situation and therefore advocated military means. The retaliation raids signalled that Israel would not tolerate attacks on its territory and hoped to compel the Arab governments to restrain anti-Israeli gangs and extremist nationalist and religious groups. Typically the army responses involved a raid on a suspected village or even on a military or police installation.

---

[12] B. Morris, *Israel's Border Wars, 1949–1956: Arab Infiltrators, Israeli Retaliation and the Countdown to the Suez War* (Tel Aviv: Am Oved, 1997), 44.

[13] On the number of casualties and economic damage see Morris, *Israel's Border Wars*, 113–21.

Dayan opted for commando operations, deep raids behind enemy lines that required surprise and guile.[14]

The retaliatory period can be divided into two different sub-periods, each one reflecting a different approach. In the first period, IDF operations were aimed at the population of the villages that allegedly encouraged and harboured raiders. Deterrence was sought by extracting a price and administering a collective punishment to the village from which the perpetrators came.[15] This period ended after 'Operation Qibya' in October 1953, which resulted in scores of dead Arab civilians. This episode led to a turning point with regard to the character and objectives of IDF operations. Dayan, sensitive to the IDF principle of 'Purity of Arms' (*jus in bello*) and public opinion, changed the targeting policy.[16] Therefore, the IDF raids in the second period, which began in late 1953, aimed to influence the leadership. Decision-makers no longer targeted villages, but raids on army and police posts were larger in scope and intensity. Though infiltration was not completely stopped, it was greatly reduced, allowing for a modicum of normalcy within Israel.

The increase in Israel's limited use of force also threatened the neighbouring Arab states with a potential escalation, which was then not desirable for the Arab regimes.[17] Yet, this change in Israeli tactics, in which the military and not the population was targeted, eventually led to an escalation that culminated in the 1956 Suez War. (That war had additional objectives beyond putting an end to terrorist acts, but a full discussion is beyond the scope of this chapter.) In any case, the 1956 campaign against Egypt in Sinai brought peace and quiet for a good decade, ending terrorist campaigns operating from bases in Egypt, as Dayan had predicted.

The retaliation raids served a number of secondary objectives. Dayan saw the raids as an instrument to enhance combat readiness and morale of the IDF. Unit 101 – founded by Maj. Ariel Sharon – carried out the raids and revolutionized small unit leadership and tactics in the IDF. After five months the unit was merged with the paratroopers' battalion under Sharon's leadership, transforming the paratroopers into the elite unit of the IDF. From 1954 onward the paratroopers led almost every military operation carried out by the IDF, setting an example for the rest of the Israeli military.[18] A corollary aim of the retaliation policy was, in

[14] Z. Drory, *Israel's Reprisal Policy, 1953–1956, The Dynamic of Military Retaliation* (London: Frank Cass, 2005), 65.
[15] Ibid., 65–7.   [16] M. Dayan, *Story of My Life* (Cambridge: Da Capo Press), 115.
[17] Drory, *Israel's Reprisal Policy*, 46.   [18] Ibid., 101–2.

Dayan's view, the uplifting of domestic morale that seemed to approve of an activist approach.

The end of hostilities on the Egyptian border led the Palestinian leadership to search for alternatives to attack Israel. The Palestinian Fatah organisation, established in 1959, was not supported by all Arab regimes. Only in 1965, when it moved to Damascus, did it gain the support of the Syrian regime. During the two years leading up to the 1967 War, Fatah initiated more than seventy terrorist attacks from bases in Lebanon, Jordan and Syria. In response, Israel launched retaliatory raids, the largest of them in 1966 in the village of Samua, Jordan. As a result, Jordan and Lebanon made efforts to curb Fatah activity, while the Syrians continued to encourage it.[19] Israeli retaliatory activities against Syria, partly to compel Syria to stop sanctioning terrorist activities, led to the 1967 War.

Low-Intensity Conflict, 1967–2000

The 1967 conquest of the West Bank (Judea and Samaria) and the Gaza Strip, two areas with large Arab populations, created a new strategic situation. Defense Minister Moshe Dayan was in charge of shaping the policy towards the Israeli-administered territories in the early years following the 1967 War. Dayan believed that coexistence with the local Arabs was possible and devised his own version of 'Hearts and Minds', more aptly described as a 'carrot and stick' policy. This formula included three elements: minimum presence of Israeli military and civil administration, maximum autonomy to local authorities, and freedom of movement between Israel the territories and Arab states.[20] His policy for allowing continuous access to Hashemite Jordan via bridges over the Jordan River was known as the 'Open Bridges' policy, which also served as a metaphor for the desired relations between the two nations.[21]

This policy assumed that economic prosperity and improvement in public services would reduce potential pressure for a national uprising, which Dayan feared. Israel made it clear that while it did not expect the local population to fight religiously or nationally motivated insurgents, it would not tolerate any collaboration on the part of the local population with insurgents.[22] It also promised fair and humane treatment. This

---

[19] B. Michelson, 'Insurgency and Counterinsurgency in Israel, 1965–1985', in M. Bar-On (ed.), *Never Ending Conflict* (Mechanicsburg: Stackpole Books, 2002), 180.

[20] Shlomo Gazit, *Trapped* (in Hebrew) (Tel Aviv: Zmora-Bitan, 1999), 62.

[21] Arie Brown, *Moshe Dayan and the Six-Day War* (in Hebrew) (Tel Aviv: Yediot Aharonot, 1997), 114.

[22] Ibid., 124.

meant respect for places of worship, for local, family and tribal structures, and avoidance of unnecessary contact between soldiers and civilians (especially women). Moreover, it provided decent social and medical services. Such policies partly explain the tranquillity that existed in the West Bank and Gaza for two decades.

Following the 1967 War, armed elements of the Palestinian Liberation Organisation (PLO) infiltrated the Israeli-controlled territories in order to mobilize the population against the Israeli occupation. Inspired by various guerrilla movements, the PLO attempted to initiate a popular revolt. However, these attempts failed, as the IDF successfully managed to hunt down the terrorists by separating them from the rest of the population, mainly through the policies described above.[23]

After failing to establish a base in the West Bank and Gaza, the Palestinian armed organisations moved to Jordan. They continued to send militants into Israeli-controlled territories for sabotage and terror. Those who managed to infiltrate were often tracked down by highly mobile IDF units specifically designed for 'Pursuit', a new tactic developed by the IDF along its long border with Jordan. The infiltrations also led to retaliatory raids. The largest, involving tanks and a paratrooper brigade, was launched against a PLO complex next to the Jordanian town of Karameh in March 1968. Such military operations forced the Palestinians to move their headquarters farther eastward into the Jordanian heartland. The PLO presence in Jordan acquired the form of 'a state within a state', which led eventually to a clash with the Jordanian authorities in September 1970 (known as 'Black September'). The Jordanian army crushed the Palestinian armed organisations, killing many thousands and driving the rest out of the country.

Weak Lebanon became the main host country for the PLO. Following the 1969 Cairo Agreement between the PLO and Lebanon, the Palestinians were given autonomy in the refugee camps and were permitted to establish their new base for operations against Israel in South Lebanon. Syria also allowed limited Palestinian attacks against Israeli targets. With the exception of short breaks, the 1970s saw a continuation of violence against Israel that included kidnapping hostages, planting mines and sniping against civilians. The Israeli response included a series of raids aimed primarily to deter the host governments of Lebanon and Syria and the construction of a fence system along the Israel–Lebanon border.

In 1970–1971 there was also a rise in the terror activity in the Gaza Strip. The IDF formed a new reconnaissance unit to combat the terrorist

---

[23] Michelson, 'Insurgency and Counterinsurgency in Israel', 181.

cells in a 'Search and Destroy' mode. Additional infantry units were deployed in Gaza in order to become familiar with the area. The persistent military pressure in a small area led to the destruction of the insurgents' cells, and most of the leaders were killed or captured. As a relative calm was achieved, most IDF units were withdrawn from the area.

The failures of the PLO to generate a popular uprising in the territories turned their attention to alternative courses of action. They started attacking Israeli and Jewish targets abroad (sometimes in cooperation with other terrorist organisations), in order to attract international attention to the Palestinian issue. Palestinians hijacked airplanes, attacked international airports, mailed letter bombs to Israeli diplomats, and attempted to assassinate Israeli officials. Well-known examples of such terrorist attacks include the Lod Airport Massacre of May 1972, perpetrated by three members of the Japanese Red Army recruited by the Palestinians, and the kidnapping and killing of Israeli athletes during the Munich Olympics in September 1972.

In response, Israel developed procedures to defend its installations and delegations abroad and went on the offensive. The hijacking of a Sabena plane in May 1972 was foiled by an IDF elite unit. A spectacular rescue operation took place in Entebbe, Uganda, in July 1976, when Israeli troops saved almost all of the hijacked passengers of an Air France plane. This seriously weakened the motivation of the PLO to carry out such operations. The Mossad also went onto the offensive, eliminating terrorist leaders throughout the world. In parallel, the IDF attacked terrorist bases in Lebanon that were training terrorists for attacks abroad.

Lebanon also served as a base for attacks on Israel proper. The Avivim bus attack (May 1970), Ma'alot Massacre (May 1974), Savoy attack (June 1974), Highway 2 attack (March 1978) and Nahariya attack (April 1979) are remembered by Israelis as terrorist attacks originating from Lebanon that left dozens of Israelis dead and many more injured.

In March 1978 Israel responded with Operation Litani. The IDF invaded southern Lebanon, only to return to the international border as a result of international pressure. However, a security zone controlled by Christian militias supported by Israel was formed along the Israeli border. The security zone and the fence system along the border denied the PLO access to Israeli territory, leading to infiltrations from the sea and the launching of rockets into Israeli towns across the border. These events led to the June 1982 invasion of Lebanon that also featured Israeli–Syrian armed clashes.[24]

---

[24] For an analysis of the 1982 Lebanon war, see A. Yaniv, *Dilemmas of Security: Politics, Strategy and the Israeli Experience in Lebanon* (Oxford: Oxford University Press, 1987).

One consequence of the 1982 Lebanon War was the expulsion of the PLO from Lebanon (to Tunisia). Another consequence was the rise of Shiite elements, primarily militant Hezbollah, which has operated as an Iranian proxy. Israeli willpower further declined as a result of the Sabra and Shatila refugee camps massacre, where Maronite militias killed hundreds of Palestinians. Since the IDF was in control of Beirut, the incident created wide international criticism as well as a severe internal dispute within Israeli society.[25] Unable to achieve a peace treaty with Lebanon, the IDF retreated in 1985 to a security zone in southern Lebanon that was formally ruled by its ally, the South Lebanon Army, a militia trained and financed by Israel. For the next fifteen years, Israel's main foe in Lebanon was Hezbollah, whose fighting capabilities improved due to Iranian aid. Continuous Hezbollah attacks caused an average of twenty-five casualties a year. Eventually, a few operational blunders, such as the 'Shayetet Disaster' in September 1997 and the death of Brigadier General Erez Gerstein, commander of the IDF's Liason Unit to Lebanon (Yakal), from a Hezbollah bomb on 28 February 1999,[26] brought about a growing domestic outcry against the presence in Lebanon. This gradually led to the decision to withdraw all IDF troops back to the international border in May 2000. The Lebanese experience indicated Israel's limits of power and the preference to disengage from areas populated by hostile populations.

The tarnished image of Israel's military might as a result of its Lebanese imbroglio eroded Israel's deterrent power and renewed Palestinian determination to fight Israel. In December 1987, a popular uprising, named the Intifada, started in the West Bank and Gaza. Its causes were complex, consisting of economic problems, Islamic radicalization and growing incitement, combined with expansion of Jewish settlement activity. The Intifada was a rebellion of a new Palestinian generation, frustrated with the old Palestinian leadership outside the territories, which tried to rock the status quo and force an Israeli withdrawal.[27]

The tactics used in the Intifada were mostly stone throwing, petrol bombs, mass demonstrations, strikes, intensive use of graffiti and hoisting Palestinian flags. The IDF was surprised and unprepared for such a contingency. It had to adapt and learn the lessons of constabulary duties in an era where the media was almost omnipresent. The IDF expanded its military presence, lowering the proportion of reservists in

---

[25] E. Zisser, *Lebanon Blood in the Cedars: From the Civil War to the Second Lebanon War* (in Hebrew) (Tel Aviv: Hakibutz Hameuchad, 2009), 86.

[26] Regarding both incidents see R. Bergman, *Point of No Return: Israeli Intelligence against Iran and Hezbollah* (in Hebrew) (Or Yehuda: Kinneret Zomra-Bitan Dvir, 2007), 352–5.

[27] For an analysis of the Intifada, see Z. Schiff and E. Yaari, *Intifada: The Palestinian Uprising – Israel's Third Front* (New York: Simon and Schuster, 1990).

the deployed force, upgraded the level of commanding officers, improved intelligence and training, and supplied its troops with better equipment to suit the new circumstances.[28] Seeing no military solution to the problem, Israel adopted a patient strategy of attrition whose goal was 'to reduce violence to a bearable level', which was instrumental in lowering the amount of attention given to the Palestinian issue by Israeli society and the international community.

The First Intifada petered out for a number of reasons. The IDF managed to limit Palestinian mass riots and arrested many of the leaders. Moreover, the weak Palestinian economy was dependent upon Israel, pushing major sections in the territories into cooperation with Israel. The 'carrot and stick' method did work. Furthermore, the attention of the international community was diverted to other issues, such as the August 1990 Iraqi invasion of Kuwait. Yet, the main Palestinian achievement was to make the Israeli public more aware of the need for a political solution and some form of separation between the populations.

Following the victory over Iraq in 1991, the United States was in a better international position to restart a peace process. In October 1991 it convened the Madrid peace conference, which eventually led to the 1994 Israeli-Jordanian peace treaty. Israel's peace treaties with Egypt in 1979 and with Jordan in 1994, combined with a growing acceptance of Israel by Arab governments in the Maghreb and the Gulf, signalled the practical end to the Arab-Israeli interstate conflict and lowered the chances for large-scale conventional war.

Subsequently, Iran's quest for nuclear weapons and the low-intensity conflict challenges became Israel's main concerns. Israel tried to solve its conflict with the Palestinians by signing the 1993 and 1995 Oslo Accords. High hopes for peace were entertained, but by the year 2000 a second Intifada erupted, opening up a new chapter in Israeli counterinsurgency.

'Mowing the Grass' of Armed Non-State Organisations, 2000–2013[29]

During the last decade the magnitude of threat from non-state actors increased, as a result of acquisitions of advanced capabilities, primarily projectiles and missile fire. Israel's main challenge was no longer Arab

---

[28] E. Inbar, 'Israel's Small War: The Military Response to the Intifada' *Armed Forces & Society* 18 (1991), 29–50.

[29] For an exposé of this mode of thinking, see E. Inbar and E. Shamir, 'Mowing the Grass': Israel's Strategy for Protracted Intractable Conflict', *Journal of Strategic Studies*, 37/1 (2014), 65–90.

conventional armies, but rather non-state militias. The turmoil in the Arab world expanded this trend, as the Sinai became a safe haven for jihadists launching operations against Israel. The area along the Israel–Syria border on the Golan Heights seems to be undergoing a similar transition.

The Second Intifada (2000–2005)

The new century started with two significant military events that are arguably connected. In May 2000 the last Israeli soldier left Lebanese territory, and in September 2000 riots erupted in the West Bank and Gaza, known as the 'Second Intifada'.[30] The immediate background for the Intifada was the failure of the Camp David Summit, where President Clinton hosted Palestinian Authority (PA)[31] leader Yasser Arafat and Israeli Prime Minister Ehud Barak, in an unsuccessful attempt to end the conflict.

The Second Intifada was not a popular uprising, but rather a campaign waged by armed Palestinian militias, characterized by shootings, sniping, riots and placement of explosives. When these tactics were contained by the IDF, the Palestinians groups, led by the radical Islamic Hamas terror group, initiated a campaign of suicide bombings in Israel's urban centres which was extremely destructive.

In March 2002, at the end of a particularly bloody month, the IDF invaded almost all of the major cities in the West Bank that had been under the control of the PA since the signing of the Oslo Accords. The operation was known as Defensive Shield and was triggered by the 'Park Hotel' suicide attack that killed thirty Israelis and injured sixty-four. The Palestinian terror campaign elicited much sympathy for Israel, granting international and domestic legitimacy for a strong military riposte. Moreover, military action was seen as a necessity following the terror that struck in Israeli public places.

For Operation Defensive Shield the IDF used many regular formations and a limited number of reservists. The military goal was to dismantle the terror infrastructure through a systematic destruction of weapons caches, bomb-making laboratories, training camps and the

---

[30] While the connection between the two events is tenuous, several Palestinians leaders said that Israel's lack of resolve in Lebanon led them to believe that inflicting casualties on Israel could precipitate a similar Israeli withdrawal from the territories. See A. Harel, *The Face of the New IDF* (in Hebrew) (Tel Aviv: Kinneret, Zmora Bitan Publishing House, 2013), 221.

[31] The PA was established following the Oslo Accords in order to run the Palestinian population beyond the Green Line.

capturing and killing of militants. The intelligence gathered was useful in disrupting additional Palestinian terrorism. Defensive Shield marked the beginning of the end of the Palestinian terrorist campaign. The number of suicide bombings gradually declined, and the number of successful attacks fell dramatically by 2004.[32] The Israeli offensive combined with defensive measures, such as the security barrier, proved very effective in eliminating the suicide bombing threat.[33]

The political objective of Defensive Shield was 'to create a different security reality for Israel'.[34] The IDF aimed at gaining security control of the West Bank without the necessity to administer the population.[35] Israel had no plans to change the PA or its leadership in any way. More and more Israelis recognized that they were locked in a protracted intractable conflict with the Palestinians, whose goals were incompatible with Israel's.[36]

The two Intifadas and Israel's experience in Lebanon sensitized Israel to the difficulties in controlling land populated by hostile elements, which led to a preference for disengagement. In 2000 Israel withdrew from the security zone in Lebanon, and in 2002 Israel started building its security barrier in the West Bank. Notably, in 2005 Israel evacuated its military and settlements from the Gaza Strip, as well as an additional four isolated settlements in North Samaria. Polls indicated popular support for these steps.

Because of the proximity of the West Bank to Israel's heartland, the Jerusalem–Tel Aviv–Haifa triangle, Israel could not disengage totally from this territory, which turned into a base of terror under the PA rule. Therefore the IDF retained military control over large parts of the West Bank but refrained from taking civil responsibility. This thin presence allowed the IDF to continue to fight effectively against the terrorist threats by preventive arrests and preemptive actions without attempting to eradicate them totally, to be termed in Israel's strategic parlance 'Mowing the Grass'.[37]

[32] H. Frisch, 'Motivation or Capabilities? Israeli Counterterrorism against Palestinian Suicide Bombings and Violence', *Journal of Strategic Studies*, 29/5 (2006), 849, 852; D. Byman, 'Curious Victory: Explaining Israel's Suppression of the Second Intifada', *Terrorism and Political Violence*, 24/5 (2012), 837–9.

[33] Frisch, 'Motivation or Capabilities', 860–4.

[34] G. Hirsh, 'From "Solid Lid" to "Other Way": Campaign Development in Central Command 2000–2003', in H. Golan and S. Shay (eds.), *Low Intensity Conflict* (in Hebrew) (Tel Aviv: Maarachot, 2004), 246.

[35] S. Catignani, 'The Security Imperative in Counterterror Operations: The Israeli Fight against Suicidal Terror', *Terrorism and Political Violence*, 17/1–2 (2005), 256.

[36] Palestinian terrorism during the second Intifada was a turning point in Israel's public opinion on the Palestinian issue.

[37] IDF officers often use the phrase 'Mowing the Grass', usually in a tactical sense. An example is a briefing for academics by senior officers in the Central Command, 20 February 2013. See also www.ynet.co.il/articles/0,7340,L-4340652,00.html and the IDF website, 'Did We Bite Palestinian Terror?', www.idf.il/1613-15468-he/Dover.aspx.

Despite Israel's withdrawal from Lebanon in 2000, Hezbollah continued to provoke the IDF. In Gaza, Hamas organised a coup against the PA in 2007, taking control over the Strip. Hamas emulated Hezbollah, smuggling weapons into Gaza from Syria and Iran, and acquiring an arsenal of rockets and missiles capable of hitting Israeli population centres. The two organisations wanted the freedom to harass Israel while deterring Israel by their threat against its population centres. Moreover, they hoped to establish an effective defensive parameter designed to exact a high cost in case of an Israeli ground invasion.[38]

In realising the difficulties in affecting the behaviour of radical ideological non-state actors, Israel's use of force had a limited effect and could achieve only temporary deterrence. Therefore, Israel adopted a patient military strategy of attrition, designed primarily to destroy enemy capabilities. Only after absorbing a series of attacks and showing much restraint in its offensive actions did Israel act forcefully to destroy the capabilities of its foes, hoping that occasional large-scale operations would also have a temporary deterrent effect in order to create periods of quiet along its borders. From an operational and tactical point of view, Israel prefers the use of accurate stand-off munitions, primarily from the air, which minimizes the risk of casualties within its own forces as well as on the other side. Ground forces were used in a limited way and are held in reserve as a threat of escalation. Indeed, the three major operations launched since 2005 – the Lebanon War (2006) and Operations Cast Lead (2008), Pillar of Defence (2012) and Operation Protective Edge (2014). all carried similar strategic and operational logic.[39] The following sections will describe and analyze each of these operations.

The Second Lebanon War (2006)

The 2006 Lebanon War (12 July–14 August 2006) was initiated following a series of provocations by Hezbollah, including several

The use of this term, nonexistent in any IDF doctrinal document, is typical of the organisational culture in the IDF, which allows the use of informal operational and doctrinal concepts. On the IDF's informal culture, see D. Adamsky, *The Culture of Military Innovation: The Impact of Cultural Factors on the Revolution in Military Affairs in Russia, the US, and Israel* (Stanford: Stanford University Press, 2010), 111; E. Shamir, *Transforming Command: The Pursuit of Mission Command in the US, British, and Israeli Armies* (Stanford: Stanford University Press. 2011), 83.

[38] On the development of military doctrine of these organisations, see I. Brun, 'While You're Busy Making Other Plans – The "Other" RMA', *Journal of Strategic Studies*, 33/4 (2010), 535–65.

[39] Inbar and Shamir, 'Mowing the Grass', 65–90.

attempts to abduct Israeli soldiers. Moreover, Hezbollah established a large missile arsenal capable of covering most of Israel. The war was a reaction to a rocket barrage against Israeli military and civilian targets that was used as a diversion for a successful abduction of two Israeli soldiers and the killing of three others.

The IDF was ordered to 'destroy Hezbollah's long-range rocket launchers and to damage the organisation's launch capability, attack its soldiers, commands, and infrastructure, strike its symbols and assets, and destroy Hezbollah infrastructures next to the Israeli border in order to establish a special security zone'.[40] Col. Gur Laish, head of the Campaign Planning Department in the Israeli Air Force (IAF), summarized the Israeli strategy in 2006 as 'a heavy assault against Hezbollah – its military assets, the centre of the government and its deployment in Beirut, and its communal infrastructure in southern Lebanon'.[41] In contrast to the criticism voiced, Israel's strategy neither attempted to target civilian infrastructure, nor planned to pressure the population to rise against Hezbollah.

The war began with a massive and successful air attack on Hezbollah's long-range missiles. Some in the defence establishment thought that no additional action was necessary. Subsequent limited ground incursions near the border indeed appeared ineffective. Moreover, the failure to halt the firing of rockets into Israel, the hesitations to commit troops for a large-scale ground offensive and the indecisive way the war ended all contributed to the widespread perception that Israel was militarily ill-prepared and botched up the war.[42]

Israel reckoned that seven hundred Hezbollah fighters had been killed and more than a thousand wounded – a high price for a militia consisting of three to four thousand professionally-trained fighters – many of them well trained by Iran. In addition, the symbol of Hezbollah's rule in Lebanon, its Beirut headquarters, was severely damaged. Hezbollah leader Sheikh Hassan Nasrallah admitted that he would not have ordered the abduction of Israeli soldiers had he known its price.[43] Israel paid a

---

[40] I. Brun, 'The Second Lebanon War, 2006', in J. Andreas Olsen (ed.), *A History of Air Warfare*, (Washington, DC: Potomac Books, 2010), 305.

[41] G, Laish, 'The Second Lebanon War – A Strategic Reappraisal', *Infinity Journal*, 4 (2011), 23.

[42] See A. Kober, 'The Israel Defense Forces in the Second Lebanon War: Why the Poor Performance?', *Journal of Strategic Studies*, 31/1 (2008), 4–6; E. Inbar, 'How Israel Bungled the Second Lebanon War', *Middle East Quarterly*, 14 (2007), 57–65; B. S. Lambeth, 'Israel's War in Gaza: A Paradigm of Effective Military Learning and Adaptation', *International Security*, 37/2 (2012), 85–91.

[43] 'Hezbollah Chief Revisits Raid', *The Washington Post*, 28 August 2006, www .washingtonpost.com/wp-dyn/content/article/2006/08/27/AR2006082700769.html, last accessed accessed 20 August 2013.

moderate price for the 2006 Lebanon War. The economic damage was bearable, and its casualties were 144 killed (121 of them soldiers) and about two thousand wounded (660 of them soldiers). Yet the country's vulnerability to missile attacks became clear. To some extent, the war also amplified the international misperception of Israeli excessive use of force. UN Resolution 1701 seemed to be the right exit strategy at the time, but did not drastically change the state of affairs in southern Lebanon, which remained under Hezbollah control. Additionally, the ground forces showed unsatisfactory performance during the war. Getting used to years of low-intensity wrangling with the Palestinians, the IDF's conventional warfare readiness diminished dramatically, a capability that proved acutely wanting against semi-conventional Hezbollah in southern Lebanon.[44] Thus, the IDF obviously needed to rethink its military doctrine and organisation.[45]

Since the war ended, Hezbollah has been rebuilding its military strength, acquiring many more missiles capable of hitting every point in Israel. However, the 2006 Israeli response appears to have strengthened Israeli deterrence against Hezbollah. In addition, Israeli covert operations against the terror group, as well as the increasing Hezbollah involvement in Syria, have kept Israel's border with Lebanon mostly quiet as of this writing.

Operation Cast Lead (2008–2009)

The decision to launch Operation Cast Lead (27 December 2008–21 January 2009) was made following a long period of escalation in rockets and mortars fired from Gaza towards Israel's civilian communities next to the Strip.[46] Overall, since Israel's unilateral disengagement from Gaza in August 2005, more than six thousand rockets and mortars were fired by Hamas and other Palestinian terrorist organisations against towns and communities in southern Israel. During 2008 alone – prior to the operation – there were more than four hundred rocket attacks. The daily lives of more than one million Israelis within range of Hamas rockets were affected.

---

[44] M. M. Matthews, 'We Were Caught Unprepared: The 2006 Hezbollah-Israeli War', *The Long War Series Occasional Paper*, 26 (2008), 61–4; A. H. Cordesman, 'Lessons of the 2006 Israeli-Hezbollah War', *Significant Issues Series*, 29/4 (2007), 91–2; S. Biddle and J. A. Friedman, *The 2006 Lebanon Campaign and the Future of Warfare: Implications for Army and Defense Policy* (Strategic Studies Institute, 2008), 73–90.

[45] Lambeth, 'Israel's War in Gaza', 85–91.

[46] U. Rubin, 'From Nuisance to Strategic Threat', *BESA Center Mideast Security and Policy*, 91(2011), 20.

Overall, Operation Cast Lead followed a similar pattern to that of the war in Lebanon in 2006, only this time, the Israeli operation was better planned and executed.[47] The IDF prepared three operational plans with incremental ambitions for the government's consideration. The political leadership opted for the minimalist option, which called for only a large raid aimed at damaging the Hamas military wing to a degree that would deter it from further firing into Israel.[48] Brig. Gen. Zvi Fogel, then a senior officer at the Southern Command headquarters, later said that the objective was 'to cripple Hamas military capabilities as much as possible'.[49] Neither toppling the Hamas rule in Gaza nor the re-conquest of the entire Gaza Strip was an objective of the mission.

In contrast to the reactive 2006 war, Israel caught Hamas off guard in 2008. Capitalizing on accurate intelligence, Cast Lead operation commenced with a powerful airstrike: eighty-eight aircraft hit one hundred preplanned targets in 220 seconds.[50] A conservative estimate suggests that 225 Hamas militants were killed and 750 injured in that incident alone. In addition, the Israeli Air Force attacked Hamas government offices, weapons depots and factories, and other critical infrastructure in Gaza. About one hundred warplanes and helicopters dropped more than a hundred bombs within the first hour of the operation.[51] The shock was immense, and there were indications that Hamas was practically paralyzed. While some IDF officers believed that this was an opportunity to topple Hamas,[52] the government resisted the temptation to expand the operation to this end.

The ground phase started a week after the air strikes, when the IAF exhausted the list of valuable targets. A key difference between the operation in Lebanon and Gaza was the growing realisation for the need of a ground manoeuvre. The notion that airpower strikes alone can be a decisive factor was rejected; it was the combined air-land manoeuvre that was to be the decisive phase of the operation.[53] Conquering territory was

---

[47] For an evaluation, see Lambeth, 'Israel's War in Gaza', 96–118; D. E. Johnson, *Hard Fighting: Israel in Lebanon and Gaza* (Santa Monica, CA: RAND, 2011), 111–12.

[48] Maj. Gen. Yoav Galant, at the time the Chief of Southern Command, Lecture at the IDF Staff and Command College, 15 April 2009.

[49] See Shay Fogelman, *Haaretz*, 24 October 2010.

[50] Quoted in Johnson, *Hard Fighting*, 113.

[51] S. Catignani, 'Variation on a Theme: Israel's Operation Cast Lead and the Gaza Strip Missile Conundrum', *RUSI Journal*, 154/4 (2009), 66–73.

[52] Interview with IAF Lt. Col. R, who took part in the planning of the operation, Tel Aviv, 25 December 2010.

[53] Lieutenant General S. C. Farquhar, *Back to Basics: A Study of the Second Lebanon War and Operation CAST LEAD* (Fort Leavenworth, KS: Combat Studies Institute Press, 2009), 89–99.

not a goal in itself, but allowed for a reduction in enemy fire and the destruction of its operational infrastructure.[54] The operation ended with an Egyptian-brokered ceasefire.

Because Hamas operated among civilians, innocent people were harmed. This led to increasing international criticism of Israel that culminated with the Goldstone Report, which accused Israel of war crimes and severe human rights violations.[55] These unintended consequences raised the question of whether in the future Israel would be able to initiate a similar operation, given the constraints posed by the international community.

Overall, the operation temporarily achieved its objective, bringing tranquillity to the border with Gaza. For a few years the number of rockets dropped to a minimum (from hundreds per month to isolated cases), which allowed the citizens of Israel's south to maintain a normal life. However, 'Mowing the Grass' was once again a necessity, as deterrence eroded over time and the number of rocket and mortar attacks increased once again.

Operation Pillar of Defence (2012)

Operation Pillar of Defence (14–21 November 2012) was an immediate response to more than a hundred rockets fired towards Israel from Gaza within twenty-four hours, as well as to an attack of an Israeli patrol and IED explosion on the Israeli side of the border. Unlike previous incidents, Hamas also fired rockets. The Israeli government again decided on a minimalist approach.[56] No statements about toppling Hamas or about attaining a decisive victory were issued. Instead, Defence Minister Ehud Barak presented the following objectives: strengthen Israel's deterrence, severely impair Hamas and other terror organisations, specifically crippling their rockets capabilities, and minimize attacks on Israel's home front.[57]

---

[54] G. Siboni, 'War and Victory' (in Hebrew), *Military and Strategy*, 1/3 (2009).

[55] United Nations Fact Finding Mission on the Gaza Conflict, www2.ohchr.org/english/bodies/hrcouncil/specialsession/9/FactFindingMission.htm for a refutation of these findings, see D. Gold, 'The Dangerous Bias of the United Nations Goldstone Report', *US News*, 24 March 2010, accessed 20 August 2013, www.usnews.com/opinion/articles/2010/03/24/the-dangerous-bias-of-the-united-nations-goldstone-report. Goldstone himself retracted the findings of his report on 2 April 2011, www.washingtonpost.com/opinions/reconsidering-the-goldstone-report-on-israel-and-war-crimes/2011/04/01/AFg111JC_story.html.

[56] G. Eiland, 'Operation Pillar of Defense: Strategic Perspectives', in S. Brom (ed.), *In the Aftermath of Operation Pillar of Defense: The Gaza Strip*, November 2012 (Tel Aviv: INSS, 2012), 12.

[57] Z. Zinger, 'The Political Echelon Is Hoping for a Quick Ending but Preparing for a Ground Operation', *Megafon*, 14 November 2012, http://megafon-news.co.il/asys/archives/98500, accessed 20 August 2013.

Similarly to the Second Lebanon War in 2006 and Operation Cast Lead in 2008–9, the major achievements were gained in the first hours of the operation due to the effect of accurate, surprise air strikes. The IDF initially eliminated Ahmed al-Jabari, the Hamas supreme military commander, and many junior Hamas terrorists were killed as well. Additional Hamas targets were attacked, such as underground rocket launchers and ammunition warehouses stocking Iranian-made, long-range Fajr-5 missiles. The idea was simultaneously to decapitate the leadership of the Hamas military wing and destroy its strategic assets. In the next few days the IDF continued its stand-off fire campaign against military targets. However, the impact of the strikes dissipated as the targets became less valuable, while the Palestinians continued to fire rockets and mortar shells into Israel. By contrast, the IDF took measures, unprecedented in the history of warfare, to minimize civilian casualties. Almost 100 per cent of attacks used precision-guided munitions, in comparison to 63 per cent in the Second Lebanon War and 81 per cent in Operation Cast Lead.[58] Moreover, the IDF spread leaflets, made telephone calls, aborted airstrikes and engaged in roof knocking by small munitions to warn about impending airstrikes. Indeed, the number of civilian casualties was less than a third of the two hundred total Palestinian fatalities.

Just as impressive were the defensive measures. The Iron Dome batteries intercepted 422 rockets that were fired into urban areas, an 88 per cent success rate. The fifty-eight rockets that did fall in these areas killed only three civilians, reflecting the disciplined behaviour of the civilian population that followed the instructions issued by the authorities. The success of the defensive measures reduced the pressure for a ground offensive.

In parallel to the air campaign, the IDF made preparations, including the mobilization of tens of thousands of reservists for a ground invasion that did not materialize.[59] These preparations were also meant to increase the psychological pressure on Hamas. Yet it was obvious that Israel was reluctant to put boots on the ground. This operation again ended with an Egyptian-negotiated truce.

It was the first major military operation Israel launched following the Goldstone Report and the events of the 'Arab Spring' that led to the Muslim Brotherhood takeover in Egypt. These factors, as well as reluctance to commit boots on the ground for fear of potential casualties,

---

[58] A. Rapaport, '100% Precision Munitions from the Air', *Israel Defense* (2012), 13.
[59] According to IDF, it mobilized between sixty and seventy thousand reservists – a greater number than in Cast Lead and similar to the figure in the last stage of the 2006 Lebanon War. O. Heler, 'The Reserve in Pillar of Defense', *Israel Defense* (2013).

constrained Israel's reaction. Importantly, Jerusalem was successful in maintaining international support for its operation in Gaza. The absence of a ground operation posed, however, two problems. First, Hamas could claim victory by insisting that Israel was deterred from conducting a ground offensive. This could further encourage Hamas and other terror groups to continue provoking Israel. Second, without a ground offensive that regained operational control over all or parts of Gaza, the terrorist infrastructure remained partially intact.

Operation Protective Edge (Summer 2014)

Operation Protective Edge (8 July–26 August 2014) resulted from two coinciding causes. The immediate cause was the kidnapping and murder on 12 June of three hitchhiking Israeli teenagers by a team of Hamas terrorists[60] in the West Bank, to which Israel responded with arrests of hundreds of Hamas-affiliated suspects.[61] The main cause of the operation was the Hamas attempt to rock the boat with fire on Israel to extricate the organisation from a budgetary crisis and increasing regional isolation as it lost its Muslim Brotherhood Egyptian patron following the takeover by Abdel Fatah al-Sisi and its Iranian support because of its opposition to al-Assad in the civil war in Syria.[62] Finally, with the loss of income from the PA unity government,[63] Hamas leadership felt compelled to escalate the conflict in hope that a serious crisis would lead to a better strategic future.

Operation Protective Edge can be divided – from the Israeli point of view – into three main phases: the first period consisted of increasing air strikes (8–17 July), the second included the short-term ground incursion against the Hamas network of offensive underground tunnels (17 July–4 August), and the third phase (after destroying thirty-two offensive tunnels) was made up of continuous air raids while negotiating a cease fire through the Egyptian mediators. The Israeli government considered but

---

[60] Initially Hamas denied involvement, but later admitted that the killers were indeed Hamas. See *CNN*, 23 August 2014, http://edition.cnn.com/2014/08/22/world/meast/mideast-crisis/index.html?hpt=hp_t2.

[61] 'News of Terrorism and the Israeli-Palestinian Conflict (June 18–24, 2014)', *The Meir Amit Intelligence and Terrorism Information Center*, 24 June 2014, www.terrorism-info.org.il/en/article/20661.

[62] E. Trager, 'Sisi's Egypt and the Gaza Conflict', The Washington Institute Policy Analysis, 14 July 2014; 'Egypt Army Destroys 13 More Gaza Tunnels', *YNET News*, 27 July 2014, www.ynetnews.com/articles/0,7340,L-4550797,00.html; On the Iranian issue see H. Frisch, 'The Flimsy Palestinian "Unity" Government', *BESA Center for Strategic Studies Perspective Papers*, 251, 26 June 2014.

[63] Ibid.

rejected a full-scale invasion of Gaza due to the expected number of Israeli military and Palestinian civilian casualties and the preference for leaving Gaza in the hands of a weakened Hamas, preserving the division within the Palestinian national movement between Hamas and Fatah.[64] Aware of the limited Israeli war objectives, Hamas felt it could act with impunity – rocket and mortar fire intensified again. Finally, on 26 August, apparently beginning to feel the pressure, Hamas agreed to an Egyptian-sponsored ceasefire with no preconditions. In return, Israel, as a minor concession, agreed to increase the size of the fishing zone off Gaza.

In contrast to the two previous operations in Gaza, Protective Edge was exceptionally lengthy (lasting fifty days) and witnessed a high number of Israeli casualties: sixty-seven soldiers and five civilians. However, in the strategic context, Protective Edge maintained the same logic and patterns as other operations. Beginning with a heavy airstrike, a ground operation ensued in order to destroy Hamas infrastructure. The IDF faced an innovative tactical threat – a network of offensive tunnels built to allow terrorists access to Israeli communities close to the border.[65] The ground operation was specifically designated to thwart this threat. In the meantime, the second major arena of events involved the continuous rocket fire employed by Hamas against Israel's southern and central population concentrations. Israel's Iron Dome batteries proved extreme effectiveness, intercepting more than 90 per cent of Hamas rockets that could strike targets within the Israeli defence perimeter.[66]

Conclusion

This chapter reviewed Israel's counterinsurgency experience, whose roots are in the pre-state period. An offensive spirit emphasizing the need of good intelligence for preventive and preemptive actions is present through the various periods. Realising the deep-rooted enmity towards the Jewish state, Israel did not find the classic 'Hearts and Minds' approach very appealing. The remaining options were a variety of military responses intended primarily to create deterrence. The IDF's learning curve was generally satisfactory, adopting effective tactics to minimize the impact of the insurgents on Israel. Over time, the main challenge to the IDF came from non-state radical organisations, as

---

[64] E. Inbar, 'A Strategic Assessment of Israel's 2014 Gaza Operation', *Middle East Quarterly*, 22 (Spring 2015).

[65] E. Hecht, 'Gaza: How Hamas Tunnel Network Grew', *BBC News*, 22 July 2014, www.bbc.com/news/world-middle-east-28430298.

[66] U. Rubin, 'The Performance of Air Defense System', Conference at BESA Center for Strategic Studies, Ramat Gan, Israel, 29 September 2014.

conventional warfare became less likely. The IDF seems to adapt to changing circumstances, although not always adequately, as the short-comings of the 2006 Lebanon War indicate. While there is greater acceptance of Israel by Arab states, the current socio-political crisis that beleaguers such states increases the chances for a proliferation of failed states and subsequent non-state armed organisations. Currently these non-state actors are operating from outside of Israel's borders, from territories they control and operate as 'mini-states' such as are the cases of Hamas and Hezbollah. Israel therefore does not view them as insurgents, that is, internal groups fighting to overthrow a government or foreign occupation, but as an external threat. The ability of such non-state actors to acquire and operate advanced weapon systems coupled with state support received in finances, training and equipment, turned them into formidable enemies.

Throughout its history the IDF has implemented a variety of methods from the COIN toolbox in order to curtail the threat of insurgency. The Israeli ethos of small-unit commando warfare has been an ongoing characteristic of the army's counterinsurgency policy. These elite units were sent to retaliate against Palestinian militants, and later also against Lebanese transgressions. Another method used by the IDF derived from the French notion of '*quadrillage*', a strategy meant to split and destroy insurgency nests by dividing the combat arena into small fighting zones. This policy was intended to ward off terrorist infiltrators from Israel's northern border during the 1970s. To some extent this method was also implemented in Judea and Samaria, via the defensive barrier constructed in 2002. In the recent decades, the IDF has also turned to targeted killings of terrorist leaders, most notably in the ensuing fighting against Hezbollah in Lebanon and against Hamas in the Gaza Strip. In recent years, as we have shown, vis-à-vis new and emerging threats the IDF has largely adopted the strategy of 'Mowing the Grass' – creating temporary deterrence through short and very aggressive operations with the purpose of causing maximum damage to militant organisations' infrastructure in the minimum time necessary in order to gain a period of quiet on its border.

While the IDF's COIN experience underlines a dominance of military instruments, other methods were more compatible to traditional 'Hearts and Minds' activities, the most noticeable of which is Dayan's 'Open Bridges' approach after the Six-Day War.

In conclusion, we have seen that the Israeli notion of COIN relies mainly on military operations, which the IDF has gradually modified according to the operational and political requirements of the time.

Part II

Insurgency Strategies

9 National Liberation, Algerian 'Style'?

Jacques Frémeaux

General Conditions

Geography plays a crucial role in any insurgency. Algeria extends over 2,204,860 square kilometres (km^2), most of it desert, the Sahara.[1] The region in which the Algerian War (1954–1962) took place belongs to the Mediterranean littoral, a rectangle of approximately 210,000 km^2, spanning roughly 1,000 km from East to West (from the Tunisian border to the Atlantic), and 200 km from North to South (from the Mediterranean to the southern limit of the high plains). The terrain is for the most part mountainous, averaging 800 meters in altitude, with steep slopes and numerous natural caves. The plains are separated by mountain ranges and connected mainly through narrow valleys or gorges. The rail network built by the French (4,375 km, i.e., 2 km/100 km^2) basically followed the large East-West axes, only partly mitigating the geographic obstacles. The more developed road network (22,971 km of good roads) did not cover the entire country, especially not the more mountainous regions.[2]

The sociological conditions are no less important. The population comprised both French and Algerians, with a ratio of 1 to 9 (1,000,000/8,700,000 on 1 January 1958).[3] Algeria contained both modernised areas, predominantly big cities such as Algiers and the great agricultural plains (Mitidja, Chélif, Oranie). Cities and fertile plains contrasted starkly with a more traditional Algeria, largely unaffected by modernisation. In the towns, the French (around 35 per cent) and Algerians (65 per cent) cohabited, although generally in separate suburbs. By contrast, only 3 per cent of the French population lived in rural areas, their number slowly decreasing. In spite of some reforms,

Translated by Callum Hamilton and Julie Jacquet.

[1] J. Frémeaux, 'The Sahara and the Algerian War', in M. S. Alexander (ed.), *The Algerian War and the French Army, 1954–1963* (London: Palgrave, 2002), 76–87.
[2] R. Gendarme, *L'Économie de L'Algerie* (Paris: Armand Colin, 1962), 102–7.
[3] *Statistique générale de l'Algérie. Tableaux de l'économie algérienne* (Alger : Baconnier, n.d.), 19.

these two peoples existed, as sociologist George Balandier put it, in a 'colonial situation'. Their status was profoundly unequal, with the French minority enjoying political and economic dominance, gained by conquest over an Algerian population with a distinctly Arab-Berber language and culture.[4]

The 'National Liberation Army' (ALN) that was to rise against French rule was formally created at the Soummam Conference of Algerian nationalists in August 1956 and constitutes the military force used by the Algerian FLN (National Liberation Front) during the war.[5] At the time the Muslim population of Algeria was the ALN's principal source of recruitment and main target of propaganda. It promised an independent Algeria and a 'democratic, social and sovereign state, based on Islamic principles'.[6] The majority of this population was rural, with more than 80 per cent of the Muslim population living in the countryside. This majority lived in extremely difficult conditions, owning small plots of land or many being merely employed as agricultural workers. Traditionally very poor, these people lived in this deteriorating condition as agrarian reforms in response to explosive demographic growth were sorely lacking. In short, the people in the countryside lived in misery. All these conditions created the perfect terrain for rural guerrilla warfare, exacerbated by a dearth of local government.

Not all circumstances favoured the ALN. The forests with the shelter they offered to the fighters, lying in the mountain regions near the sea, thinned out to the north, while the steppes made the secret movement of people impossible, at least during daylight. Furthermore, the proximity of France and conscription made the needed saturation of Algeria with French armed forces possible. Sociological and historical conditions aggravated the inequality. Contrary to French propaganda, Algeria was not France, nor was it a completely foreign country. The relationship between the French and Algerians was not entirely hostile; among the elites, which included both Europeans and Muslims, in every-day life friendly relationships existed. Some prominent figures, such as Albert Camus, strove to raise awareness of the situation in Algeria. By the time the Algerian War broke out, a significant number of Algerians had already emigrated to France in search of work (around 200,000 were living there in 1953). Over the previous 120-odd years, the French had acquired an

---

[4] See, for example, P. Bourdieu, *Sociologie de l'Algérie* (Paris: Presses Universitaires de France, 1974).

[5] For more details, see J. Frémeaux, *La France et L'Algérie en guerre, 1830–1870, 1954–1962* (Paris: Economica, 2002).

[6] '*Proclamation. Au peuple algérien. Aux militants de la cause nationale*', 31 October 1954, M. Harbi and G. Meynier, *Le FLN, documents et histoire* (Paris: Fayard, 2005), 36–8.

excellent knowledge of the country. French was the official language and was widely spoken. There was no lack of experts on the Arabic language, ethnography and sociology, such as Louis Massignon, Jacques Berque, Georges-Henri Bousquet, Jean Servier or Germaine Tillion.

Historical Continuity?

Algerian resistance against French rule had a long tradition. The combatants of the ALN presented their struggle against the French as standing in the tradition of the heroic insurgencies of 1830–1870 against French colonial domination.

Nevertheless, apart from this claim that there was a continuity, the commonalities between the Algerian insurgencies of the nineteenth century and the Algerian War of Independence (in short, the Algerian War, 1954–1962) are few. True, the nineteenth-century insurgents were motivated by hostility to the foreign invader, just as the twentieth-century fighters wanted the French out. In both cases, Islam was an essential element of the identity of the inhabitants of Algeria, and the militants of the 1950s still proudly called themselves '*Mujaheddin*' (fighters of the Jihad). But there the similarities end. In the nineteenth century, the mobilisation of the resistance was organised through the tribal system, under the leadership of traditional chiefs. The main strategy of the resistance fighters consisted of the defence of their own tribal territories, either by ambushing the occupation forces or by defending villages or strategic positions. Even if the nineteenth-century insurgents were in many ways merciless, they did not terrorise or otherwise use force against French (let alone indigenous Arab) civilians.

By contrast, during the Algerian War, the recruitment of combatants was carried out by organs of the FLN that produced their commander; the strategy was a mix of terrorism and harassment of the French military forces. The targets of the terrorism were mainly civilians, and, although the European population was affected, it was numerically the Muslim majority that suffered most. The discourse revolved around Algerian nationalism – oddly engendering a sense of identity that the colonial power had first instilled in the various tribes living in this area artificially soldered into one state – and thus anti-colonialism, with a pronounced revolutionary accent.[7]

[7] J. Frémeaux, *La France et l'Algérie en guerre,1830–1870, 1954–1962* (Paris, Economica, 2002).

Objectives and Ideology

The main objective of the ALN was not merely to conduct attacks on the French army and police in order to liberate Algeria completely from colonial rule. It was also to bring the FLN to power, and the ALN therefore fought to exclude all other Algerian political forces not aligned with their movement. To achieve this, it was necessary to charge these other factions with treason, without any room for compromise. Through the war, the FLN tried to forge a united Algerian nation behind leaders who, having called the nation to arms, had acquired revolutionary legitimacy. Parallels to many revolutionary uprisings of the past, not least the French Revolution, are obvious. The imposition of this union was even more important than being able to establish an Algeria independent from French rule: effectively, it meant the establishment of an administrative system, education, health service, public services and a functioning economy totally independent from metropolitan France. The colonisation had created strong links of interest and sometimes even amity, along with the French domination, which had to be destroyed, or at least weakened. Yet the Algerian Muslim populations were not homogeneous; there were strong regional differences in identity between East and West, North and South, between the Berber- (Kabyles and Chaouïa of the Aurès region) and Arab-speaking communities. '*Iqlimyya*' (particularism, regionalism) was therefore a perennial problem.

As always, nation building went along with a constructed historical narration. Opposing the French interpretation that Algeria had only been created from scattered tribes by France, the FLN claimed that there had been an Algerian nation for a long time, and that it had been associated with a state, indeed one of the first Muslim states to appear in North Africa. A store of collective memories furnished a number of historical dates that could be drawn upon to construct a narrative of continuous resistance to colonial domination and a continuous existence of an Algerian identity. The long insurgency lead by Emir Abd el-Kader (1832–1847) and the tribal uprisings of 1845, 1871, 1864, 1881 and 1916 were presented as evidence of such a persistent resistance. As Ferhat Abbas wrote, 'the amount of suffering is ignored by most people who today claim to be "Algerians" [the French of Algeria]. But we know it. We were taught it as children, while sitting on our grandmothers' knees.'[8] The memories of the Second World War and the German occupation of French territories made it possible to demonise the French

---

[8] F. Abbas, *Le Jeune Algérien* (1931) (Paris, Garnier, 1981), 117.

by associating them with the Nazis. The repression of the Algerian nationalist uprisings of May 1945 by the French in the wake of VE Day was still fresh in the minds of both the Algerians and the Europeans of Algeria.

The conflict was driven by a twofold ideology. Even if the FLN was not mobilised under the banner of a 'holy war', it still drew on this idea as a means of legitimisation. The war was cast as a struggle for God and nation ('*fisabilallah ouel watan*'),[9] and the people were forced rigorously to observe Ramadan fasting. The consumption of tobacco and alcohol was strictly forbidden, homosexuality was prohibited and religious teachings were encouraged.[10] Yet the party denounced popular 'superstitions' and '*marabouts*', the so-called miracle makers, as agents of 'colonialism'. In this the FLN followed the '*Islah*' thinkers, who since the nineteenth century had striven to reform Islam to make it compatible with modernity. '*Ulama*' reformists were thus welcomed into the FLN. A number of their militants had come out of the FLN-created school or youth groups (such as the Muslim Scouts).

This form of ideology was perhaps best expressed in combat. The division commanders frequently imposed the observance of strict religious rites on the soldiers, exhorting them to behave like the legendary pious warriors of early Islamic expansionism. The fighters were given names which explicitly referred to Jihad, which inter alia means the struggle against the enemies of Islam. The newspaper of the FLN, first published in the summer of 1956, was thus aptly called *El-Moudjahid* (literally fighter of Jihad). The term *mujahid* (plural *mudjahiddin*) was used for the insurgent combatant (or *jounoud*, soldier). Other words were also taken from the vocabulary of Holy War. *Moussebilin*, which the ALN translated into French as *partisans* (in fact referring to any ALN supporters, not only the combatants), eroded the religious connotations of the word (with the root *sabil*, 'the way of God'). The polemic, pejorative term *terrorist*, used by the French authorities to denote suicide bombers, was replaced by *fida'i*, another religious term implying total sacrifice for a sacred cause.[11]

The FLN, however, also claimed other values. The ALN professed to lead a revolutionary struggle, whose goal was to establish a more just society and a true democracy. The people were celebrated as the only

[9] O. Carlier, *Entre Nation et Jihad, Histoire Sociale des Radicalismes Algériens* (Paris: Presses de la FNSP, 1995), 308.
[10] DST report on the organisation of the FLN at the Paul-Cazelles camp, 24 August 1959, cited in P. Vidal-Naquet, *La raison d'État* (Paris: Éditions de Minuit, 1962), 254.
[11] See J. P. Charnay, *Principes de Stratégie Arabe* (Paris: L'Herne, 1984), 207.

true heroes of the fight. There were numerous references to socialism. The Algerian nationalist movement had its roots in French militant proletarian circles, supported by militants from the Fourth International. While this dimension was short-lived, the FLN managed to retain an anti-imperialist and anti-capitalist ideology which was applied to the colonial situation in Algeria. Franz Fanon, the physician-turned-writer from Martinique, established similar ideas towards the end of the colonial period. He sought to theorise the struggles of Third World revolutionaries from what he saw of the actions of the FLN, supported warmly by Jean-Paul Sartre, feeding into more general Leftist thinking.

The Military Apparatus

As in other leftist movements, the army was presented as the symbol of the new Algeria, a meritocracy in which it was possible to rise from humble origins. Algerian nationalism had originated in a movement created by Messali Hadj in 1926 under the name *Étoile Nord-Africaine* (Star of North Africa), which then became the PPA (Algerian People's Party) in 1937, and then the MTLD (Movement for the Triumph of Democratic Liberty) in 1946. The militant wing of the MTLD turned against Messali Hadj, deciding to establish a new movement in 1954, the FLN, and to initiate the uprising. Some of these men had a little military experience which they had gained in the French army, mostly as non-commissioned officers (Ahmed Ben Bella and Mohammed Boudiaf were adjutants, Omar Ouamrane a sergeant, Belkacem Krim a corporal; Ben Bella had fought in Italy, France and Germany). Most of them also belonged to the paramilitary *Organisation Spéciale* (OS), created in February 1947 within the MTLD, organised under the direction of Hocine Aït Ahmed, from which they acquired basic military knowledge. In 1950 the French discovered a text produced by the ALN, more than twenty pages long, containing 'a thorough examination of questions relating to the recruitment of guerrilla fighters, their moral and technical preparation as well as their tactical use in every phase of the fight'. The French judgement was laudatory: 'in precision and conciseness this could stand up to comparison with the best-conceived of our own operations, every possible situation was cited along with suggested solutions'. The text prescribed 'gymnastic and shooting lessons, notions of maritime warfare and a framework of order and account records which appeared to be taken from a commando instruction manual'.[12] These instructions

---

[12] General Morlière, commander of the 10th military region, following synthesis of information no. 3 (March 1960) following the discovery of the OS, *La Guerre d'Algérie*

were distributed among the carefully recruited militants during military instruction sessions. These were spread over a year and were composed of weekly meetings and training sessions, organised in safe regions including France.

The OS consisted of just under two thousand men, including six hundred in Kabylie.[13] The majority of personnel survived its dismantlement at the hand of the French police in March 1950. The prisoners, released quickly where they had not managed to escape, could swiftly resume their previous activities. From within this organisation most of the 'historical leaders' were recruited (such as Aït Ahmed, Abdelhafid Boussouf, Lakhdar Bentobbal, Didouche Mourad and Rabah Bitat), as well as many of the first FLN militants. After the outbreak of the conflict, some senior officers deserted from the French army to join the resistance, such as Ali Khodja, a former sergeant, who formed a formidable commando force in the Palestro region in October 1955.[14] The majority of leaders, however, came to prominence during the mid-1950s and had little previous experience. This was the case, for example, for the employees of the Solal clinic in Algiers, who came from the village of Iveskryen near Azazga, and who went on to become officers in the Wilaya IV.[15] One of the best military chiefs of this Wilaya, commander Azzedine, made a quick switch from a normal life to the resistance.

In reality, the number of active soldiers had never been very high. If we take a look at the censuses of the Algerian ministry for former *mujahidin*, 132,000 people (mostly male) served in the ranks of the ALN between 1954 and 1962.[16] In August 1956, during the Soummam Conference, the head of the FLN estimated that its forces within Algeria were composed of around twenty thousand men, including around seven thousand soldiers and fifteen thousand active supporters. It is possible that this number increased thereafter. In August 1957, Abbane Ramdane, at the time one of the foremost leaders of the organisation, guessed the number of soldiers to be around fifty thousand, with forty thousand active supporters.[17] In November 1958, French sources suggested that the number

---

par les Documents, documentation established under the direction of J. C. Jauffret, T. II, *Les Portes de la Guerre: des Occasions Manquées à l'Insurrection*, 10 March 1946–31, December 1954 (Vincennes: SHAT, 1998), 181.

[13] H. A. Ahmed, *Mémoires d'un Combattant* (Paris: Sylvie Messinger, 1983), 204.

[14] Y. Courrière, *La Guerre d'Algérie, part 2, Le Temps des Léopards* (Paris: Fayard, 1969), 320.

[15] D. Amrane, *Les Femmes Algériennes dans la Guerre* (Paris: Plon, 1991), 232.

[16] Ibid., 232.

[17] M. Harbi, *L'Algérie et son Destin, Croyants et Citoyens* (Paris: Arcantère, 1992), 109–10.

of combatants was in fact around twenty-one thousand men.[18] In August 1960, this number dropped to only eight thousand, to which an estimated fourteen thousand supporters must be added. These were labelled as 'infrastructure' by the 2nd French *Bureau* and were composed of politicians and militants charged with resupplying, communication and intelligence, or simply of soldiers taking a brief break from the combat.[19] The number of combatants fluctuated. In addition to the commandos who formed the backbone of the resistance, there was also a second category of combatant called the *moussebilin*. They formed sabotage groups, provided logistical support and still lived in the villages. It became ever more difficult to maintain their secrecy, because of the French strategy of population transfer. In 1958–1959 they were therefore forced to re-join the rank and file of the ALN.[20]

The ALN relied on a network of individuals charged with passing on and supervising orders, as well as intelligence officers, supply officers, fundraisers, men, women, sometimes children, making up for the limited military personnel. The French translated the Arab term *nizâm* as organisation and gave this network the name of Politico-Administrative Organisation (OPA). Initially the French were in awe of this organisation, imagining it to be similar to what they had encountered in Indochina. On closer observation French officers noted, however, that the Algerian 'rebels' were incapable of organising the population in a network of parallel hierarchies of the sort developed by the Vietnamese communists.[21] In reality the OPA was less formally structured, varying in scale depending on the zone and depending on the effectiveness of the repression. The OPA, founded more on individual devotion than on hierarchical connections, proved to be invaluable to the ALN. It survived the dissolution of the ALN after the French offensives of 1958–9, remaining a key tool of the FLN.

Technology

The arms of the ALN came from various sources. At the beginning they were of local origin, including hunting weapons and supplies left over from the Second World War and bought on the black market. This was

---

[18] Découpage politico-militaire et implantation à la date du 1er octobre 1958, SHAT 1 H 1682.
[19] État-Major interarmées, 2nd Bureau, Évolution des structures et des méthodes de la rebellion de 1957 à 1960, 8 August 1960, SHAT 1 H 1942.
[20] M. Teguia, *L'Algérie en Guerre* (Alger: Office of Academic Publications, 1988), 154.
[21] Commander Cogniet, *Fondements idéologiques et principes d'emploi de l'action psychologique* (Conference at the École Supérieure de Guerre, 6 Jan. 1960), 31.

followed by the acquisition of contraband items. The OS had already bought a stock of Italian arms from Libya in 1948 (Statti shotguns), which were used in the Aurès in November 1954. During the war the FLN was supplied by Eastern Bloc countries or the Arab world with World War II arms that were mainly German, Italian or British. Soviet or Chinese arms did not appear until late 1961. Another, smaller number of these arms were stolen from French army stores, often by deserters, or taken during combat. The ALN eventually succeeded in seizing arms supplied by the French secret service to those nationalist rebels hostile to the FLN, who were supposed to help the counter-insurgency. The failure of both Operation Affaire K in Grande Kabylie (October 1956) and the defection of a group of armed men to the ALN resulted in more French arms being seized by the ALN.[22] The same applied to the collapse of the 'Kobus' anti-ALN resistance in the Chélif plain (April 1958) and of the 'National Army of the Algerian People', led by 'General' Bellounis, in the Saharan Atlas (July 1958).[23]

While the supply of arms and munitions continued to be a major problem for the ALN throughout the conflict, its leaders succeeded in equipping small units who could cause real damage to their adversaries. In 1958, a *katiba* (the equivalent of a French company) was provided with six to eight FM-type arms per 100 to 120 men, twenty PMs and forty rifles, often miscellaneous (old Mausers and Lebels from the First World War, French Mas-36s or American Garands, or even Italian Statti and American rifles from the Second World War), as well as the same number of hunting rifles. The latter, loaded with buckshot or bullets, had a formidable effect from a distance of fifty metres, which made them especially suitable to forest fighting.[24] During the same period a single French infantry company had nine FMs, thirty-nine PMs and thirty-nine rifles at their disposal, which did not give them much technological superiority.[25] Conditions thus imposed on the ALN a 'commando' strategy, consisting of small raids and ambushes, always conducted with a large margin of superiority, avoiding long drawn-out engagements with the enemy.

The quality of these units was high from the outbreak of fighting in Aurès. During an engagement fought in the Aurès mountains between the Grine Belkacem 'band' and an airborne unit on 29 November 1954,

---

[22] See General M. Faivre, 'L'Affaire K, comme Kabyle', in *Guerres Mondiales et Conflits Contemporains* (1998), 37–67.

[23] See J. Valette, *La Guerre d'Algérie des Messalistes* (Paris: L'Harmattan, 2001).

[24] J. Servier, *Adieu Djebels* (Paris: France-Empire, 1958), 212.

[25] Commander Granotier, École Superieure de Guerre, 73rd promotion, *Le Bataillon d'Infanterie Face à la Guerre Subversive* (1960), 6.

the *Gendarmerie* captain in Batna noted that 'the rebels, entrenched in natural shelters, which were genuine blockhouses, proved their remarkable manoeuvrability and inflicted severe losses on our troops from the outbreak of the fighting'.[26] This combative capacity continued to improve afterwards. At the end of 1956, General Salan estimated that 'the band of *"fellaghas"* is now replaced by the organised group, which is well equipped with automatic weapons, machine guns, mortars, and more importantly a means of command, and all this implies'.[27] Around one year later, Colonel Jeanpierre of the 1st REP (Régiment étranger de parachutistes – Foreign airborne regiment), at the end of a particularly tough engagement between Tablat and Médéa, declared that he had met a 'new [type of] rebel', who was especially efficient. In the defeat of the Legion, in which his regiment lost thirteen men and ten weapons, he saw a 'turning-point in the history of the war in Algeria'.[28] The self-sacrifice of the ALN soldiers was equalled only by their offensive spirit. A document destined for officer training quoted in bold the following citation taken from an officer of the 1st RIC (Regiment d'Infanterie Coloniale): 'the outlaws will always fight until the very end'.[29]

And yet one must not exaggerate their military capabilities. For General Marcel Bigeard, who would always emphasise the qualities of the hard-fighting enemy, 'the *"fells"* (*fellaghas*) were not [as good] as the Vietnamese'.[30] According to François Coulet, who was both a diplomat and the father and chief of the airborne commandos, they practiced only 'rudimentary ambushes'; they were never able to capture weakly defended positions from the outside, to destroy airplanes in advanced positions or to carry out assaults, with the exception of breaking an encirclement. It took them a long time to adapt to airborne attacks, and only rarely were they able to react to helicopter assaults.[31] Some of these shortcomings may be due to the fact that unlike the Vietnamese, the ALN was unable to form genuine regular units capable of confronting the enemy in destructive battles. The differences in terrain were also a major factor. Also an excessive trust in morale, religious loyalties and

[26] Report on *La Guerre d'Algérie par les Documents*, part 2, 849–50.
[27] Chairman of the Joint Chiefs of Staff, General directive n°1, Algiers, 18 December 1956, SHAT 1 H 1929.
[28] Extract from a letter joined to a circulation sent by the Chairman of the Joint Chiefs of Staff, 20 March 1958, 1 H 1930. See also P. Sergent, *Je ne Regrette Rien* (Paris: Fayard, 1972), 383–5.
[29] *Training, Pacification and Guérilla Arzew* Centre, adapted by the army in operation in Algeria, SHAT 1 H 2524.
[30] M. Bigeard, *Pour une Parcelle de Gloire* (Paris: Plon, 1975), 403.
[31] F. Coulet, *Vertu des Temps Difficiles* (Paris: Plon, 1967), 19.

psychological factors was widespread in the Arab world and proved to be detrimental to training and organisational abilities.

Furthermore, these men easily became dispirited. First, they were not all volunteers. The young people who joined the resistance were not prepared for the dangers, the exhaustion or the violence. Some farmers were recruited by force. Provisions, already frugal, were often rationed, along with water. The necessity to be on the move constantly, either within an area to control it and avoid being spotted, or between central areas and border regions, where they could replace men and access weapon and ammunition supplies, meant physical exhaustion. There was insufficient medical care for injuries or sickness because of a lack of physicians, medicine and hospitals, in spite of all the efforts made to improve the situation.[32] Morale was therefore not high. The behaviour of certain ALN leaders (such as the famous Amirouche, the leader of the Wilaya III), who were often abusive, contemptuous and overly suspicious to the point of being paranoid, discouraged many from fighting. From 1959, the large-scale French campaigns of the Challe Plan (see below) were extremely challenging for morale, not only because of the losses that they inflicted on these *katibas*, forcing them to disperse and hide, but also because they made them feel forgotten by the outside world. All this fed a wave of desertion which led to a significant number of combatants crossing to the French camp.

Strategy

Central Organisation

At first the strategy was essentially one of a general uprising, which required neither a structured organisation nor a central command. Instead, it required conforming to the orders of the 'traditional leaders', who later constituted the party leadership and managed to round up and reassemble the scattered forces of the nationalist movement, which was in crisis at the time. It was only during the Soummam Conference of August 1956 that the army was organised into a regular hierarchy. The Algerian territory was then divided into six constituencies or *wilayas*, with each placed under the command of a single politico-military leader with the rank of colonel (*sagh ethanni*). The leader was assisted by a political commissioner, who does not seem to have had an important

[32] Dr. B. S. Djamel-Eddine, *Voyez nos Armes, Voyez nos Médecins* (Algiers: Entreprise Nationale du Livre, 1992).

position, because of the lack of a Marxist-style organisation of the party.[33] The central command remained weak; it was not until 1958 that an operational Military Committee was organised. This was divided into two areas of command, east and west, although this proved to be almost ineffective. The efforts made by Commander Mouloud Idir, an ex-French army officer turned deserter, to organise a real army, created suspicions among the resistance leaders and proved to be excessively ambitious in its aims of raising 160,000 men. Centralisation became effective only from the beginning of 1960 with the appointment of the General Staff, under the command of Colonel Houari Boumediene, which was mainly responsible for the border armies.[34] The strategy followed was concentrated in three main areas: the towns, the countryside and the border regions.

Urban Strategy

The ALN's urban strategy was probably what was most distinctive about its way of war and reflected the particular demographic configuration of Algeria, given that the Europeans, whom the ALN wanted to drive out, lived mainly in the towns. The towns, which in the past had not been important for any resistance because they were so difficult to defend, now assumed great importance for the insurgency. They presented a number of targets, comprising local government institutions and European civilians. The attacks began as soon as the war broke out; the FLN planned to carry out major urban offensives in Algiers even from 1956. This form of action presented an opportunity to strike at the heart of the colonial apparatus, which was much more spectacular than patient political negotiation or guerrilla actions in the countryside. As widely visible operations they would draw the attention of foreign public opinion to the FLN's cause. At first the strategy aimed to create an atmosphere of general insecurity, by multiplying individual attacks and by targeting European civilians with explosive devices. Moreover, the leaders set the date of 28 January 1957 for a general strike which would coincide with the opening of talks on the Algerian question at the UN General Assembly. This strike was designed to show international public opinion what authority the FLN enjoyed over the Algerian people. This could constitute the beginning, or at least a dress rehearsal, of an insurgency movement designed to administer the fatal blow to the French cause from both within and without.

[33] Text in Y. Courrière, *La Guerre d'Algérie*, 575–604.
[34] G. Meynier, *Histoire intérieure du FLN, 1954–1962* (Paris: Fayard, 2002), 315–19.

To achieve its objectives, the FLN had an organisation in Algiers, directed by Larbi Ben M'hidi, leader of the 'Autonomous Zone of Algiers', and for whom Yacef Saâdi was one of the principle lieutenants. Their plan involved a small number of militants (possibly fifteen hundred), who managed, through conviction or fear, to build up a vast network of support and complicity. One group produced timed bombs (so-called ticking bombs). Some young women, less likely to raise suspicion, deployed them in public places. This operation was countered in an efficient, if not morally defendable, manner by the French army; it resulted in a crushing defeat, the dismantling of part of the FLN's network, and the rest were forced to go into hiding for an extended period.[35] Nevertheless, the repression led to an increase of membership of the FLN and helped to win over the sympathies of French intellectuals.[36] Moreover, insecurity did not disappear entirely. This insecurity, although barely significant from a military point of view, led to the maintenance of a state of emergency with controls, blockades and curfews which gradually undermined the morale of the French population.

From December 1960, the FLN reappeared mainly in the towns during mass demonstrations which took place in urban areas. The crowds came from the so-called native suburbs, often slum areas surrounding the colonial cities. They marched through the central European suburbs brandishing green flags of independence. From March 1962 this takeover by the population went hand in hand with targeted actions, including systematic kidnappings. This strategy contributed to the exodus of Europeans from Algeria, as it was presented as a reprisal for the attacks carried out by the nationalist French OAS (Secret Armed Organisation).

Rural Strategy

The real focus of the ALN was in rural areas (known as the *bled*). The FLN units were only small in size; the largest unit was the battalion (*faïlek*, 350 men), itself divided into companies (*katibas*, 110 men), each divided into sections composed of combat groups of around ten men.

Each FLN unit was stationed most of the time in a 'defence zone', generally situated at the point where several valleys merged in order to

---

[35] G. Pervillé, 'Le terrorisme urbain dans la guerre d'Algérie (1954–1962)', in J. C. Jauffret and M. Vaïsse (eds.), *Militaires et Guérilla dans la Guerre d'Algérie* (Paris: Complexe, 2001), 447–67.

[36] Depicted in Gillo Pontecorvo's famous docufiction *La Battaglia di Algeri* (1966).

facilitate movement, but also in close proximity to villages, which allowed them to access supplies. This zone was covered by a 'line of defence' made up of small groups positioned in natural shelters, caves or crevices. If they were attacked, reserve troops could intervene to reinforce the most threatened positions. A unit of two hundred men could cover a zone with a perimeter of three or four kilometres. In order to increase security, the occupation of these areas was temporary, and these groups were continuously moving from one zone to another.[37] As before, their familiarity with the country and intelligence provided by permanent or part-time agents were a great help. In addition to these networks of agents they could also use radio, although this was often subject to heavy interference.

Most of the time, like most successful insurgents, the ALN units avoided battles where they would be outnumbered. They preferred to operate through ambushes along the enemy's fixed routes, especially on their lines of supply, and abrupt attacks on enemy positions, followed by a swift retreat. If they were encircled, they would carry out a fierce attack on a precise point of the French army, known as a *boule de feu* (fireball), in order to break through the French lines. Even if this failed, they could try to escape if they were able to hold out until nightfall, as darkness allowed them to flee in small groups.[38] However, the 'harassment and attacks on the forces of order' (to use the French terminology, i.e., the police) represented only a small part of the activities of the ALN, perhaps only a quarter in 1958. The rest was divided, again using the French terminology, between 'attacks on individuals' and 'attacks on assets'.[39]

Commanding an armed unit was first and foremost a political mission for the ALN. The purpose of this armed force was to impose a new authority by liquidating potential enemies, by crushing the myth of French omnipotence and by allowing the creation of the famous *nizâm* or OPA, as we have seen, a clandestine network or organisation whose goal was less to participate in armed engagements than to control the population and maintain the revolutionary spirit. There was no need for large battalions to carry out these missions; at the end of 1955, therefore, the Kabylie contained only twenty groups, each with no more than fifteen rifles at their disposal; in Constantine, the average number of each group was estimated to be around twenty men, supported by a network of

---

[37] Lieutenant-Colonel Monteux, *Comment Détruire les Bandes* (April 1957), SHAT 1 H 1942.
[38] Commander Granotier, *Le Bataillon d'Infanterie Face à la Guerre Subversive*, 6.
[39] 'Manifestations de l'activité rebelle et terroriste', SHAT 1 H 1929.

supporters.[40] The ALN detachments arrived in the villages by night, rounding up the men and appointing leaders. The inhabitants on pain of death had to obey the orders that were given, pay taxes, supply the resistance and provide volunteers for armed action. The armed group was therefore the 'vehicle of the system', which favoured the political and psychological control of the population, which in turn formed the ALN's indispensable infrastructure.[41] The ALN thus in part used terror to gain the support of the Algerian population.

This form of political-military action had never been considered an end in itself. From the beginning, the leaders of the FLN, undoubtedly inspired by the success of the Chinese and Vietnamese communists, had been planning eventually to turn from mere guerrilla fighters into a regular army. The programme of the Soummam Conference announced 'the development of an incessant armed struggle until the appearance of a general insurrection' and hoped to help the insurgency 'to develop in such a way that conformed to international law (personalisation of the army, recognisable political power, respect for the laws of warfare, normal administration of the zones liberated by the ALN').[42] They were unable to achieve this, however. The French army succeeded in preventing the ALN from gaining control of vast areas and assembling large units in them. The plan, called the 'Challe Plan', after General Maurice Challe, who was Commander in Chief in Algeria at that time, consisted of the eradication, region by region, of both the military and political organisations of the FLN. This plan proved to be extremely efficient despite the resistance. Between February 1959 and April 1961 the ALN's strength was halved – from seventeen thousand military weapons (army rifles, machine guns and submachine guns) and twenty-five thousand hunting rifles, to eight thousand and eleven thousand, respectively. There were practically no more battalions, and the *katibas* were on the brink of dissolution.[43] The resistance leaders had to accept that it was necessary to dismantle their units in order to form smaller groups. Harder to catch, they presented a new problem for the French, who were in the end unable to overcome it. These small groups, frequently ignored, especially by counterinsurgency theoreticians, in the end probably represented the most important threat to the French armed forces.

---

[40] Lieutenant P. Giraud, 'Adaptation Tactique de nos Unités à Leur Mission en Afrique du Nord', in C. Paillat, *Vingt ans qui Déchirèrent la France, part 2, La Liquidation, 1954–1962* (Paris: Presses de la Cite, 1972), 311.

[41] Instruction personelle et secrète no. 3, 11 June 1957, SHAT, 1 H 1929.

[42] Text in Y. Courrière, *La Guerre d'Algérie*, 587–8.

[43] EM, 2nd bureau, Évolution des structures et des méthodes de la rebellion de 1957 à 1960.

The Border Army

Meanwhile, the number of rebel soldiers on the Moroccan and Tunisian borders was growing. These troops, formed of exiled Algerians, had first been trained to help supply and reinforce the interior resistance forces. The frontier barriers constructed by the French army from 1957, however, were increasingly hermetic. Rebel losses here were considerable, so much so that attempts to break through the barriers which the French had established along Algeria's borders were abandoned at the beginning of 1960. The leaders under Colonel Boumediene, however, organised demobilised units into a regular army. Around 1961, their number is estimated to have been around thirty thousand men, two-thirds of whom were on the Tunisian side of the border. Deprived of armoured vehicles and air support, they began equipping themselves with heavy artillery (105 and 75 mm canons, 106 and 120 mm mortars, all of Chinese and Soviet origin). They also possessed light vehicles (jeeps). Training was well organised and discipline was very strict. The leadership was made up of resistance leaders, cadres trained in the Arab camps (especially in Egypt and Iraq) and officers who had deserted from the French army and joined the border army without going through the Resistance.[44]

Although this army did not have the heroic acclaim of the fighters within Algeria, it nevertheless played an important part. While it did not attack the frontier barriers directly, it was a constant threat for the French command, which had to station a large number of soldiers along the barriers. On the other hand, they had the means to reconcile the rival factions that fought for power once it became clear that independence was imminent (following the negotiations which began in June 1960). Their presence, often ignored by COIN scholars, was essential, with consequences that would prove as important then as it would be for the future of the region.

Ideology and Violence

Nothing contributed more to the ALN's style of combat than its ideology, which, as we have seen, had its roots both in a Muslim heritage and Stalinist revolutionary practices. For the FLN, each adversary was not only an enemy or a traitor to the homeland, but also a renegade or schismatic who undermined the fundamental unity of the Muslim community (*umma*). Mohammed Harbi wrote about the FLN that 'its conceptions of war, like *jihad*, its tendency to see heresy and deviation within

---

[44] G. Meynier, *Le FLN, documents et histoire*, 310.

the opposition, claim to be representative based on consensus, its approach to the problem of minorities, and finally its practice of elimination as elimination of the impure, were all based on tradition'. This totalitarianism was reinforced by the notion of 'democratic centralism', inherited from communist models and used to exclude or suppress all internal opposition. It was also based on 'revolutionary justice', justifying special measures (such as the execution, without trial, of supposed traitors), as opposed to 'bourgeois justice' (which, admittedly, was more of a 'colonial justice' in Algeria). For the FLN, as before them for the French Revolutionaries and the Bolsheviks, treason went together with war. It justified both their mistrust and radicalism and therefore allowed them to identify and eliminate their eventual rivals.

This ideology naturally justified violence towards opponents and those who did not rally to the FLN's cause, either because they supported the French or because they hoped to reach a compromise with France. More Muslims thus became victims of the FLN than French civilians. This included civilian officials in French service, such as policemen in towns and in the countryside, and also those who were unwilling to comply or were simply lukewarm in their support of the FLN. At the same time a merciless war was being fought against the party of Messali Hadj, the MNA (Algerian National Movement), which had a few combatants in Algeria but also solid positions within the immigrant community in France.

The same ideology also explains the internal violence of the movement. Thus most of the struggles over the direction of the war were settled by physical elimination. The most famous example of this was the assassination of leader Abbane Ramdane, who was killed in Morocco by supporters of Boussouf in December 1957. The suspicions of treason or desertion, not always unfounded, could lead to genuine paranoia. The French secret service managed to convince Colonel Amirouche that he was surrounded by traitors secretly allied with the French. This operation, codenamed *Bleuite* (after the blue boiler suits worn by the Algerian back-up troops of Captain Paul Léger, the organiser of the operation), was more successful than expected: in the summer of 1958, the purges aimed at eliminating the supposed traitors, conducted by Amirouche, led to several thousands of victims in the Wilaya III. Students who had joined the resistance were particularly suspect to the leadership and were therefore killed in particularly high numbers.

The ALN's tactics were derived from classical subversion doctrines. Among the material targets were farms and schools, which were denounced as bastions of colonialism. In the countryside the harvests were burned and cattle slaughtered. Attacks took place not only against adult men, but also women and children. Besides individual assassination, the FLN resorted to attacks using grenades and bombs in public places; real carnage was created, for example, in Melouza, a small village where three hundred MNA supporters were killed (May 1957). The FLN also often resorted to kidnappings; most of the victims were never found alive.

More than the killings themselves, it was the atrocities that went along with them that left the most traumatising memories. The French authorities recorded five hundred murders between 1958 and 1959, which, without mentioning those victims who were burnt or beaten, were often followed by mutilation of the bodies (castration for men, gutting for women). During the period of independence, the liquidation of *harkis* (auxiliaries) or former Muslim supporters of France was part of a series of acts that cannot qualify as anything other than barbarity. The rape of European women, and of even larger numbers of Algerian women, was another sad reality. In truth some ALN soldiers privately demanded 'sexual service' from their 'sisters', sometimes camouflaged as (temporary forced) 'marriage'.

These methods, inspired by tradition and supported by the Muslim authorities, were consciously used to terrorise. It was also evident that the FLN, at least in some of its actions, provoked their adversaries into using violent means. Admittedly, they operated on a favourable terrain. They shared the darkest part of the Mediterranean heritage with their enemies; many of the French Algerians were ready to use violence in preference to simple verbal abuse. However, many soldiers, shocked by the sight of atrociously mutilated bodies, were prepared to retaliate and to go even further.[45] Already as early as following the events in Constantine in August 1955, which started with the massacre of seventy European civilians, the number of Muslim victims of the repression exceeded a thousand. The lynching of innocent Muslims by Europeans too often followed the funerals of the FLN's European victims.

Conclusion

It has often been said that the ALN lost the war on the ground, and their strategy has therefore been contrasted with that of the victorious Viet Minh at Dien Bien Phu. It is true that the ALN never won great military victories. The activities of the resistance, however, along with the constitution of a military destined to become the national army, allowed the FLN to claim to be the only true representative of the Algerian people. In

---

[45] R. Branche, *L'Embuscade de Palestro, Algérie, 1956* (Paris: Armand Colin, 2010).

this respect, the fight led by the ALN has strong traits in common with other African independence movements, notably those in former Portuguese colonies. Its uniqueness undoubtedly came from its particular mix of nationalism, Islamism and revolutionary spirit. It also lies in the fact that the war was unable to unite Algerians: the fight was marked by the leaders' suspicions of one another, as well of the Algerian people as a whole.

Notwithstanding the discontinuities and differences between the ALN's war and the civil war of the 1990s, Algeria is still paying the price for this mistrust today. This raises, finally, the question of similarities between the conflict of 1954–62 and the civil war of the 1990s. The first characteristic they have in common is precisely that element of civil war. Although the Algerian War was presented to the outside world as a war of liberation, it was also a war by means of which the FLN imposed its authority on both on those who were hostile and those who had come to terms with the French presence. Similarly, thirty years later, the Islamist groups sought to impose their power on the whole society, which thus became their principal war aim. In both cases, this explains the large-scale resorting to terrorism in order to eliminate opponents and to get the population to obey them, and the will to create, through irregular warfare, areas of outside the control of the central government, by creating rival regional governments.

A fundamental difference can, however, be identified by the function of Islam. During the Algerian War, the FLN supported Islam as a state religion, as found in states throughout the Muslim world, but a state religion subjected to the state's political power that strictly set its limits. In the 1990s, the Algerian state's claim to legitimacy remained national and populist. By contrast, the Islamist insurgents proclaimed their will to create a state that would impose religious norms on all aspects of society, in both the public and the private sphere. It is also important to note that the combatants of the Algerian War could return to sanctuaries in Morocco and Tunisia and had strong diplomatic support from these neighbouring countries. This was not the case for the Islamists in the 1990s. And yet in all this, the Islamists of the 1990s presented themselves as the successors of the Mujaheddin of the Algerian wars, just as those had presented themselves as the successors of the rebels of the nineteenth century. This created a false image of continuity for an insurgency movement which probably had more in common with contemporary movements elsewhere than with its own indigenous predecessors and successors.[46]

---

[46] B. Stora, *La Guerre invisible. Algérie, années 1990* (Paris: Presses de Sciences Po, 2001), 51–68.

10 Irish Republican Insurgency and Terrorism, 1969–2007

Jim Storr

Terminology

In the context of Northern Ireland, the term 'The Troubles' refers to an internal conflict that ran from August 1969 for almost forty years. They can be best described as a short insurgency, from 1969 to 1976, followed by a terrorist campaign from 1976 to 2007, conducted by Republican paramilitary organisations. Opposition Loyalist paramilitaries also played a significant role. The Troubles were highly significant to domestic life in Northern Ireland. A total of 3,720 lives were lost as a result of the Troubles (of whom 395 were Republican terrorists and 1,012 were members of the security forces). The Troubles had some impact both on the British Mainland and in the Republic of Ireland. They affected events in continental Europe and to a limited extent the United States. They are not, however, particularly well studied. The focus here is on the conduct of operations by Republican paramilitary organisations. The role of the security forces and loyalist paramilitaries are not considered in any detail.

Some aspects of Republican insurgency and terrorism were quite particular to Ireland and its history. Other aspects were common to many conflicts. A small number appear to be unique to the Troubles. Before considering those aspects, however, it is necessary to look at the background to and the course of events in Northern Ireland in the last decades of the twenty-first century.

In what follows, 'insurgency' is taken to be the (military) conduct of an insurrection or uprising. 'Terrorism' is taken to be the use of violence to create fear for political purposes. 'Republicanism' refers to a political desire for the six counties of Northern Ireland to be united with the Irish Republic. Conversely 'Unionism' is the desire for Northern Ireland to remain part of the United Kingdom. Ardent or extreme Unionists are referred to as 'loyalists' due to their purported loyalty to the British crown. 'Catholic' and 'Protestant' are used narrowly to refer to Christian religious confession. The population of Northern Ireland had, and has, a small but absolute majority of Protestants. Although the great majority of Republicans were Catholic and the great majority of Unionists were Protestants, the converse were not necessarily the case. For many Protestants and Catholics religion was a personal issue. They did not see their religious political affiliations as being sufficient to justify violence.

Historical Background

The history of Irish disaffection with the English crown originates in 1166. In that year Richard FitzGilbert de Clare, better known as 'Strongbow', led a force of knights from the British mainland to assist Dermot MacMurrough, King of Leinster, in a conflict against other Irish rulers. Soon thereafter King Henry II of England visited Ireland to impose his sovereignty over Strongbow. England, and later Britain, ruled Ireland more or less effectively from then on.

There were several Irish uprisings, but after the Act of Union of 1800 Ireland was largely peaceful. The peace was interrupted briefly by minor disturbances by the Young Irish in 1848, the Irish Republican Brotherhood (IRB) in 1867 and the Phoenix Park murders in the 1880s. The end of the nineteenth century saw a developing movement for independence on the part of the Catholics, who form a large majority of the population outside of Northern Ireland. That movement was generally expressed politically, not least in the British Parliament at Westminster where Irish MPs formed a significant minority bloc. They were able to influence legislation to the extent that a bill to create home rule in Ireland (that is, a separate parliament) was passed in 1914. The outbreak of the First World War prevented its enactment.

Unionist disaffection in Ulster had led to the formation of a paramilitary force, the Ulster Volunteers, in 1912. They numbered about 100,000 men with several thousand rifles. That was mirrored by the formation of the republican Irish Volunteers and much smaller Irish Citizen Army. Both republican organisations had been infiltrated by the IRB, which had become an undercover revolutionary movement. Before the outbreak of war, however, all parties kept the peace.

The Citizen Army staged an uprising at Easter 1916, which was swiftly put down by the British Army. Despite a General Election within weeks of the end of the War (which elected seventy-three Republican MPs to Whitehall) and the passage of Home Rule, Republicans initiated violence in February 1919. The Irish Republican Army (IRA) had emerged as a single organisation encompassing IRB, Irish Volunteers and Citizen Army members. It numbered about fifteen thousand men.

By July 1921 about five thousand had been imprisoned and five hundred killed. The IRA estimated that it had perhaps two to three thousand men left and was within weeks of collapse. A peace treaty agreed with Whitehall granted southern Ireland the status of a dominion within the British Empire (akin to, say, Canada). British security forces withdrew. Northern Ireland, comprising six counties (of a total of nine) in Ulster, was created as a separate entity within the United Kingdom.

A section of Irish society was, however, opposed to the Treaty and took up arms against the newly-formed Irish government. The IRA split into pro- and anti-Treaty factions. After a brief civil war the anti-Treaty party was defeated. The rump of the anti-Treaty IRA dumped its arms and largely abandoned the armed struggle in 1924.

The 'Troubles', 1970–1998

From 1924 to 1969 Ireland was largely peaceful. The Republic declared independence from Britain and existed as a small, poor, undeveloped and neutral state. The Catholic church played a major role in education, health care provision and social life. Northern Ireland prospered after the Second World War on the strength of traditional industries, dominated by Protestants, such as shipbuilding and linen weaving. It attracted migration of Catholics from the Republic, who formed significant enclaves in the industrial suburbs of Belfast and Londonderry. The traditional industries then went into decline. Unemployment rose, particularly amongst Catholics. There was widespread, flagrant and institutionalised discrimination against Catholics, seemingly justified by the existence of Northern Ireland as a Protestant entity.

Immigration and a high birth rate gave rise to a growing, dissatisfied, often unemployed and increasingly organised Catholic minority. The US Civil Rights movement partly inspired a similar organisation in Northern Ireland, which organised marches and protests in the late 1960s. One such march was ambushed by a loyalist mob at Burntollet Bridge on New Year's Day 1969. On 12 August that year the traditional Loyalist Apprentice Boys' March in Londonderry sparked rioting when it passed through the Catholic suburbs of Shankill and the Creggan. The rioting spiralled out of control. The British Army was called in to reestablish public order on 14 August 1969. That was the start of the Army's operations in Northern Ireland, which continued until 2007.

Public disorder degenerated into insurgency by early 1970. The British authorities responded with Operation Banner.[1] The insurgents, organised initially as the IRA and thereafter splinter organisations (discussed below), rapidly grew in numbers. They reached a strength of about 2,800 by May 1972. They had a conventional structure of companies, battalions and brigades, and formed enclaves (called 'No Go areas') within Catholic districts. The No Go areas were contested by the Army, resulting in an escalating series of clashes. In 1972 the Army conducted a troop surge (Operation Motorman) which cleared the No Go areas. Coupled with greatly improved intelligence, that broke the insurgency. Levels of violence rapidly diminished. Hundreds of Republicans had been interned or imprisoned. The mainstream or 'Official' branch of the IRA declared a ceasefire which it has never broken.

The most active IRA faction, however, had been defeated but not destroyed. The Provisional IRA (PIRA) regrouped, reorganised as a classic terrorist organisation and developed an increasingly sophisticated terrorist campaign. After hunger strikes in 1980 and 1981 it developed an overt political organisation, increasingly known just as 'Sinn Fein'. (The original Sinn Fein had been the umbrella party for the MPs of the 1919 General Election; the Official IRA had had its own Sinn Fein; and what became today's Sinn Fein was for a time known as 'Provisional Sinn Fein'.)

Political, social and economic developments from 1969 onwards changed Northern Ireland significantly. Discrimination, unemployment and poverty were all engaged through a series of government initiatives. The Troubles were eventually resolved politically, through measures originating in John Major's government in the early 1990s. Republicans, Unionists, the government of Ireland and the British government all contributed to the signing of the Good Friday Agreement of 1998. That agreement brought about a peace which has, broadly, held until the present day.

Some aspects of Republican insurgency were quite particular to Ireland and its history. Many can be referred to as the 'Republican

---

[1] The author was the writer of the British Army's account of the Troubles, published as *Operation Banner: An Analysis of Military Operations in Northern Ireland*, Army Code 71842. That was declassified, shortly after publication, contrary to military advice. It was then reclassified, on Ministerial direction. Copies of the declassified document can be found online at www.vilaweb.cat/media/attach/vwedts/docs/op_banner_analysis_released.pdf and wlstorage.net/file/uk-operation-banner-2006.pdf. Note that the version cited here does not show a security classification at the header and footer of each page. Sources used in the preparation of the present chapter are generally those used in the Operation Banner publication.

legacy' and have obvious genesis in the Irish War of Independence and Civil War. Firstly, the anti-Treaty IRA did not formally disband. Some of its members continued a form of armed struggle. They undertook some attacks on the Irish Army until 1948, and attacks in Northern Ireland and the British Mainland into the early 1960s. It was that body which first organised armed action against the security forces in Northern Ireland in 1969 and 1970.

The legacy was more than simply organisational. The IRA of the 1920s had a moderately sophisticated structure and internal systems, which were carried down through the decades. It developed its own training and induction manual, which was revised at least twice. Perhaps more importantly, the legacy was used as a source of inspiration and legitimacy for subsequent splinter organisations. The terminology and processes of the IRA of the 1920s were adopted to justify and legitimise new developments. For example, as PIRA reorganised from an insurgent to a terrorist organisation it named its front-line elements 'Active Service Units'. These can be recognised as self-contained terrorist cells, but the name was first used to describe undercover IRA groups in the 1920s. Similarly, in the 1920s IRA officers jailed by the British were required to resign their appointments, allowing the appointment of a replacement still at liberty. That process was retained right through the Troubles. Republicans did not consider the families of security forces to be legitimate targets and never attacked them directly, nor did they attack Territorial Army (i.e., volunteer reserve) units. Both behaviours originally sprang from the dynamics of the War of Independence.

Splinter organisations were (and still are) a significant aspect of Republican paramilitary activity. Almost as soon as the Treaty had been signed in 1921, the anti-Treaty IRA broke away. In February 1970 a radical, activist branch of the IRA broke away and became PIRA. After the Official IRA declared a ceasefire, disaffected members formed the Irish National Liberation Army (INLA) and its associated political wing, the Irish Revolutionary Socialist Party. Some years later, dissident INLA members formed the Irish Peoples Liberation Organisation (IPLO) and its political wing, the Republican Socialist Collective. IPLO moved a long way from Republican ideals; its main impact was an internecine feud against INLA. During this period PIRA remained the pre-eminent Republican paramilitary organisation. PIRA's response to IPLO's activities is described below.

The politics of the Republican movement were, clearly, republican but also largely left-wing. This developed into a dalliance with Marxism until the early 1970s. As late as the 1990s Republican political organisations were all broadly left-wing. With the move towards a political settlement in the 1990s, it can be suggested that Sinn Fein moved more towards the political centre ground in order to broaden its electoral appeal. Sinn Fein MPs elected to Westminster in 1919 refused to take their seats. To this day no Sinn Fein MP elected to Westminster (there have been up to five in various parliaments since 1982) has ever taken up his seat. To do so would strongly compromise their legitimacy in the eyes of their supporters.

A further peculiarly Irish dimension is afforded by the Catholic religion. The great majority of Republicans come from Catholic communities and are opposed to Unionists or Loyalists, who are largely Protestant. The outward demonstration of religious faith is not the key issue; few Republicans are notably devout. The key issue is that they cannot risk alienating the support of their almost universally (and often devout) Catholic popular support. This has had major consequences. For example, during the hunger strikes of 1980–1981 Catholic priests persuaded the families of several strikers that, since suicide is a sin in the eyes of the Catholic Church, they should insist on resuscitation once a striker had gone into a coma and was no longer capable of expressing his wishes. That made it impossible in practice for the strikers to actually kill themselves. The strike collapsed and its political impact was greatly reduced.

Republicanism was also identified with Irish nationalism, which was manifested in a fashion for the Irish Gaelic language. Few if any leading Republicans speak Gaelic fluently, and do not do so in major policy speeches. However, some have transliterated their given names (so, for example, John Stephenson became Seán Mac Stíofáin). A few words of Gaelic added into speeches has usually been well received, and a few Gaelic terms were in widespread use. Examples include 'Ard Fheis', which effectively means 'annual congress'. An Phoblacht (The Republic) was, and is, the name of the major Republican newspaper. 'Sinn Fein' literally means 'we ourselves'. This occasional use of Gaelic resonates well in the Irish Republic, where two of the main political parties for many decades were 'Fine Gael' ('Family ~' or 'Tribe of the Irish') and 'Fianna Fáil' ('The Republican Party').

Several incidents in Irish history were (and are) commemorated with public marches. They generally originated in loyalist commemoration of incidents such as the Siege of Londonderry (Derry, in Republican parlance, in 1689) or the Battle of the Boyne (1690). Republicans responded with marches to commemorate events such as the Easter Rising of 1916. In the early days of the Troubles they mere manipulated and exploited by both sides. Such issues are highly symbolic and stir up strong sentiment, as protests over restrictions to flying the Union flag over Belfast City Hall demonstrate. Scheduling and controlling marches became a routine part of governmental activity in Northern Ireland. Arguably, however, such events had little to do with the overall course and outcome of the campaign. Much the same can be said of the funerals of paramilitaries killed in the course of the Troubles.

The Republican legacy has also had generational consequences. Members of the Young Irish in the 1840s went on to form the IRB. At least one IRB man jailed for his part in the Phoenix Park murders of the 1880s went on to revive the organisation as an undercover movement in the 1900s. They recruited many of the members of the IRA of the 1920s, who were still active in the late 1960s. However, some of its leaders in the later 1960s were recruited by people whom the 1920s generation had recruited and trained for campaigns in the 1940s and early 1960s. Many prominent Republicans of the Troubles, such as Gerry Adams, have impeccable Republican ancestry.

The geography of the British Isles makes the Mainland an important target, not least for symbolic reasons. Terrorism conducted on a separate landmass from the main conflict is a notable (although not unique) characteristic of Republican terrorism. It is not restricted to the Troubles. The Chief of the British Imperial General Staff, Field Marshal Sir Henry Wilson, was assassinated by the IRA in London in 1922.

Similarities to Other Insurgencies

Several aspects of Republican insurgency have been seen in other uprisings. For example, although splinter organisations have been an aspect of Irish republicanism for some time, factionalism is by no means peculiar to Ireland. Palestinian resistance to Israel spawned Fatah, the PLO, PFLP, the al Aqsa Martyrs' Brigades and Hamas (amongst others – see Chapter 11). Several other insurgent movements have displayed factionalism. The plethora of Iraqi militias that sprang up after 2004 illustrate the point.

A related aspect is that of discipline. Discipline is a serious problem for an insurgent movement for several reasons, which are fundamental to their nature and not particular to any one conflict. Firstly, insurgent movements need to recruit widely and have limited selection and screening apparatus. That makes them wide open to infiltration by security forces. Their relatively loose structure provides all sorts of temptations for informants and opportunities for personal gain. One problem, therefore, is that of poor operational security. Another is that the movement may gain a bad name in the eyes of those it seeks to represent or protect. 'They're no better than gangsters' would be a stereotypical complaint. The use of bank robbery to gain funding is a particular risk in that regard.

The discipline issue manifests itself in three types of punitive activity. All were displayed in the Troubles. The first is internal discipline within an organisation. PIRA had its own counterintelligence group which was quite prepared to undertake beatings, torture and even execution. Not least, this may serve to discourage groups from breaking away. At one stage the counterintelligence group was itself infiltrated, in a devilishly effective security force operation. If the leadership cannot trust their own executioners, who can they trust?

The second kind of punitive activity is that of maintaining appropriate standards of behaviour in the civilian population. This may be the prevention of gossiping or collaboration, intimidating would-be informants or punishing betrayal. Some sanctions have been common, others idiosyncratic. Republican activists undertook tarring, feathering and beatings. In Northern Ireland kneecapping was a particularly widespread, gruesome and very largely Republican sanction. Between 1973 and 1976 alone there were 756 reported kneecappings. Of these 531 victims were Catholics and most of the perpetrators were Republicans. The major paramilitary organisations even developed a scale of charges, or tariff, in order to apply some form of equity of (rough) justice.

The third form of punitive activity was inter-factional violence. Where the parties were largely coequal this can be seen as feuding. However, where one party is clearly pre-eminent it can impose some form of discipline among smaller groups. In Northern Ireland, IPLO undertook a feud against INLA: indeed, its main aim seems to have been to destroy INLA. Its activities became so counterproductive to the Republican movement as a whole that PIRA effectively decapitated it and forced it to disband in 1992. There are many analogies with, for example, Palestinian or Iraqi paramilitary organisations. To put the issue of discipline into perspective, during the Troubles the security forces killed 121 Republican paramilitaries. Republican paramilitaries killed 162 Republican paramilitaries

Republicans share some form of insurgent ideology with many other insurgent organisations. They also show similarities in their choice of military tactics. The great majority have created irregular light infantry forces. Very few have acquired anything more than a rudimentary indirect fire capability: Hamas and Hezbollah are unusual in that regard. PIRA developed a very rudimentary mortar capability which it used primarily for attacks on police stations and barracks.

More typically, all have demonstrated the use of terrorism in addition to, and at times instead of, insurgent light infantry tactics. Terrorism typically manifests itself as bombings and shootings, with the emphasis on creating maximum damage at least cost to the attacker (although suicide attacks are a variant to the pattern). To an insurgent body which operates openly, such as the IRA of the 1920s or the early 1970s, terrorism is a useful and relatively low-cost adjunct. To a movement which cannot operate openly, such as PIRA after Operation Motorman, terrorism is a tactic of weakness and exposes the absence of other alternatives. PIRA, INLA and IPLO all operated under such circumstances.

Largely because of the need to retain operational security, PIRA attacks on security forces generally involved very few people. Urban shootings typically involved one shooter, one weapon, one or two couriers and a couple of lookouts or scouts: perhaps half a dozen people. The couriers (who took the weapon in and out covertly) were sometimes women, to reduce the risk of loss of the weapon to Army searches; hence the word 'people'. Even the largest rural operations rarely involved twenty people, with (at most) a dozen actually using weapons.

PIRA took advantage of the border between Northern Ireland and the Republic of Ireland for operational reasons. For much of the Troubles PIRA had about sixteen ASUs, of which ten were based, and operated from, south of the border. British security forces could not, and did not, operate south of the border: one SAS patrol was arrested and tried for firearms offences when it got lost and strayed over the border by mistake. Irish security forces did not necessarily support Republican paramilitaries and during the later stages of the campaign actively sought to defeat them. It was a fact, however, that PIRA could, and did, operate more freely south of the border than within Northern Ireland. Once again, there are similarities with (say) Palestinian insurgents, who have variously operated across every single one of Israel's borders. The Basque separatist movement ETA could for some years enjoy sanctuary across the border with France.

Although the details of the confessional divide in Northern Ireland are unique, religious differences are common in insurgencies. Care is needed to identify just what role religion plays. It is generally true to say that, in the first instance, theology plays no part. Catholics and Protestants do not hate each other, where they do, because of differences over the proper number of holy sacraments or the details of the Miracle of Transubstantiation. The key issue is that of identity, which differences of confession or religion highlight. Catholics and Protestants in Northern Ireland attend different churches. Church ritual is different, and the dress and form of address of clergy is different. Catholic women are far more likely to be called 'Mary' and wear crucifixes. All of these issues are recognisable differences of identity. Differences of identity underpin issues of politics. In a heterogeneous society much of politics is factional, so politics (the manner in which power is brokered in a society) tends to be dominated by differences of identity.

Differences of theology can *underpin* differences of identity, and hence politics. This is clearly the case in Northern Ireland. It obviously was in Iraq, where differences between Sunni and Shia (and to some extent Kurds) were in large part those of identity underpinned by confessional differences. It clearly also underpins the Palestinian struggle: Palestinians generally have little trouble with other Muslims per se; their main opponent is the Jewish state. Yet Jews, Christians and Muslims are all 'peoples of the Book'.

Having said that issues of theology play no part in the first instance, religious teaching can drive the extent to which religious aspects of identity drive public attitudes. Care is needed, however, in following that line of reasoning. Some Islamist extremists or ultraorthodox Jews can preach hatred and violence against Jews or Muslims per se. However, more moderate interpretation of core beliefs (as demonstrated by many adherents of both religions) tends to be far more tolerant. Differences are not typically based in the Scriptures, but rather in how certain parties interpret them. There may be even a degree of circularity, in which some groups chose a radical interpretation of the Scriptures to highlight differences of identity. The underlying reasons for differences in religious interpretation are, of necessity, human.

Much the same is true of confessional differences in Northern Ireland. As one example, as a newly-ordained priest Dr Ian Paisley effectively founded his own radical church in 1951. He went on to be one of the most staunchly Loyalist politicians (and eventually First Minister of Northern Ireland in 2007). At one stage he denounced the Pope as 'the Antichrist'. Thus although the details of confessional differences in the Troubles are particular to that conflict, the general pattern is similar. Difference of identity can be underpinned by differences of faith, but lead to major political (and economic and social) difficulties.

Republicans developed a possibly surprising sensitivity to civilian casualties. After the bombing of the La Mon restaurant in 1978, in which twelve civilians died and thirty were wounded, PIRA consciously avoided causing large numbers of civilian casualties. For example, all of the bombs in London in the bombing campaign of the 1990s were planned to create massive damage and considerable public attention but few casualties. When INLA bombed the Droppin Well, a pub frequented by off-duty soldiers in 1982, eleven soldiers and six civilians died and about thirty were injured. PIRA publicly distanced itself from the attack. The reason was simple. PIRA had learnt that large numbers of civilian casualties were counterproductive in terms of popular support.

Similarly, in 2005 Al-Qaeda bombed three hotels in Amman, Jordan. They killed sixty and wounded 115, mostly Muslims. Al-Qaeda then ordered its adherents to avoid causing large numbers of civilian casualties. Insurgents seem to learn that mass casualties amongst civilians are counterproductive. This observation demands a caveat, however. For some Islamic groups, Jews (hence Israeli citizens) are seen not as innocent civilians but as the enemy. Thus theology, and particularly perceptions of identity, plays some role.

Peculiarities of the Irish Case

Own-force deaths are another consideration. During the 1980s the British security forces ambushed PIRA ASUs on several occasions, killing Republican paramilitaries red-handed. Whenever that happened, PIRA would suspend activities for several weeks. It was partly an opportunity to investigate why the operation failed, and partly an opportunity to bolster morale after losses. In another example, of the 121 Republican paramilitaries killed by the British Army twelve, or 10 per cent, were killed in a single battalion's area in the few weeks immediately before Operation Motorman. PIRAs' general response to Motorman, after the first few hours, was to withdraw south of the Border. Nobody should suggest that PIRA was not brave. It does seem, however, that irregular paramilitary organisations have difficulty sustaining human loss without tangible gain. PIRA survived long enough to learn that lesson and develop measures to counter it; not least, through avoiding casualties. That became linked to PIRA security measures. From the early 1980s, whenever PIRA believed that an operation had been compromised it would be abandoned. It quite consciously learnt to live to fight another day.

At first sight this is contrary to experience in other conflicts. The phenomenon of suicide terrorists appears to contradict it. Reflection suggests that that is not the case. Firstly, suicide terrorists have clearly come to an understanding with their own beliefs and their commanders that their own death is worth the effect sought. Secondly, commanders have made some form of calculation concerning the supply of those prepared to undertake suicide attacks and the potential gains. Those calculations do not prejudice the survival of the insurgent force as a whole. One might sensibly ask why some suicide campaigns have stopped. Part of the reason will be a perception that the loss does not merit the likely gain. There were no suicide bombings in the Troubles, although a large number of terrorists (perhaps as many as a hundred) were killed by their own home-made bombs.

In 2005 the Republican Army Council ordered its forces to 'dump arms'. It used precisely the same terminology which its predecessors had in 1924. That did two things, and implied a third. Firstly, it gave the order legitimacy in the eyes of traditionalists. Secondly, as in 1924, it left open the possibility of a subsequent resort to arms. Thirdly, it highlighted the importance of a peace acceptable to all members. In 1924 the great majority of anti-Treaty IRA gave up the struggle. A few dissidents did not. In 2005 the great majority of PIRA gave up the struggle. Several other Republican organisations also did so at or about the same time. It is now clear that, firstly, a few did not; as in 1924. Secondly, it is clear that those few can recruit individuals for the next generation: as was the case after 1924. Once again, this can be seen at first sight as being particular to Ireland, but reflection shows a similar pattern elsewhere. In the United States some people really do act as if the South will rise again, 150 years after the Civil War.

Some aspects of Republican insurgency appear to be completely unique. They have no basis in either Irish or Republican circumstances and are not seen elsewhere. As one example, PIRA undertook continental campaigns between 1979 and 1990. Targets in Germany (belonging to the British Army of the Rhine) and Gibraltar (the site of a British garrison) were selected for attack. Eight servicemen were killed. The ASU sent to Germany was arrested. The team sent to Gibraltar was killed by the SAS. The European mainland was on, or beyond, the effective reach of PIRA. The continental campaigns can be seen simply as a sensible adaption to geographic circumstances. Unusually, Britain had a network of military bases overseas. PIRA believed that they would make easy and highly symbolic targets. That is, however, fairly unremarkable. Seeking easy and highly symbolic targets is what terrorists do, and by that stage PIRA was, effectively, a terrorist organisation. The only unusual issue was the peculiarities of geography. Arab terrorists have occasionally attacked Jewish or Israeli targets in London, for example. Palestinian terrorists attacked the Israeli team at the 1972 Olympic Games in Munich.

Some aspects of PIRA's tactical methods were highly unusual. Knee-cappings do not seem to have been particularly widely used outside Northern Ireland. Similarly, however, necklace murders are not common outside southern Africa. PIRA mortars, often based on ready-to hand hardware such as 40-gallon oil drums or 47 kilogramme Calor Gas bottles, were entirely unique to Northern Ireland. What is not unique, however, is the adoption of home-made explosives and material on hand to make improvised explosive devices. The Taliban do the same. Seen from a distance, the precise details are unimportant. They represent understandable adaption to local circumstances. Of themselves, they make little difference to the conduct or outcome of an insurgent campaign.

During the Troubles Republicans employed few if any of the typical tools of the insurgent's arsenal (such as repression, indiscriminate killing, mutilation, assassination, destruction of symbolic buildings, desecration of places of worship etc.). Neither did the security forces. Conversely Republicans conducted virtually none of the 'hearts and minds' measures (such as of social welfare programmes, economic aid, building schools, hospitals and roads, building new villages, deposing the (bad) government and bringing in a new one, setting up democratic government structures, holding elections, reforming and retraining the police and the judiciary system). Conversely the UK government (and its agencies) conducted almost all of them. Perhaps that is why the outcome was as it was.

It is perhaps worth considering why Republicans carried out so few of those measures during the Troubles. One might simply point out that they were not part of the Republican legacy of the 1920s, but that is to beg the question of 'why not?' It seems more accurate to say that Ireland, and particularly Northern Ireland during the Troubles, was a developed country with an educated population, functioning institutions and a well-developed media. During the Troubles that media included television: from the British perspective, the Troubles were the first truly televised conflict. It seems that an educated population, functioning institutions and a well-developed media (and the popular revulsion that would probably have resulted) largely prevented or inhibited Republican (but also security force) acts of repression. The lack of success of the Republican insurgency meant that they were never in a position to deliver 'hearts and minds' measures; which the government could, and did. To repeat: perhaps that is why the outcome was as it was.

The Troubles went on for a particularly long time. They constituted about thirty-seven years of continuous violence. That illustrates, however, little more than PIRA's ability and determination to persist as a terrorist organisation, together with the absence of political resolution for decades. Its length is not particularly remarkable: the Tamil Tigers were active for thirty-three years, in large part due to the inability of the Sri Lankan armed forces to defeat them for much of that time. In the case of Northern Ireland, the lack of political resolution is remarkable, but beyond the scope of this chapter.

Conclusion

In summary, some aspects of Republican activities appear to reflect peculiarly Irish and Republican issues. The Republican legacy from the 1920s included aspects of: military organisation and tactics;

nomenclature; political structure and orientation; continuity of person-nel between generations; factionalism; and disciplinary problems. The particular details of geography, including the national boundary known as the Irish border, the location of the British mainland and the contin-ental landmass of Europe, all shaped the conduct of the Troubles by Republican paramilitary organisations.

Many aspects can, however, be seen as the particular manifestation of problems which are typical of insurgent movements. Many insurgencies display factionalism. Discipline is a widespread problem. Access to sophisticated weapons is often difficult, so recourse to locally-produced weapons (which are almost inevitably unique to that conflict) is common. The particular details of confessional differences between Irish Catholics and Ulster Protestants are unique. However, many theological and liturgical differences exist world-wide. The general issue is that such differences can become symbols of identity and underpin political issues. In many societies there is a revulsion against civilian casualties, so the fact that PIRA learnt to avoid large-scale civilian casualties is not particularly unusual. Irregular paramilitary organisations may not be as resilient as regular armed forces, so a tendency to avoid unwonted casualties is not surprising. Adapting insurgent tactics to the geography of a conflict is scarcely surprising, either.

To conclude, insurgency occurs when a proportion of a disaffected community resorts to violence. That element will tend to display extreme social, political and cultural views. Within 'cultural' one might include 'religious', but theology (of itself) is rarely a primary factor in insurgency. The insurgents will, at least initially, have problems recruiting, arming, equipping, training, operating and commanding their forces. That is inevitable in an irregular force. The ways in which it does so will be strongly conditioned by the real circumstances pertaining at the time. Those circumstances will be geographical, political, social, economic and cultural. Irish Republican insurgency shows how one faction tackled those problems. Other organisations have done things differently, and will continue to do so. At that level of analysis, things are very much the same. Much of the reason lies in the realities of human behaviour.

11   The Evolution of the Palestinian Resistance

Carmit Valensi

> The idea of the resistance is a grand one, one which saw the
> development of its arms from the rock, to the knife, to the gun and
> ultimately to rockets. The development continues. The resistance will
> never stop. The resistance has developed and expanded just like means
> of transportation, and so have its plans and goals. Man first rode beasts
> of burden, then drove a cart pulled by these beasts, continued to
> develop and drove a car, and ultimately flew in an airplane. Does the
> use of the internet by the resistance movement indicate that it has
> changed? No. It only refines and expands its means.[1]

The insurgency of Palestinian movements in their current form
embodies both continuity and innovation. These organisations which
define their military operative methods as guerilla warfare were deeply
influenced by ideas which emanated from China, Cuba, Algeria and
most markedly Vietnam during the 1950s and 1960s. The Arab term
for the concept linking guerilla warfare with more general ideas is
muqawama. The literal and common translation of this concept is
'Resistance', which usually means a physical action against an enemy.
However, some argue that this does not reflect the full meaning of the
term and a more accurate translation would be 'the doctrine of constant
combat', or 'persistent warfare'.[2]

Although there is no direct connection between Islam and *muqawama*,
the concept of *muqawama* gained unprecedented influence in the Middle
East and was perceived as a type of modern reincarnation of the Islamic
term *jihad*. Hence, the organisations associated with the idea of
muqawama find no contradiction between these two concepts.

This chapter argues that the concept of 'Palestinian resistance' is more
dynamic, adaptive and accumulative than is often assumed. It should

---

[1] Al-Zahar, Mahmud, co-founder of Hamas and a member of the Hamas leadership in
Gaza Strip: an interview on the 21st anniversary of Hamas (11 December 2008), *Palestine-
info*, available at http://tinyurl.com/jypaz46.

[2] Y. Ehud, 'The Muqawama Doctrine', The Washington Institute, available at www
.washingtoninstitute.org/policy-analysis/view/the-muqawama-doctrine.

therefore be viewed in a more comprehensive and multi-dimensional manner transcending the conventional focus on military aspects. Indeed, the Palestinian common strategic goal of self-determination and sovereignty over Palestine has in part manifested itself in a general Palestinian 'national style' of resistance. In its early years, the military aspect was the prime means to achieve this goal and included various tactics. Over time, however, it became clearer that the Palestinians have relied mostly on a 'random', yet selective instrumentarium of tools, maintaining their over-arching strategic goal as well as some basic military patterns of resistance. The Palestinians adopted a more pragmatic approach that resulted in the implementation of various modes of operation parallel to military means. This evolution challenges the notion of a single and unified Palestinian 'national style'. Moreover, the fact that the Palestinians have historically learned from foreign insurgent groups – thus making them similar to other insurgencies around the world – strengthens the argument that a general 'tool kit' for insurgents exists, rather than a separate and divergent 'national style'.

The Concept of Resistance

The term 'resistance' goes back to the Second World War when it was used to refer to the underground movements throughout occupied Europe (particularly in France). The term was adopted a few years later by national liberation movements fighting colonial forces in the Third World. This historical legacy lends positive associations to the term and to those associated with it, granting a legitimate and even heroic image of freedom fighters struggling against occupying forces. The phenomenon gradually spread throughout the Middle East, with the National Liberation Front in Algeria having been the first to use the term, although the strongest associations with it are derived from its adoption by Palestinian groups and individuals since the mid-1950s.

The Palestinians reinforced the idea of resistance with practical interpretations, some of the elements of which are still pertinent today: devoted adherence to the armed struggle as a strategy and a way of life; preaching absolute sacrifice (martyrdom); demonstrating determination and persistence in the struggle; targeting Israel as the central focus of the struggle and defining the conflict with Israel as an all-out war where no compromise is possible; working towards gaining worldwide sympathy and support while overcoming the aversion resulting from any particular government's narrow political interests and the tendency to work towards a diplomatic compromise.

Palestinian nationalists as well as radical Muslims do not attempt to reach strategic parity, or aim at reaching a decisive victory over Israel, recognising their own inferior military power. While that may be so, they share with other guerrilla forces the conviction that they can offset the enemy's technological and military superiority through superior mental endurance and their willingness to make sacrifices. When considering the military elements of resistance, there is a significant common denominator between Palestinians and other nationalist military groups (e.g., Lebanese Hezbollah). This may be attributed to their proclivity to select generic patterns used also by other foreign nationalist insurgency groups.

Key military concepts that characterise the Palestinian way of war (however, not exclusively) include a constantly sustained attrition of the enemy, maintained by improving the endurance of their fighting forces and establishing a credible deterrence. These aims have been achieved as follows:[3]

Survival of guerrilla troops whilst maintaining a persistent attrition of the enemy is prolonged by the use of protective structures (bunkers and tunnels), camouflage and deception, deliberately locating military facilities in the midst of civilian buildings, adopting guerilla warfare techniques and inciting terror by targeting civilian populations. As a Hamas spokesman indicated:

Our defence plans are based on a matrix of trenches and tunnels dug underneath a broad area within the (former) security zone. The army will be surprised by fighters emerging from underground to meet it with the extraordinary equipment and weapons that were hidden there.[4]

In the 1990s and early 2000s, the Palestinian insurgency has aimed at inflicting high numbers of casualties amongst civilians and the armed forces by using suicide bombers and various improvised explosive devices (IEDs) or roadside bombs. The choice of using suicide bombers as a key element of asymmetrical warfare was facilitated by the high availability of volunteers and the high impact of this tactic on Israeli morale and media.

From 2001 Palestinian warfare has included the use of high-trajectory ballistic surface-to-surface missiles (SSMs) and surface-to-surface rocket launchers (SSRs), whose advantages are their technical simplicity, low

---

[3] I. Brun and C. Valensi, 'The Revolution in Military Affairs of the "Other Side"', in D. Adamsky and K. I. Bjerga (eds.), *Contemporary Military Innovations* (London & New York: Routledge, 2012), 185–7.

[4] Ubeida (spokesman for Hamas), 'Hamas Defense Plans in Case of a Possible Israeli Invasion', *Al Hayat* newspaper, 17 December 2007.

cost and ability to penetrate deep into enemy territory without triggering a significant response, thereby creating an effect of constant attrition and deterrence.[5]

Resistance Typology

'Palestinian Resistance' encompasses various possibilities and modes of operations. New operating techniques did not replace old ones, but were used alongside those already existing creating a large pool of options. Palestinian history shows that an adaptive and flexible approach, enabling sustained mediation between the grand vision and the changing reality, was required. This situation led to a wide range of means which included military, diplomatic, popular, internationalised and agitprop.

Starting in late 1950s, the Palestinian *military resistance* developed, with violent actions inspired by the fundamental goal of national liberation. *Diplomatic resistance* has been developed in parallel with negotiations and the attempt to reach political agreements with Israel.[6] A third type of struggle is *popular resistance*, the relatively unorganised involvement of the masses whether in violent (*Intifada* – 'uprising') or non-violent resistance (mass protests and demonstrations). An additional dimension of resistance activity is *internationalised resistance*, namely directing the struggle through external channels in the international arena. It is not based on direct or mediated contact with Israel, but is a unilateral approach, mainly interpreted as being confrontational, to international institutions (in particular the UN) as a platform for furthering political aspirations. Palestinian membership in international institutions and conventions enables pressing charges against Israeli military and diplomatic personnel and demands that they be held personally responsible for their actions[7]. The final means of struggle discussed here is *agitprop* (agitation and propaganda, a term originating with international Communism in the early twentieth century). Palestinian organisations use 'deligitimisation' extensively through the international media and through propaganda directed locally and internationally. They aim to challenge Israel's legitimacy, to isolate Israel in the international arena and to impinge upon Israel's defensive capacity by denouncing its attempts at self-defence. One of the key means of

---

[5] A senior commander on Hamas 'military council' (1 January 2009), *Al-Qassam*.

[6] It should be observed that an engagement in institutional or state politics does not imply an adoption of the diplomatic approach. Hamas, for example, has been an active political actor since 2006, but has yet to adopt diplomatic resistance vis-à-vis Israel.

[7] S. Brom and E. Oded, 'The September Process: The Bid for UN Recognition of a Palestinian State', *Strategic Assessment* (October 2011).

propaganda resistance is the strategy of a Boycott of Israel, appeals for the Divestment of the Israeli state and Sanctions against it, sometimes abbreviated as BDS. This approach is multifaceted, including the creation of an anti-Israel atmosphere through defamation and demonisation of Israel by taking concrete actions directed at groups, authorities and organisations throughout the world, concentrating on Israeli diplomatic, economic, academic and cultural targets.[8]

The growth of heterogeneous approaches to resistance has been derived from four main factors.

(1)   The Type and Characteristics of Actors Involved in Resistance

These include Violent Non-State Actors (VSNA)[9] like the Palestinian Liberation Organisation (PLO) from the 1960s and up to the early 1990s and the Palestinian Islamic Jihad (PIJ); Quasi-State Actors like Hamas or even sovereign states like Syria and Iran. Due to the differences between these parties there are varied interpretations of the concept of resistance. In the case of Hamas, the organisation's developing political identity has influenced its mode of operations. Its new status has imposed substantial limitations on its operations and has gradually made Hamas more cautious, restrained and vulnerable. In contrast, classic VNSA such as the PIJ are not expected to demonstrate the same extent of accountability and disciplined restraint as Hamas. The PIJ are uninhibited by the security considerations of the Palestinian Authority. Palestinian casualties and material damage suffered through Israel's responses to terror attacks are either not taken into consideration by the PIJ or may be considered collateral benefits. Hamas, on the other hand, operates as a political entity and a ruling authority, taking into account 'cost-benefit' equations.

(2)   The Historical Experience and Friction with the Opponent

The Palestinian insurgency has been influenced by friction with the Israeli Defence Forces on the battlefield, starting with early military operations in Jordan and Lebanon (battle of Karameh 1968; the South Lebanon conflicts from 1978 to 1982); continuing through the Palestinian *intifadas* (of 1987 and 2000) and in military operations in the West Bank and Gaza Strip (Operation Defensive Shield 2002 and Operation Cast

---

[8]   Reut Institute, 'The BDS Movement Promotes Delegitimization of the State of Israel', Available online at: reut-institute.org/en/Publication.aspx?PublicationId=3868.

[9]   K. Mulaj, *Violent Non State Actors in World Politics* (London: C. Hurst & Co., 2010), 3–6.

Lead 2009). A series of statements made by Palestinian leaders and combatants demonstrates the impact of these military campaigns on their learning process.[10] The latter has clearly been evolutionary, leading to the selective survival and development of the most effective warfare methods. Palestinian warfare has also been influenced by observing and learning from external military operations, including the Second Lebanon War.[11]

(3)   Geographical and Physical Features

The geophysical terrain in which the Palestinian organisations conduct their combative operations has greatly influenced their military mode of operations, and possibly has also impacted the adoption of alternate types of resistance. The Gaza Strip is relatively small and lacks logistic depth. It is also densely populated with extensive urban development being advantageous to defensive forces while making combat difficult for regular armed forces. The presence of the Israeli military in Gaza obviously impacted upon the Palestinian pattern of combat as this, together with Gaza geography, complicated the delivery of military support from Iran and Syria to the strip (in comparison, for example, with Lebanon). Due to its isolation, distance from external distribution points and the strict control by Israel (and to a lesser degree by Egypt) of the borders, Hamas had to develop facilities for homemade arms production alongside a supply network for smuggling weapons and ammunition, allowing it to maintain a military capability against Israel. With the Israeli withdrawal from Gaza in August 2005 the territory became marginally less complex with reduced Israeli surveillance of Palestinian activities.

In contrast to Gaza, the West Bank became a separate political entity under the control of the Palestinian Authority (PA) following the takeover of the Gaza strip by Hamas in June 2007. Nevertheless, it is still territory occupied by the IDF, which was able to reduce Hamas military activities in the West Bank significantly over recent years, particularly in the early years following the outbreak of the second *intifada* in 2000. This reduction is also due to the increasing control by the PA over other Palestinian resistance organisations and to the building of the Separation Barrier. The main avenues of resistance used by the PA today are diplomatic and internationalised resistance.

---

[10] See, for example, Abu Ubeida (spokesman for Hamas), 'Brigades Are Fully Prepared for War against Israel', *Palestine-info*, 5 January 2009; Hamas's senior commander in *Al-Qassam*, 1 February 2009, available at www.alqassam.ps/arabic/.
[11] Brun and Valensi, 'The Revolution in Military Affairs of the "Other Side"', 179–80.

(4)   New Technology

New technology has helped military resistance. As technological capabilities increase there may be a decreased incentive to utilise alternative non-violent means in the struggle. The main actors identified with the resistance assumed that they did not have the capability to reach strategic parity with Israel, and therefore developed the approach of asymmetric warfare, assuming that while one side is technologically superior, parity between the two sides can be attained in other areas, and that the scales may in fact be turned in favor of the technologically weaker side.

Palestinian resistance movements have made significant technological improvements to their means of combat. This was achieved in part independently, though they also received logistic support, funding, training and instruction from Syria and Iran. Iran has supplied Hamas and the PIJ with operative knowledge as well as vast amounts of weapons which were smuggled into Gaza. These weapons allowed the Palestinians to build explosive devices similar to those that Hezbollah employed in Lebanon. Operatives have also been smuggled out of the strip in order to undergo advanced military training in Iran, Syria and Lebanon.[12]

The Historical Development of Palestinian Resistance

Dividing Palestinian history into three main periods shows how the different types of resistance developed chronologically and were implemented as a result of the four factors mentioned above.

Even though it is customary to attribute the origin of Palestinian resistance to the 1950s, some scholars argue that the Palestinian resistance started long before with the beginning of Jewish settlement in Palestine and culminated in the Arab Revolt of 1930–1936.[13] This popular uprising constituted the continuation of an existing violent struggle dating back to 1919 that aimed to foil the Jewish plan for self-determination. The Arab Revolt in essence was a violent nationalist uprising by Palestinian Arabs against British colonial rule in Mandatory Palestine, and reflected both a demand for independence and opposition to Jewish mass immigration.

In spite of the different political landscape, the Arab Revolt exhibited similar patterns of resistance that are found in later forms of the

[12] S. Eldar, *Getting to Know Hamas* (Jerusalem: Keter, 2012), 259–62.
[13] See, for example, K, Stein, *The Intifadah and the 1936–1939 Uprising: A Comparison of the Palestinian Arab Communities*, Occasional Paper series (Atlanta: Carter Center of Emory University, 1990), vol. 1, no. 1; N. Caplan, *The Israel-Palestine Conflict: Contested Histories* (West Sussex: John Wiley & Sons, 2011).

Palestinian struggle. Among them is the deliberate aim to gain the support of international public opinion for recognition as an independent national entity, and to persuade the Palestinian-Arab community to join the struggle – directly or indirectly. A major difference, however, is that in spite of maintaining the same ideological vision, during the Arab Revolt the Palestinians lacked the institutional platforms that would have facilitated their goals as can be seen in later periods. For example, the Arab Higher Committee was only established a few days after the inception of the Arab Revolt, hence its leadership found it difficult to control the latter.

(1) From the Late 1950s to the Late 1980s The main actors operating in this period were the member organisations of the PLO (headed by Fatah and left-wing organisations) categorised as classic VNSAs. The concept of military resistance was central to the ideology of these Palestinian organisations. This approach was first developed in the founding documents of Fatah at the end of the 1950s. These writings expressed criticism for the Arab strategy in the conflict with Israel led by the Egyptian President Gamal Abdel Nasser. The founders of Fatah rejected the Arab strategy, which postulated that the regular Arab armies should first be united and prepared for combat before engaging in further military conflict with Israel. The PLO's leaders perceived such conventional warfare to be inappropriate due to the difference in capabilities between the two sides. The Palestinians understood that classical warfare aimed at a limited military victory, whilst they were interested in a complete liquidation of the Zionist society in the occupied land. For achieving this goal, the Palestinian covenant of 1968 stated that 'the Jews who had normally resided in Palestine until the beginning of the Zionist invasion[14] will be considered Palestinians', thus would be allowed to stay in Palestine if they were willing to live peacefully and loyally.[15] The question of how to reduce the number of non-Palestinian Jews often revolved around the idea of driving out or killing the Jewish inhabitants (terms used included 'putting an end', 'eradicating', 'throwing into the sea' etc.). Another, non-violent proposal was to send the Jews back to their countries of origin.[16]

---

[14] The covenant does not specify in which year the Zionist invasion began; however, later statements refer to the year of 1917.

[15] Y. Harkabi, *The Palestinian Covenant and Its Meaning* (Jerusalem: Merkaz ha-Hasbarah, 1977), 30–3.

[16] Ibid.

Finally, Fatah's leadership believed that guerrilla warfare would not provoke Israel into a full-scale war, yet they also hoped that whatever response Israel did make might force the Arab states into a war with Israel.[17]

During the 1970s and in particular after the October 1973 war, an additional type of struggle, diplomatic resistance, was adopted when armed combat did not achieve effective results. The Fatah leadership became aware that exclusive dependency on guerrilla warfare was not achieving its goals and that the armed struggle must be complemented by diplomatic means.[18] In June 1974 the Palestinian National Council officially adopted a program of 'gradual' liberation of Palestine known as the 'phases program', which maintained that there was no point in continuing solely in the armed struggle and that any territory offered to the Palestinians through diplomatic means would be accepted as a phase towards the liberation of Palestine. Through this decision the PLO gave up the principle by which they would not negotiate with Israel and in practical terms prepared the ground for a policy of compromise.[19]

An examination of these early phases demonstrates that the Palestinians had an evolving approach to their struggle. While this was derived in part from their historic experience and from their friction with reality's challenges and opportunities, the geographic environment was also significant. These included the often hostile attitudes of other countries from whose territory the Palestinian resistance fighters operated, limiting their freedom of operation.

The armed struggle, headed by Fatah, was moved from Jordan in the 1960s (due to the 1968 Karameh battle and the 'Black September' uprising of 1970) to terror bases in Lebanon during the 1970s and 1980s (Operation Litani in 1978 and the first Lebanon War in 1982). Their limited technological abilities and outside support (aid was mainly received from Syria, Iraq and Libya), as well as their hostile relations with other countries (mainly Jordan) made it difficult for the Palestinian organisations to achieve significant military gains. These factors all apparently contributed to the Palestinians' decision to broaden the canvas of their struggle by including a political front.

The comparison between the initial approach of armed struggle (as in the early 1960s) and that of the latter stages reveals several significant

[17] M. Steinberg, *Facing Their Fate* (Tel Aviv: Yediot Aharonot, 2008), 78–82.
[18] The decision was officially reached at the Fatah conference in October 1972 that guerrilla warfare would be one of the means used by the Liberation movements, but not the only one. See Abu Iyad, *Without a Homeland – Conversations with Eric Rollo* (Jerusalem: Mifras, 1979), 104–5.
[19] Steinberg, *Facing*, 186.

differences: while the armed struggle was originally perceived as a means to an end, namely the destruction of the Zionist state, it later became a means to attaining a further means – a means to including the PA in a diplomatic process which in turn would achieve the final goals. Thus, if Israel reached an agreement with the PA, the armed struggle would become unnecessary.

There is no doubt that the 'glory' of the armed struggle in its original exclusive version gradually diminished for the PLO leadership as they received widening international recognition and realised the limitations of guerrilla warfare. The diplomatic approach became the central strategy with military operations being subordinated to it. This era witnessed the first expansion of the resistance beyond the classical military means and the initiation of diplomatic resistance with the option of negotiations which were to accompany the PLO and the PA through the coming years.

(2)   From the Late 1980s until 2010 At the start of this period the Palestinians were led by Fatah, which operated an integrated campaign combining diplomatic and military resistance. During the 1980s other actors entered the campaign such as the Palestinian Islamic Jihad and primarily Hamas, which would later compete with Fatah, first for leadership of the resistance program and then for the monopoly of representing the Palestinian people politically.

The PIJ movement, massively supported by Iran, had been initially established in Gaza under the leadership of Dr Fathi Shaqaqi, gaining numbers and influence throughout the 1980s. Members of the movement operated under a fervent commitment to a rigid ideological code. The movement was particularly popular amongst Palestinian youth, as it was inspired by the Islamic revolution in Iran. The PIJ wants to free all Palestine through *jihad* and to found an Islamic Palestinian state. It differs from Hamas (and from Hezbollah in Lebanon) in that it focuses solely on military activity with its 'al-Quds Brigades', without investing any resources in social or political activities. Halfway through the first decade of the twenty-first century the PIJ replaced Hamas as the most dominant terrorist group acting within Israel. Using suicide bombers they carried out a series of lethal attacks in Israel's main cities.

As an alternative to the PIJ and Fatah, Hamas was founded in 1987 as a liberation movement within the Palestinian national struggle. Alongside those movements who championed national liberation based on universal values such as the right to self-determination, Hamas preached Islam. Hamas openly declared Jihad against the Israeli occupation, relying on its own social infrastructure (*Da'wah*) to promote its religious ideological approach, alongside the violent struggle, as part of a wider trend of Islamic fundamentalism in the region.

The outbreak of the first *Intifada* in December 1987 heralded the advent of another kind of resistance: popular resistance. Consequently, more attention was gradually paid to 'internal' issues. The population in the occupied territories indicated that they had grown tired both of waiting for external political initiatives and of the limited military role which the PLO had designated to them in the past. The Palestinian street realised that the Israelis seemed incapable of controlling unarmed attacks by mobs that were only using slingshots, bottles and rocks.[20] According to Thomas Hammes, popular resistance requires a deeply discontented population alongside an organisation that could focus the anger of the discontented people. By the mid-1980s these factors were in place. Apart from coordinating the activities and providing general guidance, the local leadership was also dealing with 'military' aspects and instructed the people not to use weapons. The motive behind this decision was to avoid giving the Israelis an excuse to use lethal force and to maintain the so-called asymmetric image of unarmed Palestinians facing heavily armed Israeli troops.

This decision changed when Hamas took advantage of the *intifada* and emphasised the paramount importance of 'military resistance' by using more lethal methods, mainly based on guerrilla warfare. Although the PIJ had originated the idea of Palestinian suicide bombings, it was Hamas which first carried one out (April 1993). This 'new' method was used by the Palestinians following their growing frustration with the lack of progress attained by diplomacy and negotiations (the non-implementation of the decisions made at the Madrid conference of 1991). Hamas recognised the strategic importance of this type of attack:

The way of Jihad and resistance based mainly on suicide bombings is the only way to liberate Palestine ... Hamas will exact a high price from Israel by means of suicide bombings which caused in the past hundreds of casualties and injuries and led to a continuing sense of emergency.[21]

Alongside the military resistance used by Palestinian organisations the diplomatic activity of the PLO eventually became the organisation's primary modus operandi. This trend reached a climax in 1993 with the signing of the Oslo Accord, the 'Declaration of Principles' by Israel and the PLO. The signing of the agreement placed Hamas in danger of becoming obsolete with the imminent implementation of Palestinian autonomy and interim self-governing arrangements in the territories.

[20] T. X. Hammes, *The Sling and the Stone: On War in the 21st Century* (St. Paul, MN: Zenith Press, 2006), 91–3, 99.

[21] Muhamad Def (and other senior members of Hamas's military wing), interview, *Al-Jazeera TV*, 4 July 2006.

The armed struggle by Hamas became in part a means for the organisation to ensure its own continued existence in the face of attempts by the PA to limit its operations.

With the outbreak of the al-Aqsa *intifada* (September 2000) Fatah returned to the armed struggle, this time mainly through subsidiary organisations led by the 'Al-Aqsa Martyrs Brigades', which served as the military wing of Fatah carrying out terrorist attacks inside Israel. The brigades became the leading militant organisation in the West Bank.[22]

Some argue that by eliminating the new generation of leaders, who understood and guided the first *intifada* while implementing old and failed tactics under organised brigades, 'the PLO managed to destroy the Palestinian's hard-won image as a peaceful people resisting a brutal occupying force'.[23] In addition, arguably, the PLO gave the Israeli forces an organised, armed and partly uniformed enemy who could play to their strength.

Despite the Palestinian movements' openness to additional types of resistance there was no absolute transition from one type to another. Rather, the movements utilised a broad selection of tools from which the most suitable means could be chosen at any particular time. The military capabilities of Hamas developed with time. The second half of the first decade of the twenty-first century marks the changeover of the military wing of Hamas in Gaza from terrorist units into an organised body with a well-defined military doctrine. The concentration of Hamas's activities within the Gaza strip influenced its warfare. The fact that the Gaza strip, unlike the West Bank, was completely surrounded by security fences built by Israel led to a marked decrease in the number of suicide bombings. The solution, from the perspective of Hamas, was to find a different weapon which would enable them to continue the resistance in spite of the Israeli presence. Thus, alongside shooting attacks, explosive devices and suicide bombings Hamas adopted the use of a new type of weapon – the Qassam rocket. As one senior member of Hamas's military wing explained, 'when all of the advanced means [of Israel] could not prevent the falling of these primitive rockets inside Israeli territory, the firing of Qassam missiles from within the Gaza strip became a historic turning point in the struggle'.[24]

---

[22] During the *intifada* and after it Fatah was dissolved into independent organisations like the popular resistance front in Gaza and the Abu Rish Fatah group active in Rafiah. Some of these act on instructions from the Fatah leadership; some are independent, and others get funding and instructions from Hezbollah.

[23] Hammes, *The Sling*, 116.   [24] Abu Ubeida, interview, *Al-Jazeera TV*, 4 July 2006.

In addition, a new tactic was developed alongside the rockets system, with tunnels previously used as smuggling routes for armaments and combatants now being booby trapped with explosives to prevent the Israeli Defence Forces from penetrating into them.[25]

During the following years, closer connections between the 'external' leadership (then in Syria) and Iran brought about the situation whereby the military wing of Hamas in the Gaza Strip began to receive funding and professional direction from Iranian intelligence organisations. The Hamas military wing was further strengthened after confirmation in August 2005 that Israel would withdraw from the Gaza strip. It was understood that the completion of this process would result in a power struggle within the strip.

The friction-based evolution of Hamas's military resistance in this period has been described in a fascinating way by one of the movement's leaders, Mousa Abu Marzuq:

Hamas continues its resistance in different ways, after the withdrawal of the Israeli troops from Gaza, and the lack of direct contact between the Israelis and the resistance forces. New techniques and inventions have been put to use – like the rockets. I mean that there was a stage of car bombs, after which came the phase of suicide bombings, and now we have a new phase that is no less important, even if it causes fewer casualties. In addition, its sociological impact on society and the consequences on sovereignty are more significant than the suicide bombings ... the missiles are an expression of our determination to end the occupation and to win liberation. Everyone is involved in the production of al-Qassam missiles, which are produced in kitchens, as only in this way can we resist the occupation.[26]

Institutionalisation of organisations often impacts on the ways in which they use their powers. Following their significant achievements in the Palestinian parliamentary elections in January 2006, Hamas made an abrupt change in status from being an armed opposition group outside of the 'existing order' into being a governmental political party. This required a conceptual shift from a narrow sectarian approach to a national-political approach. The new role of Hamas as a political actor contradicts their traditional role as 'keepers of the resistance flame', and they have consistently had to make adjustments in order to bridge the gap between their military commitment and their political one.

[25] G. Aviad, '"Hamas" Military Wing in the Gaza Strip: Development, Patterns of Activity, and Forecast', *Military and Strategic Affairs*, 1/1 (2009), 6–8.
[26] Abu Marzook, Mousa, 'Interview on Hamas', *Islamonline*, available at www.onislam.net/english/politics/asia/424701.html.

Unlike Fatah, Hamas never abandoned military resistance in favor of diplomatic means. They claim that their involvement in politics will bring about the overall liberation of Palestine and the return of the Palestinian people to their country. Their political involvement would support the resistance and *intifada*, which the Palestinian people have adopted as a strategic plan for ending the occupation.[27] In spite of its political responsibilities, Hamas has continued to arm itself in preparation for the next conflict with Israel.

The Lebanese Hezbollah's modus operandi was a role model for Hamas. After Hamas took over the Gaza Strip in June 2007, they were able to make use of operational knowledge gained by Hezbollah as a result of the war in Lebanon. Such knowledge included the technical skills needed to install explosive devices similar to those used in the Second Lebanon War. Iranian support continued in the form of weapons and expertise smuggled into the Gaza Strip, including rockets with a range of 20–40 kilometres, as well as anti-tank missiles. Hamas's military capacity was applied against the Israelis in what the Israelis called Operation Cast Lead, which began in late December of 2008 and ended in early January of 2009.

The defensive concept for the Gaza Strip was based on inflicting large numbers of casualties on the IDF, through minimising friction in open areas and conducting urban warfare in densely populated areas. Within these areas, the IDF would encounter landmines, snipers, anti-tank missiles, explosive devices and suicide bombers. Hamas made its disappearance techniques more sophisticated when it made extensive use of tunnels and hid its fighters within the civilian population. At the same time, Hamas attempted to wear down Israel's home front, by continually launching rockets even during the IDF military operations. Hamas also made extensive use of the media, in order to undermine the legitimacy of Israel's operation. Based on the Second Lebanon War, Hamas estimated that continuous firing would undermine Israel's sense of military achievement and lead to frustration and the perception that the IDF had failed in its mission.[28]

(3) From 2010 until 2014 While propaganda had always played a significant part in the Palestinian struggle, this period was characterised by a noticeably more intensive application of agitprop. Since Operation Cast Lead, ever increasing efforts have been made by (Palestinian and foreign) NGOs to

---

[27] A, Regular, 'Hamas's Zahar: More Kidnappings if Israel Doesn't Release Prisoners', *Ha'aretz*, also available at www.haaretz.com/print-edition/news/hamas-zahar-more-kidnappings-if-israel-doesn-t-release-prisoners-1.172536.
[28] Brun and Valensi, 'The Revolution in Military Affairs of the "Other Side"', 199–200.

promote boycotts, sanctions and divestment of Israel. The intention is to isolate and delegitimise Israel. Amongst these organisations is the Boycott-Divestment-Sanctions movement, whose goal is to put pressure on individuals to promote cultural and economic boycotts of Israel, on organisations and institutions to stop investing in Israel and on governments to encourage sanctions. The battle to delegitimise Israel reached a new peak after the sailing of the 'Gaza Freedom Flotilla' of May 2010 and the ensuing flotillas throughout 2010 and 2011.[29]

Other VNSAs which became active in Gaza, particularly after 2010, are Salafist Jihadist groups, which are identified with the ideology of Al-Qaeda. These organisations aspire to liberate Palestine and to establish a state based on *Shari'a* law. These organisations prospered under Hamas rule in the context of the Islamification of the Gaza strip since Hamas took power in June 2007. They view Hamas policy as being too restrained and have to some extent filled in the void which, from their perspective, had emerged in the military resistance. After Egyptian President Mubarak's fall in January 2011 it became easier for these groups to move through the Sinai Peninsula and cross the border from Egypt into Gaza.

The most prominent Salafist group has been 'The Mujahidin Council in the Environs of Jerusalem', which became known after it claimed responsibility for an attack on Israeli targets on the Sinai border in June 2012. It appears that the group's primary modus operandi is cross-border raids. In contrast to Hamas or PIJ the Mujahidin Shura's prime focus is less on military achievements against Israel. The organisation is more interested in spreading their ideology in the Palestinian arena and in recruiting volunteers for the global jihad.

A more marginal group – Ansar al-Jihad and Al-Qaeda in the Sinai Peninsula – announced its formation in 2011 and pledged to 'fulfill the oath' of Osama bin Laden and Al-Qaeda. The group claimed responsibility for several attacks on the Egypt-Israel natural-gas pipeline that crosses the Sinai Peninsula.[30]

Movements affiliated with global *jihad* within the Palestinian territories reject the idea of resistance identifying it as an invalid tool under *shari'a* law. The reason for this is that resistance not only limits the true struggle of Islam against occupying forces but also involves gaining legitimacy from the international community and giving this precedence over

---

[29] Reut Institute, 'The BDS Movement Promotes Delegitimization of the State of Israel', 1–3.

[30] E. Ya'ari, 'Sinai: A New Front', The Washington Institute for Near East Policy, no. 9 (2012), 4.

legitimacy given by God. They therefore prefer the Islamic term *jihad*. As a VNSA their military activities are still broad, placing little or no importance on political or social considerations. Global *jihad* organisations share some characteristics of anarchists, amongst these being their distaste for anything connected with state-like characteristics or other processes of institutionalisation which in their eyes diverts attention and resources from the armed struggle.

The 'Palestinian Resistance' and the 'Arab Spring'

At the time of writing, the 'Arab Spring' that started in late 2010 may not yet have fully affected the Palestinian arena. Still, it has influenced the organisations operating within it, with the popular protests having stressed the importance of public opinion.

The recent upheavals have renewed the relevance of non-violent popular resistance. Such popular protest stands in contrast to the armed struggle of the two *intifadas*. The youth in Arab societies realised that they have the power to change their reality and can organise themselves through social networks and gain political achievements through nonviolent mass protests. In this context, Hamas leader and chairman of Hamas Political Bureau Khaled Meshaal's statement in November 2011 that popular protest has the 'power of a tsunami' is particularly noteworthy: 'We and Fatah currently have a shared basis which can be worked upon, with this being popular protest, which expresses the power of the people'.[31]

As a quasi-state actor Hamas recognises the importance of public opinion and the need to be accountable to the population it represents. Hamas therefore operates a policy of military restraint in Gaza, which tries to maneuver between the Jihadist approach and the overall demands and constraints under which they operate. This creates an atmosphere conducive to pragmatic policies, including an attempt to avoid irreparable damage to the infrastructure of the Gaza strip and to the population there as a result of military response by Israel.

Hamas is also attempting to co-ordinate other military organisations operating within Gaza. While Hamas itself has refrained from firing missiles into Israel, it allowed other organisations to continue doing so, including the PIJ, the Popular Resistance Front, Fatah's military wing and Salafist Jihadist groups identifying with Al-Qaeda. As part of its commitment to the armed struggle Hamas has attempted to promote its own 'low signature' attacks without taking responsibility. This includes

[31] 'Mishaal Abbas Meeting in Cairo', *Felesteen Alyoum*, available at paltoday.ps/ar/post/123687/.

carrying out terror attacks within Israel through the Sinai Peninsula. Hamas has also taken advantage of the relative quiet after military operations with Israel in order to rearm as quickly as possible.

Although Hamas invested much effort in calming the volatile dynamic, past experience revealed that it was only a matter of time until the next round of conflict. As the second part of Meshaal's statement that is mentioned above indicates, Hamas did not give up the armed struggle against Israel. 'For as long as our land is occupied we have the right to defend ourselves by any means, including military struggle'.[32]

Indeed, the restraint was violated in November 2012 with the beginning of an eight-day military operation in Gaza (Operation Pillar of Defence). This operation was preceded by a period of mutual Israeli-Palestinian responsive attacks. Two years later, another military operation was launched (Operation Protective Edge). With Hamas being in an increasingly complex position (regional isolation, political and financial crises) this military operation could pose an opportunity to restore its reputation as an effective resistance movement. In addition, Hamas was given the opportunity to project its strength into Israel as well as in the Palestinian arena. These two military operations demonstrated, once again, the lack of a total shift from armed resistance to complete institutionalisation.

In parallel, the leadership of the PA in general and of Fatah in particular (headed by Mahmoud Abbas, also known as Abu-Mazen) has not abandoned diplomatic activities as a primary means for realising Palestinian national aspirations. However, they continue to stress that military resistance still has a central position in their ideology and clarify that in the light of the stalled peace talks and political stagnation, there is a possibility that they would abandon the relative restraint that they have displayed in recent years and return to the armed struggle.[33]

Since 2011 the PA has operated a different type of resistance, focused mainly on the international arena, in order to realise the goal of establishing a Palestinian state. Disappointments and issues of contention over recent years have included the stalemate in the political process with Israel and internal political crisis have forced Mahmud Abbas to explore new options to retain the confidence of the Palestinians.

Thus, in contrast to the endeavours of diplomatic resistance based upon negotiations with Israel, this new resistance is based on direct approaches made to international organisations. In September 2011,

[32] Ibid.
[33] A. R. Arnaout, 'Fatah's Sixth General Conference in Bethlehem', *Al-Ayyam* newspaper, 4 August 2009, 21.

the Palestinians unilaterally approached the Security Council of the United Nations and requested that they accept Palestine as a full member of the organisation. After efforts to promote the vote in the Security Council failed, they switched to a second track – a vote in the UN General Assembly. In November 2012 it was determined that the general assembly of the UN would recognise Palestine within the 1967 borders as 'an observer state which does not have full membership of the UN'. It was also decided that negotiations should be renewed immediately between Israel and the Palestinians so as to realise the two-state solution.[34]

The political deadlock that continued to characterise the years 2012–2014 pushed the Palestinian leadership to concentrate efforts in the international arena in a manner that bypasses the direct diplomatic channel. A series of declarations, started in late 2014, by several European parliaments and governments regarding their recognition of a Palestinian state, strengthened the significance of the internationalised resistance.

Conclusion

Palestinian history shows that many different strata have been added through the years to the concept of resistance, making it a heterogeneous concept incorporating a wide variety of options and modes of operation. To a certain extent, a Palestinian 'national style' can be identified, however, only as a general notion of resistance that includes some basic patterns, rather than defined, permanent and deterministic modes of operation. The Palestinian actors associated with the ideas of resistance have had to adopt an adaptive and flexible approach which consistently negotiated between a well-defined ideological vision and a dynamic reality.

The term 'resistance' indicates a constantly existing entity, implemented intermittently through various means. As in Spinoza's metaphorical description of individual waves whose existence is dependent on the eternal ocean, so military actions, diplomatic efforts, popular protests and propaganda are all different 'waves' which exist in their entirety in the ocean of resistance. Resistance gives the broad context and the ideological justification to the variety of means available to the actor in the struggle. By nurturing these many varied meanings, resistance gains support from different sectors and is empowered in the struggle for hearts and minds.

---

[34] United Nations, Sixty-seventh General Assembly, available at www.un.org/News/Press/docs/2012/ga11317.doc.htm.

Over the years in the Palestinian struggle, there has been no complete transition from one type of resistance to the next. Instead, new tactics were developed in parallel to the continuation of older ones. Recent declarations do not indicate that Hamas will give up armed resistance altogether and adopt popular protest in its place. The dynamic between military and other types of resistance is not binary but multidimensional and changeable.

Changes in the strategic environment of the Palestinian arena, the experience with the Israeli opponent, the evolving military capabilities, the geophysical features and the various parties involved have all had a dramatic impact on the strategic and operational concept of *muqawama*. In addition, similar causes under the same national flag are defended by different factions with varying interpretations of *muqawama*. While some actors prefer to emphasise the military meaning, others allow themselves to cherry-pick the relevant means which serve them best in a specific context.

For those states dealing with the resistance these developments have created two complex challenges: firstly, on the military front, some resistance movements have adopted a modus operandi of a regular army while maintaining their capability to function as terror units and guerrilla forces.[35] This has created a complex pattern of warfare which conventional armies find difficult and confusing. Secondly the increase and diversification of means and the adoption of accepted political and diplomatic rules of engagement have, to a large extent, increased the legitimacy enjoyed by terrorist organisations in the eyes of the international community and global public opinion.

However, it is not only states which have been challenged by this diversification, with the resistance movements themselves also having had to face a variety of resultant drawbacks. In the Palestinian context, the PA's current diplomatic strategy played a significant role in the split which occurred between Hamas and the PA in 2007 and resulted in the creation of two mini-states (in Gaza Strip and the West Bank). This development has come at a considerable political cost for the Palestinians. Moreover, adding non-violent means of resistance raises the need to operate according to international norms and produces a certain trade-off between international legitimisation and the pursuit of military resistance. Finally, expanding the means of resistance has not always been the result of a deliberate choice but rather the result of

---

[35] Hoffman has termed this type of warfare as 'Hybrid Warfare'. F. Hoffman, *Conflict in the 21st Century: The Rise of Hybrid Wars* (Arlington, VA: Potomac Institute for Policy Studies, 2007).

some constraints. Hamas's lack of ability to gain significant military achievements against Israel has led them, at least partially, to switch arenas from a focus on the military to the political-propagandistic and governmental level.

Either way, leaders facing the challenges presented by the Palestinian resistance are well advised to develop a deeper understanding of the geo-strategic reality developing in the area and to redefine goals and methods of operation in order to cope with this unique challenge, rather than to attempt to apply general COIN recipes.

12   The Taliban

Rob Johnson

The Taliban, literally 'disciples', or better 'seekers' for the right path (Islam), is an atavistic, largely Pashtun insurgent movement in Afghanistan. The 'Taliban' is a collective term for a number of resistance organisations including the Taliban senior leadership, based mainly in Pakistan, and mid-ranking leaders and large groups with extensive networks across Afghanistan, through to the Taliban groups that exist at a local level with very small numbers. Separate network titles are accorded to the Haqqani-inspired groups, originating in Pakistan but with strong ties to eastern Afghanistan, and further distinctions are made from groups inspired or acting for Hezb-e Gulbuddin and its leader Hekmatyr. Overlaying these neat divisions are local Qawmi allegiances, and it is not uncommon to find certain clans fighting for different parties or even with the government in order to fulfil local or regional objectives, power politics or suppression activities against long-standing rival clans or leaders. Taliban has become the term used to describe resistance, of whatever hue, to the government and its international backers, a handy reference point for defining the 'enemy' in a protracted conflict, the Western phase of which began in 2001.[1] Tarak Barkawi and Keith Stanski have shown how war drives stereotyping to particular extremes, especially when it comes to interpretations of non-Western adversaries like the Afghans.[2] The Taliban are synonymous with indiscriminate violence, brutality and oppression, particularly against women and minorities. The temptation is to see all their 'essentialising' tendencies as

---

[1] Western operations against the Taliban began in 1998 with missiles strikes against alleged Al-Qaeda training camps. It is not clear when the Taliban first entered the consciousness of the Western media, but the term has entered the vocabulary of the British press to describe resistance to the diktats of central authority. See 'The "Turnip Taliban" Are Fighting to Save the Tory Party from David Cameron's Blairite Dictatorship', 2 February 2009, *The Daily Telegraph*.

[2] See also D. Welch and J. Fox (eds.), *Justifying War* (London: Routledge, 2012).

negative, but Orientalism was rarely so singular.[3] The misunderstanding over who constitutes the *real* Taliban, and what it is fighting for, is familiar in other studies of insurgencies. There is often confusion over who is doing the fighting and who is commanding, what the boundaries of its jurisdiction are and what its relationship with the people really is.

To 'know' the Taliban, a handful of journalists have attempted to embed briefly with fighters in Afghanistan, including the intrepid David Loyn of the BBC.[4] Other reporters have sought conduct face-to-face discussions in 'safe' locations, although it is not always clear whether the individuals they encountered are reliable, typical or even authentic.[5] Alex Strick van Linschoten and Felix Kuehn have worked in Kandahar and published the rants of Mullah Abdul Salem Zaeff, a 'former Taliban', and have made extensive enquiries about the origins of the organisation, concluding that it was not, as many assumed, a product of the civil war in the 1990s, but a movement that dates back to the anti-Soviet jihad of the 1980s.[6] Through commissioned interviews, Theo Farrell and Antonio Giustozzi, in an outstanding work, have made a thorough and highly original account of the adaptation of the insurgents of southern Afghanistan, which is far more comprehensive than anything that has gone before, except, perhaps, in classified material. Yet, they too acknowledge the difficulty of examining an on-going insurgency as 'immensely difficult for scholars'.[7]

It is not just the difficulty of clarifying who the enemy is, but also the Western struggle to defeat the Taliban insurgency since 2001, that has

---

[3] It was the exoticism of the east, more precisely the fact that it was so *unknown*, that was a source of both fear *and* fascination. The very mystery of the Taliban to Western audiences in recent years has replicated the mixed sentiments of previous eras, a point made forcefully by Hugh Gusterson and Patrick Porter. H. Gusterson, 'Can the Insurgent Speak?', in T. Barkawi and K. Stanski (eds.), *Orientalism at War* (London: Hurst & Co., 2012), 84; Porter, *Military Orientalism* (London and New York: Hurst & Co., 2009).

[4] David Loyn travelled alongside the fighters in Helmand in 2006. He documents some of his experience in *Butcher and Bolt* (London: Hutchinson, 2008). See also Refsdal, 'Living with the Taliban on the Afghan Frontline', *Channel 4 News*, 4 August 2010; N. Rosen 'How We Lost the War We Won: Rolling Stone's 2008 Journey into Taliban-Controlled Afghanistan', *Rolling Stone*, 31 January 2011.

[5] S. Yousafzai and R. Moreau, 'The Taliban in Their Own Words', *Newsweek*, 5 October 2009.

[6] S. Zaeff, *My Life with the Taliban*, ed. and trans. Van Linschoten and Kuehn (London: Hurst & Co., 2011); Van Linschoten and Kuehn, *An Enemy We Created* (London: Hurst & Co., 2012); Van Linschoten and Kuehn (eds.), *Poetry of the Taliban* (London: Hurst & Co., 2012). For detail on the origins see Alex Strick van Linschoten, 'Mullah Wars: The Afghan Taliban between Village and State, 1979–2001', unpublished doctoral thesis, King's College London, May 2016.

[7] T. Farrell and A. Giustozzi, 'The Taliban at War: Inside the Helmand Insurgency, 2004–2012', *International Affairs* (2013).

an impact on the portrayal of the movement in the West. Protracted operations in mountainous, densely vegetated or populated terrain have compelled the Western-led Coalition armed forces to investigate the historical socio-cultural aspects of their adversaries, and to look deeply into the British and Soviet historical experience of fighting the Afghans to see if there was a 'national style' and where, in fact, the opportunities lie for driving a wedge between the people and insurgents. However attractive it might be to try to 'isolate the insurgent from the people', or to use templates from a military manual, the familiar problem here is applying historical models to entirely new situations in the present or to assume that all insurgencies follow a standard pattern.[8]

It is hard to define and understand an enemy that one cannot encounter, know or even see. This is a common problem for all security forces on the modern 'empty battlefield'.[9] The guerrilla fighter, unable to confront the stronger conventional or state power militarily with any hope of success, strikes at night, through ambushes, raiding and assassination. The Soviets referred to the Afghan fighters as 'ghosts',[10] while the British of the nineteenth century complained that the Afghans preferred to raid lines of communications and attack isolated detachments, but they tended to melt back into the civilian population the moment they were overmatched by colonial forces, to 'play the part of a peaceful peasant'.[11] One American journalist noted recently: 'the Taliban watch the Marines' habits carefully, including how small units react in the first instants of a firefight' before emplacing mines or initiating ambushes.[12] Guerrilla operations in Afghanistan through history appear to fit the classic model. The Afghans seem to have a mastery of war by a 'thousand cuts', using ambushes amidst broken terrain, trading space for time, and severing lines of logistics, while adding costs and sapping the strategic patience of occupiers and central government. The Afghans have often tried to cut off the supplies of their enemies, gradually strengthening a ring of steel around urban areas, denying access along important routes and conducting passive resistance in rural areas.

---

[8] D. Galula, *Counterinsurgency Warfare: Theory and Practice*, reprint (Westport, CT and London: Praeger, 2006), 52.

[9] M. Boot, *Invisible Armies: An Epic History of Guerrilla Warfare from Ancient Times to the Present* (New York: Liveright Publishing, 2013); R. Holmes, *Firing Line* (London: Penguin, 1985).

[10] A. Borovik, *The Hidden War: A Russian Journalist's Account of the Soviet War in Afghanistan* (New York: Hippocrene Books, 1990); G. Bobrov, *Soldatskaya Saga* (Moscow, 2007), 202–3.

[11] H. Hensman, *The Afghan War of 1879–80*, reprint (New Delhi: Lancer, 2008), 321.

[12] C. J. Chivers, 'In the Taliban, U.S. Marines Find Evolving Foes', *New York Times*, 2 February 2010, 1.

Nevertheless, such broad generalisations are not enough to identify a distinctive 'national style'. What matters here is to understand that the geographical setting and the disparity of resources are the features that have sometimes determined what appears to be a 'national' preference for guerrilla war. Nonetheless, a unique historical setting also shapes the response of the Afghan insurgents. For example, the difficulty of forming a strong central authority, because of the weaknesses in systems of national organisation and absence of resources, meant that regional or local politics, small-scale organisation, and local security predominated. There were few full time military forces until the nineteenth century and even then the national army was dependent on the continued flow of foreign aid. Local and ad hoc forces were more common. Even in the early 1900s, when the state was relatively secure, the numbers of irregular armed groups dwarfed the regular army. Yet, these groups were kept in small formations to prevent them becoming a threat to the state: 'Lashkars' (war parties) rarely reached two thousand and might be typically no more than two hundred. These local forces knew their own lands and were motivated strongly to fight for them. If defeated, they might make use of the local mountains or desert, to 'spread themselves broadcast across the country', and blend back into rural life.[13]

It is often asserted that the Afghan is a religious warrior and that ideology has characterised the national style throughout history, including that of the Taliban. The opposition to the Afghan government and its Soviet military support in the 1980s was described frequently as a struggle for liberation from foreign ideologues in defence of Islam. The resistance believed their interests were not so narrowly defined: they were defending the people and the very fabric of their life in an existential people's war. One fighter remarked to a journalist: 'Why do you differentiate between fighters and old men, women and children? If you have courage and treasure freedom, you are mujahed. We are all mujahedeen'.[14] Within Afghan resistance ideology, myths and symbols have played a powerful role of mobilisation. Protection of the faith, of the people and of the weak, are themes endlessly recycled. Paradigmatic moments in Afghan history, and sometimes in family history, are magnified and reworked to glorify particular characteristics or prowess. Ustad Rafeh, a professor of Pashtun history at Kabul University, stated:

Then you British came, 150 years ago. You had 60,000 troops and the best artillery, but it was *Pashtuns* who surrounded Kabul and killed 17,000 [*sic*] of you

[13] Hensman, *The Afghan War of 1879–80*, 213.
[14] Cited in E. Giradet, *Afghanistan: The Soviet War* (London: Croom Helm, 1985), 163–4.

as you tried to escape. The rulers of your empire thought this was an accident: they couldn't accept such a defeat, so they attacked again, in 1880. We killed 12,000 [*sic*] of you that time, at Maiwand. The same with the Soviets in 1979: most of their original army was destroyed [*sic*]. What makes you think it will be any different for America this time?'[15]

Popular Support

In 2008, one village elder in the south expressed anger with foreign forces, a typical reaction which characterised both official 'Taliban' complaints and that of many Afghan civilians. He announced: 'Foreign forces always employ bullying tactics. They humiliate elders in front of their relatives; put a bag on their heads and body-search their female family members. It obviously benefits the Taliban [who] have photographs of such incidents and now send them via mobile to each and every one'. Those who joined the Taliban often cited the same motivations: foreign occupation, and overbearing or corrupt security forces. The complaint by one Western diplomat that 'this is a country where during the day they speak like great friends and at night they become the Taliban movement' hints at the uncomfortable fact that the civil population often sympathised with or actually constituted the 'Taliban'.[16] In 2006 British troops in Helmand found that the Taliban were usually local men, sometimes augmented by a stream of volunteers from Pakistan.[17] Nevertheless allegiances were often determined by local situations. Many Ishaqzai families in Sangin district in Helmand regarded the British as the enforcers for a sustained campaign of dispossession.[18] To the Ishaqzai, the British were supporters of their arch rivals, clans who had styled themselves as the local police or ingratiated themselves with the new Karzai government for their own personal gain. The British found themselves drawn into an inter-clan conflict, with the people engaged in denunciations or flocking to sources of power for protection: a textbook example of Stathis Kalyvas's theory on the logic of violence in civil war.[19]

[15] J. Ferguson, 'Taliban: Greatest Guerrilla Insurgency?', *Channel 4 News*, 16 August 2010, cited in R. Johnson, *The Afghan Way of War* (London and New York: Hurst & Co., 2011), 289.

[16] F. Stockman, 'Anthropologists War Death Reverberates', *Boston Globe*, 12 February 2009, cited in Gusterson, 'Can the Insurgent Speak?', 89.

[17] M. Martin, *An Intimate War* (London: Hurst, 2014).

[18] F. Ledwidge, *Losing Small Wars: British Military Failure in Iraq and Afghanistan* (New Haven: Yale, 2011), 81.

[19] S. Kalyvas, *The Logic of Violence in Civil War* (New York: Cambridge University Press, 2006).

The degree to which the Taliban were local and developed as a response to unrest and were angry at the Afghan government extending into their communities and the violence of foreign intervention also helps to resolve the 'origins' debate. Ahmed Rashid locates the origins of the Taliban to Kandahar in 1994 – a spontaneous response to abuse of the population by *mujahidin* commanders and their militias during the civil war.[20] Alex Strick van Linschoten and Felix Kuehn argue that the Taliban movement had been operating as *mujahidin* in the 1980s against the Soviets, and they cite the testimony of Abdul Salam Zaeef as evidence.[21] The claims about the beginning of the Taliban have to be treated with caution, and so do assertions about the absence of a merger with more radical ideologies.[22] The younger neo-Taliban emulate the old *mujahidin* but they also reject moderate voices, seeing themselves as more pure fighters engaged in a divine mission. Zaeef represents an older generation of 'Taliban sitting at home'.[23] It is clear that local resistance surged when the International Security and Assistance Force (ISAF) increased its strength in southern Afghanistan, and this gave the Taliban, which was attempting to reconstitute itself after its bloody defeat in 2001, the impetus to recruit and organise at the local level across the south. Tom Coghlan referred to this as the 'coalition of the angry'.[24] Mohammed, a Talib, explained how the situation was transformed:

[In 2004] The Afghan Taliban were weak and disorganised. But slowly the situation began to change. American operations that harassed villagers, bombings that killed civilians and Karzai's corrupt police and officials were alienating villagers and turning them in our favour. Soon we didn't have to hide so much on our raids. We came openly. When they saw us, villagers started preparing green tea and food for us. The tables were turning. Karzai's police and officials mostly hid in their district compounds like prisoners.[25]

In Afghanistan, there are some enduring elements that shape the character of each conflict. The terrain militates against occupiers and centralising rulers. One Soviet officer noted: 'The country is extremely well adapted to a *passive* resistance. Its mountainous nature and the

---

[20] A. Rashid, *Taliban: The Story of the Afghan Warlords* (London: Pan, 2001).
[21] A. S. Zaeef, *My Life with the Taliban*, ed. and trans. A. Strick Van Linschoten and F. Kuehn (London: Hurst & Co., 2010).
[22] Linschoten and Kuehn, *An Enemy We Created: The Myth of the Taliban/Al Qaeda Merger in Afghanistan, 1970–2010* (London: Hurst & Co., 2012).
[23] Farrell and Giustozzi, 'The Taliban at War', 10.
[24] T. Coghlan, 'The Taliban in Helmand: An Oral History', in Antonio Giustozzi (ed.), *Decoding the New Taliban* (London: Hurst & Co., 2009), 119–53. D. Kilcullen famously called it the 'Accidental Guerrilla'.
[25] Yousafzai and Moreau, 'The Taliban in Their Own Words', 11.

proud and freedom-loving character of its people, combined with the lack of adequate roads, makes it very difficult to conquer and even harder to hold'.[26] The weaknesses of infrastructure means that resources have to be brought in, which, in turn creates an opportunity for raiding by impoverished irregular fighters.

The Taliban have been prevented from establishing a national revolutionary movement by the fissures of Afghanistan's social structure. Thirty years of civil war has left deep divisions, despite the unifying rhetoric of Islam. One Pakistani Intelligence officer, reflecting on the attempts to unify all resistance groups against the Soviet occupation in the 1980s, cautioned: 'There was no discernible pattern to their activities; they fought when they saw an opportunity or they needed loot, and when the time suited them'.[27]

Popular perception is an important, perennial issue in Afghanistan, and, indeed, in all insurgencies. Regardless of how professionally the ISAF forces behaved towards Afghans, they remained *'Kufr'* and foreign. For rural populations, so long immune from the developments even in nearby cities, all outsiders can threaten power relationships, land holdings and profits; furthermore, they can potentially damage family honour, faith and status. Therefore it matters less what benefits the West has brought to Afghanistan than what many Afghans believe about foreigners. Some Taliban fighters referred to the Americans as 'monkeys', 'bastards', 'pigs' and 'kids'.[28] Mahmud Khan, an insurgent leader, told one journalist: 'We gained our freedom from Britain 160 years ago, and should remain free. We don't accept their claim that they are here to rebuild our country. They have done nothing for us'.[29] These sentiments have a wide appeal.

What Are Taliban Characteristics?

Journalists, pressured by the time limitations of their profession, have been apt to reach for simple devices to explain the fighting style of the Taliban. When added to the desire to demonise an adversary, a prevalent and common sentiment in wartime, then the stereotypes became even more pronounced. Concealment for survival becomes 'deception'; the hit and run attack is deemed to be 'treacherous', even 'cowardly'. Hugh

[26] General A. Snesarev, *Afganistan* (Moscow, 2002), 199.

[27] M. Yousaf and M. Adkin, *Afghanistan: The Bear Trap* (London: Leo Cooper, 1992), 43.

[28] E. Rubin, 'Battle Company Is Out There', *New York Times Magazine*, 24 February 2008, Also available at www.nytimes.com/2008/02/24/magazine/24afghanistan-t.html ?pagewanted=all&_r=0.

[29] Cited in D. Loyn, *Butcher and Bolt* (London: Hutchinson, 2008), 295.

Gusterson draws attention to the media device of wild animal analogies, the Taliban labelled as those occupying dens, lairs and sanctuaries.[30] He contends that Taliban violence is not contextualised but portrayed as indiscriminate and frequently aimed directly at the killing of civilians.[31] They are defined by the most violent episodes of their fighting, such that all Taliban are seen as eager to behead their captives. Typically for insurgents throughout time and space, the media siding with the embattled state do not regard them as a political movement, but a criminal one.[32]

The difficulty with this analysis is not that the Taliban are misrepresented, but that the Western interpretation portrays them as though they were monolithic. Professional military officers do not share the views of many journalists, and, in fact, they often despise the simplistic tropes of the media world. The lower the tactical level of analysis, the more accurate and sophisticated is the military assessment. The level of detail achieved by British and American forces by 2013, for example, would be the envy of many anthropologists and is the product of over a decade of sustained 'human terrain' investigation. Their long-term proximity to Afghans, detailed assessments of the Taliban and their modus operandi, and interviews with prisoners reveal a more sophisticated perspective – one that the Afghan insurgents themselves could recognise.[33] ISAF attributed the strengths of the Taliban to their freedom of movement and skills of observation; adaptability, local knowledge; patronage and civilian support, the fact they have been unhindered by any complex rules of engagement, and their decentralised command structure which allowed for rapid decision-making. Unofficially, many troops also expressed admiration of the Taliban fighters' courage and acceptance of casualties. One American officer, after a sharp fire fight in the Korengal Valley, concluded: 'I wish I was made as strong as "Haj" [nickname for insurgents] ... They were balls[y] to do what they did'.[34]

---

[30] Gusterson, 'Can the Insurgent Speak?', 90.   [31] Ibid., 93–4,

[32] Ironically, a Talib, following the American bombing in 2001 who made the analogies Gusterson disapproved of. Akhunzada reported: 'We walked four days in the deep snow without food or water. Kids started shooting at us from the hilltops, hunting us like wild animals'. Yousafzai and Moreau, 'The Taliban in Their Own Words', 2; Fergusson, Taliban, 113.

[33] This reflects a long pedigree of mutual respect the closer the proximity, as well as denigration. Colonel C. E. Callwell described Afghan fighters as 'exceptionally fine mountaineers', 'admirable marksmen' and 'ferocious adversaries'. C. E. Callwell, Tirah, 1897, republished with a new Introduction by Rob Johnson (Williamsburg, VA, 2010), 34–5.

[34] E. Rubin, 'Battle Company Is Out There', New York Times Magazine, 24 February 2008, available at www.nytimes.com/2008/02/24/magazine/24afghanistan-t.html?pagewanted=all&_r=0.

Stereotypical interpretations, misperceptions and misinterpretations play an important part on both sides. In 2006, the Taliban were able to make use of the existing national sentiment and present the idea to the southern Pashtuns that the British task force, for example, were coming to occupy their land, to break up their livelihoods with a counter-narcotics programme, and to get their revenge for the Battle of Maiwand. Nevertheless, despite the myths and the tendency to see only the ideological commitment of the Taliban and their Afghan allies, counter-myth, opportunism and pragmatism continued to reassert themselves. The Taliban's interpretation of the past and the present is often contested by other Afghans, if not openly, then certainly privately. One of the commonly-held assumptions by Afghans in the rural south, for example, is that the Taliban is an American organisation.[35] This astonishing assessment is founded on the idea that, since the Americans are so very powerful, they could not possibly permit any opposition without their express encouragement; therefore, it follows the Taliban is American, designed to crush the genuine Pashtun aspirations in the south. A similar line of argument is used to suggest the Taliban is entirely Pakistani in its composition on the grounds that Pakistan's objective is to keep Afghanistan weak. It is a reminder that the sheer diversity of internal groups, each with their own narrative, is no less authentically 'Afghan'.

Who, then, are the Taliban in reality? In Pashtu, the name 'Taliban' does not convey the same meaning when used by Westerners, and 'religious students' is an inadequate translation. The Taliban are an amalgam of various groups, and Emile Simpson, a British officer and author who has served in Afghanistan, believes this coalition 'is better understood as a franchise than as a unified, centrally-controlled movement'.[36] Some Afghans claimed to be Taliban for opportunistic reasons. Many local fighters call themselves *mujahidin*, partly to reflect the past and partly to describe their identity. Yet the Taliban is also a movement with a clear command structure. According to Theo Farrell and Antonio Giustozzi, it is an organisation which seeks greater centralisation.[37] Nevertheless, what is striking is that, despite co-operation at the local level, even from formerly rival *Qawm*, the Taliban is not a national movement, as they claim, but a regional one centred on the Pashtun-populated south and its smaller enclaves in the north. Among the Taliban, there are different roles which

---

[35] My thanks to Mike Martin, whose own interviews corroborated what seemed to be an impossible anomaly. PhD dissertation, King's College London, January 2013.

[36] E. Simpson, *War from the Ground Up: Twenty-First Century Combat as Politics* (London: Hurst & Co., 2012), 46, 76–7.

[37] Farrell and Giustozzi, 'The Taliban at War'.

are not without contention, including 'shadow government' leaders, *Mahez* (front) commanders, 'Nizami' military committees, part-time fighters, legal specialists and bomb-makers. There is a significant emphasis on discipline from the senior leadership, but the repeated injunctions of the *Laheya*, the Taliban's 'code of conduct', suggest that there have been episodes of misconduct, periodic confusion over money or lines of jurisdiction and counter-productive criminal activity.[38] One Talib captive, Zabihullah, apparently complained: 'I'm worried that Taliban who are fighting for Islam are decreasing, and those who have dirty intentions to kidnap and make money are increasing'. He concluded: 'Too many fighters are fighting for their own interests'.[39]

National style is a problematic concept if one attempts to extend its apparently enduring features over a long period, since war is a phenomenon that endlessly changes its character; and insurgents must adapt in order to survive or succeed. The weaknesses of any 'national way of war' paradigm when applied to the Taliban are thus twofold: one, how to assess and incorporate change, and, two, to identify what constituted an identifiable and distinctive 'culture' through time. The dynamics of war, the reciprocal adaptation of methods, strengths and systems and the changes in institutions and personalities indicate that cultures are time-bound as much as they geographically and thematically limited. Yet even here there are problems: Afghanistan's insurgent forces do not match any of John Lynn's famous seven models of armies, for example.[40] Similarly, behavioural and organisational studies of insurgency do not provide a full set of criteria beyond motivation. One might reasonably ask: is it actually possible to identify taxonomies of insurgents and insurgencies that incorporate all the critical facets? The answer is a paradox. The Afghan 'way', if it can be identified at all, is characterised by adaptation and change to each adversary and situation, and so it is change itself which becomes the culture of the insurgent.

Terror and Discipline

Is there a special Taliban fighting style? During the civil war, Taliban tactics left much to be desired. There were no elements of organisation which typify regular armies: there were no standard military procedures.

[38] N. Shah (trans.), 'The *laheya*', *Studies in Conflict and Terrorism* 25, 6 (2012).
[39] S. Yousafzai and R. Moreau, 'How the Taliban Lost Its Swagger', *Newsweek International*, 7 March 2011.
[40] J. A. Lynn, 'The Evolution of Army Style in the Modern West, 800–2000', *International History Review*, 18 /3 (1996), 505–45.

Instead, rockets or light artillery were 'fired in the general direction' of the enemy, accompanied by a 'hail of bullets from automatic weapons' whereupon 'hopefully the rival militia surrenders'.[41] If there was any sort of resistance, a hastily organised attack was mounted. If very stubborn resistance was encountered, the Taliban simply assembled more men, sometimes upwards of a thousand fighters. Ordinarily, Taliban units rarely exceeded five hundred, which reflected the guerrilla structure of their forces and the problem of obtaining large volumes of supplies in a penurious country (the general sizes of units employed thus differed little from those of the *Lashkars* a century earlier). Guerrilla tactics, of 'hit and run' or a short rocket fusillade without any actual attack by foot soldiers to follow it up, were common.

Like so many of the historical resistance movements in Afghanistan, it was plagued by disunity, a lack of coordination, the temptation to seek personal or collective gain through collaboration with central government or foreign forces, and the need to conduct conflicts against rival groups inside Afghanistan rather than against foreign occupation forces. The senior *Ruhbari* leadership of the Taliban, allegedly based in Quetta, was initially dominated by Ghlizai Pashtuns close to Mullah Omar, the *Amir ul Moomineen*, but, within the first few years, the composition of the *Shura* changed to incorporate other *Qawmi* and groups. According to Taliban interviewees, there has been better co-ordination with the Peshawar Shura of the Pakistan Taliban and the headquarters of Shirajuddin Haqqani in Miranshah.[42] Nevertheless, attempts to central-ise the movement were not entirely successful. Supplies and logistics remained vulnerable, increasing local tensions. Crucially, it failed to develop its popular support, and did not transform its regional move-ment into a national one.[43] It was forced to adapt itself to the new political realities of the Afghan state, and, with foreign forces present, it failed to overthrow the Kabul government. It developed a reputation for coercion, based in part on its record of government in the 1990s. A much divided and localised movement, the Taliban was warped by the dynamic of war itself and forced to adapt and transform, just as the international Coalition had done. There is some evidence, for example, that it softened its previously tough line against government schools. That was not

---

[41] K. Matinuddin, *The Taliban Phenomenon: Afghanistan, 1994–1997* (Oxford: Oxford University Press, 1999), 59.

[42] J. Dressler, 'The Haqqani Network', Washington: Institute for the Study of War, 2010; Farrell and Giustozzi, 'The Taliban at War', 43; Correspondence with (name withheld), Security Advisor, March 2011.

[43] See O. Roy, *Islam and Resistance in Afghanistan* (Cambridge: Cambridge University Press, 1986).

determined by any national style, but rather by the dynamic pressures of multiple factors, all identified as themes within this volume, including, crucially, a particular perception of their own past.

Discipline is demanded through adherence to a strict and narrow interpretation of Sunni Islam, strongly influenced by Deobandi theology and practice from Pakistan and the slogans of war. To command Taliban units, fighters must have a proven meritorious track record, the approval of more senior commanders and demonstrate strict religious observance. Nevertheless, like so many other insurgencies, the most frequent exercise of disciplinary actions are against suspected collaborators from the population. Nir Rosen, while accompanying a Taliban commander called Shafiq, was told 'of the trials that the Taliban frequently hold to prosecute collaborators'. He noted: 'The suspects are given a hearing by a *Qazi*, or judge, who orders those convicted to be beheaded'. Such disciplinary action against their own people risks generating resistance, and can compromise operational security, leading to betrayal – often the greatest vulnerability of insurgents. A Talib complained: 'They [local informers] gave names of anyone who was supporting the Taliban [and] they are one reason for our heavy casualties'. Moreover, disciplining the local population by killing them can also affect the morale of the Taliban. One fighter, Yahya, claimed: 'I'd like to delete my past from my memory ... I'm worried about how Allah will treat me for what I have done'.[44] Another stated: 'We were playing with the lives of people ... We killed and harmed innocents, just as the infidel Americans do ... The commanders didn't care'. Between 2009 and 2011, it is estimated that some twenty-five hundred civilians were killed by the Taliban and other insurgent groups.[45]

The brutality of Taliban actions against the Afghan people, both in the 1990s and as insurgents, represents an attempt to control the population and discipline them, and there is evidence of tensions in the movement that caused some fragmentation after the Western forces' withdrawal in December 2014. The fight against foreigners had long been the unifying cause of resistance. In 1992, following the Soviet withdrawal, hard-line Jihadist insurgents were defeated by the Afghan regular forces and their militias, while divisions between *mujahidin* factions escalated the civil war. The demands on the population for money and supplies, another common alienation factor in insurgencies, have also caused logistical

[44] Yousafzai and Moreau, 'How the Taliban Lost Its Swagger'.
[45] I. S. Livingstone and M. O'Hanlon, 'Brookings Afghanistan Index', figures 1.23 and 1.24, *Brookings Institute* (31 January 2013), 15–16; also available at www.brookings.edu/~/media/Programs/foreign%20policy/afghanistan%20index/index20130131.pdf.

problems for the Taliban. One Helmandi Talib lamented: '[Formerly] we got lots of money from the traffickers as *Zakat* [tax]. At that time we didn't need our leaders to support us; we could find the money for everything, weapons, ammunition, food and other necessary stuff. But now it's completely different. We have few villages under our control and collecting *Zakat* from those villages is not enough. Most of our supplies are coming from Pakistan ... we can only get our food here'.[46]

Strengths and Weaknesses of the Taliban since 2013

The Taliban have thus a series of weaknesses; that stemming from a lack of centralisation has already been discussed. Although support or sympathy for the Taliban among the Afghan population seemed to grow between 2006 and 2008, the Taliban could not prevail against the firepower, mobility and strength of the ISAF forces. Not one Western outpost was overrun, and despite inflicting a handful of casualties, their own losses were heavy. Reliance on local, charismatic commanders created vulnerability: the loss of a field commander tended to bring operations to a halt. Moreover, the problems of co-ordination and discipline were serious enough to merit urgent reform. According to the research carried out by Farrell and Giustozzi, the Taliban established military or Nizami commissions at provincial and district levels, attempting to adopt a more hierarchical command and control system. Theoretically commissions rewarded loyalty with arms and supplies.[47] The change was not easy to implement, not least because ISAF forces, whose intelligence operations were becoming more effective, were able to target individual commanders. The Taliban's original aspiration, to establish both shadow civil governors alongside fighting 'front' commanders, was not accomplished. Local people and fighting men tended to seek out the front commanders on almost all issues.

The tendency of groups to cluster around charismatic leaders also threatened to undermine the command decisions of the senior Taliban leadership, and so, for a brief period, the Taliban tried to rotate field commanders from one area to another. Once again, the disruptive effect of ISAF operations seemed to have caused the system of rotation to be abandoned by 2011 in at least one province. A Talib interviewee reported:

In fact over the last year, many Taliban commanders with their soldiers were targeted by American drone attacks while they were moving from one district to

---

[46] Farrell and Giustozzi, 'The Taliban at War', 47.   [47] Ibid., 29, 34.

another district. That's why the rotation has been decreased, because moving became difficult for Taliban commanders.[48]

The areas that saw the most fighting tended to produce a leadership system that heeded the military commanders. In Helmand, for example, one village elder remarked that they simply did not know who the Talib 'shadow' governor was.

For the Taliban rank and file, there has been a repeated emphasis on the war of defence. The fighting is both the ends and the ways. One fighter boasted: 'We will attack in larger numbers, with new recruits from Waziristan and with more *Madrassa* students [in 2011]: You watch – we'll cause more American casualties this year than last'. Another, Mohammed, stated: 'We will fight until victory no matter how long it takes. The U.S. has the weapons, but we are prepared for a long and tireless Jihad. We were born here. We will die here. We aren't going anywhere'.[49] For all the defiance, some more experienced Taliban were concerned that money and power over local people mattered more than adherence to the religious struggle to drive out the foreigners. The implication of this militarisation and this focus on the tactical fight, with little or declining political work, implies failure in the future political landscape of Afghanistan. Even without the presence of international forces, the Taliban are in danger of winning the war and losing the peace, or perhaps even losing both.

The adaptation of the Taliban, and the improvements in their tactics, has been hard won. Initially the Taliban had to overcome the collapse in morale when they were driven out of government. Fighters spoke of the importance of 'Arab' leaders and the availability of training to the regeneration of the movement. Younas, who had not been through the devastating bombing of 2001, was attracted to the neo-Taliban by these means:

At first I didn't hear the Afghans talking about going back to fight. But the Arabs did, and they encouraged the Afghans and the local tribal people [in Pakistan] not to give up. Nothing much happened for the first year or so, but then the Arabs started organising some training camps.[50]

The Taliban hope was that, by 2006, they would be able to embark on a more effective counter-offensive, but the extension of the presence of ISAF and Afghan security forces into the south that year, and the heavy losses the Taliban suffered in direct assaults, meant a shift in tactics and in training. Some groups were able to use the terrain to conceal camps

[48] Farrell and Giustozzi, 'The Taliban at War', 32.
[49] Yousafzai and Moreau, 'The Taliban in Their Own Words', 16.   [50] Ibid., 6.

and conduct regular training or rehearsals. Others were not. Some regarded training as unnecessary. Sharing observations about ISAF and Afghan government forces' methods and procedures was particularly important though. As ISAF deployed new vehicles to protect their personnel against improvised explosive devices (IEDs) and improved their detection and defusing capabilities, the Taliban had to adapt: they used larger quantities of explosives, developing plastic containers and fewer metal parts. Yet this also meant bringing in expertise.[51] These 'enablers' became the target of ISAF operations, leading to a constant attrition of skilled personnel.

Insurgencies are, in essence, political struggles where military means should serve the agenda of mobilising the population against the central government.[52] The Taliban movement has been prevented from making any headway in the political arena in Afghanistan, and their focus on military operations has, from this perspective, been counter-productive. Legitimacy also remains a related challenge. They failed to gain the same degree of international recognition and support which the old-Taliban had during the Soviet period, specifically from Pakistan. According to Iftikar Malik, elements in Pakistani ISI (Inter-Services Intelligence) and the Pakistan Army may still support the Taliban as a means of trying to keep their influence in Afghanistan, particularly vis-à-vis India, but the Taliban's dependence on international networks can be seen as an indication of their weakness.[53] The vast numbers of Afghans, not just from the north, who reject the Taliban's injunctions on religious and social behaviour, and condemn the detonation of bombs in busy markets or the use of suicide terrorism, have remained a significant obstacle for the movement.

Strategy, Victory and Defeat

Insurgent groups are often weakened by an inability to formulate and pursue a strategy as tactical fighting tends to predominate. The Taliban's asymmetrical stance has been a direct result of being too weak to confront Western and Afghan security forces any other way rather than being

[51] T. Farrell, F. Osinga and J. A. Russell (eds.), *Military Adaptation in Afghanistan* (Stanford, CA: Stanford University Press, 2013).

[52] I. Arreguin-Toft, *How the Weak Win Wars: A Theory of Asymmetric Conflict* (Cambridge: Cambridge University Press, 2005); B. O'Neil, *Insurgency and Terrorism: Inside Modern Revolutionary Warfare/From Revolution to Apocalypse*, rev. ed. (Dulles, VA: Potomac Books, 2005).

[53] I. Malik, 'Pakistan in 2001: The Afghanistan Crisis and the Rediscovery of the Frontline State' *Asian Survey*, 42/1 (2001), 204–12; Zaeff, *My Life with the Taliban*, 62, 65.

a strategy of choice. In the 1980s the *mujahidins'* failure to combine quickly to take advantage of their enemy's weakness was the result of a similar asymmetry in military capability. Moreover, personal rivalries, prejudices and hatreds often clouded their views and dictated their actions, reflecting the fact that the conflict in Afghanistan since 1978 has been a civil war, rather than a classic insurgency against the government. It is striking that, after the Soviet withdrawal in 1989, the Afghan government under Najibullah eventually employed 100,000 former insurgents in government service as militias. One civilian advisor to ISAF forces in Afghanistan commented in 2013 that the Afghan National Army 'is still essentially a confederation of tribal militias [with] well understood vertical fracture lines running through most units – but made even more complex by horizontal fracture lines [of] three distinct generations of officers'.[54] Latif, an Afghan NGO worker, also explained how three generations of Afghans saw the solutions to Afghanistan's problems in distinct terms.[55] The Taliban senior leadership struggles with internal divisions as much as the rest of the population and has tried to impose greater cohesion and discipline on its forces, and its strategy amounts to maintaining a fighting force. The lack of a clear plan for converting a military campaign into political power is a significant problem.

Losses have been heavy. ISAF estimates that in some areas, the Taliban suffered an attrition rate of 20 per cent, and this appears to be borne out by the fighters' own estimates, but the variations across time and region are enormous, making generalisation hazardous. Deaths through accidents with IEDs and weapons malfunctions or the inability to extract wounded fighters has also taken its toll. Quarrels in 2012–2014 between the Peshawar Shura and the Taliban in the south, perhaps reflecting changed priorities amongst the insurgent leadership or inside Pakistan, reduced the tempo of operations, giving the Afghan security forces the opportunity to deploy in larger numbers and replace the outgoing ISAF troops.

On the other hand, inexperienced Afghan security forces working for the government may decide to cut deals with insurgents at local level as the transition to Afghan government control of security gathers pace, just as they did at the end of the Soviet occupation. Self-preservation of isolated units has, in the past, fostered ceasefires, truces and even a form of collusion. Edward Giradet visited an Afghan army outpost in 1982 and found 'a group of bored conscripts ... kicking an empty can about.

---

[54] (Name withheld) email to the author, 20 February 2013.
[55] Correspondence with the author, 2010.

We shook hands and they watched as dozens of guerrillas marched by, leading strings of pack mules loaded with arms, ammunition and other supplies'.[56] Clearly a deal had been struck. Antonio Giustozzi noted that, even in Takhar in the north, communication between government officials, the police and the Taliban was common.[57] Family relationships, smuggling deals and the supply of arms or money can cause collusion to flourish. Officially, the Taliban and the Afghan government deny any contact. The shadow governor of Herat was sacked by the Taliban for unauthorised negotiations, but that has not prevented its occurrence elsewhere. The increase in 'green on blue' attacks against ISAF personnel and generally within the ranks of the Afghan National Army was, it is thought, largely the result of frustrations rather than a premeditated plan of infiltration, but this process in the police was less clear cut. Giustozzi and Mohammad Isaqzadeh suggest that defections to the Taliban from the police between 2001 and 2011 were 'relatively frequent events', and examples indicate sometimes entire units would desert the government.[58]

Paradoxically, the mutual weaknesses of both sides, and the absence of foreign forces, may make it more likely that the current conflict will be concluded, like previous ones in Afghan history, with a negotiated settlement. The Taliban, during their offensives that brought them to Kabul in 1995–1996, often acquired allegiances by offering deals rather than fighting every militia they encountered: a reminder, perhaps, that striking a bargain is as much a part of the supposed Taliban 'way of war' as the fighting.[59] Nevertheless, there is no guarantee of a peaceful conclusion to the civil conflict in the short term. The paradox for the Taliban is that the desire to preserve a particular conservative, Islamic, Afghan way of life has been made unrealisable by the war they have waged. Despite any military success they might claim, their strategic ends have slipped further and further away with each year of fighting: the Taliban's war

---

[56] Giradet, *Afghanistan: The Soviet War*, 61.

[57] A. Giustozzi, 'Local and Tactical Political Accommodation: Evidence from Afghanistan', paper delivered at the Understanding Transition: Frameworks, Lessons and Observations from Global History Conference, Oxford University, 17–19 December 2012.

[58] A. Giustozzi and M. Isaqzadeh, *Policing Afghanistan: The Politics of the Lame Leviathan* (London: Hurst & Co., 2013), 122–3.

[59] The usual process was to halt and send forward a mullah under the white Taliban flag with its green *Kalima* and entreat the opposition to lay down their arms because the Taliban had come to end all fighting in the country. Their aim was to gain support by consensus, to appear to be a neutral force, and to avoid taking sides in inter-clan fighting. Johnson, *The Afghan Way of War*, 256.

will appear in retrospect to have hastened the very modernisation and transformation they had hoped to prevent.

Conclusion

Assessments of the Taliban, either as a collection of local movements and 'fronts', or as a national organisation, have to take account of both specific 'traditional' or 'warrior' conceptions and more generic insurgent structures and tactics. The Taliban are, in short, a *blend* of common and also distinctive, contingent and historical influences. Moreover, the characteristics of the Taliban are in no way fixed, but are adapted to the environment and to the capabilities of their adversaries. Afghan insurgents, sometimes styled as *mujahidin*, have inherited traditions of *Qawm* (clan/locality) rivalry, periodic or sustained rural antagonism with central government and, in some areas, a *habitus* of violence in dispute resolution. Nevertheless, they have been forced to adapt. A surge of more powerful foreign military forces after 2001 rendered the rather disorganised tactics that had brought success in the 1980s and 1990s as costly and irrelevant. Some innovations, such as mine warfare and improvised explosive devices, proved effective tactically, although, on their own, they could not bring about a strategic success. Other changes, such as the attempt to rotate front commanders in order to overcome clan allegiances and make the movement more centralised, proved unsuccessful in most cases.

There have been recognisable areas of continuity in the style of Afghan insurgency. Personal esteem and exhibitions of courage or fighting prowess have been more attractive than the ability to orchestrate a shadow government. There has been a long tradition of negotiating during combat, using violence as another form of communication. Changing sides is a common survival mechanism in civil conflict, and this too has featured strongly in the last thirty years of fighting in Afghanistan. The mercenary motive, with opportunism regarding money or a share in local profits, has been a constant source of criticism within the Taliban movement in recent years but which stems back into recorded Afghan history. Afghan insurgents have always been compelled to adapt to the strength of their rivals' and enemies, changing their modus operandi accordingly.

At the tactical level, in common with many insurgent forces, the Taliban have been vulnerable. Those dependent on local support can be overrun, outflanked or encircled, and therefore forced to suspend operations. In terms of leadership, reliance on charismatic commanders with their emphasis on being active in operations, makes the movement vulnerable if these men are killed. High casualty rates have meant that less experienced individuals were placed in positions of responsibility or became dependent on outsiders. While religion was a sustaining ideological tool for mobilisation, it did not appeal to all fighters as the primary motivation, and, at times, such cosmological interpretations were not as powerful as nationalistic or pragmatic concerns about land, money and clan solidarity. In other words, the Taliban and their equivalent insurgent organisations in Afghanistan in the 2000s[60] exhibited quite traditional motivations, tactics and vulnerabilities.

Nonetheless, the Taliban were not entirely traditional. Neither their nature and nor their intent can defined as 'national'. The Taliban had a distinct brand of 'imagined community' that was not limited to one nation when it imposed itself or co-opted its former rivals in the 1990s. Its conception of an emirate, embracing Sunni Muslims who followed particular practices in belief and lifestyle, made it accommodating to foreigners of Al-Qaeda, while, at the same time, condemning Shia Afghans and other ethnic groups of the north, west and centre as apostates, heretics or simply '*tarburi*' (enemies). Nevertheless, at a local level, from the 1990s onwards, there was a significant difference. More material and pragmatic concerns, and judicious coercion, could ensure allegiance. The Taliban celebrated a cult of the religious warrior, but they used a narrow and militaristic interpretation of Islam to support it. They claimed to have brought peace and security to Afghans, but, in the name of protecting the virtue of the people, they exhibited great brutality and injustice. They insisted on 'disciplining' the population and seemed to have a moral insecurity that could only be compensated by further violence. After the Western military operations broke the Taliban's grip on power in 2001, many Afghans felt confident about defying the edicts of the former regime. Others saw an opportunity to exploit the change in the political landscape to gain the favour of the new government in Kabul, the Western powers or the resurgent neo-Taliban from 2003.

In summary, the Taliban cannot be defined purely as traditional or as an entirely new phenomenon. They are a hybrid: a blend of some recognisable older Afghan approaches which, ironically, are part of a history of adaptation to specific strategic situations. An enduring faith in Islam, a unique geographical environment and a rural habitus of violence, self-preservation and opportunism have shaped the Taliban. Yet so too has the need to adapt to Western military power, to discipline

---

[60] Excellent examples can be found in M. Martin, *An Intimate War* (London: Hurst, 2014).

their own population and to evolve their tactics to sustain their resistance. However, despite a determined resistance to Western and Afghan governments, the tactics and motivations of this movement and its local affiliates has not offered a strategic solution to a more fundamental dilemma: how to govern a transforming Afghanistan with consent. Violence has proven an inadequate tool for winning the peace.

Part III

Interaction

13 Guerrilla and Counter-Guerrilla Greece
Tradition and Change

Spyridon Plakoudas

With a thousand names, one nature, *Akritas* [frontier guard] or *Armatolos* [gendarme]/*Antartis* [guerrillero], *Kleftis* [brigand], *Palikari* [hero], I'm always the people itself.

(From the Ὑμνος͜του ΕΛΑΣ (hymn of the ELAS) resistance movement of World War II)

The Guerrilla Tradition in Greece

The question of strategic culture in counterinsurgency (COIN) has stimulated endless debates on the actual existence and impact of a distinct national style in conducting guerrilla and counter-guerrilla warfare. Greece stands out as an ideal case to test the hypothesis that such a national style does actually exist, since the phenomenon of insurgency constitutes a constant and prime theme in modern Greek history. The mountainous terrain, the predominantly agricultural structure of a conservative society, the recurring phenomenon of banditry and the uninterrupted tradition of rebellion against Ottoman despotism decisively contributed to the appearance of a distinct guerrilla tradition that influenced Greek history from the end of the Ottoman rule to the onset of the Cold War.[1]

The period between 1831 and 1912 could be regarded as the heyday of banditry in Greece. Numerous large groups of well-armed bandits pillaged and terrorised the villagers with impunity as the Athens-centric state could not fully control the mountainous countryside of Greece. Surprisingly, the very same bandits could be found hunting down other bandits or fostering rebellions in Ottoman-ruled territories in the Balkans whenever the Greek kingdom bought them off with state offices and riches. For more than a hundred years, armed irregulars (part-time bandits and part-time guerrillas) roamed across the mountainous regions of Greece.[2]

[1] S. N. Kalyvas, 'Comparing Three Greek Unorthodox Wars', in B. C. Gounaris et al. (eds.), *Unorthodox Wars: Macedonia, Civil War, Cyprus* (Athens: Patakis, 2010), 14.
[2] J. S. Koliopoulos, *Brigands with a Cause: Brigandage and Irredentism in Modern Greece, 1821–1912* (Oxford: Clarendon Press, 1987), 105–236; E. Hatzivassiliou, '"Unorthodox

The true nature of these irregulars in modern Greek history still remains a matter of debate. The ordinary people praised them as national heroes, while the romantic and Leftist-oriented thinkers portrayed them as apostles of socio-political revolution. In reality, until the early twenti-eth century, guerrillas comprised a unique social class, homogenous but fragmented, that no Greek government could afford to ignore.[3] Specific regions (such as Crete) bred generations of tough warriors who fought with the time-tested guerrilla methods of '*Kleftopolemos*' (bandit war in Greek) – hit-and-run tactics and night raids by small units of seasoned warriors who followed a charismatic captain. These fighters usually operated only close to their place of origin and relied on their families and fellow villagers for support; and although they observed an unwritten code of honour, they remained extremely unruly and often resorted to banditry and rampant violence against civilians. The various militant groups that operated simultaneously within an area did not cooperate with each other and, in fact, fought each other quite frequently,[4] much like the rivalling mafias that sprang up in Italy in the nineteenth century.

The First Modest Deviation from the Guerrilla Tradition

The history of modern Greece has been marked by numerous insurgen-cies. And although most of them failed, they hold an immense symbolic capital for the Greek people.[5] The Greek Civil War (1946–1949) stands out as the most representative case of this paradox.[6] Although the Greek Communist insurgents were defeated on the battlefield, after several years the Left established a long-lasting political and ideological hegem-ony over Greek society.[7] The Greek Civil War did not just bring old passions and rivalries within Greek society to a bloody climax;[8] this conflict was also a laboratory for guerrilla and counter-guerrilla warfare in modern Greece.

The civil conflict between the Right and Left began during World War II, when small civil wars were fought among Greeks in the midst of the main war against the occupying Axis Powers. The brutality of the Axis occupation of Greece must be stressed, and the experience of that war

War as Politics" Lever in Greek History, 1904–1959' in Gounaris et al. (eds.), *Unorthodox Wars*, 24–5.

[3] Koliopoulos, *Brigands*, 25–6, 31–50.

[4] Koliopoulos, *Brigands*, 20–35, 39–66, 239–92.   [5] Kalyva, 'Comparing', 19–20.

[6] N. A. Marantzidis, *Democratic Army of Greece (DSE), 1946–1949* (Athens: Alexandreia, 2010), 15–28.

[7] G. T. Mavrogordatos, 'Revanche of the Defeated', *To Vima* (10 September 1999).

[8] D. H. Close, *Origins of the Greek Civil War* (London: Longman, 1995).

had a brutalising effect on all sides that would make itself felt well into the late 1940s.[9] The Second World War also witnessed the development of new types of guerrilla groups and tactics that diverged from the old tradition of *Kleftopolemos*. Many non-Communist resistance movements set up a dual structure (a political one in the towns and a military one in the countryside) or operated solely in an urban environment; however, all the non-Communist resistance movements that waged a guerrilla campaign against the Axis Powers built on the old Greek guerrilla tradition of *Kleftopolemos*.[10]

Then came the first significant change: the National Liberation Front (EAM), a resistance movement established in late 1941 under the aegis of the Greek Communist Party (KKE), critically deviated from the old Greek guerrilla tradition. The Communist-dominated EAM quickly grew into the most powerful and popular resistance movement in occupied Greece and gained substantial support from a wide range of socio-economic strata by implementing a series of radical reforms (e.g., suffrage for women) in the context of a 'patriotic and democratic programme' (the concept of the 'people's rule') – without triggering the Soviet-style Communist revolution imagined by radicals within the movement. Apart from propaganda and reforms, the EAM also used coercion to cow its opponents to submission and control the population.[11]

The EAM's military wing, the Greek People's Liberation Army (ELAS), stood out as a wholly new type of guerrilla movement. The ELAS operated under civilian supervision and stuck to old tactics of *Kleftopolemos* only for the first few months, but then radically changed its configuration and tactics. It integrated inexperienced recruits, primarily youngsters but also, for the first time, women; women had played an important part in Tito's partisan movement in neighbouring Yugoslavia during the Second World War. From mid-1943 onwards, the ELAS in every respect resembled a regular army. A military academy was opened, military insignia and an anthem were introduced, a general headquarters and a military hierarchy were instituted, and different types of units were set up. In the final stages of the occupation, the ELAS's units were organised into battalions and divisions to confront the Germans and their Greek allies in

[9] See the contribution of Henning Pieper to this volume.
[10] J. L. Hondros, *Occupation and Resistance: The Greek Agony, 1941–44* (New York: Pella Publishing Co., 1983).
[11] M. Mazower, *Inside Hitler's Greece: The Experience of Occupation, 1941–44* (New Haven, CT: Yale University Press, 2001), 271–91; D. H. Close, 'Introduction', in D. H. Close (ed.), *The Greek Civil War, 1943–1950: Studies of Polarisation* (London: Routledge, 1993), 17–20, 22; Close, *Origins*, 80–3.

pitched battles.[12] Such determined resistance compelled the three Axis Powers (Bulgaria, Nazi Germany and Italy – the last until its capitulation in 1943) to retain more than three hundred thousand occupying troops in Greece and foster the development and growth of Greek Quisling military forces.[13]

The EAM did not want to share power with other parties and one by one wiped out the antagonistic resistance movements (several of them had turned to collaboration or sought British protection for their own survival). After the withdrawal of the Wehrmacht in late 1944, the ELAS overwhelmed the military forces of the Quisling Greek government and seized control of most of Greece. However, the EAM's hegemony did not last long. When in December 1944 the EAM tried to overthrow the restored Greek government by capturing Athens, the British army intervened and routed the ELAS. In February 1945, the EAM capitulated by signing the Varkiza Agreement, which inter alia stipulated the disarmament and dissolution of the ELAS.[14]

The Radical Deviation: The Communist Insurgency in the Greek Civil War

Resurrecting ELAS?

The peace treaty, however, did not bring peace. The Right, which by mid-1945 controlled the security and state organs, unleashed a vindictive persecution of the Left while Britain, the hegemon of Greece, watched passively.[15] In response, by mid-1945, several Communist guerrilla bands had sprung up in northern Greece without official support from the KKE that opposed the Rightist paramilitary groups. Meanwhile, though officially committed to peace, from late 1945 onwards the KKE secretly rebuilt its fighting capacity and sought support from Moscow for an armed uprising.[16]

In February 1946, the KKE (following Stalin's prescriptions) adopted a dual strategy of mass political struggles in the towns and a low-intensity guerrilla campaign in the countryside in order to compel the Greek government to accept a political compromise.[17] In February, the KKE

---

[12] Mazower, *Inside Hitler's Greece*, 297–321.
[13] Ibid., 144–5, 323–5; Kathimerini, 14 April 2013.
[14] Close, *Origins*, 102–6, 113–19, 137–45.   [15] Ibid., 150–65.
[16] Ibid., 150–73, 176–84; S. Rizas, *From Liberation to Civil War* (Athens: Kastaniotis, 2011), 177–80, 214–16, 220–2.
[17] T. D. Sfikas. *War and Peace in the KKE's Strategy, 1945-1949* (Athens: Filistor, 2001), 65–6.

took another fateful decision: to boycott the upcoming elections of March 1946 (the rest of the Left followed soon afterwards). When in April Stalin and Tito gave the KKE the green light for an uprising, the party moved swiftly. In July, the KKE's Secretary General, Nikos Zachariadis, instructed Markos Vafeiadis, a senior ex-ELAS commander, to organise the Communist insurgents in the mountains of northern Greece.[18] In the last quarter of 1946, the KKE intensified its efforts to compel the government to reach a compromise: on the one hand, the party submitted peace proposals to the government and wooed the Centrist parties and personalities; on the other hand, the KKE set up the General Headquarters of the Insurgents (GAA) and created a 'Democratic Army of Greece' (DSE) in October and December respectively.[19]

In February 1947, the KKE stepped up the military pressure on the government and, in April, Vafeiadis, the DSE's Commander-in-Chief, received secret orders to progressively convert the Communist insurgents into a regular army that would carve out a 'Free Greece' in northern Greece with Thessaloniki, Greece's second largest city, as its capital.[20] In May, growing tensions with the West prompted Stalin to reassure Zachariadis that the Soviets would support the KKE's plans for a 'Free Greece'. At Stalin's orders, from mid-1947 onwards, the European Communist states started supplying the KKE with military and economic aid.[21] In essence, Moscow and its Balkan satellites waged a 'proxy war': they used the Greek insurgents to subvert a Royalist regime supported by Britain (and, since early 1947, the United States).

During the first phase of the insurgency, the Communists followed the traditional *Kleftopolemos*: small units of tough ELAS veterans and volunteers under the command of seasoned ELAS captains used hit-and-run tactics with impressive results. Though deficient in numbers and weapons, these units possessed superb intelligence, tactical skill and military leadership and used the mountainous terrain to their own advantage. Supported by the Communist Balkan countries and the mountainous Greek villagers whom the Royalist regime

---

[18] T. D. Sfikas, *The British Labour Government and the Greek Civil War, 1945-1949: The Imperialism of 'Non-Intervention'* (Keele: Ryburn and Keele University Press, 1994), 85–6, 105–6, 113–14.

[19] Rizas, *From Liberation*, 293–300.

[20] Iliou, *The Greek Civil War: The Entanglement of the KKE* (Athens: Themelio, 2004), 77–8, 82.

[21] J. O. Iatrides, 'Revolution or Self-Defense? Communist Goals, Strategy, and Tactics during the Greek Civil War', *Journal of Cold War Studies*, 7/3(2005), 24–6.

had either neglected or maltreated, the insurgents quickly seized a sizable part of northern and central Greece.[22]

Although the KKE used the arms and human expertise of the defunct ELAS, the party proved unwilling to resurrect the ELAS. Many seasoned ELAS captains had been imprisoned in violation of the Treaty of Varkiza. From the remaining ELAS captains, the KKE recruited only a small number whom they regarded as politically reliable. Even these veteran commanders were treated with suspicion and scorn by the KKE's leadership and occupied few senior posts in the DSE.[23] In fact, the DSE ended up completely subservient to the KKE, whereas the ELAS had enjoyed a considerable degree of operational autonomy.[24]

Meanwhile, the KKE still pursued a *dual strategy* and, thus, continued to search for a negotiated settlement to the conflict. In the summer of 1947, the precarious peace negotiations between the Left and the Greek government reached their zenith. However, neither side was sincerely committed to the peace process and, instead, strove to improve its negotiatory position vis-à-vis its suspicious opponent by scoring military victories. Upon American insistence, the Greek government suspended the peace negotiations.[25]

The Socialist Revolution – Discarding the Kleftopolemos

In September 1947, the KKE decided to declare open war on the Greek government and, to this end, approved Operation Limnes – a plan drawn up with Yugoslav military assistance due to start in early 1948, to build up a sizable regular army (including a navy and an air force) and set up the secessionist 'Free Greece' as planned.[26] Interestingly, the KKE's decision was reached just days before the founding conference of the 'Cominform' – the international organisation designed to co-ordinate the political line to be taken by Communist parties across Europe (much as the 'Comintern' had done before World War II).[27] In late December 1947, the KKE set up the Provisional Democratic Government (PDK)

---

[22] D. H. Close and T. Veremis, 'The Military Struggle, 1945–9', in Close (ed.), *Greek Civil War*, 100–101; C. R. Shrader, *The Withered Vine: Logistics and Communist Insurgency in Greece, 1945–1949* (Westport, CT: Praeger, 1999), 216–17, 219–21.

[23] Close and Veremis, 'Military Struggle', 103; Shrader, *Withered Vine*, 143–4; Marantzidis, *Democratic Army*, 67.

[24] Close and Veremis, 'Military Struggle', 101; Marantzidis, *Democratic Army*, 65.

[25] Sfikas, *War and Peace*, 88–92; Rizas, *From Liberation*, 328–41.

[26] Roussos (official of the KKE's Politburo) to the Communist Party of the Soviet Union (September 1947) in Iliou, *Greek Civil War*, 185–8.

[27] Sfikas, 'Revolution or Self-Defence', 26.

and set into motion Operation Limnes. Unfortunately for the KKE, not a single Communist country recognised the PDK.[28]

From late 1947 onwards, the KKE sped up the creation of the DSE (now also referred to as the 'people's revolutionary army') and the transition from irregular to regular tactics. A standard uniform and rank insignia were introduced, supporting arms (e.g., artillery) and services (e.g., communication and logistics) were established, training centres (e.g., a military academy) were expanded and army units were enlarged (first to light brigades, then to heavy brigades and finally to divisions). The KKE's dogmatic leaders used Soviet-style models of military organisation to wage a 'people's revolutionary struggle'. Democratic assemblies in each rebel unit reviewed political and military issues, political commissars shared power with the military commanders in each rebel unit, and an internal security service oversaw and purged officers and conscripts they distrusted. The KKE's leadership also used Soviet-inspired tactics to overpower the 'monarcho-fascists'. The DSE intended to confront the government army head-on and overwhelm it in a decisive battle and, for that reason, staged a series of determined assaults against towns held by the government.[29]

The dogmatic Zachariadis wanted to set up a Soviet-style 'people's republic'. During World War II, the EAM had refrained from staging a socialist revolution that would antagonize the conservative rural society it controlled. From early 1948 onwards, however, the KKE established Soviet-inspired institutions and implemented radical Communist reforms that alienated the rural population.[30] In the first half of 1948, the KKE also moved thousands of children from northern Greece to Communist Europe – a decision that cost the Communists dearly in terms of legitimacy and popular appeal and still causes debates among scholars. These were in part the children of Communists who wanted to see their offspring protected from the Greek government or other children more or less kidnapped by the Communists.[31] This seems to be a feature largely unique to the Greek civil war, as the children were treated relatively well and not turned into child-soldiers, prostituted or otherwise exploited.

---

[28] Iliou, *Greek Civil War*, 267–9.
[29] Shrader, *Withered Vine*, 69–71, 94–9; Close and Veremis, 'Military Struggle', 109–11; Marantzidis, *Democratic Army*, 76–86.
[30] Shrader, *Withered Vine*, 123–4; Marantzidis, *Democratic Army*, 155–83.
[31] L. Bœrentzen, 'The "Paidomazoma" and the Queen's Camps', in Bœrentzen et al. (eds.), *Studies in the History of the Greek Civil War, 1945–1949* (Copenhagen: Museum Tusculanum Press, 1987), 127–58.

The creation of a sizable regular army remained an unrealisable objective. The DSE suffered from a crippling shortage in fighters. Even at its peak in early 1948, the DSE's combat strength did not exceed twenty-six thousand fighters (plus twenty thousand reserves spread out across the neighbouring Balkan states).[32] Repeated police sweeps had sent tens of thousands of Communists to prison camps or execution squads; the remaining Communist supporters could not slip past the vigilant security organs or simply refused to risk their lives for an unwinnable civil war. In addition, the KKE's extreme socialist experiments alienated a significant part of the conservative and pious peasantry, and, worse, the army resettled hundreds of thousands of Communist peasants in state-controlled refugee camps.[33] The insurgents resorted to forcibly recruiting youngsters (even children) from captured towns and villages; by late 1947, impressed recruits made up the vast majority of the DSE's fighters. By early 1949, women and youngsters below the age of twenty-five constituted over one-third and four-fifths of the DSE's combat strength respectively.[34] Despite continuous military support of Communist Europe, the DSE had not developed the military capabilities envisioned by Zachariadis. The DSE possessed insufficient and, often, defective weapons and an inadequate number of professional officers, whereas the supporting arms and services remained primitive and the training of recruits and officers rudimentary.[35]

By late 1948, the KKE had not succeeded in setting up the big regular army imagined by Zachariadis; nor did the DSE's navy and air force come into being. Without realising any of the KKE's overambitious objectives, the insurgents only seized a series of small mountain towns, while suffering heavy and irreplaceable losses themselves. In typical Communist fashion, Zachariadis silenced the critics of these military failures. When in November 1948 Vafeiadis protested against the resort to regular warfare and proposed a return to guerrilla tactics, Zachariadis denounced him as a defeatist and, in January 1949, relieved him of his post. Reigning supreme over the DSE and KKE, Zachariadis continued his unsuccessful strategy and sided with Stalin against Tito. Intent on isolating Tito and increasing the DSE's combat strength, the KKE offered significant concessions to the Slav Macedonians – a sizable

[32] Shrader, *Withered Vine*, 110–11.
[33] Close and Veremis, 'Military Struggle', 104; Shrader, *Withered Vine*, 258–9; Marantzidis, *Democratic Army*, 138–9.
[34] Close and Veremis, 'Military Struggle', 102–3, 104, 120; Shrader, *Withered Vine*, 108–13, 158–214; Marantzidis, *Democratic Army*, 32–51, 52–4, 137–41.
[35] Close and Veremis, 'Military Struggle', 102–3; Shrader, *Withered Vine*, 159–214; Marantzidis, *Democratic Army*, 32–51, 101–13.

minority in Greek Macedonia that had been seeking independence – in exchange for their support and, consequently, creating resentment among the Greek population.[36]

By early 1949, the KKE had been isolated both domestically and internationally; not even Stalin supported the Communist insurgency any longer. Weakened by unwise military policies and cut off from the population, in late 1949 the insurgents were defeated by the growing military might of the government forces.[37]

The Tradition of 'Anti-Banditry Campaigns'

There are interesting parallels between Spain and Greece in the early nineteenth centuries. In both countries, many of the irregulars who fought, respectively, against the French occupiers or the Ottoman authorities, had been, were or would later be engaged in banditry, contraband, extortion or other forms of criminal activities. For that reason, both the Greek and Spanish states developed fairly consistent anti-banditry strategies.[38]

Although banditry does not constitute an insurgency, the Greek kingdom did not distinguish between the two irregular threats. The general characteristics of this policy remained consistent for more than a century. In summary, the Greek governments passed draconian laws that collectively punished the brigands and their civilian supporters (e.g., their families) by sentencing them to imprisonment, deportation or execution, while the gendarmerie and other paramilitary forces relentlessly pursued the brigands and, in the old Byzantine and later Ottoman tradition, forcibly moved their (predominantly pastoral) communities to other regions. When such coercive policies failed, the Greek governments bought off the bandits with lavish gifts and a general amnesty. Indeed, the weak Greek kingdom from time to time hired bandits to hunt down other brigands or to foment revolts in Ottoman-ruled lands.[39]

The aforementioned anti-banditry strategy, implemented from 1831 by a succession of Greek governments, was once again applied in the Second World War. When in mid-1943 National Socialist Germany nominally transferred the responsibility for internal security to the Quisling anti-Communist Greek government, the latter put into effect an aggressive anti-banditry policy against the EAM. Although the Wehrmacht retained

---

[36] Shrader, *Withered Vine*, 67–8.   [37] Iatrides, 'Revolution or Self-Defense?', 31–2.
[38] M. Lawrence, 'Poachers Turned Gamekeepers: A Study of the Guerrilla Phenomenon in Spain, 1808–1840', *Small Wars and Insurgencies*, 24/4 (2014), 713–27.
[39] Koliopoulos, *Brigands*, 107–16, 120–1.

responsibility for the overall COIN campaign,[40] they exploited the anti-Communism of a part of the Greek political élite to fight the EAM in a way that spared German blood and treasure. The government instituted courts-martial and security committees that condemned the accused to execution or deportation and, in addition, subjected the urban and rural populations that supported the insurgents to cruel punishment (including burning and bombings of villages and mass executions of civilians). The Greek Quislings also reinforced the gendarmerie and created auxiliary military forces (the Security Battalions) and cooperated with anti-Communist resistance groups.[41] In effect, they used classic scorched earth tactics, which, nonetheless, proved rather ineffective. When in late 1944 the Wehrmacht withdrew from Greece, the Quisling security apparatus collapsed in the face of the ELAS's vigorous campaigns.[42] The ensuing Greek Civil War of 1946–1949 would put the old anti-banditry strategy to its most serious test.

The Critical Rupture: Counterinsurgency in the Greek Civil War

Business as Usual

When in mid-1946 the KKE began its insurgency, the Greek state did not understand the character and scope of the threat early enough either to act preventively or to react resolutely. After winning the elections of March 1946, the Royalists concentrated on reinstating the monarchy, seizing control of the state and security apparatuses, and repressing the still powerful Communists.[43]

In the summer of 1946, the newly-elected Royalist government, which considered the Communist insurgency as little more than Communist banditry, decided to confront the irregular threat by using the old anti-banditry strategy. The government adopted emergency legislation and established special courts-martial that punished the insurgents and their sympathisers mercilessly. In addition, the government instructed the gendarmerie to pursue the insurgents and even used anti-Communist guerrillas and bandits who had clashed with the EAM during the Second World War. However, these measures proved utterly ineffective.[44]

---

[40] See Henning Pieper's contribution to this volume.
[41] Mazower, *Inside Hitler's Greece*, 322–49.   [42] Close, *Origins*, 118–19.
[43] Sfikas, *British Labour Government*, 99–105; Rizas, *From Liberation*, 274–8.
[44] Close and Veremis, 'Military Struggle', 106; Close, *Origins*, 190–3.

The First Phase of COIN

In late September 1946, the Royalist government realised that the Communist insurgency could not be contained with outdated anti-banditry methods. Thus, the government resorted to vigorous economic, political, military and diplomatic measures. The government tried to increase its control over the population and cow the Leftists into submission. The trade unions and state organs were purged of Leftists, the emergency courts-martial tried thousands of Leftists under new harsh laws, and the new Rightist governing bodies in the countryside punished the pro-insurgent villages (e.g., by withholding humanitarian aid). The army now led the fight against the Communist insurgency and launched the first clearing operations in the mountains of central and northern Greece. In addition, the army sporadically evacuated pro-insurgent villages and established Rightist militias to defend the pro-government villages.[45]

In late December, the Greek government complained to the UN that the support of Balkan Communist countries for the insurgents threatened Greek sovereignty and territorial integrity, and the Security Council set up the UN Commission of Investigation Concerning Greek Frontier Incidents. This ad hoc agency monitored the civil war between January and May 1947 and wrote a report that condemned Greece's three Balkan neighbours (Yugoslavia, Albania and Bulgaria) for supporting the Greek insurgents.[46]

In early January 1947, a fragile coalition government of seven anti-Communist Rightist and Centrist parties was set up after persistent pressure from the Anglo-Americans and the Greek king. The new government under Dimitrios Maximos vowed to restore public order and put into effect a twofold policy: a policy of leniency for the Communist political prisoners and a general amnesty for all armed irregulars (Rightists and Communists alike).[47]

However, these policies did not yield results. The Communists did not trust the new government to keep its word. Their suspicions were soon vindicated. While the government released thousands of deportees, the anti-Communist Minister of Public Order seized others and sent them to prison camps. Just a few insurgents surrendered their weapons since they feared, quite rightly, that the anti-Communist security organs would violate the amnesty as they had done after the Treaty of Varkiza.[48]

---

[45] G. Margaritis, *History of the Greek Civil War, 1946–1949*, Vol. I (Athens: Vivliorama, 2001), 205–12, 227–30, 244–50.
[46] Sfikas, *British Labour Government*, 134–5, 155–63.   [47] Ibid., 136.
[48] S. Plakoudas, 'Counterinsurgency in the Greek Civil War, 1946–1949' (University of Reading, PhD thesis, forthcoming).

In addition, the army proved utterly unfit for COIN duties and scored only minor tactical victories. After the Treaty of Varkiza, Britain had shouldered the task of rebuilding the Greek army from scratch. However, the almost bankrupt Labour government could not sustain a massive army. Worse, the British were still training the army for regular warfare. In short, the army did not possess the necessary military capabilities (size, structure, training and weapons) for COIN operations and suffered from low morale as there were numerous Communist sympathisers within its ranks. Political interventions in the appointment of the senior military leadership and operational planning further impaired the efficiency of an army which was short of trained and capable officers. The army used unproductive operational concepts (search-and-destroy) and tactics (poorly timed and coordinated pincer movements) against a tactically superior irregular opponent.[49]

In the summer of 1947 the military failures spurred the government to open exploratory peace negotiations with the Communists. These negotiations soon collapsed because neither side could credibly commit to the peace process: the KKE stepped up the preparations to create its 'Free State' in the North, whereas Rightist government officials sabotaged the parleys by clamping down on the still legal Left. Foreign intervention burried all hopes for peace. The United States opposed the negotiations and pressed the government (and the other Centrist personalities and parties to whom the Left had submitted peace offers) to sever all links with the Left. In March 1947, the Truman Doctrine had clearly demonstrated the willingness of the United States to prevent a Communist take-over in Greece and, in general, contain Communism in the eastern Mediterranean. To this end, in mid-1947 the United States took control of the economy and, gradually, of the political and military affairs of Greece to ensure the defeat of the Communist insurgency.[50]

The US intervention drastically changed the course of the war. In early September, the United States dictated the establishment of a coalition government between the two most powerful parties of the Republican Centre and the Royalist Right – the Liberal and the Populist Parties, respectively.[51] This move proved rewarding as the new government under the aged Republican leader, Themistocles Sophoulis, commanded high levels of popularity and legitimacy amongst Greeks. The government initially employed a twofold policy: on the one hand, a policy of leniency and amnesty for Communist prisoners and insurgents

---

[49] Close and Veremis, 'Military Struggle', 104–7.
[50] Sfikas, *British Labour Government*, 168–75.   [51] Ibid., 184–5.

respectively and, on the other hand, a programme of dynamic military operations.[52] However, the government did not intend to implement a reliable policy of leniency and amnesty, and the Rightist-controlled state and security organs continued the persecution of Communists. Consequently, these two policies failed miserably – as did the military operations launched during the same period.[53]

The Second Phase of COIN

The KKE did not intend to pursue a peaceful policy either. As noted previously, the KKE declared open war in September 1947 and established its 'Provisional Democratic Government' in December. Shocked by the twin developments, the government responded with repression by outlawing Communist organisations and proscribing Communism as an ideology. The state organs, labour unions and even agricultural co-operatives were systematically purged of Communists. The Greek Communists were officially vilified as anti-national and atheist agents of the Communist Slavs who wanted to surrender northern Greece to their foreign masters and wipe out the traditional social values and the Christian religion of the Greek nation. Obviously, no quarter would be granted to traitors to the Greek race. Roughly five thousand people were executed and fifty thousand more were deported to prison camps where terrible conditions prevailed. Tens of thousands of Communists fled to the northern Communist Balkan states.[54]

The KKE's overtures to minorities (in particular the Slav-Macedonians), the radical socialist experiments and the transfer of thousands of children to the Communist European countries seemed to vindicate the narrative of the Royalist regime. Therefore, the majority of the nationalist, pious and conservative Greek population threw in its lot with the government. While the latter's repressive policies gave rise to vehement international protests, the Americans felt compelled to defend the Greek Royalist regime.[55]

The countryside's domination by the insurgents prompted the Greek government to resort to the ancient Byzantine, then Ottoman,

---

[52] Service of Diplomatic and Historical Archive (ΥΔΙΑ): Ministry of Foreign Affairs, (1947), File 134.2, No. 42433: Griswold (Chief of the AMAG) to Sophoulis (Prime Minister), 19/9/1947.

[53] Sfikas, *Peace and War*, 93–4.

[54] Close, 'Introduction', 10; Voglis, *Becoming a Subject: Political Prisoners during the Greek Civil War* (New York: Berghahn Books, 2002), 61–3.

[55] L. S. Wittner, *American Intervention in Greece, 1943–1949: A Study in Counterrevolution*, (New York: Columbia University Press, 1982), 143–9.

nineteenth-century Greek and Russian/Soviet practice of population transfers. From late 1947 onwards the army intensified its policy of evacuating peasants suspected of Communist sympathies from their mountain villages to state-run refugee camps. Despite strong American objections, the army resettled more than 750,000 peasants (over 10 per cent of Greece's population) to such camps – thus, to use Mao's metaphor, 'draining the sea' within which the 'fish' swam.[56] Ironically, Stalin was at much the same time employing this strategy of population transfer to quell internal rebellions.[57]

The refugee crisis brought to the fore the urgent need for a comprehensive reconstruction programme in a country wrecked by years of war. After the Second World War, hundreds of thousands of Greeks (around one-third of the population) had been left homeless, hungry and poor. Therefore, Greece had become over-dependent on foreign aid to feed its starving population and get the anaemic economy back on track.[58] Greece became the beneficiary of two massive aid programmes: one in July 1947 (in the context of the Truman Doctrine) and another one in July 1948 (in the context of the Marshall Plan). Both aid programmes included a civil and military part because the United States realised that the victory over the Communist insurgency and the reconstruction of the Greek state went hand in hand. As noted, US officials took control of the economy because they, quite correctly, regarded the Greek political élites as hopelessly corrupt and incompetent to tackle the country's economic problems. The two aid programmes underwent repeated revisions due to the civil war's escalation, and, ultimately, the United States cut back on the reconstruction projects in order to pay for the repeated increases in the Greek army's size. Thereafter, US officials relaxed their strict austerity policy and subsidised the Greek government's populist policies (more than one-third of the population depended on the government for salaries and pensions) and the massive repatriation programme for more than seven hundred thousand refugees.[59] The government won the 'battle for the stomachs' of the population.

US officials intervened more than once in Greek political affairs to resolve the political crises that the incorrigible opportunism and

---

[56] Close and Veremis, 'Military Struggle', 118.

[57] A. J. Joes, *Guerrilla Warfare: A Historical, Biographical and Bibliographical Sourcebook* (Westport, CT: Greenwood Press, 1996), 226.

[58] G. Stathakis, *The Truman Doctrine and the Marshall Plan* (Athens: Vivliorama, 2004), 33–6.

[59] Stathakis, *Truman Doctrine*, 163–213; 227–92; K. E. Botsiou, 'New Policies, Old Politics: American Concepts of Reform in Marshall Plan Greece', *Journal of Modern Greek Studies*, 27/2 (2009), 209–26.

sectarianism of the Greek political élites and the growing interference of powerful non-political players (the army and the palace) repeatedly caused. Thanks to US interventions, the fragile coalition government between the Right and Centre stayed in power until the insurgency's suppression in late 1949.[60]

The continuous outside support for the Communist insurgents remained a problem with no easy solutions. The Greek government wanted to use the UN to cut off outside support for the insurgents, and the Anglo-Americans threw their weight behind the Greek government's plans. Upon a US initiative, in October 1947 the UN General Assembly set up a second monitoring agency, the United Nations Special Committee on the Balkans (UNSCOB), to determine whether Yugoslavia, Albania and Bulgaria still supported the Greek insurgents. Heavily influenced by the United States, UNSCOB wrote incriminatory reports and sent them on to the UN General Assembly, which in turn issued a series of resolutions that condemned the three Balkan states for their policies. In addition, the General Assembly repeatedly called for the repatriation of the Greek children that the insurgents had transferred to Communist Europe.[61]

After the establishment of the independent Communist government in December 1947, the US policymakers debated among themselves whether they should deploy US troops to Greece in anticipation of an invasion from Communist Europe. Truman wisely decided not to dispatch US troops so as not to escalate the internal conflict into an international one. The rumours about a Communist invasion or the operation of Communist International Brigades proved a figment of the imagination of panic-stricken Greek officials, while the US diplomatic efforts deterred even Communist governments from recognising the Greek Communists' Provisional Democratic Government.[62]

Britain shrewdly discerned a golden opportunity in the rivalries that shook the Communist camp from 1948 onwards. In June 1948, Yugoslavia was expelled from the 'Cominform' after a serious quarrel with the Soviet Union, and, in January 1949, the Greek Communists sided with Stalin in the Tito-Stalin feud and tried to wrest the Slav-

---

[60] Sfikas, *British Labour Government*, 230–1, 293.

[61] Van Coufoudakis, 'The United States, the United Nations, and the Greek Question, 1946–1952', in J. O. Iatrides (ed.), *Greece in the 40s: A Nation in Crisis* (Hanover, NH: University Press of New England, 1981), 285–8.

[62] H. Jones, '*A New Kind of War*': America's Global Strategy and the Truman Doctrine in Greece (New York: Oxford University Press, 1989), 79–94, 117–21, 137–9; Sfikas. *British Labour*, 205–11, 214–16.

Macedonians away from Belgrade. After intensive talks behind the scenes, in mid-1949 Yugoslavia agreed to terminate support for the insurgents in exchange for British (and American) economic aid. In July 1949, Tito closed the border to the KKE. The Greek insurgents found themselves at an all-time low. By that time, Stalin had ordered the KKE to stop the insurgency and instructed the other Communist states to cease support to the KKE. The Greek government had threatened to invade Albania because its Communist regime supported the insurgents, and, thus, Moscow chose to terminate the uprising rather than lose another Balkan satellite.[63]

Every war must be won on the battlefield. Victory did not come early or easily. First, the Greek army needed to develop the required military capabilities for COIN duties. In December 1947, the United States set up the Joint US Military Advisory and Planning Group (JUSMAPG) and started immediately reinforcing and reorganising the Greek army. The British Military Mission provided training on COIN, whereas JUSMAPG concerned itself with the logistical and organisational issues of the armed forces. In addition, JUSMAPG terminated the political interventions in the army and radically changed the operational concept of the Greek army. Instead of periodically staging poorly timed and coordinated pincer movements within a short campaigning season, the army would henceforth relentlessly pursue the insurgents and clear methodically one region at a time without sticking to rigid timetables.[64]

In early 1948, the revitalised Greek army was ready to strike against the insurgents. The army's size and structure had improved, new units for COIN operations (commando and light infantry units) had been created, and new weapons (e.g., mountain artillery) had been supplied in vast quantities. Implementing an operational plan that had been worked out jointly with JUSMAPG, the Greek army staged a series of clearing operations that intended to first rout the insurgents' units in central Greece and then capture the insurgents' strongholds in the north. By July 1948, the army had scored several tactical victories but the insurgents refused to submit. In late August, the insurgents launched a counter-offensive that threatened the whole front with collapse, and only the timely intervention of the Greek air force saved the day. Despite these reversals, a growing number of Greek officers acquired experience and

---

[63] B. Heuser, Western *'Containment' Policies in the Cold War: The Yugoslav Case* (London: Routledge, 1989); Sfikas, *British Labour Government*, 241–5, 251–2, 255–60.

[64] Close and Veremis, 'Military Struggle', 114–15.

expertise in COIN that they would later utilise under the orders of a capable commander.[65]

In early 1949, the Greek Commander-in-Chief during World War II, Alexandros Papagos, took office as the Field Marshall of Greece with quasi-dictatorial powers after his exacting conditions were met by the Greek government and its allies. Assuming office three years before General Gerald Templer took charge of the British COIN campaign in Malaya and applying similar measures, as we shall see, Papagos personified the imperative of unity of effort and command in COIN. He restored meritocracy and orderliness in the armed forces and inspired an offensive spirit and a sense of commitment to the Greek officer corps. Although he insisted on retaining supreme decision-making authority, he cooperated with the allied military missions in an exemplary manner. He largely followed the advice of General Van Fleet, the JUSMAPG's aggressive commander, and formulated a simple operational plan: the government army would first destroy the insurgents' weak and isolated units in southern and central Greece and then capture the insurgents' strongholds in northern Greece. The army also adopted an operational concept which was fairly new for Greece – although it had been practiced by the French for considerable time in the form of the *'quadrillage'* ('clear-and hold' tactics) and would once again be applied in the 1950s to Algeria. The army first sealed off a specific region and pre-emptively destroyed the insurgents' clandestine structures within the population that provided intelligence, manpower and material resources. Thereafter, the army cleared the region by staging spirited offensives under capable commanders. After the end of the operations, the army shifted its forces to another region, while the gendarmerie and the National Guard restored governmental control in the region and resettled the refugees in their villages.[66]

The insurgents, on the other hand, under the leadership of Zachariadis, a megalomaniac and militarily unskilled leader, had moved to a strategy requiring a regular military force (which, as we saw, they were unable to muster) and regular 'hold and defend' tactics, with disastrous effects for them. Without outside support and shrinking resources, the Communist insurgents were sentenced to an inescapable defeat. By September 1949, the army had captured the insurgents'

---

[65] D. Zafeiropoulos, *Anti-Bandit War, 1945–9* (Athens: n.p., 1956), 274–5, 283–4, 267–8, 346–503, 512–13; Close and Veremis, 'Military Struggle', 106, 108, 113–14.

[66] Zafeiropoulos, *Anti-Bandit War*, 522–38; Close and Veremis, 'Military Struggle', 115–16; 122–3.

strongholds on mounts Vitsi and Grammos in northern Greece and cleared the whole of Greece.[67] The insurgency had been completely defeated.

Tradition Cast Aside

From the early nineteenth to the mid–twentieth century, an insurgency broke out almost every twenty years in the territories that today form the modern Greek state, generating a rather distinctive and consistent tradition of guerrilla warfare. Preserved and reproduced by a distinct 'social class' of irregulars (often part-time bandits), the guerrilla tradition of *Kleftopolemos* remained in use by every insurgent movement until World War II.

The strategy of the Communist-led EAM during World War II represented the very first rift with the guerrilla tradition. Its military wing, the ELAS, only temporarily followed the guerrilla tradition of *Kleftopolemos*, and, by the end of the Axis Occupation in 1944, the ELAS had grown into a regular army that fought with regular tactics. However, this insistence on regular tactics cost the ELAS dearly when in late 1944 the EAM tried to seize power by staging an ill-executed offensive against the Greek government and its British patron.

In 1946, the Greek Communist Party staged a rural insurgency that would differ radically from every other insurgency in the history of modern Greece. The Greek Communists strove to observe rigidly Communist orthodoxy as interpreted by the pope of Communism, Stalin. Under the leadership of the dogmatic and vainglorious Zachariadis, the party set up Soviet-style political and military institutions and even strove to trigger a 'socialist revolution' in Greece. These policies, however, did not secure the support of the Greek people, and, increasingly isolated from their external allies, the insurgency suffered a sudden and painful defeat.

For more than a century, the ailing Greek kingdom strove to cope with banditry and, thus, had gradually established a fairly coherent anti-banditry strategy. The Communist insurgency, however, represented a threat that strained the traditional form of COIN almost to breaking point and compelled a succession of short-lived coalition governments to work out alternative approaches. Not merely the result of internal Communist schisms, the victory of the Royalist regime, paid for by Greek blood and American arms and money, should be credited to a critical deviation from the old anti-bandit strategy. The Greek army's

[67] Zafeiropoulos, *Anti-Bandit War*, 503–11, 522–655; Close and Veremis, 'Military Struggle', 115–16, 122–3.

commanders went through a painstaking trial-and-error process and took advantage of their own strengths and their enemies' errors to the fullest. Although the Royalist regime did not ultimately resort to the use of chemical weapons as certain military officers proposed,[68] in the end the Greek strategy-makers managed to make their strategy fit well with President Truman's global strategy of containment, with the effect that they gained the upper hand in this bloody conflict.

[68] Archive of Konstantinos Tsaldaris: File 28.2, No. 17: Lieutenant General Stylianos Kytrilakis to Army General Staff, 16/2/1948.

14   Syria: Insurrection and Suppression 2011–2016

Eyal Zisser

Syria with its several ethnic and religious communities became an independent state in April 1946. A struggle for the country ensued. This came to an end in November 1970 with the rise to power of Hafiz al-Assad. Under his regime Syria became a regional great power casting its shadow over the nearby countries and manoeuvring for influence and control over areas beyond its borders. Syria continued successfully to project an image of strength and stability even after Hafiz's death in June 2000.

All this changed in a flash in March 2011 when the Arab Spring reached Damascus and the Syrian Revolution broke out. The country was once more thrown into an internal struggle. Limited acts of protest turned into a popular insurrection and ended up as a full-scale civil war.

As soon as the disturbances erupted the regime responded with an iron fist, but was unable to suppress the rebellion, which spread and took root among large segments of the Syrian population all over the country. The regime managed to survive the first waves of protest, maintaining its cohesion and keeping its grip on the state's institutions and the military. Based on their support, the regime launched all-out war against its rivals, which was characterized by brutal large-scale repression, the use of terror and intimidation through the launching of advanced surface-surface missiles and the use of chemical weapons against civilian populations which gave support to rebel forces, and in many cases even the starvation of rebel areas and the systematic 'cleansing' of entire areas of their inhabitants.

As the struggle proceeded, Syrian society broke down step by step into its component parts, along the fault lines that had already existed in the country before its establishment. These separated geographical regions and ethnic and religious communities, as well as tribes and families. An even more divisive factor emerged as Syria turned into a theatre of Jihad, when young volunteers from all over the Arab and Muslim world flowed into the country with the aim of fighting the heretical Alawite regime in Damascus.

This situation was further complicated in the summer of 2014 by the emergence of the Islamic State in Iraq and Syria (ISIS) from the deserts of Syria and Iraq, and its achievements in the battles against the Iraqi army, the Syrian army, the Kurds and rival Syrian rebel groups. The rise of ISIS further changed the balance of forces in Syria. For the first time since the rebellion broke out in Syria, a military and political alternative to the Syrian regime was created, however abhorrent it is and however it threatens to shatter whatever remains of the Syrian state. Moreover, the rise of ISIS led to the division of Syria into small sub-states: an ISIS state in eastern Syria and western Iraq, a Ba'ath stronghold under the Assad dynasty in central Syria, and autonomous enclaves of rebel groups fighting against both the Syrian regime and ISIS.

The accomplishments of the rebels in Syria since the summer of 2014 have reignited questions regarding Bashar al-Assad's ability to remain in power and led many to conclude that only a miracle could save him. Such a miracle took place in September 2015, when Russian forces landed on Syrian soil, accompanied by members of the Iranian Revolutionary Guard, with the aim of saving the Assad regime. The war in Syria, however, has a dynamic of its own, and the Russian-Iranian involvement may prove to be a recipe for continued fighting in the country. Moreover, limited accomplishments via Russian and Iranian protection did preserve Bashar's rule over approximately one-quarter of Syrian territory but further entrenched the division of Syria between Assad and his opponents.

The Struggle for Syria

The roots of this 'Struggle for Syria' include the weakness of the state because it lacked sufficient legitimacy in the eyes of its population, especially since it had no historical antecedent that it could use to justify its existence; the deep divisions that existed in Syrian society on the basis of ethnic, religious, regional, socio-economic and social class and ideological divisions; the tension and even the rivalry between the two major urban centres, Damascus and Aleppo; and finally, the great gulf separating the cities from the rural and periphery regions.[1]

Foreign powers did not remain impartial observers of the ongoing struggle for Syria. Neighbouring Arab states as well as the superpowers

---

[1] For more see Patrick Seale, *The Struggle for Syria: A Study of Post-War Arab Politics, 1945–1958* (Oxford: Oxford University Press, 1965).

sought to gain a hold on the Syrian state, which was viewed as an important key to attaining influence and regional hegemony. This struggle contributed more than anything else to Syria's image as a weak, unstable state fraught with protracted crises and chronic military coups. In 1958, the crisis that began with independence peaked when the Syrians decided to merge with Egypt in forming the United Arab Republic (UAR). What at first seemed national suicide turned out well until, disillusioned with the merger's aftermath, the Syrians decided to dismantle the UAR in September 1961. From that point on they were resolved, come what may, to adhere to the political framework of an independent Syria.

Domestically Syria was torn apart for many years by power struggles involving several political, ideological and social forces, while Syrian society underwent a major transformation. At its centre was the rise to power of new actors from the margins of Syrian society, members of the minority religious groups and the Sunni rural periphery. These newcomers burst into the centre of the country's political stage, displacing the Sunni urban elite that had ruled high-handedly until then. Later, these forces fought among themselves. The members of the Alawite community, led by the Assad family, finally emerged as the victors.[2]

These struggles for power during the 1950s and 1960s did not develop into a civil war of all against all. For the most part they pitted factions within the army against each other and, later, within the Ba'ath party. Thus during those two decades, Syria was a witness to a spate of military coups that ended quickly and with little bloodshed.

The struggle inside Syria took on a different character after the Ba'ath Party's rise to power in the early 1960s and the establishment of the the Ba'ath regime by revolution on 8 March 1963. Islamic circles originating among the Sunni middle class in Syria's big cities began to protest against the Ba'ath regime. In the 1960s these popular protests did not spill over into violent clashes and did not provoke the use of military force against civilians (apart from the case of the riots in Hama in 1964). Between 1976 and 1982, however, under the rule of Hafiz al-Assad, Islamists declared a revolt against the regime. At first, the revolt was limited to widespread popular protests, strikes and demonstrations. Eventually armed groups joined the struggle, which culminated in the

---

[2] See also Hanna Batatu, *Syria's Peasantry: The Descendants of Its Lesser Rural Notables and Their Politics* (Princeton: Princeton University Press, 1999). Nikolaos Van Dam, *The Struggle for Power in Syria* (London: I. B. Tauris, 1996).

uprising in the city of Hama in February 1982. The scope of the revolt was relatively limited overall, ultimately making it possible for the regime to suppress it completely.[3]

Hafiz al-Assad's rise to power in November 1970 brought about a basic change in Syria's circumstances and, it seemed, heralded the end of the foreign powers' 'struggle for Syria'. Assad brought the country a degree of political stability that it had never known and thereby enabled it to transform itself from being passive and weak on the international stage into being a major player in the struggle with Israel, and on other fronts as well. At the same time, with the exception of the October 1973 (Yom Kippur) War, which began with a joint Egyptian-Syrian initiative to attack Israel, Damascus was careful not to initiate or be drawn into a direct military confrontation with Israel or to allow the quiet along the Golan Heights front to be disturbed, perhaps because of lessons it drew from the 1973 War. Even when the two countries clashed in Lebanon in June 1982, it was not the result of a Syrian initiative, but rather as a result of an Israeli effort to push Syria out of Lebanon. Damascus did, however, make wide use of the services of Palestinian and Lebanese terrorist organizations, while avoiding a direct confrontation with the Jewish state. Proxies of Syria were used not only against Israel in the Lebanese and Palestinian arenas, but also against other adversaries of Syria and its interests, whether Lebanese, Palestinian, Turkish or even American.[4]

During Operation Peace for Galilee in the 1982 War, units of the Israel IDF directly attacked Syrian troops in Lebanon. In the 1980s, following this war, Assad's Syria adopted a policy of 'strategic balance', the aim of which was to strengthen the Syrian army with Soviet assistance to the point where it would be equal in strength to the IDF. Initially, the aim was to build a conventional army able to oppose Israel head-on. Towards the end of the 1990s, after the collapse of the Soviet Union, Syria adopted a new approach. The aim now was to achieve a deterrent ability vis-à-vis Israel based upon a balance of fear or terror. This was to be accomplished by the purchase or development of non-conventional weaponry, mainly chemical weapons, as a kind of 'poor man's arsenal'. At a later stage, drawing conclusions from the First Gulf War, Syria sought to acquire long-range missiles as well. During the early 2000s it was discovered that Syria was trying

---

[3] For more see Umar F. Abd-Allah, *The Islamic Struggle in Syria* (Berkeley: Mizan Press, 1983).

[4] Patrick Seale, *Assad of Syria, the Struggle for the Middle East* (London: I. B. Tauris, 1988).

to develop nuclear weapons. In response, Israel attacked and destroyed the nuclear reactor the Syrians were trying to construct in the north of the country.[5]

Another change in Syrian policy that followed the collapse of the Soviet Union was Hafiz al-Assad's decision in the early 1990s to join the Arab-Israel peace process then under way. He began direct negotiations with the Israeli government with the aim of reaching a peace agreement. However, both Assad and Israel had before them clear red lines that limited their flexibility, so the efforts to reach an arrangement ultimately failed.[6]

Hafiz al-Assad died in June 2000 and was succeeded president of Syria by his son and heir, Bashar al-Assad. Many people inside and outside Syria were doubtful of his ability to fill his father's big shoes and continue on his path. However, the young ruler successfully secured his position and that of his regime both inside the country and abroad. Bashar's 'soft' image as a Westerner, as someone who favoured reform and change, mutated rather quickly into the image of a 'despot', determined to advance economic reforms, but not in state and society.

Bashar generally continued his father's policies towards Israel, but with noticeably less caution and prudence. On the one hand he declared his commitment to the peace process and allowed discussions with Israel during the first months of 2008 when Ehud Olmert was Prime Minister of Israel. Like his father before him, Bashar maintained the quiet along the Golan Heights border. On the other hand, he greatly strengthened his ties with Iran and the Hezbollah organization in Lebanon and enabled the latter to acquire advanced weaponry, some of it of Syrian manufacture. This, together with his decision to construct a nuclear reactor with North Korean aid in the Dayr al-Zur region of northern Syria, indicated that he was ready to take the risk of challenging both Washington and Jerusalem, and even of engaging in a conflict with the Jewish state. Still, after Israel destroyed the Syrian reactor in September 2007, Bashar refrained from any belligerent reaction.[7]

---

[5] Moshe Ma'oz, *Assad: The Sphinx of Damascus* (London: Weidenfeld and Nicolson, 1988), 119–57. See also Eyal Zisser, 'An Israeli Watershed: Strike on Syria', *Middle East Quarterly*, 15/3 (Summer 2008), 57–62.

[6] Eyal Zisser, 'What Went Wrong', *Orient*, 42/2 (2001), 25–49. For historical background on the Israeli-Syrian peace negotiations see Itamar Rabinovich, *Brink of Peace* (Tel Aviv: Yedi'ot Aharonot, 1998); Moshe Ma'oz, *Syria and Israel from War to Peace-Making* (Oxford: Oxford University Press, 1996).

[7] For more on Bashar al-Assad's first years in power see Eyal Zisser, *Commanding Syria, Bashar al-Assad's in Power* (London: I. B. Tauris Academic Press, 2006); David W. Lesch, *The New Lion of Damascus: Bashar al-Assad and Modern Syria* (New Haven, CT: Yale University Press, 2005).

The Arab Spring Reaches Syria

In December 2010 the Arab Spring broke out, initially in Tunis. From there the flames spread to Egypt, Libya and Yemen. At first it looked as though the wave of Arab revolutions might spare the Syrian state. Some analysts, but also the Syrian leadership, including Bashar al-Assad, suggested that this was so because the Syrian regime had an image of being committed to the 'resistance' (*Muqawama*) and to the struggle against Israel. After all, this regime was, along with Iran, Hezbollah and Hamas, a member of the 'axis of resistance' in the region. However, the conflict with Israel which was at the centre of the Arab public opinion's attention during the first years of the 2000s, had lost much of its importance and relevance by 2010, as Bashar al-Assad was to learn when on 18 March 2011, at the end of Friday prayer services in the mosques, demonstrations began in several Syrian cities, including Dar'a, Hama and Banyas. Since then Syria has known no peace.[8]

When the demonstrations first broke out in Syria, it seemed they might be much less extensive than those in Egypt. While hundreds of thousands, if not millions, of people were taking to the streets in Cairo and other Egyptian cities, only hundreds or at most several thousand demonstrators took part in the Syrian disturbances. Even more important was the fact emphasized by news correspondents, commentators and scholars, namely, that the demonstrations were confined to peripheral areas, at first to the town of Dar'a in the south and the small towns and villages nearby. From there disturbances spread to the rural areas around Damascus. The turmoil reached the capital itself, with its millions of inhabitants, only after several months.[9]

Perhaps surprisingly, it was precisely the peripheral areas of Syria that had constituted the stronghold of power of the Ba'ath Party and the Ba'ath regime. Clearly, something has changed. The Syrian periphery that gave the Ba'ath Party its support over the years, and from which the Ba'ath regime drew its strength, and its leaders as well, has turned its back on it. This is the culmination of a long process, extending over several decades, during which the regime allowed the support it enjoyed among the popular bases to decline and dissipate. Since its establishment

---

[8] For more on the Syrian revolution see Fouad Ajami, *The Syrian Rebellion* (Stanford, CA: Stanford University, 2012).
[9] David W. Lesch, *The Fall of the House of Assad* (New Haven, CT: Yale University Press, 2005), 55–69.

in 1963, and even more, following the November 1970 seizure of power by Hafez al-Assad (the corrective movement – *al-Haraka al-Tashihiyya*), the Ba'ath regime reflected the social changes that had occurred in Syria's society during the 1950s and 1960s, especially the emergence centre-stage of the minority religious communities and the Sunni Muslim residents of the Syrian periphery. The regime and the Ba'ath Party did not, however, adapt to further social changes since the 1970s, which included the deepening of the economic gap between the periphery and the urban centers and the spread of radical Islamism within the Sunni periphery and the growth of Shia-Sunni tension and of Kurdish national sentiments.[10]

Thus with the passage of the years, and especially from the beginning of the 2000s, the Syrian regime ceased to reflect Syrian society. It even seems to have turned its back on the Sunni population in the villages and peripheral areas that had until then been its own flesh and blood. Indeed, already in March 2004 serious rioting involving the Kurdish population broke in the city of Qamishli, and from there the protest spread to Kurdish towns and cities in the region, and even to the Kurdish quarters of Damascus and Aleppo. Dozens of Kurds were killed in the clashes, and hundreds were wounded. The disorders died down after a while, but the embers continued to glow.[11]

During the second half of the first decade of the 2000s Syria experienced one of the worst droughts the state had ever known. The damage done by the drought was felt most intensely in the Jazira region of northeastern Syria and in the south, especially in the Hawran region and its center, the city of Dar'a. In addition, these regions were adversely affected by the government's economic policies, which aimed at changing the Syrian economy from a socialist one into a 'social market economy'. The aim of the latter was to open Syria to the world economy, encourage foreign investment and promote activity in the domestic private sector as well. While the Syrian regime did indeed manage to preserve its image of strength and solidity during the first decade of the 2000s, its base of support was crumbling.[12]

---

[10] Raymound A. Hinnebusch, *Authoritarian Power and State Formation in Ba'athist Syria: Army, Party and Peasant* (Boulder, CO: Westview Press, 1990); Eyal Zisser, *Decision Making in Assad's Syria* (Washington, DC: Washington Institute for Near East Policy, 1998).

[11] *New York Times* (14, 15 March 2004).

[12] Eyal Zisser, 'The Renewal of the "Struggle for Syria": The Rise and Fall of the Ba'ath Party', *Sharqiyya* (fall 2011), 21–29. For economic data, see EIU (Economist Intelligence Unit), *Syria – Country Report* (April 2011).

From Protest to Revolution and from Revolution to Civil War

In Tunis and Egypt the Arab Spring uprising came to a head soon after the outbreak of demonstrations on the streets of Tunis and Cairo. In Libya and Yemen the uprisings spread rapidly to all parts of each country. In contrast to these Arab states, the events in Syria unfolded slowly and gradually, with ups and downs, condemning the country and its inhabitants to an intractable, long-drawn-out and extremely bloody conflict. Syria descended into a treacherous swamp from which it found it difficult to extricate itself. As important and significant as the initial sporadic demonstrations may have been in and of themselves, they were nevertheless limited in scope and intensity. However, they turned into a broad popular protest movement, and this in turn metamorphosed into a violent and uncompromising struggle between the regime and its opponents. Ultimately Assad had a full-scale civil war on his hands.

In general, one can point to three main stages in the development of the revolt in Syria into a major civil war and eventually into a war of Jihad:

> *The first stage:* In the spring of 2011, the uprising was limited to mass demonstrations of tens of thousands of protesters in peripheral towns and the countryside, with scant protests in some of the larger cities. These demonstrations nearly ceased following the regime's massive and brutal use of the military to forcefully suppress them.
>
> *The second stage,* beginning in the summer of 2011, was characterized by the expansion of the protests to the medium-sized central cities, Hama and Homs, and to the outskirts of Damascus and Aleppo. At the same time, armed groups, some of them defectors from the military, began to operate against targets belonging to the Syrian regime, such as checkpoints, police stations and military bases. At this stage, the death toll reached some 5,000 people.[13]
>
> *The third stage:* At this point, from early 2012 to mid-2014, the protest took on a new appearance. The strength of the rebels grew, and their ranks swelled until tens of thousands of armed men spread throughout the country, although they did not always operate under a united leadership. They took over large areas of the Syrian countryside, mostly in the east

---

[13] *The Guardian* (13 December 2011).

(the al Jazira area), the north (Idlib and areas outside of Aleppo), the Homs and Hama regions, and the agricultural areas of Damascus and Hawran. Attacks on Syrian military units became more systematic, and efforts to take over the large urban centres got underway, first Homs and now Damascus and Aleppo. However, the Syrian military's success in forcing the rebels out of Damascus indicates that rebel forces are more like disorganized irregulars than a proper army, even if they include defectors from the Syrian military. They were not capable of conducting a large-scale military campaign, but rather only specific, local attacks on limited targets. On the other hand, the Syrian army clearly failed to suppress and defeat these rebels, as some of the rebel camps that constituted safe havens were across the Syrian borders in Turkey or Jordan.[14]

The protest quickly turned into revolution. From the very start of the revolt the Syrian regime decided to use force against the demonstrators, in the hope of containing and suppressing the insurrection. From the beginning, many of the demonstrations turned violent, especially at focal points of tension and revolt, like Dar'a. Demonstrators set fire to public and governmental buildings and began attacking police stations and army and security force positions. Afraid to lose control, the regime sent police and internal security forces into action to disperse the demonstrators by shooting at them and making preventive arrests.

During the first week of the Syrian revolution in 18–25 March 2011 the result was five people killed all over the country. However, the number of slain rose quickly from week to week, and in less than a month 120 protesters were shot dead on one day, Friday, 20 April. Each victim served as an incitement to revolt for his family and friends. When the police and security forces found themselves unable to suppress the uprising, even at the price of several dozen dead each week, and when the regime found itself losing control in several regions of the country, the army was called into action. On 22 April 2011, army units were sent into Dar'a. Later the army was sent to other centres of confrontation, assisted by armoured units, artillery, airplanes and helicopters. It is interesting to note that in contrast to Egypt and Tunis, the top echelons of the Syrian military did not hesitate to join the battle on the side of the regime, and they were followed by the junior officers and most soldiers of

---

[14] For more *Syria Comment,* see www.Joshualandis.com/blog. See also Zisser, 'Struggle for Syria', 105–10.

the regular army. The Syrian army is an army of the regime and the dynasty, whose officers were closely tied to the ruler and his family and religious community by strong and intricate bonds.[15]

Yet even the dispatch of the army against the protesters did not quash the insurgency. Instead, it changed its character. What started out as mass demonstrations on the weekends turned into daily confrontations between the military and armed groups that began to get organized on a local basis, and later, on the basis of deserters from the Syrian army. A significant sign of the deterioration of the situation into a violent and bloody conflict was the killing of 120 security force personnel in the small town of Jisr al-Shughur near the border with Turkey. On 4 June 2011, Damascus reporting the deaths dramatically blamed 'armed terrorist groups' for the killings. The authorities went on to display the mutilated bodies of the victims. Military units were sent to the area, and their activities led to the flight of tens of thousands of refugees to Turkey.[16] With the intensification of the violence, the number of killed mounted quickly and reached several dozens daily, mostly civilians.

The Syrian army's failure to suppress or even contain the disturbances could be attributed to its conception of the uprising as a phenomenon led by isolated armed groups unconnected with the wider public, holding a radical Islamic worldview (*Takfiri*), which denounces their rival side as heretic. Thus, the regime's working assumption was that if it eliminated these groups and made a show of force, that that would deter the wider public from joining the rebellion, allowing peace and quiet to return to the country, the voices of dissent would be stilled, and the security forces and the police, as well as members of the Ba'ath party, would be enabled to restore their authority and control over the entire country.[17]

This, incidentally, was exactly what had occurred during the Islamic rebellion of 1976–1982, and especially during the rebellion in the city of Hama in February 1982. It seemed as though Bashar al-Assad was seeking to follow the footsteps of his late father and to fight the 2011–2012 uprising as if it were the violent Islamic rebellion of 1976–1982, without understanding that the situation in the country had changed radically. This time the protest was the result of a popular protest with a broad base of public support, a wide geographical spread, one that was much more intensive than the uprising of the 1980s. Indeed,

---

[15] See *al-Sharq al-Awsat* (London), (19, 20 March, 23, 30 April 2011); *al-'Arabiyya* TV Channel (20, 22 April 2011). See also *Syria Comment*, www.Joshualandis.com/blog.

[16] See Sana (Syrian Arab New Agency) (www.rtv.gov.sy) (4, 5 June 2011); *Reuters* (11 June 2011).

[17] Lesch, *Fall of the House of Assad*, 69–86.

in those areas where the army succeeded in restoring the regime's authority, such as Dasr'a in late April 2011 or Homs in early March 2012, it was able to conquer the territory, but not the hearts of the inhabitants. It became a garrison force not supported by the local population.[18]

The rebels, for their part, generally preferred to avoid head-on clashes with the army. Often they would retreat to the places from which they hailed: the villages, mountains and rural areas with their groves and forests. Then, when the army left the neighbourhoods and towns it had captured, the rebels returned and renewed their protest activities and the rebellion. By the end of 2011 the rebels had succeeded in taking firm control over substantial territory in the rural areas and the periphery. They even managed to gain control in several towns. In Homs, for example, they established themselves in at least several neighbourhoods.[19]

In this situation, in which military units found themselves confronting the civilian population, soldiers began to desert. With time, this phenomenon became more frequent. At first the number of deserters was negligible, encompassing some soldiers and lower ranking officers. But by the middle of 2012 the desertion rate had become sizeable and included more and more senior officers with the rank of major and lieutenant colonel, and even colonel and brigadier general. The various groups of deserters united in September 2011 into the 'Free Syrian Army', an umbrella body whose commanding officers operated out of Turkey. It controlled the armed groups, however loosely. It served mainly as a channel for transmitting weapons and funds from some Arab states, Turkey, and perhaps even France and the United States, to the rebels inside Syria. Still, the forces that rose up against the Syrian regime and carried on the struggle were not homogeneous. As noted above, they were characterized by factionalism and fragmentation based upon class and regional origins and ideological differences. In addition, the political leadership of the opposition bodies, the 'National Council' established in September 2011 by oppositional factors active outside of Syria, and supported by Arab and Western countries, and later the National Coalition formed in November 2012, did not succeed in establishing itself as legitimate and recognised representative of all insurgent factions inside Syria. Even the Free Army retained its independence and

---

[18] See, for example, Ammar Abdulhamid, *The Syrian Revolution Digest* (4 February 2012), www.syrianrevolutiondigest.com. For more on the 1982 events see Thomas Friedman, *From Beirut to Jerusalem* (London: Harper Collins, 1989), 185–200.

[19] See *Syria Comment*, www.Joshualandis.com/blog (3 March 2012).

refrained from subordinating itself to the authority of the National Council. In many instances local committees continued to carry on the struggle against the regime on a purely local basis.[20]

Most of the rebel forces are made up of local forces that organized themselves on a local basis, at the village, small town or even family and tribal level. They are controlled by a local leadership and worked mostly in defence of their villages and small towns or in areas close to their homes. Many of these groups have eventually become associated with the Free Syrian Army, but some have associated themselves with Islamic groups, or even with Jabhat al-Nusra, the local Al-Qaeda branch in Syria.

The Free Syrian Army established or extended its lose control over forces composed of deserters from the regular army. These forces are sometimes called regiments or brigades, although generally they are not large enough to merit such a categorization. These forces are loosely coordinated in their activities; they have received assistance from Turkey, Saudi Arabia and the United States, and they have managed to capture weapons from the regular army. Over time they have become a significant force in terms of numbers and their wide distribution all over the country. But they have not been acting in a coordinated fashion and under a common leadership, so they have not always been able to apply their numerical strength. Towards the end of 2013 this group lost much of its power, and many of its erstwhile supporters shifted their loyalty to Islamic forces operating in Syria.

Indeed, as the fighting escalated and became increasingly brutal, particularly as the religious dimension to the struggle became increasingly salient, new players, Islamic groups, entered the scene, jihadi fighters streaming into Syria from all over the Arab and Muslim world. These foreign volunteers, joined by native Syrians, served as the basis for the al-Nusra Front ('Support Front for the People of Syria'; *Jabhat an-Nuṣra li-Ahl al-Shām*), which became the local branch of Al-Qaeda in Iraq (known there as the Islamic State of Iraq; *al-Dawla al-Islamiyya fi al-'Iraq*). In April 2013, the Iraqi branch separated from the Syrian one and began operating independently as the Islamic State in Iraq and Syria (*al-Dawla al-Islamiyya fi al-'Iraq wal- al-Shām*). Other religious groups arose as well, for example, the Salafi group known as the Syrian Islamic Liberation Front, which is identified with the Syrian Muslim Brotherhood, and more important, the Islamic Front, based on Islamic

---

[20] See *Al-Watan* (Qatar) (11 April 2011); *al-Hayat* (London), (12 September 2011). For the Free Syrian army website see http://syrianarmyfree.com. More on Syrian opposition see BBC Guide to the Syrian opposition, www.bbc.co.uk/news/world-middle-east-15798218.

groups from all over Syria such as *Jaysh al-Islam* (The Islamic Army) or The Tawhid Brigade. These groups operated beside the Free Syrian Army or sometimes under its auspices in one form of another. At the end of 2011, some of these groups began to carry out terrorist and suicide attacks in all parts of Syria, especially in Aleppo and Damascus, against targets identified with the Syrian regime. Sometimes they even tried to take control and hold on to territories in which they found supporters. In such areas they carried out radical actions against supporters of the regime or war prisoners such as public beheadings. These radical groups also carried out systematic destructions of Alawite, Shi'ite and even Christian shrines and holy places.[21]

A False Turning Point

For a moment in mid-July 2012, it seemed that the outcome of the steadily escalating struggle in Syria, which first began in March 2011, had been determined, and that Bashar al-Assad's regime had reached its end. On 18 July 2012, explosions ripped through the National Security headquarters in Damascus, killing some of the most senior officials in the Syrian military and defence systems, who up until then had commanded the counter-insurgency campaign: Defence Minister Da'ud Rajiha, Chief of Crisis Operations Hasan Turkamani, and Deputy Minister of Defense and President Bashar al-Assad's brother-in-law, Asaf Shawkat. Also wounded in the attack were Hisham Ikhtiyar, director of the National Security Bureau, who died two days later, and Minister of the Interior Muhammad al-Sha'ar, who was the only survivor.[22]

As Syria was sinking into chaos, it became difficult for the sides to identify who was 'on their side' and who was 'against them'. The greatest testimony to this was the liquidation of Syria's top security echelon in July 2012, and even before this, the failed attempt to poison those same senior officers that was reported in the media in May 2012.

The strike against the heads of the Syrian regime was accompanied by an attack on Damascus by several armed groups, some of them belonging to the Free Syrian Army. The attackers managed to take over several of the city's districts, including al-Maydan. For a moment it appeared that Damascus would fall into the hands of the rebels within the coming

---

[21] See *al-Hayat* (London), 'Jabhat al-Nusara' (11, 25 November 2012). See also Aaron Lund, 'Holy Warriors, A Field Guide to Syria's Jihadi Groups', *Argument* (15 October 2012).

[22] See *al-Jazira* TV Channel (18 July 2012); *Sana* (18 July 2012). See also Eyal Zisser, 'Assad's Syria on a Brink', *Tel Aviv Notes* (14 August 2012).

hours or days. Several days later, the rebels launched an attack against Aleppo, the second most important city in the country, and managed to take over large parts of it. Simultaneously, it was reported that the rebels had also managed to gain control of a number of Syria's border crossings with Turkey and Iraq. Finally, it was reported that the Kurdish population in the northern and eastern regions of the country (about 10 per cent of the entire population of Syria), which until then had remained neutral, had begun taking steps to gain some degree of autonomy in the areas they inhabited, which they call Western Kurdistan. At the same time, they left the door open for dialogue, and even limited cooperation, with both the government and the rebels. This manner of acting by the Kurds was conditioned by their historical memory of what they had suffered under the heavy hand of the Ba'ath regime, but even more, of what they had suffered under the heavy hand of the regimes that came before the Ba'ath. Those regimes were headed by the Sunni urban elite that took control of the Syrian state from the time it first gained its independence. Thus, for example, in November 1962, one of the pre-Ba'ath Syrian governments deprived hundreds of thousands of Kurds in the Jazira region of their Syrian citizenship.

The areas inhabited by large numbers of Kurds, like the Jazira region and northern Syria, are also inhabited by Arabs, some of whom are organized in tribal frameworks. After the Syrian revolution broke out and the forces of the Assad regime began to withdraw from these areas, confrontations between the Kurds and the Arabs began over control of the territory, and especially over the grain storage facilities and oil fields located there. These confrontations became sharper because of the presence of radical Islamic movements, like the Al-Nusra Front or the 'Islamic State'. These radicals set the tone, with the support of the local Arab tribes that are inclined to cooperate with them. Naturally, the Muslims oppose the Kurds' efforts to gain control, and even some degree of autonomy, in these regions.[23]

At the same time, the Kurdish population continued to suffer from fragmentation within its ranks. It was divided among two main groups: The first, the Democratic Union Party (Kurdish: *Partiya Yekîtiya Demokrat*, PYD), a Syrian Kurdish political party established in 2003 by Kurdish activists, is perceived as affiliated with the Kurdistan Workers' Party (PKK), which operates in Turkey. The second, the

---

[23] *Reuters* (14 July 2012); al-`Arabiyya TV Channel (24 July 2012); al-Hayat (London) (19, 24 July 2012).

Kurdish National Council, was founded in Hawler on 26 October 2011, under the sponsorship of the Iraqi Kurdish leader, Massoud Barzani. The organization was originally composed of eleven Syrian Kurdish parties.

Several KNC parties have also on occasion come into conflict with another Kurdish group, the Democratic Union Party, or PYD. In order to reduce tensions, Massoud Barzani mediated between the two groups in July 2012 at a diplomatic meeting in Hawler. As a result, the PYD joined with the Kurdish National Council to form the Kurdish Supreme Committee along with a popular defence force to defend Syrian Kurdistan. Under the agreement, cities that fall under the control of Syrian Kurdish forces will be ruled jointly by the PYD and the KNC until an election can be held. Despite the agreement the PYD has apparently been able to take over most of the Kurdish regions, due to the fact that it maintains a significant armed wing, the YPG (defence committees).[24]

Thus in mid-July 2012 it seemed as if a significant turning point was about to take place. But as the days passed it became clear that the struggle for Syria had returned to its old pattern of unfolding slowly and progressively with an abundance of bloodshed. Hundreds of persons continued to be killed weekly with neither side being able to subdue its opponents. The rebellion in Syria had been going on for almost two years. Its most noteworthy characteristic, even in its third stage, had been the conspicuously slow and gradual pace at which the violence has spread throughout the country. It was almost impossible to point to any noticeable dramatic turning point in the stream of events. What can be discerned was a steady deterioration of the country's security situation as little by little the regime grew weaker.

Thus, all the erstwhile predictions that the fall of the Syrian regime was only a matter of time – a few days, as was the case in Tunisia, a few weeks, as in Egypt, or at most several months, as in Libya – had been rebuffed. The Syrian regime had managed to maintain its cohesion and unity, based on its supporting pillars: the army, the security forces, the governmental institutions and the Ba'ath Party. These elements continued their support of the regime, despite the severe blows they had suffered and the wave of desertions from their ranks. More importantly, the regime continued to rely on and benefitted from the support of important sections of Syrian society – mainly a coalition of minorities comprising the Alawites, along with Druze, Christians and even some Sunnis from the middle and

---

[24] *Reuters* (26 November 2011; 27 July 2012; 5, 15 November 2013).

upper classes in the large cities. In addition, the Syrian regime was benefitting from the support of powerful forces in the regional and international arenas, headed by Russia and Iran.

Indeed, towards mid-2013 the tide of the Syrian civil war had seemed to turn in favour of Bashar al-Assad's regime. Assad's forces, with the support of Hezbollah forces, had apparently halted the rebels' momentum and had seized the initiative. One noteworthy gain was Hezbollah's conquest of al-Qusair, in the district of Homs, during June 2013. The importance of this city, which had been in rebel hands since the summer of 2012, was that it was the key to controlling the link between Syria's interior – the Damascus-Aleppo axis – and the Syrian coast and Alawite heartland. In addition, al-Qusair is a strategic point straddling the main route from Lebanon to Homs and northern Syria. It was along this route that weapons, aid and even volunteers had flowed into rebel hands from the adjacent Sunni areas of Lebanon, including Tripoli. In addition, the Syrian regime solidified its grip on the city of Homs, even if it could not completely control it, and pushed rebel forces back from some of the entrances to Damascus, even though the rebels continued to control many of the surrounding villages to the city's east and west and some of the neighbourhoods in the eastern part of the city itself. The rebels also increased the pressure on regime forces in Aleppo, Syria's second largest city, and drove them from the northeastern part of the country, the al-Jazira region, and even mounted an offensive that extended as far as the southern coast of Syria, into the areas populated by an Alawite majority, the regime's stronghold.[25]

War of Annihilation

As the war in Syria entered its fourth year, it seemed as if the Syrian army was waging a campaign to exterminate or expel the rebels and the population that supported them. To be sure, this was perhaps not the regime's original objective, but this was the outcome of an inexorable brutalization by all parties to the conflict. But there was no other explanation for the massive use of deadly weapons of terror, such as aerial bombardment, concentrated artillery fire, surface-to-surface missiles and even chemical weapons against the rebels and their supporters in

---

[25] 'Does the Fall of al-Raqqa Constitute a Turning Point in the Syrian Revolution?' Arab Center for Research and Policy Studies (Doha, Qatar), Policy Paper (24 March 2013), http://english.dohainstitute.org/release. For the achievements of the Syrian regime in regaining control of various areas of the country during May, see *Reuters* (19–20 May, 5 June 2013).

densely populated areas. The regime used methods such as intimidation and starvation – for example in January 2015 in the siege of Madaya – and its militias carried out massacres in rebel areas which they occupied, which eventually led to the cleansing of entire areas of their inhabitants. One result has been that between four and eight million Syrians, around 30 per cent of the total population, became either internal or external refugees, most of them Sunni Muslim supporters of the rebels living in villages and peripheral areas.[26]

A striking example for this war of annihilation was the use of chemical weapons on 21 August 2013 by the Syrian regime against its opponents, in the area of al-Ghouta al-Sharqiyya, on the rural outskirts of eastern Damascus, killing more than 1,400 civilians including women and children. Russia was able, however, to conclude an agreement with the United States which rescued the Syrian regime from an imminent American attack in return for the disarmament of its chemical weapons.[27]

The unexpected collapse of the Iraqi army in early June 2014 in northern Iraq, and the fall of the Syrian regime's strongholds and enclaves in eastern Syria in July–August 2014, the threat of a radical Islamic area stretching from the outskirts of Baghdad to the outskirts of Aleppo, and the declaration by al-Baghdadi in early July 2014 of the formation of a Muslim caliphate in this region under his leadership, followed by a declaration in early September 2014 by Abu Mohammed al-Julani, leader of al-Nusra front, of the establishment of an Islamic emirate in the territories under his control – all have given the rebels a boost in their struggle against the Assad regime. The rise of ISIS led the United States to form an international coalition to fight ISIS, but the campaign launched by the United States and its allies was based on air strikes aimed at ISIS's targets and thus had only a limited effect.

ISIS's importance lies in the fact that it is the first organization fighting the regime to establish itself as a realistic alternative to Assad. ISIS has consolidated itself as a governing entity with government systems and economic, social and legal services, however basic and primitive they may be. It has succeeded in unifying under its banner – admittedly through the use of threats and violence – a large part of the armed groups that have been operating in Syria until now. It has thereby succeeded where all the opposition groups that arose during the years since the revolution began in Syria have failed. At the same time, it has exacerbated the tensions between the various opposing groups in the

---

[26] For estimates of the numbers of fatalities and refugees, see *Reuters* (14 May 2013).
[27] *Reuters* (1, 5, 11 September 2013).

rebel ranks and, more importantly, has generated renewed international legitimacy for the Assad regime.[28]

Saudi Arabia, Qatar and even Turkey have tried, individually and sometimes together, to unite the Islamic groups affiliated with them. The most recent such attempt was the establishment of the Islamic front in November 2013, as a coalition of seven rebel groups with fifty thousand soldiers. The driving force behind this front was apparently *Jaysh al-Islam* (the Army of Islam), under the leadership of Zahran Alloush (killed in a Russian bombing in late December 2015), who was close to Saudi Arabia. Because of concern about an American veto, the al-Nusra Front was not included in the Islamic Front, but it was reported from Syria that Alloush was in regular contact with al-Nusra operatives. The Islamic front published its platform in late November 2013, reflecting a radical Islamic philosophy. The platform stated, 'The Front is an Islamic political and social body acting to overthrow the Assad regime and establish an Islamic state. The Front's principles are based on Islam, which opposes democratic secularism and the idea of a civil state as a violation of religion and Islamic law'. The effort to unite these relatively moderate Islamic groups did not last for more than several months, as each group continued to operate on its own. But the immediate losers from the establishment of the Islamic Front were the National Coalition for Syrian Revolutionary and Opposition Forces and the Free Syrian Army, which until then were recognized by the West as the representatives of the Syrian revolution.[29]

Syria as a Regional and International Arena of Conflict

The initial response of the international community to the events in Syria was feeble and hesitant. Indeed, during the first months of the Syrian Intifada, the international community preferred to sit on the fence and observe what was happening from the sidelines. It even granted backing to Bashar al-Assad in his efforts to stabilize matters and calm the raging tempers in his country.[30]

However, as the weeks and months passed and the protest in Syria not only did not die down but even intensified, an increasingly striking change in attitude could be observed in the Sunni Arab street. The Arab states and the international community also changed their position with regard to what was happening in Syria and to Assad and his regime. This

[28] *Al-Sharq al-Awsat* (14 June, 15 July, 4 September 2014).
[29] *Reuters* (26, 27 November, 7 December 2013).
[30] Lesch, *Fall of the House of Assad*, 122–63.

change came about, first of all, because of the assessment that the Syrian regime would in the end collapse, as had happened to the regimes in Tunis, Egypt and Libya. Another factor in the change was the exposure of the regime's brutality and violence and the dozens of daily killings that it was perpetrating in its efforts to suppress the uprising.

The willingness of many Arab states, led by Saudi Arabia, to come out against Syria resulted from the Saudi understanding that Syria was becoming an arena of conflict between Shiite Iran and the Sunni Arab world, and therefore it was necessary to act with determination to tip the scales against Assad. To the Saudis this appeared to be especially so in the light of the weakness and incompetence they perceived in the way the United States was handling the problems of the Middle East. Turkey shared this assessment, particularly since it, and especially its leaders, members of the AKP, were pursuing additional interests in connection with their neighbour to the south. Under the leadership of Recep Tayyip Erdoğan, the Turks nurse aspirations of achieving a leading role in the Arab and Sunni world. Turkey continues to be determined not to allow the emergence of Kurdish autonomy in northern Syria, which may affect the Kurds living in Turkey. Qatar too, seemed eager to exploit the crisis in Syria to increase its influence in the Arab world and to appear as the champion of the revolutionary spirit that spread all over the Arab world.

At the same time, the international community found it difficult to come up with a cure for the Syrian crisis. It did not conceal its apprehensions over intervening in what was happening inside the country. Russia's opposition was not the only factor. There was also the concern that the treacherous quagmire Syria had turned into would swallow up anyone rushing in, like Indochina/Vietnam and later Afghanistan or Iraq in their day.

From the summer of 2014 onward, the Syrian regime found itself facing two primary fighting fronts: On the eastern front, in the summer of 2014, the Islamic State swooped in from the desert and seized control of significant parts of northern Iraq and eastern Syria. Since then, the organization has worked to establish its rule in the al-Jazeera region (eastern Syria – the az-Zor, al-Hasakeh and al-Raqqa districts), while also striving to destroy the still remaining regime enclaves in eastern Syria, such as the cities of al-Tabaka and Abu Kamal. In central Syria, Islamic State fighters succeeded in May 2015 in conquering the city of Tadmur, which constitutes the gateway into central Syria from the desert towards Homs and Damascus. Finally, in early April 2015, Islamic State fighters managed to establish control over a number of suburbs of Damascus and, in the course of May and June 2015, to advance to the eastern foothills of the Druze Mountain.

During the final months of 2014, *Jabhat al-Nusra* and its partners seized control of most of southern Syria – the rural areas of the Dara'a and Quneitra districts and the district of Damascus' rural areas (Rif Dimashq). The rebels surrounded the cities of Dara'a and Quneitra and seized control of most of the Syrian Golan Heights. In the north, the rebels succeeded in seizing control of most of the territory of north-western Syria, first and foremost the Idlib district. In the course of March–April 2015, the rebels conquered Idlib, the district capital, followed by the cities of Jisr al-Shughur and Arihah, which control the roads from Aleppo and Idlib to southern Syria and the coastal region. These achievements provided them with a safe region along the Turkish border, which enabled them to increase the pressure on Aleppo. It also provided them with a starting position towards the Syrian coast. The rebels' achievements raised doubts regarding the ability of Bashar al-Assad to remain in power in the long run and led many to conclude that only a miracle could save him.

Nevertheless, in September 2015, Russian combat air squadrons and combat soldiers arrived on Syria soil, in addition to members of the Iranian Revolutionary Guard, who were sent to Syria – possibly in accordance with an Iranian-Russian understanding or agreement – to provide assistance to the Assad regime and ensure Bashar's survival in Syria.[31] The Russian and Iranian forces dispatched to Syria were sufficient to enable him to maintain his control of the Syrian coast, which contains a large Alawite population whose loyalty to the regime is assured under all circumstances, no matter what the cost.

This measure reflects Russian and Iranian recognition of a reality in which the Syrian state of yore has ceased to exist and, on its ruins, an ISIS state has been established in eastern Syria, while Kurdish enclaves exist alongside rebel enclaves in southern and northern Syria, and a hard-core Bashar state, or a 'little or vital Syria', continues under Russian and Iranian influence, largely dependent on the goodwill of these two countries. In any case, over time Syria, which had been perceived as a regional great power in recent decades, became a punching bag and arena of regional and international conflict. On the one side were Iran and Hezbollah, and on the other side, Turkey, Saudi Arabia and other moderate Arab states. Also, on one side were the United States and the European states, while on the other side was Russia.

---

[31] Julian Borger, "Russian Troops in Syria Could End Up Helping ISIS, Report Claims," *The Guardian*, 25 September 2015, available at www.theguardian.com/world/2015/sep/25/russia-troops-syria-could-helping-isis-report.

The Military Dimension of the Struggle for Syria

In the course of the 2011–2012 uprising, Syria's regular army became the mainstay of Bashar al-Assad's regime. Several observations can be made regarding this development.

Firstly, from the moment the wall of fear protecting the regime collapsed, so did the security apparatuses that over the years had been the real base of power upon which the regime depended in order to secure its rule over the country. These apparatuses were capable of handling individuals and small opposition groups, but they proved ineffectual when it came to dealing with a wide-scale and deeply rooted popular rebellion. In this situation the regime had no alternative but to place its hopes in the armed forces.

Second, unlike the Egyptian army, the Syrian army's loyalty to the regime outweighed its loyalty to the state. We can understand this phenomenon against the following background factors: the ties of blood and patron-client relationships that linked the army's senior officers to the Assad dynasty; the key positions in the army held by many Alawite officers[32] in numbers far exceeding their community's relative weight in the Syrian population; the loyalty to the Assad regime of the members of the minority religious communities, led by the Druze and the Christians; and the fact that many of the army's senior officers came from the Sunni community and remained loyal to the military establishment, having become thoroughly integrated into it and having made successful careers there. It should be noted that this loyalty was felt less among the lower ranking Sunni officers, and it eroded as time passed and the fighting continued.

Third, the Syrian army was organized and trained to deal with external threats and, in particular, Israel. Its frame of reference was a conventional military campaign in which it would clash head-on with the army of the enemy or, at most, engage in an exchange of missiles, again, with an eye to Israel in particular. But quite suddenly it found itself confronting a home-grown, wide-scale and deeply rooted popular rebellion. Furthermore, the war in which it had to engage was asymmetrical, pitting the army's power against motley groups of rebels. Additionally, some of the army's branches proved to be totally irrelevant or useless in dealing with the challenge on the domestic front, for example, the air defence units, the navy and others.

---

[32] Alain Chouet, 'Alawi Tribal Space Tested by Power: Disintegration by Politics', *Maghreb-Machrek* (January–March 1995), 93–119, also published in *FBIS* (Foreign Broadcast Information Service), DR (Daily Report) (3 October 1995).

As noted above, the Syrian regime also made use of armed militias, called *shabiha* (Arabic: 'ghosts'). These were based upon supporters of the government recruited from among the Alawite community for pay. However, the true 'ghosts' were the groups of rebels, who enjoyed ease of movement and the ability to slip away into the mountainous areas and villages. Unlike the regular army forces, they were not hampered by any inconvenient dependency on supply routes and logistical bases. With the passing of time, the regime formed the 'Popular Committees' and later the 'National Defence Army' (*Jaysh al-Difa' al-Watani*) as a militia force affiliated with the regular army but based on volunteers, mainly from the Alawite community.[33]

Although the war the army was fighting against the rebels was asymmetrical, the army did not necessarily have the advantage. The need to deploy military units all over the country in order to ensure governmental control vis-à-vis groups of rebels whose goals were more limited compelled the soldiers to get into battles for which they were not trained or prepared and in which they had no numerical superiority over the rebels. Thus, military road blocks turned into easy prey for attackers, and army officers and commanders were attacked when they returned to their homes in areas of tension and rioting.[34]

The failure of the army to supress the revolt against the Assad dynasty led the Syrian regime to take drastic steps against its opponents, even the use of chemical weapons. Reports from Syria about the intention of the regime to use such weapons provoked stern warnings from the United States to Bashar al-Assad, telling him not to even think of such a step. Otherwise, as President Barack Obama warned, Washington would view this as the crossing of a red line. However, once it became clear that such a red line was crossed in August 2013, the Syrian regime was ready to make difficult compromise and agreed to the disarmament of its chemical weapons to avoid an American attack.[35] Israel, for its part, warned that the transfer of non-conventional weaponry to Hezbollah would constitute a casus belli and provoke an attack on the weapons before they reached the wrong hands.[36]

---

[33] See, for example, Harriet Alexander, 'The Shabiha: Inside Assad's Death Squads,' *The Telegraph* (London), 2 July 2012. See also BBC News, 'Syria Unrest: Who Are the Shabiha?', 29 May 2012, www.bbc.co.uk/news/world-middle-east-14482968.

[34] Eyal Zisser, 'Can Assad's Syria Survive Revolution?,' *Middle East Quarterly*, 20/2 (Spring 2013), 36–42. See also the *Syrian Revolution Digest* blog by Syrian expatriate intellectual Ammar Abdulhamid, www.syrianrevolutiondigest.com.

[35] Eyal Zisser, 'The Syrian Deadlock – Bashar al-Assad and Barak Obama's Moment of Truth', *e-international Relations* (15 September 2013), 1–3.

[36] *Ha'aretz* (3, 5 February; 5, 6 May 2013).

The struggle in Syria thus turned into a war of attrition in which the side that survives and overcomes its rivals will be declared the winner. The rebels had a built-in advantage, since they were motivated by the passionate desire to bring about change, as well as a passion for revenge. However, it should also be remembered that the Syrian opposition was just a loose coalition of separated factions that found it difficult to join ranks and raise up an accepted and agreed-upon political and military leadership. In the field itself, the armed groups acted with a certain degree of backing from the populations of the villages and slums at the edges of the big cities among whom they operated. However, they suffered greatly from their lack of heavy and advanced weapons, military skill and a logistical infrastructure, and most of all, from the absence of a skilled and coordinated military command.

The Syrian regime, the ethnic and religious groups supporting it, and the army down to the lowest ranking soldier saw themselves as fighting for their existence. Thus, it was not surprising that the struggle for Syria turned, on the side of the regime, into a war of annihilation aimed to exterminate or expel the rebels and the population that supports them. This was the result of the massive use of deadly weapons of terror, such as aerial bombardment, concentrated artillery fire, surface-to-surface missiles and even chemical weapons against the rebels and their supporters in densely populated areas. Between eight to ten million Syrians, around 30–50 per cent of the total population, became either internal or external refugees, most of them Sunni Muslim supporters of the rebels living in villages and peripheral areas.[37]

The deep-seated processes underway within the Syrian state and Syrian society have therefore raised doubts regarding Bashar's ability to remain in power for the long term and have led many to the conclusion that only a miracle can save him. However, just such a miracle seems to have occurred, following the change in position on the Syrian question among certain regional and international actors. Iran and Russia have taken another significant step forward by beginning to send military forces to fight alongside Bashar, and the United States and some European Union states are reassessing their positions regarding the future of his rule in Damascus. After all, the actors involved in the Syrian sphere, and the Americans and Europeans in particular, have reached the conclusion that a supreme effort must be made to preserve the institutions of the Syrian state to prevent the return of the Iraqi scenario, in which the destruction of the state and state institutions – and the army in

---

[37] For estimates of the numbers of fatalities and refugees, see *Reuters* (14 May 2013).

particular – is what created the vacuum that facilitated the emergence of the Islamic State. This also explains the commitment of Tehran and Moscow, which are now liable to become embroiled in the Syrian quagmire and a hopeless war with few accomplishments. However, Russian-Iranian intervention may prove to be a recipe for prolonging the belligerency and deepening the human tragedy underway in Syria. The price will be the limited accomplishment of preserving Bashar's rule over one-quarter of the territory of Syria, which in practice will further entrench the division of the Syrian state.

Conclusion: From One Insurgency to Many

Although the timing of the outbreak of the revolt in Syria, as well as its intensity, surprised many both inside the country and abroad, to a certain extent the writing had been on the wall for some time. A number of ominous factors could have been perceived in the country during the years preceding the outbreak: a gulf was opening up and widening between the rulers and their traditional social strongholds of support, leading to a narrowing of the regime's bases of support, large portions of the population were experiencing social and economic distress, and religious sentiments were becoming stronger. These were all signs that it was becoming more and more difficult for Bashar al-Assad's government to maintain the status quo that had existed in Syria ever since Hafiz al-Assad's seizure of power in November 1970.

The Assad family's forty-year reign was characterized by governmental stability, which enabled the country to become stable and strong. All this collapsed in a flash, as Syria has been effectively bisected into the east of the country, which is currently part of the ISIS caliphate, and the centre and west of the country, still held by the regime but also containing rebel enclaves, and from the Kurdish enclave in the north and east of the country to enclaves of opposition soldiers in western Syria, some of these being large autonomous areas beyond the regime's control.

Whatever the future may hold for Syria, whether the regime survives on the points of the army's bayonets or it falls and a new political order arises, it seems that the country is destined, not to advance, but rather to fall back into a situation like that of the past. One recalls the 1940s and 1950s when the governments in power were weak. They relied mainly on the urban Sunni population for support, and especially the traditional distinguished families and the bourgeoisie. Their control over the peripheral areas of the country was unsteady, as was their control over the locales inhabited by various ethnic communities, for example, the Alawites along the coastal strip, the Druze of Mt. Druze, and the Kurds in the Jazira region. Indeed, during those early years of Syria's independence the state's and society's fundamental components were not yet consolidated. It was a time of ceaseless struggle over the identity of the state, the path it should follow and who should rule. It was a time when external powers blatantly intervened in Syria's affairs and turned the country into an arena of regional and international conflict.

To be sure, there was an unexpected and surprising aspect to the outbreak of the 2011–2012 revolt in Syria. Its intensity and the speed with which it deteriorated into a blood bath were largely unanticipated. Still, the uniqueness and exceptional nature of these events in Syrian history should not be exaggerated. There is in them also a fundamental element of historical and institutional continuity that must not be ignored. The recent events should really be viewed as the continuation or rekindling of the not-fully-resolved struggle over control of the state, that same struggle that started from the moment Syria gained independence, and that never really ended.

15 Beyond National Styles
Towards a Connected History of Cold War Counterinsurgency

Élie Tenenbaum

Introduction

The strategic context of the Cold War, and especially the self-paralysis of the industrial war model by the advent of nuclear weapons,[1] made possible a resurgence of irregular warfare, which had hitherto been marginalised – even though always present – in Western strategic thought. As Communist-inspired movements, and especially Maoist doctrine of revolutionary war, started to spread to the fledgling Third World, Western strategists were quick to point out the emergence of a 'subversive threat', embodied by guerrilla and psychological warfare. This new paradigm would soon bring counterinsurgency expertise into one of the limelights of the international struggle.

After being shunned by academics for a long time, the literature pertaining to these 'twilight wars' has expanded considerably over the last twenty years, taking full advantage of the latest archival releases.[2] These studies generally focus either at the level of the theatre of operations (e.g., 'the Emergency campaign in Malaya') or at that of the national experience (e.g., 'the British way in counterinsurgency'). Now that this necessary work is considerably advanced, it seems possible to address the transnational level and thus to try to connect these different national experiences together and to study how they interacted. Such a 'connected approach'[3] is especially relevant in the case of the Western powers during the Cold War. Indeed, many counterinsurgents of this time tended to perceive themselves as part of a united – although never monolithic – front against a common

---

[1] R. Smith, *The Utility of Force: The Art of War in the Modern World* (London: Penguin, 2006).

[2] I. F. W. Beckett, 'British Counter-Insurgency: A Historiographical Reflection', *Small Wars & Insurgencies*, 23 (2012), 781–98.

[3] C. Douki and P. Minard, 'Histoire globale, histoires connectées: un changement d'échelle historiographique?', *Revue d'Histoire Moderne et Contemporaine*, 54/4bis (2007), 7–21.

threat. For instance, in the midst of the Algerian war, a French general called for 'a comprehensive response from the West [against] a threat that concerns it globally and therefore demands a counter-action if not integrated, at least coordinated'.[4]

This chapter attempts to apply the methods of connected history to the case of the three major Western powers involved in early Cold War counterinsurgency (the United States, the United Kingdom and France), in order to provide some keys to understand the links binding together Western experiences of irregular warfare. Following a three-part narrative, the chapter will first address the emergence of a strategic community during and after the Second World War; it will then take up the introduction and subsequent pooling of new tactics in Southeast Asia; and it will finally focus on how these were systematised and stand-ardised through a globalisation process that eventually failed to be imple-mented on the ground.

The Birth of a Strategic Community (1944–1954)

Most studies on irregular warfare in the twentieth century, and par-ticularly those on counterinsurgency, tend to emphasise the import-ance of the colonial legacy and its effects on Cold War practices. While this feature should not be played down, it is all the more important to underline the radical turn induced by the experience of Total War.[5] This is even more true when we turn to the circulation of expertise in matters of irregular warfare, even if evidence of a nearly as widespread circulation of knowledge about colonial warfare can be found in the late nineteenth and early twentieth centuries,[6] World War II brought about a dramatic change as it initiated the first inter-allied training in irregular warfare, under British influence.

The British Crucible of Special Warfare

The interwar period witnessed the emergence of a very fertile British thinking on covert, non-linear, behind-the-lines types of operations that often implied propaganda, sabotage and guerrilla tactics, all of which was

---

[4] C. Delmas, *La Guerre Révolutionnaire* (Paris: Presses Universitaires de France, 1959), 124.
[5] H. Strachan, 'Essay and Reflection: On Total War and Modern War', *International History Review*, 22 (2000), 341–70.
[6] É. Tenenbaum, 'Apprendre de ses Alliés. Réflexions autour de la circulation des savoirs stratégiques irréguliers en Occident', in M. Goya and C. Sicourmat (eds.), *L'Académie de la Boue. Regards croisés sur l'apprentissage des forces armées* (Paris: IRSEM, 2012) 16–26.

later called special warfare.[7] Even though these views remained rather marginal compared to the largely conventional mind-set of the General Staff, they did gain an institutional acknowledgement through the creation in 1938 of a small General Staff Research section or GS(R), then MI(R) in 1939, that was responsible for providing doctrinal support to operations designed to subvert and harass Britain's adversary on its rear front.[8] This small cell was essentially staffed with two officers with experience from both the Great War and Ireland, J. C. F. Holland and Colin Gubbins; one can also mention future Field Marshal Templer's time at MI(R), which is of some interest to the analysis of his subsequent action in Malaya.

MI(R) constituted the core of the Special Operations Executive (SOE), created in July 1940, after the fall of France and the British Expeditionary Force's expulsion from the Continent. Placed under the command of General Gubbins, SOE's very mission was, according to Churchill's own words, to 'set Europe ablaze'[9] through a network of underground organisations that would wage a subversive war in Nazi-occupied Europe. To this end, SOE would naturally rely massively on the contingents of refugees and exiles, coming to Britain from every corner of Europe. Openly inspired by the IRA techniques,[10] Gubbins organised sabotage and propaganda, then guerrilla – once popular support had been secured – so as to open a new front, on the rear of the enemy.

British strategy of irregular warfare during World War II therefore required a close collaboration with its European allies – as well as with the United States, whose new-born Office of Strategic Services (OSS) was rapidly to follow SOE's lead in covert operations.[11] Thus placed at the spearhead of an irregular coalition, London set up special training schools (STSs) where British and foreigners were taught side by side in the art of guerrilla and subversion.[12] In the same line of thinking, SOE's sister organisation, the Political Warfare Executive (PWE), in charge of propaganda and psychological warfare, would equally prove an inter-allied

---

[7] For a good review of the British strategic landscape in the interwar period, see S. Anglim, *Orde Wingate and the British Army, 1922–1944* (London: Pickering & Chatto, 2010).

[8] S. Anglim, 'MI(R), G(R) and British Covert Operations, 1939–42', *Intelligence and National Security*, 20 (2005), 631–53.

[9] D. Dodds-Parker, *Setting Europe Ablaze: An Account of Ungentlemanly Warfare* (London: Springwood 1983).

[10] A. R. B. Linderman, 'Lessons Learned by SOE from the Irish War of Independence' (presented at the Society for Military History 79th Annual Meeting, Washington, DC, 2012).

[11] A. H. Paddock, *US Army Special Warfare. Its Origins. Psychological and Unconventional Warfare, 1941-1952* (Washington, DC: National Defense University Press, 1982), 7.

[12] United Kingdom National Archives (TNA), HS 8/960, Special Training Schools Folder, 1941–1942.

experience as the British had to rely on exiles in order to organise radio broadcasts and to help in the production of propaganda leaflets.[13]

If alliances have always existed in the history of warfare, joint training appeared much more recently, and the British practice of 'special warfare' surely constituted one of the very first examples of the kind. As far as Americans and French were concerned, the so-called Jedburghs were particularly important. These three-man teams – one of them at least French – were to be parachuted into occupied France after D-Day in order to help and organise the *Maquis* in coordination of Allied conventional forces. Trained together at Milton Hall, French, British and American operatives were let alone to form their team 'on the basis of personal affinity'[14] so they would get along during the operation.

After the war, many Jedburghs played an important part in the irregular forces of their respective countries while always maintaining contact through a very active network of veterans. Human ties that were woven between these very young men were to result in a strong generational experience that would persist throughout the Cold War and would provide the social backbone for the circulation of irregular strategic knowledge.[15]

From Guerrillas to Counter-Guerrillas

In the aftermath of World War II, irregular warfare was on the brink of returning to the marginality it came from, as the political-military establishment decided to decommission most of these wartime organisations – PWE, SOE and SAS in Britain, OSS in the Unites States, and *the Service de Documentation Extérieure et de Contre-Espionnage* (SDECE)'s 'action branch' in France were all disbanded in 1945–1946.[16] However,

---

[13] T. W. Brooks, *British Propaganda to France, 1940-1944: Machinery, Method and Message* (Edinburgh: Edinburgh University Press, 2007). PWE would eventually merge with American and French counterparts to form SHAEF's Psychological Warfare Division under the command of US Army general Robert McClure.

[14] J. Sassi, *Opérations Spéciales: 20 Ans De Guerres Secrètes* (Paris: Nimrod, 2009), 49.

[15] Many accounts of the training period can be found in the memoirs of former Jedburghs: W. E. Colby, *Honorable Men: My Life in the CIA* (New York: Simon and Schuster, 1978); J. Singlaub, *Hazardous Duty: An American Soldier in the Twentieth Century* (New York: Summit Books, 1992); P. Aussaresses, *Pour la France. Services Spéciaux. 1942–1954* (Monaco: Le Rocher, 2001); Sassi, *Opérations Spéciales: 20 Ans De Guerres Secrètes*. For a general account of the Jedburgh operation, see W. Irwin, *The Jedburghs: The Secret History of the Allied Special Forces, France 1944* (London: Public Affairs, 2005).

[16] For the liquidation of SOE and OSS, see R. J. Aldrich, *The Hidden Hand. Britain, America, and Cold War Secret Intelligence* (Overlook Press, 2001), 79–85. For the somewhat more complicated fate of the 'Service Action', in post-war France, see Service Historique de la Défense (SHD), DITEEX, 3K 60, 'Témoignage de Paul Aussaresses' and 3K 71, 'Témoignage de Robert Maloubier'.

the rise of the Cold War prevented these skills, and the social networks that came with them, from disappearing. Faced with the emerging threat of a 'Communist Fifth Column within our own borders, whose aim is to rot our resistance from within, as similar methods rotted France before 1940,'[17] the Western powers surreptitiously reactivated their subversion and guerrilla experts in order to turn them into counter-subversion and counter-guerrilla specialists.

The case of Greece is quite suggestive of this trend. The pioneering work of Tim Jones showed how SOE and SAS operatives took part, as soon as December 1944, in street fights in Athens to prevent the communist coup attempted by the Greek People's Liberation Army (ELAS).[18] It is this counter-guerrilla capability that SAS proponents such as Lt. Colonel M. C. Calvert would put forward in their attempt to convince Whitehall that they still had a role to play in the post-war world. As the Truman Doctrine was formulated by March 1947, the United States' conventional forces gradually assumed responsibility for military assistance to Greece against communist subversion. Even though US assistance mostly took a conventional form, they did benefit, once again, from 'British views on counter-banditry operations.'[19] Such a knowledge transfer did not necessarily go easily, and the British soon complained that the US mission was unable 'to profit from [their] experience',[20] especially regarding SAS-type commando units, which were 'still being incorrectly employed'[21] by the Americans.

As in Greece, the transition from guerrilla to counter-guerrilla in Southeast Asia was sometime quite swift. Such was the case of Force 136's French Indochina Country Section (FICS), commanded by Colonel Crèvecœur, that was supposed to 'subvert' Japanese forces in Indochina, notably by setting up *Maquis* on their rear-guard.[22] This unit, essentially composed of former French Jedburghs, also benefitted from British tactical training in jungle warfare, and was commanded from

---

[17] TNA, AIR 75/116, 'Defence Policy and Global Strategy 1950', Top Secret, Report by the Chiefs of Staff, 20 March 1950.

[18] T. Jones, *SAS: The First Secret Wars: The Unknown Years of Combat and Counter-Insurgency* (London: I. B. Tauris, 2005), 12.

[19] United States National Archives and Records Administration (NARA), Record Group (RG) 319, 1041, Box 41, 'Intelligence Report No. 4-47' from the Office of the Military Attaché in Athens, Top Secret, 2 January 1947.

[20] Quoted in T. Jones, *Postwar Counterinsurgency and the SAS, 1945–1952: A Special Type of Warfare* (New York: Routledge, 2001), 64–5.

[21] TNA, WO 202/976, 'Maj. Gen. S.B. Rawlins to Lt. Gen. D. Yadjis', Secret & Personal, 25 December 1947.

[22] M. Thomas, 'Silent Partners: SOE's French Indo-China Section, 1943–1945', *Modern Asian Studies*, 34 (2000), 943–76.

SOE headquarters in Kandy (Ceylon).[23] Along with the Corps Léger d'Intervention (CLI) commanded by Lt. Colonel Huard, FICS operational concepts were openly inspired from British lessons on deep penetration operations like Brigadier Wingate's *Chindits* in Burma.[24] After the Japanese surrendered on 2 September 1945, French guerrilla forces were swiftly turned into a counter-guerrilla instrument of colonial *Reconquista* against a new adversary: the Viet Minh.

Countering Communist Subversion in Europe

As for guerrilla warfare, political or psychological warfare organisations had also been disbanded in the immediate post–World War II period. Western democracies distrusted these tools, which might have been justified for a total war but were considered dangerous in peacetime.[25] But as in the case of guerrilla warfare, these skills were progressively reintroduced and adapted to meet the Cold War challenge. By 1947, the state of psychological subversion in Western Europe was perceived as disastrous, especially in France and Italy where Communist labour unions had been organising a series of 'insurrectionary strikes' that threatened the fragile post-war regimes.[26]

In order to react to what they saw as a Soviet subversive offensive, Britain, the United States and, to a much lesser extent, France, reactivated psychological warfare organisations, whose concepts of employment were generally modelled on their wartime ancestors. Once again, the British appeared at the spearhead of this irregular warfare apparatus with the creation in 1948 of the Information Research Department (IRD), a replica of the PWE but placed under the supervision of the Foreign Office. IRD was prompt to engage in the circulation of information with other allies. The Americans were naturally the first to be

---

[23] SHD/DT, 1K 401, Boxes 1–5. See also P. and M. C. Villatoux, *La République et son armée face au 'péril subversif'. Guerre et action psychologiques. 1945–1960* (Paris: Les Indes savantes, 2005), 241.

[24] SHD/DT, 10H 85, 'Extrait du Rapport Wingate', appendix to the 'Avant-projet de plan d'action subversive en Indochine', Kandy, 2 October 1944; see also SHD/DT, 1K 402, 'Avant-projet d'action subversive au Cambodge' by Capt. Laure, Calcutta, 23 May 1945.

[25] Prime Minister Clement Atlee disbanded the PWE stating that 'he had no wish to preside over a British Komintern' and OSS propaganda apparatus was retired on the basis of the fear to see 'the creation of a super-Gestapo agency', both referred to in Andrew Defty, *Britain, America and Anti-Communists: The Information Research Department* (London: Routledge, 2007), 27–8.

[26] For a study of the 1947 strikes in France, see É. Méchoulan, 'Chapitre 18. Le Pouvoir Face Aux Grèves "Insurrectionnelles" de Novembre et de Décembre', in S. Berstein and P. Milza (eds.), *L'année 1947* (Paris: Presses de Sciences Po, 1999), 389–408.

engaged, as they cooperated with IRD in Italy to influence the 1948 elections. But British 'psy-warriors' soon discovered that the State Department's Office of International Information 'was not producing anything comparable to the IRD's basic papers'.[27] The same kind of disappointment came from the cooperation with French authorities, which were lagging behind even further, so that the IRD had to dispatch seven information officers to the big French cities in order to make direct contact with the press to provide it with anti-communist materials.[28]

Notwithstanding these difficulties, a meeting was held in Paris on 4 October 1948 with the heads of French, British and US diplomatic services in order to 'take a general move towards some degree of coordination of propaganda vis-à-vis the Russians'.[29] By the same token, the Foreign Office set up a Working Party to study possible cooperation with the Brussels Treaty (or Western Union, WU) Powers (UK, France and Benelux countries) on propaganda issues.[30] Even though a number of ambitious projects was formulated under the name 'Spiritual Union',[31] it was eventually decided 'to oppose the creation of a joint propaganda committee within the Western Union and to propose instead periodic discussions between information officials'.[32] As Britain considered itself to be 'the only one [among the Five Powers] to be equipped with a large and efficient information machine'[33] so that there would be 'no advantage' for them to bind themselves in too narrow a coordination.

But the idea was reactivated in the framework of the Atlantic Alliance by the United States, for whom 'the maximum degree of cooperation among the NATO members in both the fields of intelligence and information had to be achieved as soon as possible'.[34] By 1950, NATO

---

[27] Defty, *Britain, America and Anti-Communists*, 106–7. As a matter of fact, it took some time to the British to understand that it was the CIA that was doing most of the job that IRD was doing.

[28] For the French organisation of psychological warfare in 1947–50, see Villatoux, *La République et son armée*, 131–4. For the work of IRD officers in France see, for example, TNA, FO 1110/229, Dispatch 3395/G, 'Minutes of a conference of provincial information officers held in Paris 24–25 October 1949'. It was not until June 1950 that France engineered an information policy that spared IRD the 'very difficult task' of contacting directly the French newspapers.

[29] TNA, FO 1110/126, PR860/G, 'An exchange of views between France, the United States of America and the United Kingdom on the co-ordination of their propaganda', 4 October 1948.

[30] TNA, FO 1110/126, PR914/G, 'Co-ordination of measures to counter Soviet propaganda between the Brussels Treaty Powers', 21 October 1948.

[31] TNA, FO 953/145, P253, 'Spiritual Union', 19 March 1948.

[32] L. Risso, 'A Difficult Compromise: British and American Plans for a Common Anti-Communist Propaganda Response in Western Europe, 1948–58', *Intelligence and National Security*, 26 (2011), 330–54, 333.

[33] TNA, FO 1110/126, PR860/G.   [34] Risso, 'Difficult Compromise', 339.

Information Service (NATIS) called on the allied powers to 'study the effective measures capable to reverse the current defensive posture in the counter-propaganda field'.[35] NATO's work relied heavily on IRD and CIA materials, passed on to British and US delegations and then circulated among Western powers.

The same year, 1951, the Supreme Headquarters Allied Powers Europe (SHAPE) set up a Psychological Warfare (PW) Branch whose task was 'to plan and prepare for the conduct of psychological warfare in time of war'.[36] This small office – occupied by two American officers, one French and one British– was supposed to reinvest the 'PsyWar' field on the military side. Even though the PW Branch was limited by Britain's reluctance to give away political autonomy to military staff, it proved a doctrinal convergence between allied armed forces. For the French, this decision proved to be a wake-up call to catch up with the British and the Americans in this matter – Paris decided to send some officers to Fort Bragg as soon as possible in order 'to receive PsyWar training'.[37]

In 1952, another step was taken with a series of NATO council memoranda regarding the planning of civil organisation in wartime regarding 'subversion' and 'fifth columns'.[38] These led to the creation of a Special Information Committee, whose role was to 'exchange intelligence on the methods employed by hostile forces to infiltrate NATO countries and more generally to engage in subversive activities'.[39] The general term 'subversion' now embraced in a single phrase both legal (political activism, propaganda) and illegal (espionage, sabotage and guerrilla) activities. In December 1952 the Committee's name was changed to 'Special Committee' at the request of the UK but kept on its work of monitoring communist subversive activities through regular meetings between the different intelligence services.[40]

As the European theatre was progressively frozen by the Cold War stalemate, irregular warfare became increasingly limited to propaganda

---

[35] NATO Archives, AC/1-D/6, 'Resolution on Initiative in the Counter-Propaganda Field, 16 April 1951'.

[36] TNA, FO 371/102555, WU16912/1/G, 'Suggestion by Lt Col Chesshyre that a NATO authority should be set up to give Gen. Eisenhower political guidance on Psychological Warfare, 16 November 1951'.

[37] SHD/DT, 'L806/CAB/SS, Aide-mémoire des question d'actualités en matière d'action psychologique et d'information, 30 October 1952'.

[38] NATO Archives, CM(52)27, 'Memorandum of the Secretary General (Lord Ismay), 5 June 1952'.

[39] NATO Archives, CM(52)110, 'Groupe de travail chargé d'étudier la coopération contre les activités subversives, 27 November 1952'.

[40] NATO Archives, CR(52)31, 'Minute of a Council Meeting', 4 December 1952. The Special Committee archives (AC/46 series) are closed to the public, and the committee itself is still active today.

and occasional covert actions. During this time, a new chapter of knowledge circulation was being written in Asia, where the Cold War was
considerably hotter.

Southeast Asia – A Laboratory for Irregular Warfare (1949–1959)

Facing the Maoist Strategic Revolution

The Chinese communist victory in November 1949 and the fear of a
Communist tide submerging Southeast Asia prompted the new wave of
knowledge exchange between Western powers. By the end of 1949, the
French and the British, soon to be joined by the Americans, started to see
China as 'the common enemy that had arrived [on] the borders of the
Western world'.[41] Such an enemy was all the more threatening that it
claimed to resort to a new strategic concept, codified by twenty years of
civil war and anti-Japanese struggle, and known as 'revolutionary warfare'. The West essentially interpreted this concept as a combination of
guerrilla tactics and intensive propaganda – thus projecting its own
experience of World War II.

The Chinese Communists had not waited for their victory over
Kuomintang to preach their strategic gospel to other liberation movements across Asia and the world.[42] Therefore, the Communist insurgencies launched against the French in Indochina in 1946, against the
British in Malaya and against the US-friendly regime in the Philippines
in 1948 were quick to turn to the Chinese model – depending on the
cases, the Chinese offered diplomatic support, military advisers or war
material.[43]

The Western powers in the area quickly recognised the challenge posed
by China through its revolutionary warfare strategy. The need to meet
such a threat prompted a strong desire for cooperation as shown by US

---

[41] SHD/DT, 10H 144, 'Aide-mémoire sur la conférence tenue à Singapour, 26 November
1949', 10–11.

[42] That is the message of Liu Shaoqi (Vice-Chairman of the PRC) at the Conference of the
labour unions of Asia and Australia in November 1949: 'The armed struggle must be
the main form of struggle. .... This is the way followed by the Chinese people to obtain
the victory in its own country. This is the way of Mao Zedong. This may be the way to be
followed by the colonised people in their struggle for liberation'. In L. Shaoqi, 'Speech of
November 23, 1949', *Collected Works of Liu Shao-ch'i*, vol. 2 (Hong Kong: Union
Research Institute 1969), 185.

[43] É. Tenenbaum, 'L'Asie Du Sud-Est, Laboratoire Stratégique De La Guerre Irrégulière
Depuis 1945', in P. Journoud (ed.), *Le débat stratégique en Asie du Sud-Est depuis 1945*
(Paris: IRSEM, 2012), 147–203.

National Security Council document NSC 90, entitled 'Collaboration with friendly governments on operations against guerrillas' and suggested by Philip Jessup to Dean Acheson in 1950.[44] This memorandum intended 'to develop a parallel program for the exchange of current information on Soviet and communistic inspired guerrilla activities with our allies and friends'. The only two allies explicitly mentioned in the document were the French and the British given their counter-guerrilla experience Southeast Asia.

NSC 90 did not produce much of a result: it failed to create any ad hoc exchange structures as the NSC staff eventually decided to limit this process to the already existing ways (liaison officers, intelligence forms, etc.).[45] But this certainly did not preclude the Western proponents of irregular warfare from working together.

A Regional Cross-Learning Process

Given the Maoist strategic challenge, the pivotal role of the region in geopolitical representations, and the concomitant presence of three main Western powers, Southeast Asia emerged as a seminal laboratory for irregular warfare in the first decade of the Cold War. Within this area, counter-guerrilla, counter-subversion and soon counterinsurgency techniques were widely tested, pooled, dispatched and adapted in a cross-learning process.

From the outset, Indochina appeared as a focal point for knowledge circulation, due to its strategic position, in the front line against 'Red China'. As soon as they decided to back the French fight against the Viet Minh,[46] the Americans tried to foster the creation of irregular operational groups on the pattern of their inter-allied experience in World War II.[47] This is why the CIA called on a young French-American OSS veteran with a 'behind-the-lines' combat experience in

---

[44] Digital National Security Archives (DNSA), Intelligence Community Collection, 'NSC 90, Report to the National Security Council by Executive Secretary on Office of Special Projects, October 1950'.

[45] NARA, RG59, A11586E, Box 13, Report to the National Security Council by Executive Secretary on Office of Special Projects, Secret, NSC 90, 8 May 1951.

[46] This decision can be roughly dated from the NSC 64 (27 February 1950). See Department of Defense, *The Pentagon Papers: The Defense Department History of United States Decisionmaking on Vietnam*, Senator Gravel Edition (Boston, MA: Beacon Press, 1971), 179.

[47] NARA, RG59, 751G.5 MAP/6-2050, 'Telegram from Saigon, 20 June 1950'. See also R. H. Spector, *Advice and Support: The Early Years, 1941–1960* (Washington, DC: United States Department of Defense, 2009), 161.

China: Thibaut de Saint-Phalle.[48] The proposal he made to Saigon in November 1950 was to provide US training to local 'irregulars' to operate as *Maquis* at the Viet Minh rear.[49] It seems that an agreement in principle was given by High Commissioner Pignon, but was eventually rejected when General de Lattre de Tassigny took over both civilian and military command in December. Nevertheless, de Lattre did apply the American concept on a purely French basis with the creation of a SDECE action branch called GCMA (Composite Airborne Commando Groups).[50]

In spite of these recurring rivalries, Franco-American cooperation continued in the field of irregular warfare. Psychological operations in particular became a central concern as they appeared instrumental in securing popular support – a central aspect of the communist people's war. Thanks to French officers training in the United States, Paris was soon able to provide its army with a state-of-the-art psychological warfare apparatus[51]. For instance, loudspeaker and leaflet companies, created by the US Army in 1950,[52] were introduced in the French Army under the name *Compagnies de Haut-Parleurs et de Tracts* (CHPT).[53] Another example of inter-allied cooperation is the 1953 Pearl Harbor conference where working groups were set up to discuss psychological and guerrilla warfare. This provided an opportunity for French, American and British representatives to discuss the possibility of resorting to Second World War–style unconventional joint operations in the event of a Chinese invasion of Indochina.[54]

Finally, even though the French-American relations in Indochina were tarnished by the the failure of the US to support France at Dien Bien Phu in 1954,[55] this bitter handover also proved the occasion for knowledge transfers, this time from the French to the Americans. Some French

---

[48] T. de Saint Phalle, *Saints, Sinners and Scalawags: A Lifetime in Stories* (Brookline, NH: Hobblebush Books, 2004), 291–316.

[49] SHD/DT, 10H 608, 'Extrait d'une lettre de M. du Gardier à M. Baeyens, directeur d'Asie-Océanie', 17 November 1950.

[50] Philippe Pottier, 'GCMA/GMI: A French Experience in Counterinsurgency during the French Indochina War', *Small Wars and Insurgencies*, 16 (2005), 125–46.

[51] SHD/DT, 10T 1013, 'Rapport de Mission du CBA Jacques Rousset sur le Deuxieme cours de Guerre Psychologique suivie à l'Army General School', 8 April 1952.

[52] NARA, RG319, UD 148, Box 1, 'Major Accomplishment of the Office of the Chief of Psychological Warfare', 24 March 1953. See also Paddock, *US Army Special Warfare*, 200n.

[53] Even though some will be introduced by 1952 in Indochina, they will only be systematised in Algeria from 1956 onwards; see Villatoux, *La République et son armée*, 387.

[54] SHD/DT, 10H 151, 'Report by Staff Planners to the Military Representatives of the Five Powers on the Conference held 15 June to 1 July 1953 at Pearl Harbor', undated.

[55] Beatrice Heuser: 'Dunkirk, Dien Bien Phu, and Suez, or why France doesn't trust allies and has learned to love the bomb', in id. & Cyril Buffet (eds.): *Haunted by History* (Oxford: Berghahn, 1998), pp. 157–174.

structures like the Mobile Administrative Groups (GAMO) were adapted by the CIA's Saigon Military Mission – headed by Colonel (later General) Edward G. Lansdale and turned into the Civic Action Teams.[56] The later years of the decade also witnessed the CIA reactivation of the GCMA *Maquis* – the very operation proposed by Saint-Phalle in 1950 – especially in Laos, where the power struggle was continuous from the Geneva Conference onwards.[57]

Even though all eyes were undoubtedly on Indochina during the early Cold War, Malaya was at least as important in terms of knowledge transfer. The British campaign against the communist insurgents offered an original model of operations based on a combination of colonial pacification (food and population control, resettlement to new villages) and special operations (police-type operations against communist infrastructure through special branch and jungle warfare counter-guerrilla with Special Air Service (SAS) units, recreated after being disbanded in 1946).[58]

Once more, the British posed as concept- and training-providers for their allies: by 1951, they provided French, Vietnamese and American-Filipino officers with counter-guerrilla training courses.[59] By 1956, a CIA representative visited Malaya and 'seemed very impressed by [British] police training methods in anti-communist and security techniques [particularly Special Branch and anti-guerrilla activity]', including the idea to 'offer graduate scholarships [to officers from SEATO countries] in British institutions'.[60] Around the end of the decade, a permanent exchange convention had been passed between the 22nd SAS regiment and US Army 1st Special Forces Group in Okinawa, which used to 'send approximately ten men per year to the operation month course at the FARELF (Far East Land Forces) Training Centre, Kotta Tingi, Malaya'.[61]

[56] Personal interview with Rufus Philipps, a close collaborator of E. Lansdale in the SMM, in Washington, DC, 14 March 2012. See also Edward Lansdale, *In the Midst of Wars. An American's Mission to Southeast Asia* (New York: Harper & Row, 1972), 217.

[57] Jean-Marc Le Page and Élie Tenenbaum, 'The "Unquiet Allies": French and American Intelligence Relations during the First Indochina War, 1950–54', *Studies in Intelligence*, 55 (2011), 25–37.

[58] For Special Branch work, see L. Comber, *Malaya's Secret Police 1945–60: The Role of the Special Branch in the Malayan Emergency* (Pasir Panjang: Institute of Southeast Asian Studies, 2008). For SAS operations, see Jones, *Postwar Counterinsurgency and the SAS, 1945–1952*, 114 ff.

[59] TNA, FO 371/92947, FP 1192/G, 'Visit of Lt. Col. Banzon, Philippine Army to Malaya', 13 March 1951; SHD/DT, 10H 704, 'Compte-rendu du stage en Malaisie par le Cne Robert Ferry', 26 February 1952.

[60] TNA, CO 1030/170, 'Letter from A.A. Landymore (DO/FED) to A. G. Gilchrist, Esq., Singapore', 17 February 1956.

[61] US Center for Military History (CMH), Andrew Birtle Personal Papers, Malaya C3, 'US Military Forces Benefits Resulting from British Anti-Guerrilla Warfare in Malaya', top secret memo, 4 March 1960. See also J. F. Kennedy Presidential Library (JFKL),

Finally, the Southeast Asia Treaty Organisation (SEATO), established in February 1955, also functioned as a forum for exchanging knowledge on irregular warfare issues. In the aftermath of the Manila Treaty, the creation of a Security Expert Committee was decided to monitor and possibly coordinate counter-subversion activities in the region 'with the Brussels Treaty Security Committee as our model'.[62] By July 1955, a 'Counter-Subversion Committee' composed of civilian and military experts was established, relying mostly on British, US and, to a lesser extent, French materials. Before drawing away from SEATO, Paris did send some of its best experts on these issues, including Charles Lacheroy and David Galula, to attend the first meetings.[63] In the later years of the decade, SEATO counter-subversion committee became a major purveyor of security personnel training (especially Vietnamese officers sent to Malaya or to the United States) as well as for the exchange and diffusion of psychological warfare materials, usually issued by British IRD.[64]

At the end of the 1950s, the Western powers had pooled a vast repertoire of counter-subversion and counter-guerrilla tactics. But such a repertoire still needed to be taken out of its specific regional context in order to provide a comprehensive strategic model capable of meeting the new insurgency challenge anywhere.

Theorisation and Globalisation of the Strategic Knowledge (1955–1965)

While in the first decade of the Cold War, the French and the British were certainly at the forefront of the counter-subversive movement, they gradually withdrew from 'East of Suez' as they wrote the final chapter of their respective colonial empires. As decolonisation processed, the United States felt a need to take up the 'White man's burden' wherever Soviet influence was to be countered. Such a containment strategy, which had initially been thought for Europe, progressively extended to the 'Third World'. In order to meet this new challenge, the United States

National Security Files, Box 279, 'Special Warfare Activities Field Inspection Visits to Okinawa, Laos, Vietnam and Malaya', 14 February 1962.

[62] TNA, FO 371/111897, D1074/835/G, 'Subversion in S.E. Asia – Manila Treaty', 30 December 1954.

[63] Archives du Ministère des Affaires Étrangères in Nantes (AMAEN), Fonds OTASE, Series B, boxes 25 and 48; See also TNA, FO 371/116928, FO 371/116929, FO 371/116930.

[64] For both these SEATO activities see TNA, DO 35/8871 and CO 1030/170.

took an even more central role in the circulation of what was getting to be known as counterinsurgency (COIN) strategy.

America in Search of Strategic Inspiration

American strategic and operational thinking in the 1950s was largely dominated by the nuclear issue and was therefore wrong-footed by the emergence such an indirect approach as the communist insurgency strategy.[65] This lack of knowledge on this issue – with the exception of the CIA – led the Pentagon to start monitoring the reflections on the subject carried out within the UK and French governments and defence communities. In the former, a general review was well under way of the various experiences from Palestine to Kenya.[66] Comparative studies were being conducted 'with a view of discovering ... any general features, and, particularly, methods of conduct likely to be applicable to future Emergencies of this nature'.[67] In France, an even more ambitious reflection process had started towards the formulation of a Revolutionary War doctrine.[68] The US defence community was aware of these evolutions abroad thanks to a close strategic watch: copies of French and British military articles were published in US military journals,[69] observation missions were sent to operations theatres, especially in Algeria and Malaya,[70] and comprehensive studies were commissioned on the lessons learned from the Indochina War.[71]

[65] A. Long, On 'Other War': Lessons from Five Decades of RAND Counterinsurgency Research (Santa Monica, CA: RAND Corporation, 2006).

[66] D. French, The British Way in Counter-Insurgency, 1945–1967 (Oxford: Oxford University Press, 2011).

[67] TNA, WO 291/1670, 'Operational Research Report. A comparative study of the emergencies in Malaya and Kenya', 6 June 1957.

[68] G. Périès, 'De l'action militaire à l'action politique. Impulsion, codification et application de la doctrine de la "guerre révolutionnaire" au sein de l'armée française, 1944–1960' (unpublished doctoral thesis, Université de Lille III, 1999).

[69] In the French case, see, for instance, J. Némo, 'The Place of Guerrilla Action in War', Military Review, 1957, 99–107; A. Souyris, 'An Effective Counterguerrilla Procedure', Military Review, 1957, 86–90; Ximénès (pseud.), 'Revolutionary War', Military Review, 1957, 103–8.

[70] US Army Heritage and Education Center (USAHEC), UG1232.T72 J69, Joy, D. P., 'Operations Research Study to Determine Optimum Transport Helicopter Characteristics for Military' (Vertol Production, 1957), 55; See also Victor J. Croizat, Journey among Warriors. The Memoirs of a Marine (Shippensburg, PA: White Mane Pub. Co., 1997), 129–32.

[71] G. K. Tanham, 'Defeating Insurgency in South Vietnam: My Early Efforts', in H. C. Neese and K. O'Donnel (eds.), Prelude to Tragedy: Vietnam, 1960–1965(Annapolis, MD: Naval Institute Press, 2001), 155–79. Tanham is the author of the first RAND study on irregular warfare, for which he was sent to Paris in 1955 and had access to French

The pace of the learning process accelerated considerably from January 1961 with the inauguration of President Kennedy, who decided to make irregular warfare a top priority of his national security policy.[72] This short period (1961–1963) marked the relative and temporary empowerment of irregular warfare, as well as an acceleration of the knowledge transfer process in the direction of the United States. Indeed, at the immediate request of the White House, experts and the experiences of the Western world were pooled, interviewed and taken into account by the politico-military administration, eager to learn as rarely before. By 20 March 1961, General Trudeau, then Chief of Research and Development, US Army, circulated a letter 'from an individual who has given much thought to the field of guerrilla warfare'.[73] This anonymous expert expressed the view 'that foreign armies have moved further in anti-guerrilla warfare than we have. The French, British, Belgian and South East Asian experiences would provide the best initial basis for doctrine and teaching. There are already regional schools where this new responsibility could be placed. One could be formed in the NATO area, perhaps Paris, where we could benefit from the French experience'.[74]

A Network-Centric Circulation and Learning Process

This US-led knowledge transfer took various forms but generally rested on a relatively small number of circulation networks. The first of these networks related to doctrinal and operational research, as illustrated by the numerous reports produced or commissioned by the Department of Defence. Federally funded research centres

---

military records from Indochina and to the leading figures of French Revolutionary War doctrine.

[72] 'Letter from Secretary of State Rusk to Secretary of Defense McNamara', *Foreign Relations of the United States* (FRUS), 1961–1963, Volume VIII, National Security Policy, 26. Developments on Kennedy's enthusiasm for these issues can be found in D. Blaufarb, *The Counterinsurgency Era: U.S. Doctrine and Performance, 1950 to the Present* (New York: Free Press, 1977); M. McClintock, *Instruments of Statecraft: U.S. Guerrilla Warfare, Counterinsurgency, and Counter-terrorism, 1940–1990* (New York: Pantheon Books, 1992); L. Freedman, *Kennedy's Wars: Berlin, Cuba, Laos, and Vietnam* (Oxford: Oxford University Press, 2002).

[73] USAHEC, B5/FA/S4/Box 14/Folder 226, 'Some Comments on Guerrilla Warfare', 20 March 1961.

[74] Ibid. Even though the author of the memo is unknown, we found a letter attributing it allegedly to Edward Lansdale, then Assistant Secretary of Defence for Special Operations. See Hoover Institution Library and Archives (HILA), Lansdale Collection, Box 38, 'Letter from Col. George M. Jones [former chief of Special Warfare School] to Brig. Gen. E. G. Lansdale', 9 May 1961.

(FFRDCs) such as the Special Operations Research Office or the RAND Corporation had an instrumental role in extracting lessons learned from various foreign experiences. Here again, Malaya and Algeria were the top two models.[75] The United States soon sponsored a dozen symposia and conferences under close patronage of Edward Lansdale, then Assistant Secretary of Defence for Special Operations[76]. It is through this network that French officer David Galula was invited on Lansdale's advice to take part to a symposium in April 1962 along with British and US experts – he would then be commissioned to write a report on his Algerian experience and then spend a year at Harvard University where he would write his seminal essay, *Counterinsurgency Warfare: Theory and Practices.*[77]

Another important network was that of the foreign Liaison Officers Instructors (LOIs) detached to a dozen US military schools. Only three countries had such a dense liaison network in the United States: France, Great Britain and Canada.[78] It is hard to overstate how much these LOIs were appreciated in military circles as they provided the school boards – in charge of writing doctrine– with their practical experience, foreign doctrinal documents and oral performance. For instance, Col. Richard L. Clutterbuck, British LOI at the US Army Command and General Staff College (CGSC), performed between 1961 and 1963 'about 150 lectures, mainly to Universities and armed forces colleges (in addition to those at CGSC)', all of them pertaining to his Malayan experience.[79] On the French side, Lt. Colonel Aussaresses was also very much appreciated as a LOI:[80] a former Jedburgh fluent in English, he was a perfect example of the 'SOE generation', but also a devoted proponent of French

---

[75] SHD/DT, 10T 1073, 'L'Armée Américaine face à la Guérilla, exposé du Lt. Col. Aussaresses, officier de liaison à l'US Army Infantry School', 25 November 1963. See also A. J. Birtle, *United States Army Counterinsurgency and Contingency Operations Doctrine, 1942–1976* (Washington, DC: US Center for Military History, 2006), 229–30.

[76] HILA, Lansdale Collection, Box 40, 'Correspondence with Rand Corporation', 16 April 1962.

[77] S. T. Hosmer (ed.), *Counterinsurgency. A Symposium, April 16–20 1962* (Santa Monica, CA: RAND Corporation, 2006); D. Galula, *Pacification in Algeria. 1956–1958* (Santa Monica, CA: RAND Corporation, 2006); D. Galula, *Counterinsurgency Warfare: Theory and Practice* (Westport, CT: Greenwood Publishing Group, 2006). A biography of Galula has been recently published by A. A. Cohen, *Galula: The Life and Writings of the French Officer Who Defined the Art of Counterinsurgency* (Westport, CT: Greenwood Publishing Group, 2012).

[78] NARA, RG319, NM-3/47P, Box24, 'Report of Educational Survey Commission', 20 November 1962.

[79] Churchill Archives Centre (CAC), Clutterbuck Collection, Box 1, 'Comments on lectures given by Richard Clutterbuck in the USA', undated.

[80] SHD/DT, 10T 1077, 'Visite à Fort Bragg, Caroline du Nord', 13 February 1963.

Revolutionary Warfare, who had been in charge tracking down FLN cadres during the battle of Algiers.[81]

A third means of circulation was the creation of third-country assistance missions in US-led operations. The most famous of these was certainly the British Advisory Mission (BRIAM) in Saigon, led by Sir Robert Thompson – another offspring of British tradition and a protégé of Orde Wingate, with whom he fought in the *Chindits* before being sent to Malaya where he served as a security civil servant for more than fifteen years.[82] BRIAM was supposed to help the governments of South Vietnam and the United States to fight the communist insurgency in 'applying the lessons of Malaya'[83] and proved of especially important influence in the decisions leading to the Strategic Hamlet program.

By the end of 1963, some degree of standardisation had clearly been reached in the realm counterinsurgency, thanks to the active amalgamation orchestrated by the United States. A strategic narrative, typically illustrated by Galula's 'five-stage insurgency',[84] was set up and widely shared among counterinsurgency practitioners across the Western bloc. Even though some aspect of 'national styles' could still pervade respective doctrines, counterinsurgency thinking was marked by a considerable degree of convergence. Nevertheless, this convergence was not necessarily reflected by the political and military practice, thus setting an important limit to strategic cosmopolitanism.

Conclusion: The Limits to Strategic Cosmopolitanism

Admittedly, there were structural limits that restricted the circulation of counterinsurgency knowledge all along. For each proponent of knowledge transfer, one could find a fierce opponent to it, raising their voice against a tendency to 'copy and paste' foreign experiences to situations that were only superficially similar. Robert Thompson's mission to Saigon is a good example of the reluctance that the international transfers

---

[81] P. Aussaresses, *Je N'ai Pas Tout Dit, Ultimes Révélations Au Service De La France* (Paris: Le Rocher, 2008).

[82] R. G. K. Thompson, *Make for the Hills. Memories of Far Eastern Wars* (Londres: Leo Cooper, 1989).

[83] P. Busch, *All the Way with JFK? Britain, the US, and the Vietnam War* (Oxford: Oxford University Press, 2003), 67. On the same subject, see also I. F. W. Beckett, 'Robert Thompson and the British Advisory Mission to South Vietnam, 1961–1965', *Small Wars & Insurgencies*, 8 (1997), 41–63; G. D. T. Shaw, 'Policeman Versus Soldiers, the Debate Leading to MAAG Objections and Washington Rejections of the Core of the British Counter Insurgency Advice', *Small Wars & Insurgencies*, 12 (2001), 51–78; J. McAllister and I. Schulte, 'The Limits of Influence in Vietnam: Britain, the United States and the Diem Regime, 1959–63', *Small Wars & Insurgencies*, 17 (2006), 22–43.

[84] Galula, *Counterinsurgency Warfare*.

could cause: even Lansdale, who was the first to praise the need to engage in cross-learning, clearly opposed the presence of a British advisory mission, stating that it was 'unsound to turn over US aid funds and energies to a foreigner to spend for us [in Vietnam]'.[85]

National stereotypes and cultural barriers also hampered the circulation process. American constant suspicion of colonialism vis-à-vis the French and British drove them to ignore some of their findings.[86] French contempt towards 'Anglo-Saxon pragmatism'[87] or British confidence to have nothing to learn from people they had themselves formerly trained[88] were also recurring leitmotifs that comforted the feeling of self-sufficiency. Other types of cognitive frictions also hindered international knowledge transfers throughout the period, like the language barrier in the case of the French, or the weight of conventional habits on senior officers as on NCOs, which made them sceptical of irregular warfare thinking.

These limits should not overshadow more contextual factors that explain the decrease from mid-1960s onwards. Kennedy's assassination aborted the Copernican revolution in irregular warfare he intended to force on the military establishment, while Johnson seemed less enthusiastic about 'twilight wars'.[89] The final chapter of the Algerian war and the progressive elimination of any reference to subversive warfare in the French military doctrine after France's retreat from Algeria as well as the growing distance from NATO and the United States were certainly drying-up factors on the French side.[90] Unsurprisingly, Anglo-American dialogue remained more lively, but as the Vietnam War got bogged down, Whitehall also tried to distance itself from any public engagements in controversial partnerships. BRIAM survived Thompson's departure from Vietnam in 1965 and kept on going until 1972 under the form of a public safety advisory mission.[91] Thompson himself, as other British

---

[85] 'Memorandum from Lansdale (DoD) to Williams (MAAG)', 14 April 1960, *Foreign Relations of the United States* (FRUS), 1958–1960, Volume I, 'Vietnam', 386.

[86] R. Phillips, *Why Vietnam Matters: An Eyewitness Account of Lessons Not Learned* (Annapolis, MD: Naval Institute Press, 2008).

[87] SHD/DT, 3K 18, 'Témoignage oral du Colonel Lacheroy'.

[88] TNA, FO 371/174483, DV 1017/22, 'Mr. Thompson to visit Mr. Fenner in Kuala Lumpur', 16 June 1964.

[89] This assertion must be nuanced, however, as the US Army kept on its doctrinal effort in counterinsurgency even though the pace was not the same as before. See Birtle, United States Army Counterinsurgency and Contingency Operations Doctrine, 276–8.

[90] Rémy Martinot-Leroy, 'La Contestation de la Dissuasion dans l'Armée de Terre: l'Atome et la Guerre Subversive dans les Travaux des Officiers de l'École Supérieure De Guerre (1962–1975)' (unpublished doctoral thesis, Lille III, 1999).

[91] NARA, RG286, A132, Box 60, 'Memorandum of understanding on working arrangements for the provision of public safety advisory assistance in Vietnam', 3 December 1968.

experts, was still very much appreciated throughout the Nixon era, but no longer with any official backing.[92]

Finally, a last phenomenon contributed to stall the process of international circulation of strategic ideas beyond the mid-1960s – the persistent marginality of the counterinsurgency proponents in a climate dominated by a fixation on nuclear weapons. If institutional marginality was initially a motivation for engaging in international transfers, it also prevented the counterinsurgency community from having a lasting influence on the political-military establishment. Past the novelty and exoticism of the early years, circulation networks were still struggling to expand beyond the small circle of experts, who finally ended preaching to the choir. This was certainly the feeling of General Frank Kitson, who took part in the seminal RAND symposium that grouped so many counterinsurgency experts in 1962:

Although we came from such widely divergent backgrounds, it was if we had all been brought up together from youth. We all spoke the same language. Probably all of us had worked out theories of counterinsurgency procedures at one time or another, which we thought were unique and original. But when we came to air them, all our ideas were essentially the same. We had another thing in common. Although we had no difficulty in making our views understood to each other, we had mostly been unable to get our respective armies to hoist in the message.[93]

This quotation illustrates both the reality and the limits of counterinsurgency circulation. After twenty years of cross-fertilising experience and intensive international networking, Western counterinsurgency thinkers had reached a genuine homogenisation of their strategic ideas. The international dimension is thus an essential aspect to understand the development of counterinsurgency during the Cold War. But circulation eventually remained limited to intellectual circles and never really allowed institutional decompartmentalisation capable of leading to an enduring influence on Western military practices.

[92] TNA, FCO 15/1724.
[93] Kitson, *Bunch of Five* (London: Faber & Faber, 1977), 200–201.

16 Universal Toolbox, National Styles or Divergence of Civilisations?

Beatrice Heuser and Eitan Shamir

The Toolbox

In Chapter 1 we listed tools of both COIN and of insurgencies, promising to furnish here evidence for their recurrent use by different cultures, in different ages. We wanted to find out whether the case studies in this volume also reflect the use of such a general instrumentarium, or whether there are tools particular to the traditions of one country or one insurgency movement. In our ensuing taxonomy of such instruments or tools, both of insurgencies and of counterinsurgency operations (COIN), we have endeavoured to trace them back as far as we could, with examples where we could find them, restricted in our search as we were by our own language skills and research focus on sources accessible to us. We have factored in the examples furnished in the chapters of this book. It will become apparent that, curiously, many tools are common to COIN and to insurgent movements.

Brutal Large-Scale Repression, Indiscriminate Killing and Terror

The first recurrent tool is that of brutal use of force – not only against the other side, collaborators with the other side, their dependents, but at times against neutral populations to frighten them into co-operation. Examples of brutal repressions of insurgencies through the large-scale killing not only of insurgents but also of civilians suspected of siding with rebels abound since Antiquity. Whatever refined individuals like Cicero said about the need for justice and moderation in the use of force, Rome is remembered for her bloody slaughter of subdued peoples who wanted to rid themselves of Roman domination. The people of Numantia in modern Spain, the Iceni under Boudicca in Britain, and the Jews in Palestine could bear witness to this.

To move forward in time, an infamous English tradition of COIN is well documented from the brutal Harrying of the North by the Normans in the decades after the Conquest in the eleventh century, the suppression of Welsh uprisings in the twelfth to fifteenth centuries and attempts to impose overlordship on Scotland, and the subjection of Ireland after Henry II appointed himself ruler, the repression of uprisings on the Green Island in the twelfth and sixteenth to eighteenth centuries, which are the backdrop to the Irish uprisings in the late nineteenth and then the war of independence in the early twentieth centuries, and the 'troubles' of the 1970s–1990s. After the Glorious Revolution of 1688, an intra-British dynastic quarrel, wrapped in a Catholic insurgency against Protestant rule, led to legendary examples of repression such as the massacre perpetrated in Drogheda by the English and their Dutch allies in Ireland in 1649, and the Glencoe Massacre of the Macdonald clan in Scotland in 1692. This dynastic quarrel, which took the form of the Jacobite revolts lasting until 1746, later interpreted as a last Scottish bid for independence from a supposedly dominating English, resulted not only in the killing and deportation of rebels (or suspected rebels), but also in the temporary suppression of cultural aspects of 'Scottishness', from the wearing of the tartan to the use of bagpipes.

Also within the greater British Empire, there was the bloody repression of the Indian Mutiny or Rebellion of 1857, the exceptionally asymmetric carnage of the battle of Omdurman in 1898 against the followers of Abdullah al Taashi who sought to shake off colonial rule, the brutal operations against combatants and non-combatants (with their high mortality) in the second Boer War (arguably the precedent for the population relocation which worked in Malaya and infamously did not in Kenya), and the Massacre of Amritsar in 1919. It is poor comfort and no excuse to record that more Native Americans died from disease than in massacres inflicted by the white settlers. The killings carried out in the Philippine War 1899–1902 stood in the same tradition. Unlike in the twentieth century, the COIN repressions in China, and the German- and Soviet-perpetrated killings, the aforementioned English/British and American COIN operations killed at worst a few thousand, not hundreds of thousands or even millions, but the memory of these deeds lived on to become important political factors in the twentieth century.

This pre-1919 English/British way of COIN was by no means excep- tional within Europe. In the early thirteenth century, the 'crusade' against the Cathars in southern France (the Albigensian Crusade) was treated in part as COIN and was doubly bloody as the Cathars were treated both as heretics and as rebels. The imposition of northern French (Catholic) rule amounted to the 'agony of the *langue d'oc*' or extinction of a separate southern French language and culture (comparable to the suppression of elements Scottish culture after the Jacobite Revolts cen- turies later). The Grande Jacquerie of the mid-fourteenth century and the other peasant revolts in late Medieval France ended with the hanging, drawing and quartering usual throughout Europe in such contexts. Both the armies fighting under the English and the French kings in the Hundred Years' War treated civilians in the theatre of war, especially townsfolk, as rebels if they sided with the opponent. The French Religious Wars of the sixteenth century fused COIN with the persecution of heretics and were memorable for their cruelty on both sides. The Fronde of the seventeenth century, led by aristocrats and directed against the rule of Louis XIV, ended with a negotiated settlement, but not without much bloodshed on the way. Corsican separatism today is still fired by the fierce repression of Corsican attempts to secure their independence after the island was annexed by France in the mid-eighteenth century, and the French revolutionary regime's suppression of the Catholic, monarchist uprisings in the Vendée and the Bretagne a few decades later has been referred to as a genocide.[1]

The Holy Roman Empire tended to delegate COIN to its sub-entities, but knew its fair share of revolts of townspeople and peasants in the late Middle Ages and in Early Modern times. The post-1871 German Empire by contrast can be held squarely responsible for the killing or starving of African civilians in the context of (anti-German, anti-colonial) rebellions in Africa. Another latecomer in the empire-building game, Belgium, also developed a despicable reputation for the violent suppression of revolts, in turn caused by unbearable conditions (and punishments) imposed on the indigenous workforce by their colonial masters. On the other side of the Atlantic, brutality was also the hallmark on both sides in America's Indian Wars 1790–1891.[2]

Examples of massacres of non-combatants reached, in absolute numbers, an all-time high in the first half of the twentieth century. Beginning with the atrocities carried out by the Germans (and the French) in China at the tail-end of the Boxer Rebellion (1898–1900) and the Germans in Africa to suppress the uprisings of the Hereros and Nama (1904–1907), these include the genocide practised by Germany's ally, the Ottoman Empire, against the Armenians during the First World War. (The Turks have attempted to explain this as measures to prevent an Armenian uprising in support of Russia, which was fighting against Turkey.)[3] Then came the Second World War with the tens of millions

---

[1] A. J. Joes, 'Insurgency and Genocide: La Vendée', *Small Wars & Insurgencies*, 9/3 (Winter 1998), 17–45.

[2] See Chapter 6.

[3] E. Arslan, 'Insurgencies and Measures by the Ottoman State (Armenian Rebellions and Measures)', in T. B. Zaalberg, J. Hoffenaar and A. Lemmers (eds.), *Insurgency and Counterinsurgency: Irregular Warfare from 1800 to the Present* (The Hague: Netherlands

of civilian deaths in the 'Bloodlands' of Eastern Europe at the hands of the Germans,[4] justified by them in large part as COIN.[5] While the British, the French and the Americans did not come out of this period entirely clean either, to repeat, the numbers of victims of – usually unplanned – atrocities they committed tended to be on significantly lower orders of magnitude.

Massacres have been practised by both insurgent movements and COIN forces. Some of the latter have tried to 'drain the swamp' or 'drain the sea in which the fish [= the insurgents] are swimming', or to dry out the 'breeding areas' of the 'mosquitos'.[6] Massacres and related forms of terror against civilians, culminating in mass killings, have been used also by insurgents trying to force the population to take their side or to punish them for siding with the state power. This in turn made it imperative in many COIN operations to make especial efforts to secure the villages of populations hostile to the insurgents (see below).[7] Insurgents defending the rights of the oppressed might also turn against third groups: the Ukrainian Insurgent Army who between 1944 and 1959 fought the Soviet Union's forces and civilian authorities themselves turned against the Polish minority in Ukraine, killing perhaps up to 40,000 Poles.[8]

In the case of the Taliban, usually operations against civilian populations suspected of being unsympathetic to them were unorganized and relied on a sporadic delivery of firepower. In contrast to that, other insurgent groups forged more regulated tactics, essentially using terrorism as a method of causing multiple casualties and extensive damage when using minimal manpower. Terrorism has been used for different purposes by different insurgency groups. During the 'Troubles' of the 1970s–1990s, the Provisional Irish Republican Army (PIRA) mainly targeted military bases and barracks and avoided large civilian casualties because this proved counterproductive in the public opinion.

Institute of Militay History, 2010), 595–608. See by contrast T. Akçam, *A Shameful Act: The Armenian Genocide and the Question of Turkish Responsibility*, trans. from Turkish by P. Bessemer (New York: Metropolitan Books, 2006).

[4] T. Snyder, *Bloodlands: Europe between Hitler and Stalin* (New York: Vintage Books, 2011).

[5] See Chapter 7.

[6] W. Markel, 'Draining the Swamp: The British Strategy of Population Control', *Parameters* (Spring 2006), 35–48; A. Gandolfi, *Les luttes armées en Amérique latine* (Paris: PUF, 1991), 143–63; T. Mockaitis, *British Counterinsurgency 1919–1960* (New York: St Martin's Press, 1990), 115.

[7] Gandolfi, *Les luttes*, passim.

[8] Y. Zhukov, 'Examining the Authoritarian Model of Counter-insurgency: The Soviet Campaign against the Ukrainian Insurgent Army', *Small Wars & Insurgencies*, 18/3 (September 2007), 445.

Other insurgencies have deliberately caused civilian casualties, both as a means of deterrence and as attrition of morale.

The use of suicide bombings, in particular, characterizes the aspiration to wreak havoc within population centres. When used in recent times by extremist Muslim organisations, one can surmise a link with Jihad, even though many Muslim theologians have argued that it is incompatible with the teaching of Mohammed. It is not unique to Muslim rebel movements, however: François Géré in an impressive study has traced many other uses of suicide attacks since Antiquity, including, in the more recent past, by Russian anarchists of the late nineteenth century, and in the twentieth, by Vietnamese during the French Indochina War.[9] By contrast, Hamas and Hezbollah have been unique in the use of missiles in their attempt to target civilians, obviously a relatively recent means for the weaker power to fight against a superior force.

Wreaking carnage upon the COIN-leader state's civilian population is a further tool coming under this category. This course of action is intended to undermine the commitment of the state conducting the COIN operation and diminish its population's support for the operation, not least by sapping the credibility of the government's monopoly of the use of force and its ability to protect its own population. This tactic has been widely adopted by Native Americans against the settlers in the Indian Wars, by the Algerian Front de Libération nationale (FLN) during the Algerian War 1954–1963, and in recent decades by Palestinian groups, which relied on the demoralizing effect of suicide bombings and missile launches on Israeli settlements.

Terror is also used widely to protect the insurgency movement against infiltration. In many of the organizations, internal counterintelligence services were established which were given the responsibility of dismissing recruits which were suspected of collaboration. We have learnt that the USSR's secret services devoted particular attention to the intelligence penetration of insurgents, as did the British.[10] In turn, the Provisional IRA (PIRA) was willing to undertake torture and even executions against such suspects. The Taliban also established a code of conduct, although unlike other insurgencies its main criteria were religious adherence and not only loyalty to the cause. These counter-infiltration measures are seen as so crucial since the insurgencies rely on the local population for recruitment, and this process usually does not include much screening of the new recruits. A different form of this is the persecution of rival insurgent groups, like the Irish National Liberation Army in Northern Ireland or the

[9] F. Géré, *Les Volontaires de la mort : L'Arme du suicide* (Paris: Bayard, 2003).
[10] See the relevant chapters in this book.

Algerian National Movement (MNA) in Algeria. In the latter country, not only did this measure serve as an obstacle to factionalism, but it was part of the ideology itself, that is to say, a persistent exclusion of all parties but the FLN from the political landscape.

Burning Villages and 'Scorched Earth' Tactics

Mass killings of civilians can of course be achieved in bloodless ways. The burning of harvests, but also of fields before the harvest, and of fruit or olive trees is tantamount to condemning populations to the bloodless, but slow and thus in many respects more torturous death by starvation. Apart from the usual examples of Antiquity, this was specifically put into practice by the Spanish under the infamous Duke of Alba to quash the Dutch revolt in its early phase in the late sixteenth century, by the French and Spanish reciprocally in their war over the Spanish Netherlands of the late seventeenth century, by the French against the Spanish and then the Algerians in the first half of the nineteenth century, then at the end of that century by the Americans in the Philippines and in the following century in Vietnam.[11] In America, colonists burned corn fields and food storage of the Native Americans in the East. A similar tactic was followed in the nineteenth century by white settlers against the Plains Indians by destroying the buffalo herds that their livelihood depended upon.[12] In the American Civil War, General Sherman's famous march to sea used scorched earth tactics to subdue the South.[13] The burning of rebel villages in winter, for example, by the Germans in the Second World War, especially on the Eastern Front and in Greece, amounts to cold-blooded massacring as well, as it usually condemns the populations in isolated areas to death by exposure.[14]

---

[11] B. Fonck and G. Satterfield, 'The Essence of War: French Armies and Small War in the Low Countries (1672–1697)', special issue of *Small Wars and Insurgencies*, 25/5 (Autumn 2014), 767–83; T. R. Bugeaud de la Piconnerie, Duc d'Isly, *De la stratégie, de la tactique, des retraites et du passage des défilés dans les montagnes des Kabyles* (Alger: Imprimerie du Gouvernement, 1850), 110–18; and see Chapter 6.

[12] M. Boot, *Invisible Armies: An Epic History of Guerrilla Warfare from Ancient Times to the Present* (New York: W. W. Norton & Company, 2013), 134, 147.

[13] B. Davis, *Sherman's March* (New York: Vintage Books, 1988).

[14] E. Rondholz, 'Schärfste Massnahmen gegen die Banden sind notwendig …' Partisanenbekämpfung und Kriegsverbrechen in Griechenland. Aspekte deutscher Okkupationspolitik, 1941–1944', in E. Jungfer and A. Meyer (eds.), *Repression und Kriegsverbrechen. Die Bekämpfung von Widerstands- und Partisanenbewegungen gegen die deutsche Besatzung in West- und Südeuropa* (Berlin/Göttingen: Verlag der Buchläden, 1997), 130–70; K. Arnold, *Die Wehrmacht und die Besatzungspolitik in den besetzten Gebieten der Sowjetunion. Kriegführung und Radikalisierung im 'Unternehmen Barbarossa'* (Berlin: Ducker & Humblodt, 2005), 459.

In the interwar period, other European powers hit on the destruction of villages from the air as a COIN tool, that is, as punitive measures to subdue revolts. We have examples of what some commentators called 'Air Blockades' in the interwar period, carried out by the British, the Spanish, the French and the Italians.[15] The Americans destroyed individual houses and entire villages during their search-and-destroy missions in the Vietnam War. So again, this way of suppressing revolts is not particular to one nation. Today, such measures are seen as highly problematic in international law, quite apart from being seen as highly counter-productive: Robert Pape in his study of air attacks on towns and cities has found that they have consistently strengthened the determination of the bombed population to stick by their own leadership (rather than to put pressure on it to surrender).[16]

It was a French particularity to smoke rebels out of their hiding places in the form of the notorious *enfumades* practiced under Bugeaud de la Piconnerie in Algeria in the 1840s. But the result is not much different from the American use of explosives against Al Qaeda followers hiding in Afghan caves in their 2001 campaign, only there it was directed against Al Qaeda militants, not civilian populations.

Scorched earth tactics have also been used by the weaker party to deny provisions to invading forces who would otherwise have lived off the land. The Helvetii in the early stages of the Gallic Wars documented by Caesar[17] and the Russians during Napoleon's 1812 campaign as well as in the First and Second World Wars thus destroyed their own crops in order to halt the advance of enemy forces, clearly a desperate measure of last resort.

Rounding Up and Executing Leaders: Targeted Assassinations

A further COIN tool, recourse to which can also be illustrated across time and space, is that of isolating leaders from the rank and file of insurgents, and of course from more passive sympathizers within the population itself. To pick just a handful of examples, the Romans made a point of meting out humiliating treatment to rebel leaders like Vercingetorix, who was paraded in a triumph through Rome in

---

[15] T. Mockaitis, *British Counterinsurgency 1919–1960* ((New York: St Martin's Press, 1990), 31f; J. Corum and W. R. Johnson, *Airpower in Small Wars: Fighting Insurgents and Terrorists* (Lawrence: University Press of Kansas, 2003), 58–6, 428f.

[16] R. A. Pape, *Bombing to Win: Air Power and Coercion in War* (Ithaca, NY: Cornell University Press, 1996); see also D. Chuter, 'Triumph of the Will? Or, Why Surrender Is Not Always Inevitable', *Review of Internationl Studies*, 23 (1997), 381–400.

[17] *De bello gallico* I.5.1.

46 BCE before presumably being executed in his prison cell, or the rebellious Iceni queen Boudicca and her children. In the British Isles, the fate of William Wallace, leader of the Scottish resistance to annexation by the Plantagenets, is well remembered: in 1305 he was executed successively in the most heinous ways practiced at the time in Europe. That did not stop him from being turned into a Scottish national hero, which is also true for the Counts Egmont and Horn, leaders of the Dutch revolt against the Habsburg, who were beheaded by the Spanish in the Grande Place of Brussels in 1568. Only four years later, the Spanish in Peru executed a local rebel leader by the name of Tupac Amaru, who would later give his name to the insurgent movements of the Tupamaros.[18] Another rebel leader who was immortalised in death was Che Guevara in 1967, who has been idolised by teenagers since – again an unintended consequence. Nevertheless, the immediate effect was to stymie his insurgent movement. The Americans launched large military expeditions to kill or catch guerrilla fighters and bandits such as the Apache leader Geronimo in 1886 or the Mexican rebel Pancho Villa in 1917.[19] Thus the assassination of rebel leaders is a perennial utensil in the tool box, notwithstanding the ambiguous consequences of its application.

Direct attempts to intimidate the insurgents are the most obvious measure to embrace, but it may not be sufficient for success. For nineteenth-century France, the use of gunboat diplomacy against Algeria sufficed only in the latter half of the century, while in the twentieth century, attempts to use limited military operations in this way against Egypt and Libya were unsuccessful (especially the Suez Crisis in 1956). Israeli forces sought to destroy Palestinian terrorists' hideouts in Jordan in the 1960s and Lebanon during the 1970s, but Israel suffered retaliatory measures.

Insurgents' equivalent of the COIN tool of rounding up and executing leaders of the opposite side is that of targeted assassination of state leaders or other outstanding individuals who can be portrayed as representing the oppressive powers. Famously, the legendary Swiss freedom fighter William Tell is thus said to have assassinated a tyrannical Habsburg governor, Hermann Gessler, around the year 1300. There are many

---

[18] Gandolfi, *Luttes armées*, 18–20, 51f.; on one period of counterinsurgency against the Tupamaros, see also F. A. Godfrey, 'The Latin American Experience: The Tupamaros Campaign in Uruguay, 1963–1973', in I. F. W. Beckett and J. Pimlott (eds.), *Armed Forces & Modern Counter-Insurgency* (London: Croom Helm, 1985), 112–35.

[19] D. Roberts, *Once They Moved like the Wind: Cochise, Geronimo, and the Apache Wars* (New York: Simon and Schuster, 1994); M. L. Tate, 'Pershing's Punitive Expedition: Pursuer of Bandits of Presidential Panacea?', *The Americas*, 32/1 (July 1975), 47–51.

historically confirmed assassinations, including much more recently anarchists' bombings in France and Russia in the 1890s and early 1900s, by the Ukrainian UPA in the 1940s and 1950s, or by the FLN.[20]

Like the elimination of insurgency leaders by COIN forces, such assassinations tend to serve multiple functions. Not only do they have an important value in terms of publicity for one's cause, signalling the high impact and extensive reach of one's efforts, but they can also disrupt the other side's effectiveness through 'decapitation'. As the word implies, this is an old idea, but articulated particularly in the context of air power strategy, where it conveys the promise that the other side's leadership will be killed (this is the hope in a targeted air strike) or thrown into confusion if a succession crisis ensues. For this reason this tool is attractive both to insurgents and to governments fighting them. The Israeli government occasionally uses targeted assassinations against Hamas leaders. These have usually been executed with relatively limited collateral damage, occasionally without any at all, but even then, this is a problematic approach for a state built on the rule of law.[21] Much to its credit, in 2006 the Supreme Court of Israel judged targeted killings 'a lawful part of armed conflict' only if they are the last resort (a just war criterion) and many other constraining criteria are met.[22]

Mutilations and Rape

Short of killing, but to some perhaps worse than death, are mass mutilations. It does seem that mutilations were often originally culturally specific ways of fighting. Dead enemies were often mutilated (scalped) by native Americans in their wars, something that particularly horrified Europeans, simply because such measures were not usual in Europe at the time, even though European history had known mutilation as part of war: Spaniards occasionally mutilated the corpses of French, Polish, and Nassau soldiers fighting for Napoleon, as eyewitnesses reported.[23]

Mutilations would be carried out not only by rebel forces. Mutilations were a related form of humiliating and discrediting rebel leaders. Byzantine emperors would order the facial mutilation of pretenders to the imperial crown, which somehow precluded them from being eligible

---

[20] For example, see J.-L. Brau, *Les Armes de Guerilla* (Paris: Balland, 1974), 88ff.

[21] For a highly intelligent discussion of the pros and cons of this, see the documentary 'The Gatekeepers' (D. Moreh, 2012)

[22] I. Detter, *The Law of War*, 3rd ed. (Farnham, Surrey: Ashgate, 2013), 99.

[23] Ludwig von Grolmann, 'Aus dem Tagebuche eines deutschen Offiziers über seinen Feldzug in Spanien 1808', in Friedrich Kircheisen (ed.), *Memoiren aus dem spanischen Freiheitskampfe 1808–1811* (Hamburg: Gutenberg-Verlag, 1908), 98, 107f.

for the succession. A particular tradition can be found in Africa, perhaps linked with Sharia law, perhaps developed independently from it: that of cutting off body parts which may not be vital to the organic survival of the individual but will make him or her dependent on the help of others for the rest of their lives: feet, legs, but above all hands or arms.[24] This tradition was appropriated by the Belgian administrators under King Leopold II in his African colonies in the late nineteenth century. It has most recently been practised under Charles Taylor, President of Liberia, and by the rebel movement Revolutionary United Front in Sierra Leone.

Post-mortem mutilations were at times counting devices. The scalping practised by Native Americans seems to have been turned into such a practice at the instigation of white employers.[25] In Burma in the early twentieth century, irregular forces recruited locally by the British to fight against Moplah insurgents, in order to be able to identify insurgency leaders, hacked off the heads of insurgent fighters and took them along – something that scandalised their European employers.[26] Similarly, for the body count which the American operations analysts imposed on US forces in Vietnam, the habit was formed to cut off one ear of killed Viet Cong. Thus mutilation in some cases is a culturally specific form of punishment or humiliation, such as the knee-capping practised by the IRA,[27] while in others it may be just a convenient and pragmatic way to count or identify dead adversaries.

Rape has also been a weapon of both insurgents and of COIN campaigners, and is neither specific to just one culture nor is it absent in cases of armies fighting for ideologies proclaiming either the equal rights of human beings or the liberation of the working classes (including women). Napoleon's armies practised it widely in the Peninsular War, as French eyewitnesses reported;[28] the Red Army was known for doing it throughout Eastern Europe, and not just against German women, but also against random women in the countries they 'liberated' from German oppression (the Yugoslav Communists would later protest to Stalin about this).[29] In Darfur in Sudan, rape by the Janjaweed

---

[24] Martin Ewans, *European Atrocity, African Catastrophe: Leopold II, the Congo Free State and Its Aftermath* (London: Routledge, 2002); Theo Gerritse. *Van constitutioneel monarch tot roofridder: rood rubber, de exploitatie door Leopold II van de Kongo Vrijstaat (1885–1908)* (Soesterberg: Aspekt, 2007).

[25] James Axtell and William C. Sturtevant, 'The Unkindest Cut, or Who Invented Scalping', *William and Mary Quarterly*, 31/3 (July 1980), 461f.

[26] Mockaitis: *British Counterinsurgency*, 38.   [27] See Chapter 10.

[28] 'Le petit diable boiteux', *Mes réminiscences de l'Espagne: ... tactique des guérillas et des miquelets ...* (Paris: Constant-Chantipie, 1823), 37–9; J.-P. Bois, *Bugeaud* (Paris: Fayard, 1997), 91f.

[29] M. Djilas, *Conversations with Stalin* (New York: Harcourt Brace, 1963).

paramilitaries was condoned or even ordered by the Sudanese government.[30] To cite one example of a rebel movement, the Lord's Resistance Army practised rape and child-sex slavery in Uganda and surrounding countries. It is very much a matter of individual perception whether these forms of violence are less cruel than outright killing. Quite apart from the lasting handicaps resulting from mutilations, rape and torture often add long-term trauma and mental disorder to irreversible physical effects which we know since the famous work of Bruno Bettelheim to affect not only the generation that has suffered such humiliating and painful treatment, but often also the following generation.[31]

Hostage Taking and Hostage Executions

Hostages have been taken by insurgents and by counterinsurgents in many historical cases. Famously, the Romans took away the children of allied leaders to ensure their loyalty. In the European Middle Ages, this practise assumed a more benign form when children were sent to the courts of other princes to be raised there and to ensure bonds of friendship, often even bonds of marriage.[32] But in the context of war, the taking and execution of hostages is also a recurrent phenomenon. To give just one nineteenth-century example, in the coalition campaign against the French in 1813, the Prussians resorted to taking as hostages prominent burghers from villages and towns near the French border to ensure that these communities did not support Napoleon.[33]

In the twentieth century, hostage taking assumed two forms in particular. One which was by no means the only one was what the National-Socialist regime in Germany defined as *Sippenhaft*, the liability of all members of a family or clan for the actions (crimes) of any one member. De facto it had always been a tool of COIN when rebels eluded the state authorities to turn against members of their families, punishing or even killing them. The Russian equivalent of such kin liability, which ranged from imprisoning families of rebels to punishing entire communities, is

[30] M. Lent Hirsch, 'Darfur-Sudan', in *Women under Siege* (8 Feb. 2012), http://www .womenundersiegeproject.org/conflicts/profile/darfur-sudan.

[31] B. Bettelheim, *Surviving and Other Essays* (New York: Knopf, 1979); see also A. Meijer, 'Child Psychiatric Sequelae of Maternal War Stress', *Acta Psychiatrica Scandinavica*, 72/6 (December 1985), 505–11.

[32] Perversely, the medieval German word for hostage, 'gisel-' (modern German: 'Geisel') was used as a first name and remains in wide use still as Gisela/Giselle.

[33] Major General J. G. von Hoyer, *Handbuch für Offiziere in den angewandten Theilen der Krieges-Wissenschaften* Vol. 4 *Von der Strategie* (Hannover: Helwigsche Hof-Buchhandlung, 1829), 222–8.

well testified to by Soviet treatment of reticent populations, especially in the 1920s–1950s. We find the theory spelled out by Tukhachevsky.[34] Of course, this suggests a link between this particular form of measure and the totalitarian ideologies of the twentieth century. It may have been used by the totalitarian states on a larger scale than ever before, but sadly, it was not exclusive to their instrumentarium of repressing insurgencies.

We have written elsewhere about the second form, namely punitive atrocities committed by state authorities in such a way.[35] Suffice it to say that in the early twentieth century, such actions became notorious particularly at the hands of the Wehrmacht in occupied territories and the Gestapo secret police within the German Reich. The Germans became particularly infamous for their policy of shooting large numbers of hostages – their first choice always being individuals whom they had imprisoned as Communists or saboteurs or insurgents. Even this habit goes back a long way. In 1810, Frenchman Honoré Reille in Spain ordered the execution of four captured *guerrilleros* for any French soldier killed in an ambush, and if not enough partisans were found, civilians could be put in their place.[36] This was not general practice then,[37] but in the second half of the century, we find it applied widely by the Germans in the Franco-Prussian War of 1870/1871, especially in avenging the deaths of their own soldiers through sniper fire; the Germans held whole communities responsible for such actions and shot civilians to make an example of them. The French in turn seem to have emulated this German behaviour later in their colonies.[38] Then the First World War brought further examples of German actions of this sort. John Horne and Alan Kramer estimate that the Germans killed around six-and-a-half thousand people in this way in Belgium and northern France in the short span of time of August–October 1914.[39] What distinguished the German application of such collective punishment in the Second World War from previous practices was the proportionally (and absolutely) higher number of hostages that would be shot (and that the

---

[34] M. N. Tuchačevskij, 'La lutte contre le, Banditisme', trans. Annick Pelissier, in Gérard Chaliand (ed.), *Anthologie mondiale de la Stratégie* (Paris: Robert Laffont, 1990), 1165–7.

[35] B. Heuser, 'Atrocities in Theory and Practice', in Beatrice Heuser and Dale Walton (eds.), *Atrocities in Insurgencies and Counterinsurgency*, Special Issue of *Civil Wars*, 14/1 (March 2012), 2–28.

[36] I. F. W. Beckett, *Modern Insurgencies and Counter-Insurgencies: Guerrillas and Their Opponents since 1750* (London: Routledge, 2001), 27.

[37] Von Hoyer prescribed the use of hostages exclusively to have people to trade for one's own soldiers who had fallen in the enemy's hands; see J. G. von Hoyer, *Handbuch für Offiziere in den angewandten Theilen der Kriegswissenschaften* (Hannover: Helwigsche Hofbuchhandlung, 1829), 215–21.

[38] J. Ellis, *A Short History of Guerrilla Warfare* (London: Ian Allan, 1975), 108.

[39] J. Horne and A. Kramer, *German Atrocities, 1914: A History of Denial* (New Haven, CT: Yale University Press., 2001), 74–8, 435–43.

Germans tended on the Eastern Front to equate any Jew with Communist resistance). In Serbia, Ukraine and Russia, the Germans would kill between thirty and a hundred hostages for one of their own soldiers killed.[40] Where possible, in killing political prisoners as hostages, the Germans would act as though these were executions of criminals.[41]

German habits were also adopted by Germany's client regimes in the Second World War. To give just one illustration, the Vichy French administration of Indochina persecuted the family of Vo Nguyen Giap after he fled to China in 1940. His wife died of maltreatment in a French prison, his sister was guillotined.[42] Predictably, this did not make Giap amenable to negotiate with the French.

In the context of the Nuremberg War Crimes Trials it became clear that there was no international consensus on the matter of hostage taking and reprisal killings. Was a ratio of killing ten hostages to one soldier killed by snipers acceptable (while a ratio of eleven-to-one was not)?[43] Some countries (such as the United States) accepted the practice in principle, others did not. It was only in preparing the war crimes tribunals that the victorious powers came to an agreement that henceforth the killing of hostages would be contrary to the laws of war, and it was only the Geneva Conventions of 1949 which fully outlawed the taking of hostages. The so-called Al Quaeda Kidnapping Manual of 2004, said to be written by one Abdel Aziz al-Moqrin, in giving details about the conditions and circumstances in which hostages shall be taken and killed thus advocates something that is against the current laws or war, not something lacking historical precedent.[44]

Hostage taking was also often a tool of forced recruitment, as holding their families hostage would ensure the loyalty of key individuals,

---

[40] W. Manoschek, 'Kriegsverbrechen und Judenvernichtung in Serbien 1941–1942', in W. Wette and G. R. Ueberschär (eds.), *Kriegsverbrechen im 20. Jahrhundert* (Darmstadt: Wissenschaftliche Buchgesellschaft, 2001), 123–31; D. Pohl, *Die Herrschaft der Wehrmacht: Deutsche Militärbesatzung und einheimische Bevölkerung in der Sowjetunion, 1941–1944* (Munich: Oldenbourg, 2008), 71, 78, 303; K. Arnold, *Die Wehrmacht und die Besatzungspolitik in den besetzten Gebieten der Sowjetunion. Kriegführung und Radikalisierung im 'Unternehmen Barbarossa'* (Berlin: Ducker u. Humblodt, 2005), 458.

[41] K. Schmider, *Partisanenkrieg in Jugoslawien 1941–1944* (Hamburg: E. S. Mittler und Sohn, 2002).

[42] R. J. O'Neill, *General Giap: Politician and Strategist* (Melbourne: Cassell Australia, 1969), 1–17.

[43] K. von Lingen, *Kesselrings letzte Schlacht: Kriegsverbrecherprozesse, Vergangenheitspolitik und Wiederbewaffnung* (Paderborn: Ferdinand Schöningh, 2004). See also C. Gentile, *Wehrmacht und Waffen-SS im Partisanenkrieg: Italien 1943–1945* (Paderborn: Ferdinand Schöningh, 2012).

[44] A. de Coupigny, 'Otages: constantes d'une institution archaïque et variantes contemporaines', in H. Coutau-Bégarie (ed.), *Stratégies irrégulières* (Paris: Economica, 2010), 674, 682–7.

whether this be to insurgent movements or to governments as informers or fighters. Another means of ensuring loyalty, especially on the side of rebel forces, would be to force recent recruits to commit particularly heinous crimes in the presence of witnesses, which would stigmatise them and prevent them from deserting the movement, as they would be treated as criminals wherever else they would attempt to be reintegrated into a peaceful society.[45]

Unlike the tools of hostage taking and kin liability, the mass abduction of children that occurred in the Greek Civil War, sometimes with but probably mostly against the will of their parents, seems to have been something unique to that conflict. While Spyridon Plakoudas' chapter in this volume shows the link that was made in Greek between this measure and the 'child levy' practised by the Ottoman Turks to recruit Janissaries, there was no real historical continuity. The taking of Christian boys to become Janissaries had been practised selectively; it did not affect the entire child population of villages. Nor were these children treated really badly relatively to the customs of their time, unlike children in recent African conflict zones, who have been recruited as child soldiers (mainly boys) or servants and child prostitutes (mainly, but not only, girls).[46]

While today Western governments make no open use of hostage taking or executions, targeted assassinations still take place, carried out by government organs (most famously, of Osama Bin Laden by American special forces in 2011, and murders of journalists attributed to Russian state organs in the context of the insurgencies in Chechnya) or enabled by a permissive attitude of Western governments (France's role in the killing of Muammar Gaddafi by the insurgents in Libya is still not clear). Attempts to find and arrest or otherwise eliminate key leaders are clearly topping the list of COIN measures today as much as in previous centuries, as are targeted assassinations of police chiefs, majors and other representatives of the state by insurgents.

Hostage taking and assassinations are now more commonly associated with insurgent bands for whom the priority is not to establish their legitimacy. The violent repression of insurgencies in a form that leads to massacres among the civilians, even if they were at best sympathetic bystanders, practised by both sides in the Greek Civil War, and as practised in recent decades in Chechnya by Russian forces, or in 1989 by Chinese forces in Tiananmen Square, and as currently

---

[45] See K. Mitton, 'Irrational Actors and the Process of Brutalisation: Understanding Atrocity in the Sierra Leonean Conflict (1991–2002)', *Civil Wars*, 14/1 (March 2012), 104–21.

[46] Ibid.

practised by the Syrian government, is not generally used by law-abiding governments ('Liberal Democracies') any longer, with the exception of the Sri Lankan government's 2009 campaign to round up and kill the Tamil Tigers and their families. Mutilations of adversaries are not part of the instrumentarium of any COIN force outside Africa, it seems. Rape, also a prominent feature of recent and ongoing intra-state conflicts in sub-Saharan Africa, and an intrinsic part of the Yugoslav Wars of the 1990s, as a result of a breakdown of discipline[47] occurs exceptionally among the militaries of 'Liberal Democracies', but is not used by them deliberately as an instrument of COIN.

Forced Population Transfers ('Ethnic Cleansing')

Significant continuity, by contrast, can be demonstrated in the measure of what in the late 1990s would euphemistically become known in the disintegrating Yugoslavia as 'ethnic cleansing', that is, forced population transfers. This old practice is particular to Southeastern Europe and Asia Minor. It can be traced back to the Assyrians and Babylonians, who moved unruly populations – most famously the Israelites – to their own territory to use them as enslaved workers. Later, the medieval rulers of Constantinople, concerned about the loyalty of populations living near the Persian frontier of the East Roman Empire with their dualist form of Christianity inspired by Zoroastrianism, moved them to the Balkans, from where they spread their teaching along Alps and Pyrenees across Europe to the Atlantic. Heirs to Byzantium, with Moscow as the third Rome, the Russians adopted this practice of population transfers for better and worse: for better, when Russian emperors invited skilled artisans and their families from Western Europe to come and live in Russia (such as the Volga Germans invited in by Catherine the Great), and for worse when persecuting and forcibly moving populations whose loyalty they distrusted (again, for example, the Volga Germans, moved to Siberia by Stalin during the Second World War, lest they collude with the invading Wehrmacht). Stalin's deportations also affected other minorities within his Soviet Empire, such as, during and after the Second World War, the populations of entire Ukrainian villages, as well as Tatar and Kazakh communities.[48]

---

[47] See Col. (Ret) D. Benest, 'A Liberal Democratic State and COIN: The Case of Britain, or Why Atrocities Can Still Happen', in *Civil Wars*, 40/1 (March 2012), 29–48.

[48] Y. Zhukov, 'Examining the Authoritarian Model of Counter-insurgency: The Soviet Campaign against the Ukrainian Insurgent Army', *Small Wars & Insurgencies*, 18/3 (September 2007), 439–66.

But even this instrument from the tool box has been applied in other parts of the world. A distinctive pattern of resettlement was introduced by the British. In England, the idea of resettling unruly elements of the population in colonies abroad can be traced back to the mid-sixteenth century.[49] An early example includes the colonising settlements of people from Britain in Ireland, but then also, in the 1920s, the relocation of loyalist and neutral populations within Ireland, ostensibly for their own protection.[50] Following this latter pattern, the British both in Malaya and in Kenya resettled populations susceptible of supporting insurgencies in newly constructed villages away from their original (unsatisfactory) settlements, which worked well for the Chinese populations of Malaya, but very badly for the Kikuyu, as their villages were isolated and starved of vital supplies, admittedly due to poor planning, not genocidal intentions.[51] Was this more a case of rounding up such populations in detention *laagers* – as practised by the British when they rounded up Boer populations in the Boer War in what became infamously known as 'concentration camps', with the aim of preventing them from joining insurgencies? Or was the main intention the more altruistic one of protecting them and their villages from insurgents, for their own good, and of giving them land to live off with these new settlements? Hotly debated by specialists, it was probably a bit of both.[52]

The construction of new villages and the resettlement of potentially unruly populations was not solely a British instrument. It was used by the US Army against Native American tribes in the nineteenth century, and copied in France's COIN campaigns in Algeria in the 1950s, especially in the famous plan named after General Maurice Challe.[53] While his intention seems to have been to resettle loyalist villagers in areas where they were safe from reprisals by the FLN, this often led to the creation of miserable internment camps, and their inmates were vulnerable to reprisals after all, once the French pulled out after the Evian Treaty of 1963.[54]

A widely used tool to pacify a conquered region was the resettlement of one's own trusted natives there and is a measure going back to the earliest conscious colonisations in Antiquity, one difficult to distinguish, then as

---

[49] Sir H. Gilbert, quoted in Professor Walter Raleigh, 'The English Voyages of the Sixteenth Century' (originally 1904), in R. Hakluyt (ed.), *The Principal Navigations, Voyages, Traffiqves & Discoveries of the English Nation, Made by Sea or ouer Land, ...*, reprinted in 12 volumes (New York: Augustus M. Kelley, 1969), vol. XII 35f.

[50] T. Mockaitis: *British Counterinsurgency 1919–1960* (New York: St Martin's Press, 1990), 68.

[51] W. Markel: 'Draining the Swamp: The British Strategy of Population Control', *Parameters* (Spring 2006), 35–48.

[52] See Chapter 2.   [53] See Chapter 3.

[54] Fr.-M. Gougeon, 'The Challe Plan: Vain Yet Indispensable Victory', *Small Wars and Insurgencies*, 16/3 (December 2005), 311f.

later, from population movements resulting from purely economic push-and pull-factors. Thus, for example, Han Chinese settled in peripheral lands; Protestant Scots moved to Northern Ireland; Russians settled in Ukraine, the Baltic States and the central Asian states like Kazakhstan in the time of the Soviet Union; and French families put down roots in Algeria. All these followed what might be described as Antique pattern of colonisation. As an instrument of political control and safeguarding against insurgency, this seems to have disappeared from the tool kit of Liberal Democracies who have relinquished territorial ambitions. Zionist settlements on the West Bank (Samaria and Judaea) are not endorsed by the Israeli government, although it feels obliged to protect these Israeli settlers.

At the time of writing, rising figures of refugees world-wide form the backdrop to the rise in Syrian refugees in neighbouring countries who have been displaced as a result of government or insurgent actions. In mid-2016, more than seven-and-a-half million refugees had left Afghanistan and Syria,[55] whether as a result of conscious 'ethnic cleansing' or unintended actions by the leadership of each side.

Quadrillage versus External Sanctuaries and External Support

Possibly a French invention, as the term might suggest, and if so, perhaps linked to the late eighteenth-century French efforts to provide scientific measurements of territory, was the dividing up of insurgent territory into areas which would be searched for rebels, cleared of them and then held, what today is often referred to as 'search, clear, hold' missions. This '*quadrillage*', dividing the territory into squares that are then to be combed through methodically, can be traced back at least as far as the French Revolutionary Government's suppression of the Catholic and later Royalist revolts in the Vendée, a region on France's Atlantic coast, even though the term seems not to have been used in the late 1790s or early 1800s. In aid of these measures, fortified buildings were constructed along the frontiers between the Vendée and neighbouring Britany, to which the insurgency had also spread.[56] The French built 'little fortresses called *bloc-houses*' (suggesting English origins of that practice!) at particularly dangerous road crossings during the Peninsular War, but according to one French eyewitness they had little effect as the

---

[55] http://www.unhcr.org/uk/figures-at-a-glance.html, accessed on 12 IX 2016.
[56] A. J. Joes, 'Insurgency and Genocide: La Vendée', *Small Wars & Insurgencies*, 9/3 (Winter 1998), 32–45.

Spanish *guerrilleros* found ways of going around them.[57] Nevertheless, learning from the French, the Spanish Cristino COIN operations of the 1830s used block houses better to contain the Carlist insurgency.[58] Something very similar to *quadrillage* was used by the Greek Government in the Greek Civil War, and the term itself was used for the construction of such strongpoints by the French in the Indochina War a century later; *quadrillage* is most commonly associated with French practice in the Algerian War, where on a large scale, the closing of the frontier to neighbouring countries was most effectively practised with the *Ligne Morice*, and on a small scale, the *souk* of Algiers itself was divided up and searched (brutally but effectively) for insurgents in the eponymous 'battle' for the city.[59]

Israel has also used this approach in cordoning off the Syrian and Lebanese borders, after continued terrorist infiltration from its northern borders during the 1970s. To a lesser extent, Hezbollah's seizure of al-Qusair proved a drawback for the Syrian rebels as this location had been a strategic point on the route used to continue the flow of ammunition and manpower into Syria. The fence established along the de facto demarcation line between Israel and the West Bank has successfully ended Palestinian suicide missions, but has had its own political fallout and social costs.

While in late nineteenth-century English literature, we find the French term '*quadrillage*' used, the practice of superimposing a grid on an area and combing it systematically to find insurgent fighters had by then spread to other colonial or pseudo-colonial powers. Stationary population control at crucial passage has long been an alternative to chasing the rebels. Linked closely to this were attempts to control the population, by installing check points, issuing identity cards and controlling food supplies, measures we find in the American submission of the Philippines both in the late nineteenth century and in the American COIN against the Huks in the 1950s. As a preventive measure, the Soviet Union imposed restrictions on travel, and deprived them of the right to choose their domicile, on its own citizens, even within the its state boundaries, which until its very end prevented the ethnic Kazakh and German populations who had been moved to Siberia by Stalin during the Second World War from returning to their former areas of settlement. Identity

[57] J. F. A. Le Mière de Corvey, *Des Partisans et des corps irréguliers* (Paris: Anselin & Pochard et al., 1823), 99f.
[58] M. Lawrence: 'Poachers Turned Gamekeepers: A Study of the Guerrilla Phenomenon in Spain, 1808–1840', *Small Wars and Insurgencies*, 25/4 (August 2014), 848.
[59] A. J. Joes, *Modern Guerrilla Insurgency* (Westport, CT: Praeger, 1992), 105; Gougeon, 'The Challe Plan'.

cards and food rationing were of course central measures in the total *Erfassung* (bureaucratic registration and control) of the population in all police states from National-Socialist Germany to the Communist countries of Eastern Europe.

The counterpart to such *quadrillage* and other systematic persecution was always for those persecuted to seek sanctuary in areas inaccessible to the authorities hunting them, that is, refuge beyond the legal reach of the challenged state power. Caesar invaded Britain as Celtic opponents to Roman pacification of their lands sought refuge there and obtained support from natives of the British Isles. During the Middle Ages, given the systematic rivalry between the French and English monarchs, pretenders to the English throne or 'traitors' of all sorts would seek refuge in or be exiled to France, often to reappear on English or Welsh shores with an army recruited on the Continent. In the sixteenth and early seventeenth centuries, the Dutch Eighty Years' War to establish their independence from Spain would not have led to success if it had not been for prolonged help from the French Huguenots and from Elizabethan England, and later from the Protestant powers involved in the Thirty Years' War. In 1745, Bonnie Prince Charlie, the last (Catholic) Jacobite challenger of the (Protestant) Hanoverian dynasty in Britain, arrived in Scotland transported by French ships, with French-paid Irish (Catholic) soldiers under his command, the famous Wild Geese. After the French Revolution had erupted and the extremely conservative populations of the west coast of France, in the Vendée and Brittany, staged their counter-revolution or '*Chouannerie*', Britain attempted to support the counter-revolutionaries by supplying arms and men.[60] While this misfired, the French in turn took this as an incentive to instigate an (equally unsuccessful) anti-English uprising in Ireland, Wales and the West Country, much in line with centuries of previous Spanish support for uprisings in Ireland against the British crown.[61] In the nineteenth century, Greece's establishment of its independence from the Ottoman Empire owed much to the international brigade of Hellenophile supporters who flocked to its support from all over Europe and even America, much as Muslim-led insurgencies today attract ardent young Muslims of Middle Easter origin from Cardiff and Birmingham and from Muslim communities throughout the Eurasian landmass.

[60] A. Forrest, 'The Insurgency of the Vendée', *Small Wars and Insurgencies*, 25/4 (August 2014), 783–97.

[61] S. Kleinman, 'Initiating Insurgencies Abroad: French Plans to "Choannise" Britain and Ireland', *Small Wars and Insurgencies*, 25/4 (August 2014), 767–82; E. García Hernan, *Ireland and Spain in the Reign of Philip II*, trans. L. Liddy (Dublin: Four Courts Press, 2009).

Insurgencies that have been cut off from external sanctuaries and supplies by the counterinsurgents have almost always been crushed. It is hardly possible to exaggerate the importance of sanctuaries for the insurgents – Morocco and Tunisia for the FLN, Eire for the PIRA, Jordan and Lebanon for the Palestinians, Pakistan for the Taliban, the Balkan and the USSR for the Greek Communists, and Turkey and Jordan for the Syrian rebels. In the Greek Civil War discussed in this volume, as in America's Vietnam War, the ability of the Communist fighters to withdraw into neighbouring states was a crucial element of their success. The KKE in Greece expanded this aspect of the international lifeline to include also economic and social support from the Balkan states, thus enabling the short-lived construction of 'free Greece'. The closure of the frontier by Yugoslavia and Bulgaria, by contrast, strangled the Communist uprising in Greece. In 1949 Tito's Yugoslavia, ostracized by Stalin and the Cominform, was persuaded by British-led diplomatic measures to cease aiding the Greek Communists, a major diplomatic coup for the COIN side.[62] In 1972, members of the PIRA were able to escape from Northern Ireland into Eire when the UK government launched Operation Motorman. In the 1960s members of the Palestinian Liberation Organisation (PLO), using bases in Jordan, would organize cross-border raids and return to Jordan after the operations. Even if Israel had been willing to break international law and attack the PLO across the frontier in Jordan, this action would have created a conflict with the Jordanian army, a deterrent factor that minimized Israeli retaliation.

Insurgencies often rely on external assistance for training, manpower, weapons and other provisions. The FLN, the PIRA, the Palestinians and the Syrian rebels all established training camps in neighbouring countries, preparing fighters before they enter the actual battlefields. Insurgents also often recruit new combatants abroad. The Taliban brought in fighters not only to increase their numbers, but also for the importing of technical staff highly skilled with explosives and other firearm technology. The 'Border Army' in Tunisia and Morocco could not invade the country and join the FLN insurgents because of the French barriers, but its constant threat on the Algerian border necessitated the concentration of most French forces in that area, forces which would otherwise have been free to engage in COIN activity, and thus it facilitated FLN insurgency efficiency. Furthermore, these insurgencies have relied on outside support for weapons and provisions. Since the supply of ground-to-air

---

[62] B. Heuser, *Western Containment Policies in the Cold War: The Yugoslav Case, 1948–1953* (London & New York: Routledge, 1989).

Stinger missiles by the United States to the Taliban in their fight against Soviet occupation in the 1990s, the use of missiles has always implied reliance on an outside source, usually a state.

Claiming the monopoly of force, most states attempt to control the weapons within their state boundaries very tightly, enabling them to deny any legal flow of arms to rebels. Consequently, rebels have to draw on foreign powers and/or criminal networks (usually with international links) to procure them. The latter, linking insurgents to organised international crime, is clearly not limited to any part of the world, but constitutes a problem encountered world-wide in counterinsurgency operations.

Destruction of Symbolic Buildings or Sites

The punishment, humiliation and demoralisation of insurgents have often been attempted by means of the destruction of a ritual site particularly holy to them. Particular buildings can be of importance for both insurgents and COIN forces in a symbolic way: they can stand for state power, tradition, identity or prestige, which might be targeted by insurgents to embarrass the state authorities, or (relatively more rarely) by the state to humiliate insurgents. An early and widely known example of the latter is the repeated destruction of the Temple of Jerusalem, last by the Romans to crush the Jewish revolt of 70 CE. An early medieval example of such a COIN measure has come to us from Western Europe. When the Saxons whom Charlemagne had conquered and integrated into his kingdom rose up against his rule and against his forced conversion to Christianity, he in 772 ordered the destruction of Irminsul, their pagan sanctuary, variously speculated to have been a holy tree or a sacred column.

The destruction of castles or other fortresses which generally asserted the power of and protected occupants served both a political and a practical purpose. The razing of such strong points was thus a widely utilised tool, both to prevent the opponent from seizing them or reconquering them and to express his defeat symbolically. This accounts for the many ruined castles throughout Europe and the Middle East. The destruction of a large number of British castles during the Civil War (the War of the Three Kingdoms) in the seventeenth century, mainly by Cromwell's Republican Roundheads (to deprive the Royalists of them) falls in this category, as does the storming of the Bastille in 1789 and its subsequent slighting (the Bastille was both an administrative centre and a prison at the time).

Following the French Revolution of 1848, the brutal French mastercounterinsurgent Bugeaud noted the importance of defending prestigious and administratively important government buildings against hostile crowds, such as the National Assembly, the town hall, the residence of the head of state, the Tuileries (i.e., a wing of the Louvre Palace that was burned down in the Commune), the headquarters of the armed forces and the *Garde nationale*, the telegraph station, the Bank of France, and the Treasury.[63]

He was absolutely right in his designation of key spots that might be targeted by revolutionaries or other insurgents, as many later events would demonstrate.[64] Prestigious buildings representing power centres were chosen by terrorists, in general, more for their symbolic importance: thus the King David Hotel in Jerusalem which housed the British administrative headquarters was bombed by a Zionist independence movement in 1946, and thus in 1991 the IRA launched a mortar attack on No. 10 Downing Street in London, the residence of the British Prime Minister. More recently, US embassies or military vessels have become favourite targets for Islamists and other anti-American movements. Big and famous shops such as Harrods in London (1983) and the FNAC bookshop in Paris (1986) preceded New York's twin towers and Washington's Pentagon as targets for terrorist attacks, but, in a more pragmatic way, transport nodes seem even more popular with insurgents. For more practical reasons, sabotage in the form of obstructing key transport links, cutting telegraph lines, or blowing up arms or fuel or food depots were measures explicitly articulated and applied by T. E. Lawrence ('of Arabia') and his Arab friends who rose up against the Ottoman Empire during the First World War, and prescribed by Stalin for the Soviet resistance against the Germans, once he had recovered from the surprise German invasion.[65] An explosion in airports, railway stations or underground lines has maximum disruptive effects and lends itself to maximum publicity for a cause, although it is unlikely to create much sympathy for those causing it.

High-profile events can also be targets of terrorist action, most famously perhaps the attack on the Israeli delegation at the 1972 Olympic Games in Munich or in 2015, the targeting of an international football

---

[63] T. R. Bugeaud de la Piconnerie, Duc d'Isly, *La Guerre des Rues et des Maisons* (MS of 1849, Paris: Jean-Paul Rocher, 1997), 126.

[64] A. Gandolfi, *Les luttes armées en Amérique latine* (Paris: PUF, 1991), 137ff.

[65] T. E. Lawrence, 'The Evolution of a Revolt', *Army Quarterly* (October 1920), and T. E. Lawrence: 'Science of Guerrilla Warfare', *Encyclopedia Britannica*, 14th ed. (Chicago, 1929), vol. 10, reprinted in M. Brown (ed.), *T. E. Lawrence in War & Peace* (Pennsylvania: Stackpole Books and London: Greenhill Books, 2005), 261–73 and 274–84 respectively; for Stalin's directives, see A. Hill (ed.), *The Great Patriotic War of the Soviet Union 1941–1945: A Documentary Reader* (London: Routledge, 2009), 199f.

match and a rock concert in Paris. Consequently, we regularly see enormous efforts made by governments to achieve security during such events. Paradoxically, however, the terrorists edge a little closer to achieving their goals when the public becomes irritated with the State's security measures taken in response to terrorist acts.[66]

'Bands', 'Counter-Bands' and 'Bandit-Hunters'

Turning to operational, tactical and structural features of insurgencies and COIN, there, too, we find recurrent patterns. These can be traced back to the writings of Frontinus[67] and are documented in Caesar's record of the Gallic Wars[68] or Medieval sources such as Gerald of Wales (Geraldus Cambrensis), which are clearly reinvented periodically.[69]

In the early stages of an insurgency (which may be its only stage), insurgents largely operate in small groups of trained fighters. In some cases, as in nineteenth-century Greece or in the mountainous regions in Afghanistan or Algeria, this characteristic derives from local tradition of small-scale banditry or guerrilla fighting, usually made possible by the lack of a centralized political authority. This phenomenon seems to be based less on specific traditions, however, but rather on the very definition of insurgency, that is to say an asymmetrical struggle against a foe superior in training, discipline and firepower. Hence the preference of insurgent groups for small-unit activity is mainly a result of necessity, not of choice.

Realizing the superiority of the counterinsurgents on the open battle-field, only in rare cases have there been attempts by insurgents to forge a conventional fighting force, as these have mostly proved ineffective in confronting the counterinsurgents. The Viet Minh's initial success against the French is rather exceptional in this regard. Other attempts were far less successful. The Algerian makeshift army formed of rural ALN guerrilla forces was soon dismantled, and in a short time the small-unit configuration returned. The Greek Communist KKE's attempt to transform the communist insurgency into a regular army also failed to defeat the Royalist government. In the Greek case, and to some extent also in Algeria, attempts to create a regular army constituted a

---

[66] Where terrorist acts are committed not against authoritarian and repressive states, academics complaining about the excessive 'securitization' of such problems, purportedly to increase the State's power over society, lose sight of the main issues.

[67] Sextus Iulius Frontinus: *Strategemata* (ca. 84–96 CE) trans. C. E. Bennett, *The Stratagems* (London: Heinemann, 1925), 135.

[68] Caius Iulius Caesar, *De bello gallico* (58–50 BCE), e.g., I.12.

[69] Geraldus Cambrensis, *The Historical Works of Geraldus Cambrensis*, trans. and ed. T. Wright (London: H. G. Bohn, 1863).

deviation from the small-unit banditry tradition of earlier centuries. The Chinese case – Mao's victory – still stands out as exceptional; the Vietnamese case, often cited alongside it, was less so as it was ultimately not through a conventional defeat of the American COIN forces that the Vietnamese Communists won the war.

A tool of COIN that can be traced back to the tenth century is that of forming crack units quite similar to guerrilla bands in order to fight like with like. The example of this is the Byzantine emperor Nikephoros Phokas' work on the subject on how to fight small-scale incursions by Arab raiders.[70] Throughout early modern times, the specialist partisan forces employed by empires and kingdoms – often lightly armed horsemen or infantry from particular tribes – were best fought by units similarly constituted.[71] Different governments hit on the idea of turning poachers into gamekeepers, and recruiting special units to hunt down insurgents from among former rebel bands.[72] In this context the grey area between irregular forces and criminal gangs was always particularly important, as the Spanish experience of the first half of the nineteenth century and the Greek tradition of *kleftopolemos* illustrate.[73] In the First World War, the Austrian government recruited Muslims from the Austro-Hungarian Empire to form 'Counter-Bands' to fight the many insurgent movements. These ultimately seized the opportunity of the great conflagration to secure the independence of their own people from Vienna.[74]

Stephen Blank shows in his chapter how the Soviets created counter-bands in the form of local militias to fight insurgents. The 'Black and Tans' auxiliaries formed in Ireland to support the Royal Irish Constabulary for the purpose of fighting the IRA became infamous for their excesses.[75] In the Second World War the SS and the Wehrmacht formed units to chase resistant fighters, aptly referred to as 'bandit hunters' by historian Philip Blood.[76] Specialist forces were also formed

[70] Nikephoros Phoka, *De Velitatione*, trans. G. Dagron *Traité sur la guerrilla* (Paris: Eds du CNRS, 1999).
[71] B. Heuser: 'Lessons Learnt? Cultural Transfer and Revolutionary Wars, 1775–1831', *Small Wars and Insurgencies*, 25/4 (Autumn 2014), 858–76.
[72] M. Lawrence, 'Poachers Turned Gamekeepers: A Study of the Guerrilla Phenomenon in Spain, 1808–1840', *Small Wars and Insurgencies*, 25/4 (August 2014), 827–42; see also Chapter 13.
[73] C. Esdaile, 'Guerrillas and Bandits in the Serranía de Ronda, 1810–1812', *Small Wars and Insurgencies*, 25/4 (August 2014), 798–811.
[74] A. Ehrhardt, *Kleinkrieg: Geschichtliche Erfahrungen und künftige Möglichkeiten* (Potsdam: Ludwig Voggenreiter Verlag, 1st ed. 1935; 2nd ed. 1942), 72.
[75] Mockaitis: *British COIN*, 19f.
[76] P. W. Blood, *Hitler's Bandit Hunters: The SS and the Nazi Occupation of Europe* (Washington, DC: Potomac Books, 2006).

and employed by the French in Indochina; in Algeria such units, deployed in helicopters, were referred to as *commandos de chasse*.[77] Tactically effective, such units rarely endeared themselves to the population in general as their methods tended to be as cruel as those they were tasked to fight, thus often undermining any legitimacy of the state power they represented. Still, David Charters and Maurice Tugwell found in the late 1980s that British, French and Israeli armies had begun to transform their armed forces into small units to counter insurgents, in an attempt 'to beat their opponents at their own game.'[78] In the early 2000s, confronted with insurgents in Iraq and Afghanistan, they seem to have had to re-invent this wheel.

Ensuring Survival of the Insurgency

Apart from small units and the avoidance of frontal battles, the survival of insurgencies usually depended on the ability of fighters to disappear into inaccessible areas or to vanish among the people. Irish rebels since the seventeenth century, Spanish *guerrilleros* in the Peninsular War, and more recently the Taliban and Palestinians have been known for their ability to blend in with the local population and thus avoid exposure, or in other cases for their willingness to fight from within civilian populations. Confrontation was avoided even when encircled, in which case the forces attempted to attack a weak point of the quarantine and then escape, or in other incidents took advantage of night in order to escape in small groups. In a different form of this approach, the Syrian rebels of the 2010s retreated to largely secure peripheral areas when confrontation with the Syrian army was likely to occur, but then reconquered the cities after the army had to desert them because of lack in manpower. In Algeria, the mountainous periphery was used as concealment for the FLN forces.

Another prevalent tactical approach is that of accepting a pause in order to reorganize after periods of exceptionally high losses of manpower. The PIRA, after failed operations or after having been overrun by British forces, tended to suspend activities for several weeks, as Jim Storr notes (see Chapter 10).

While in most cases the notion of preserving the resistance is regarded as an essential necessity, in particular cases this prolonged struggle has become a part of the ideology itself. The idea that an enduring resistance will eventually achieve victory through willingness and sacrifice, which

---

[77] P. Pottier, 'GCMA/GMI: A French Experience in Counterinsurgency during the French Indochina War', *Small Wars and Insurgencies*, 16 /2 (June 2005), 125–46.

[78] D. A. Charters and Maurice Tugwell (eds.), *Armies in Low-Intensity Conflict: a Comparative Analysis* (London: Brassey's Defence Publishers, 1989), 253.

will compensate for inferior military power, is especially prominent in the Palestinian ideology. Adopting the *Muqawama,* or persistent warfare, the Palestinians have idealized sacrifice and facilitated the gradual transition between different forms of resistance, including non-violent methods.[79]

Winning over the Population

We have demonstrated that insurgencies have relied on terror to garner public acquiescence in their activities, but their longevity at least in theory should rely more on the prolonged support of the local population (whose interests they usually claim to represent).[80] Popular support is critical for both sides, and logically effort should be put into obtaining and maintaining it. And yet there are many examples where insurgents or COIN forces rely on terror, rather than on 'Hearts & Minds' winning strategies. Jim Storr thinks the outcome of the Irish troubles may well have been due mostly to the absence of measures undertaken by the 'Republicans' to win over the population, and that all positive investment in Northern Ireland, in its infrastructure in all forms, was undertaken by the government in London. As Rob Johnson illustrates, despite their rule of terror, the Taliban garner support by proclaiming that the Western powers came to Afghanistan to terrorize the population and liquidate authentic Afghan traditions and ways of life. Popular support makes it possible for the insurgents to blend in with the population and to receive aid and provisions during operations. In addition, when popular support for the insurgents is high, it is possible to recruit locals into the organization. Such has been the case in all insurgencies examined in this volume.

Disaffection also plays a role. In Syria, it helped not only in recruiting locals but also in recruiting deserters from the pro-Assad military forces. Similarly the FLN recruited Algerian deserters from the French armed forces. In the Palestinian case, popular support has facilitated the implementation of a strategy of popular resistance, that is to say mass demonstrations which may accumulate to violent mass involvement in the resistance (*intifada*). In Algeria mass urban protests organized by the FLN helped give it the image of a nationalistic party.

If the insurgents terrorise the civilian population with violent measures, these usually damage their image and popular support wanes. The Taliban in recent years have encountered this problem, since their adherence to only a narrow interpretation of Islamic law separates them from most of the population, and the suicide bombings or other terrorist acts

---

[79] See Chapter 11.   [80] Heuser, 'Atrocities in Theory and Practice'.

only further this split. The most outstanding case in this regard is the Greek KKE's harrying of urban centres in northern Greece and the related removal of thousands of children into neighbouring communist countries. As Spyridon Plakoudas has shown, this inspired the Royalist government to respond in kind and in turn create children's villages for orphans but also children whose parents had joined the Communists or were interned in prison camps.

In Northern Ireland, the PIRA stopped terrorist acts against civilians as this had a bad effect on its public image and undermined public support. In Algeria in the 1950s and early 1960s, the FLN made a great effort to convince the population and the international community that its conflict with the French was a patriotic struggle of de-colonization. Image was everything, both at home and abroad. And yet the Algerians took brutal measures against collaborators or pro-French populations. This paradox resulted from the totalitarian conception of the struggle, a mix of Jihadism and Stalinism. Beyond that, public image and public support derive largely from cultural and social factors. In a society dominated by macho and feudal structures of strongmen winning the allegiance of others through shows of force, authoritarian behaviour towards subordinates and violent behaviour (especially towards traitors) might be admired rather than condemned. Cultural and social factors vary greatly from one case to the other, and a certain image that would obtain support in one culture may be regarded as appalling and reprehensible in another.

The Soviet Union sought to win the support of the Russian population in general and of strata within the populations where there was resistance to Soviet rule through deep indoctrination – the rebels were invariably identified as being in the pockets of the class enemy, paid for by the CIA (often true), enemies to the well-being of the people, etc. Since the disappearance of the Soviet Union, Moscow has played a more nationalist, anti-Islamic card in securing the support of its population against the (mostly Muslim) insurgent groups in its border regions. At the time of writing, we are seeing evidence of Russian nationalism extending to the protection of Russophone separatist insurgents outside the frontiers of the Russian Federation, especially Ukraine, a position with strong albeit not universal appeal both to domestic audiences and to Russophone communities elsewhere. Russia is clearly a culture prone to admiring strong men, with a nationalism born out of perceived humiliation which reminds any historically educated mind of the rampant German nationalism in the early 1930s, born out of the perceived humiliation of Versailles.

On the positive side, hearts-and-minds approaches are now firmly entrenched in the COIN doctrines at any rate of NATO member states and of NATO as a whole, where the military's role in support of safeguarding the human security in areas affected by insurgencies and COIN operations, in supporting economic and infrastructure development, government and the rule of law, and in improving 'societal relationships' so as to help stabilise the society post-conflict is emphasized.[81] Such measures systematically include infrastructure construction projects, including roads, repairing water supplies, digging wells, building or restoring schools and hospitals, and other social welfare programmes. In UN-backed missions, they now also tend to include state-building, with all the elements we have listed in our Introduction, including also attempts to spread democratic values. By contrast, Liberal Democracies hesitate to remove incompetent, corrupt and otherwise inadequate governments that have been elected in some form that can be called democratic or instituted by them. Examples include the American failure to remove Ngo Dinh Diem in South Vietnam, the NATO powers' continued support for Hamid Karzai in Afghanistan, and the international community's continued support for Nouri al-Maliki in Iraq.

Resettlement with benevolent intentions towards the populations concerned, including the construction of new, better, protected villages, and patrolling and defending them, has been undertaken a number of times, with varying effects. The German World War Two *Wehrdörfer* did not help pacify occupied Eastern Europe. We have already noted the positive results of British creations of such settlements in Malaya and the catastrophic results in Kenya. Secured villages, 'strategic hamlets', were set up by the Americans in the Vietnam War, ultimately without strategically decisive success. More widespread is the use of refugee camps, which of course are interim solutions with a tendency to become long-term problems, where the COIN powers do not have land to give away and to protect.

Resettlement efforts of another nature were undertaken by successive Italian governments in an effort to break the spine of the parallel Italian state structures created by the organised crime structures we commonly refer to as 'Mafias'. This consisted of moving Mafia supporters and their families away from their places of origin (mainly in southern Italy) to cities in the North, a measure called the '*confino*'. It was done since the Mafias sprang up as alternatives to the nascent national government in Italy in the context of the wars for Italian independence of the nineteenth century, then in the Fascist period, but again from the 1950s to 1970s. The underlying assumption was that the Mafias were cultural constructs

---

[81] *Allied Joint Doctrine for Counterinsurgency* (COIN) of February 2011 (AJP-3.4.4) of 2011, http://publicintelligence.net/nato-allied-joint-doctrine-for-counterinsurgency.

dependent on a particular environment, so that removing the Mafiosi from their cultural environment would make them adopt a different set of values and lifestyle. The '*confino*' tended to have the opposite effect of that intended, however, namely to spread the criminal networks to the north.[82]

A special form of winning popular support is an appeal to a special segment of the population – for example, to play off one ethnic or religious group against another. Yitzhak Shichor notes that the Chinese wielded this tool repeatedly, but so have Western powers in their appeal to the Arabs against the Ottoman Empire in the First World War, to the mountain tribes or Montagnards in Vietnam (against the Vietnamese Communists) in the 1950s, 1960s and early 1970s, to the Kurds first against Saddam Hussein and presently against the Islamists trying to establish an Islamic Caliphate in Iraq and Syria.

Propaganda, a tool in the COIN and the insurgents' box that predates the invention of the term by centuries, is assuming ever greater importance and dimensions in the cyber age. The pressure to dominate the 'narrative' and media campaign in conflicts has reached such proportions that public relations have their place centre stage in operations by both sides, to witness, the expansion of NATO and other ministerial press offices, websites, Facebook etc. In turn, if anything is new about insurgencies post '9/11', it is their use of cyber-based means of communication. The articulation of the concern for 'public opinion and the political community of States' (i.e., what today is called the 'international community') can be traced at least to the Prussian Rühle von Lilienstern, writing in 1818, who noted that the best victory was no good if the way it was obtained turned international public opinion against the victor.[83] Since then, 'propaganda' and 'media warfare' have become important lines of business for articulate civilians and military personnel alike, as much as for IT-savvy insurgents.[84] 'World opinion'

---

[82] S. Lupo, *History of the Mafia*, trans. A. Shugaar (originally 1996; New York: Columbia University Press, 2009) and F. Varese, *Mafia on the Moves. How Organized Crime Conquers New Territories* (Princeton, NJ: Princeton University Press, 2011), and all in N. Rossi, *A Modern Janus: A Study on the Mutual Constitution of the Italian State and the Sicilian Mafia* (unpublished PhD dissertation, University of Reading, 2015). We are grateful to Ms Rossi for these references.

[83] [August] R[ühle] v[on] L[ilienstern], *Handbuch für den Offizier zur Belehrung im Frieden und zum Gebrauch im Felde* (1818), 2, translation in B. Heuser (ed. and trans.), *The Strategy Makers: Thoughts on War and Society from Machiavelli to Clausewitz* (Santa Barbara, CA: ABC-Clio for Praeger, 2010), 180.

[84] See, e.g., D. Schlechter, *Media Wars: News at a Time of Terror* (Oxford: Rowman & Littlefield, 2003); M. Dartnell, *Insurgency Online: Web Activism and Global Conflict* (Toronto: University of Toronto Press, 2006).

and the struggle to capture its support, however measured, has indeed been an important factor in insurgencies and COIN throughout the twentieth century, providing the great undercurrent for the growing tide of self-determination and thus decolonisation, context for such a large proportion of uprisings against state power.

The battle for the sympathy of international public opinion is increasingly one that both sides engage in in an insurgency. In this context one can say, with Michel Foucault, that 'politics is the continuation of war by other means'.[85] The Algerians in the 1950s, and the Palestinians since the 1970, understood that the outcome of their conflict will be determined on a diplomatic battlefield. This does not mean that they neglected military methods, rather that they pursued a binary strategy. A similar dual approach could be seen on both sides in the Greek Civil War. Thus not all strategies with an important diplomatic component also imply a relinquishment of violent methods.

Tibetans have garnered much international awareness of and support for their cause through appeals to public opinion especially in Western states, but to little avail, as no one is willing to take on China as the source of their oppression. The Palestinians and the East Timorese have used international links most successfully, especially through the use of international organisations as platforms for furthering their political aspirations. As a part of the pragmatic 'persistent resistance' strategy, the Palestinians in recent years have used such public platforms to gain international support whilst pressuring Israel through a delegitimizing propaganda campaign.[86]

Public diplomacy and the use of international organisations are in principle easier for a state government with its diplomatic apparatus and permanent representation in these organisations. Thus the Greek government could use the UN against the Communist rebels. The opposite of propaganda and public diplomacy, namely, information blockage, for obvious reasons is confined to authoritarian, closed societies. North Korea, Russia and China can thus check the media in quarantined areas to ensure that no government-committed atrocity is reported to the public or the international community. This approach accepted in autocratic states could not be carried out in the free world. Thus French atrocities committed in the Algerian War of 1954–62 had a dramatic effect on public opinion both at home and abroad and contributed strongly and perhaps decisively to France's self-imposed decision to abandon the fight.

---

[85] M. Foucault, Lecture of 7 Jan. 1976, in *Society Must Be Defended: Lectures at the Collège de France, 1975–1976*, trans. D. Macey (London: Allen Lane, 2003), 15.
[86] See Chapter 11.

Exit Strategies and Long-Term Commitments

It is notable that since the wave of decolonisation that lapped over the globe, Western Liberal Democracies look upon COIN operations as temporary involvements and are ever keener to develop 'exit strategies', a term that is self-explanatory. The United States, with the exception of Hawaii and the Philippines, typically intended to come home from the beginning of any overseas intervention. France's post-1962 operations have tended to aim at most to keep military bases in the area and friendly relations with the government. The exception to the rule is made by the British in Northern Ireland, and of course Israel in the occupied territories. We would expect to find the determination to stay on more generally where the area in question is part of or close to the homeland, especially in immediately adjacent territories, and COIN is applied by governments that are or tend towards authoritarianism. Examples include Russia's treatment of Chechnya, China's of Tibet, and Turkey's towards the Kurds.

In turn, the absence of a determination to stay on influences the type of COIN strategies for which governments are prepared. The short, sharp interventions most perfectly exemplified by France's Mali expedition in 2013 are the ideal, while the reality is often one of unsuccessful short interventions (for example, the United States in Somalia 1992–1993), or of military interventions that turned into long-term state-building with varying degrees of success (Iraq in 2003–2014; Afghanistan 2001–present). Where these regions are far from the homeland, inevitably, domestic support for such long-term investment in terms of personnel and treasure becomes difficult to maintain. Militaries the world over are conditioned to aim for *military* victory, not for long-term policing and state-building operations.[87] Populations of Liberal Democracies squirm at the idea of killing even the most militant insurgents, which creates constraints on the way their militaries can fight and above all be *seen* to fight. Unlike in former times, the killing of militants cannot be celebrated in the West, even if it is generally recognised that it might be a necessary element in defeating an insurgency. It is precisely in this area that we can test the true spirit of a culture, and whether it is built on Human Rights and humanitarian principles, or on intolerant and fanatical ideologies or religious movements, for which Human Rights count for less than the triumph of one's ideology or religion. Machism, the love for authoritarian strong leaders and the apotheosis of one's own nation

---

[87] On the idea of victory, see B. Heuser, 'Victory, Peace, and Justice: The Neglected Trinity', *Joint Forces Quarterly*, 69 (April 2013), 6–12, www.ndu.edu/press/neglected-trinity.html.

over all others (as opposed to any recognition of the fundamental equivalence of all humans and their freedoms), of course fall in the latter category. An application of this test indicates that the values upheld by the UN are not as universally accepted as the signing up to them by state governments the world over would suggest.

The Choice of Tools: Evidence of a Particular 'Style'?

General Tools and Culture-Specific Tools

It appears that there is indeed a widely shared instrumentarium or tool set that has endured across time and space. To this, of course, have been added new instruments, such as air strikes (including by drones) and ground-to-air missiles, mobile phones, the use of the Internet (cyber) and other new technology. So far the balance between old and new to us seems to be weighed down by continuity rather than change. In general, insurgency warfare tactics thus seem to draw on a tool kit, adapted to political and technological circumstances. An exception to this may be constant geographical characteristics, which may create a certain insurgency style (like mountainous banditry). Another exception may be some cultural factors engendering particular tactics; one would expect a certain degree of tactical adaptation if the insurgents accept that the ends justify the means, and tactics are subordinated to a greater political purpose. The political context is likely to have a national or cultural particularity, as influenced to a far greater extent by cultural and social parameters, and change with international trends that vary from one insurgency to another.

So, yes, there are some features often shared by insurgencies, viz. often shared by COIN operations. National style or peculiarities are not necessarily the most important features of such conflicts. Moreover, there is plenty of evidence of big ruptures in ways insurgency movements in one country or region operate (see our example of Greece) and/or in the way in which government COIN in one country/region operates (see again Greece, or the fact that the Germans had little COIN tradition before 1870 or after 1945), or there are two or more rivalling trends such as in France.[88] But it is still the case that each case must still be evaluated separately.

Passing review of the examples both of COIN and of insurgencies' tools, we find some that were unique. Chinese and Soviet repression of insurgencies distinguish themselves from those of other states by the

---

[88] M. Martin, 'From Algiers to N'Djamena: France's Adaptation to Low-Intensity Wars, 1830–1987', in D. A. Charters and M. Tugwell (eds.), *Armies in Low-Intensity Conflict: A Comparative Analysis* (London: Brassey's Defence Publishers, 1989), 77–138

sheer number of victims.[89] China seems to be more inclined than other states to use brute force preventively. On a lower level, there are unique tools, such as knee-capping by the IRA and the abduction of children by both sides in the Greek Civil War.[90] Other phenomena were mainly regional, such as the deliberate punitive population transfers if these populations supported rebels. The amputation of body parts is found mainly in Islamic areas of Africa.

Crucially, the material presented in this volume leads us to the conclusion that there is not a simple national tradition of carrying out insurgencies or COIN. Instead, each country (or group of insurgents) has drawn on a mix of instruments. The degree to which they have relied on one type or another can, however, produce something of a distinctive pattern.

Styles Can Change

This leads us to our second set of conclusions: for most parties concerned, the mix has often changed widely over time. The English and later the British, for example, were known for centuries for their brutal repression of uprisings and resistance of all sorts. What collective memory in Ireland, Wales, Scotland or India (and Americans whose ancestors fled Ireland and Britain because they loathed the English/British regime) has preserved as the hallmark of any English/British way of COIN is brutal repression. This tradition was prevalent until (at least) the Amritsar Massacre of 1919 provoked a public outcry at home, arguably producing a catharsis in the thinking of the British public about what Britain's colonial forces were doing in its Empire, preparing the ground for a significant change of heart. Others trace the change of heart further back, arguing that Amritsar was so shocking to the British at home because it constituted a departure from what was assumed by then to be the norm of a more humanitarian approach (later to be subsumed under 'minimum force' and 'hearts and minds').[91] The latter position is difficult to uphold in the light of the suffering of civilians in the Boer War, which impressed the newspaper-reading world. One could argue in the opposite direction that the negligence and incompetence of the resettlement of local populations in Britain's campaign against the Mau Mau in Kenya with a horrendous outcome of mass fatality – in principle not very

---

[89] See Chapters 4 and 5.   [90] See Chapters 10 and 13.

[91] R. Thornton, 'The British Army and the Origins of Its Minimum Force Philosophy', *Small Wars & Insurgencies*, 15/1 (Spring 2004), 83–106; but see also N. Lloyd, 'The Amritsar Massacre and the Minimum Force Debate', *Small Wars & Insurgencies*, 21/2 (June 2010), 382–403.

different from what was done successfully in Malaya – stood in the tradition of the badly-run British concentration camps in the Boer War with their shockingly high fatality figures.

There does, however, seem to be a shift towards a gentler approach to COIN in Britain broadly speaking after the Second World War, even if our understanding of this more recent British 'hearts and minds' model must be adjusted to give more credit to the involvement of civilian organs alongside the military.[92] Significantly, however, the British never seem to have developed a standard operational procedure that was applied across the board. Where they did copy their own previous measures – such as population resettlements, whether in concentration camps or new villages – this sometimes worked, and sometimes went catastrophically wrong. Even their ability to learn and adapt within a spell of COIN operations, once praised by US commentators,[93] was at least initially not much in evidence in Iraq or Afghanistan.

A similar picture of radical changes in COIN emerges in France. Like most European monarchies in the Middle Ages and Early Modern times, the French were merciless and bloodthirsty in their suppression of uprisings or anything that could be interpreted as such. But a transition can be seen at the latest from the time of the French Revolution, which contained within itself the paradox of both the 'Totalitarian Democracy'[94] and the humanitarian ideals of benefitting all mankind. Accordingly, the French Republican government's COIN in the Vendée took two different forms, one cruel and repressive – exemplified by the killing of the entire population of villages by the 'infernal columns' of General Kellermann – and one taking a tolerant hearts-and-minds approach, championed by General Hoche. The subsequent French history of COIN – both at home and in Empire and colonies abroad – has been interpreted elsewhere in terms of this dualist approach, on the one hand the brutal Kellermann strategy (soon to be followed by Napoleon's forces in Spain, and then by veterans of the anti-guerrilla COIN like Bugeaud in Algeria), on the other the Hoche approach, more sympathetic to the local populations, a tradition later ascribed to Gallieni and Lyautey.[95] Jacques Frémeaux and Bruno Reis show[96] that the Gallieni-Lyautey approach in

---

[92] See Chapter 2.
[93] Most recently and famously argued by J. Nagl, *Learning to Eat Soup with a Knife: Experiences of Malaya and Vietnam* (Chicago: University of Chicago Press, 2002).
[94] J. L. Talmon, *The Origins of Totalitarian Democracy* (London: Secker & Warburg, 1952).
[95] J. Gottman, 'Bugeaud, Gallieni, Lyautey: The Development of French Colonial Warfare', in E. Meade Earle (ed.), *Makers of Modern Strategy* (Princeton, NJ: Princeton University Press, 1941).
[96] See Chapter 3.

fact consisted of both carrot and stick, and that this mix can be traced throughout the era of France's Algerian wars. Nevertheless, the emphasis on the benevolent exportation of the acquis of French civilisation (a package including democracy, education, health care, the construction of infrastructure, human rights, etc) by and by became a particular characteristic of the French way of COIN. Indeed, the faith in the benign spreading of this acquis like an oil-slick (the famous *'tache d'huile'* approach of Lyautey) came to be admired or even emulated by other democracies confronted with analogous tasks. Having originated, one might argue, in a particular French articulation of values, it became an example of cultural transfer. David Johnson has illustrated, however, that similar beliefs – albeit often minority beliefs – that insurgents can be turned into friends by imbuing them with American values also go back to the nineteenth century.[97]

After this long period of two competing approaches, we can observe a big change. It is striking how France – after the frustrating experience of the Indochina and last Algerian wars – backed away from state building and confined itself, as far as possible, to COIN operations which were limited in scope and duration, and had no or barely any non-military element. Obviously, this came in a post-colonial context where France itself no longer provided the government against which uprisings took place, but merely supported (mostly) friendly governments against such revolts. But we might see here a tendency in French overseas operations (OPEX) after 1962, a third phase in French COIN history,[98] which is likely to spread to other democratic powers in the coming years, given their frustrating experiences with comprehensive state-building COIN strategies, especially in Iraq and Afghanistan. Washington is not alone in murmuring the mantra of 'No more Afghanistans'.[99]

Because of the nature of the Israeli-Arab conflict, Israel has mostly not attempted to implement a pacification approach of COIN, with the exception of Moshe Dayan's policy towards the Gaza Strip and the West Bank in the years following the Six Day War.[100] Instead, the IDF has maintained a policy of deterrence against insurgents and neighbouring countries in order to ensure Israel's security. Large-scale retaliatory measures were conducted in the 1950s against infiltrators, initially targeting civilians but soon after shifting to more state-affiliated targets such as public buildings.

---

[97] See Chapter 6.   [98] Martin, 'From Algiers to N'Djamena'.   [99] See Chapter 6.
[100] E. Shamir, 'From Retaliation to Open Bridges: Moshe Dayan's Evolving Approach toward the Population in Counter Insurgency', *Civil Wars*, 14/1 (2012), 63–79.

We thus see ample evidence that the conduct of irregular war by individual states and also insurgent movements underwent change. In recent decades, as terrorism has become more deadly, Israel has adopted a more offensive strategy. It relies on accurate intelligence on the one hand and on the tradition of small-unit 'pursuit' warfare in the IDF on the other hand. Since the first Intifada, Israel has adopted attrition as a strategy in order to avoid direct conflict with Palestinian population. Additionally, following the pressure and cost associated in controlling populations, Israel has favoured disengagement from hostile population when possible, as in south Lebanon and the Gaza Strip and the construction of a separation barrier in the West Bank. Against terrorist groups located in disengaged regions, posing a bigger threat than before, the IDF has concluded a 'mowing the grass' approach, aiming to deter Palestinian militants with short-term military operations targeted specifically at the insurgents, their weapons systems and ammunitions depots. This strategy cannot solve the problem but merely maintains the status quo. Its limitations were demonstrated in the operations in Gaza in 2012 and 2014 where after much destruction and death (including of civilians) very little was achieved politically for either side.

Change can result from a learning process from own disasters (see, e.g., Russia's lessons from Chechnya).[101] Other lessons might be learnt, but again forgotten, because there has been a preference within a state to conclude from past disasters that this sort of engagement must be avoided altogether. But we have also given evidence of a transfer of lessons, from state to state, from insurgency movement to insurgency movement, across boundaries. Individuals such as David Galula and Roger Trinquier were the chief vehicles of such transfers.[102]

At present we see a convergence of British, French and American towards a reluctance to intervene in intractable situations (Syria), or to intervene only in operations limited in time and quantity and quality – namely to the military arm (Mali, against ISIS), or to furnish weapons and air support, and otherwise to rely on the locals to battle it out (thus the support for the Kurds against the Islamic Caliphate fighters). Diffidence as to the extent to which one can export Western values and civilisation is growing; the belief that anybody can be turned into 'little Americans', to borrow Robert Ramsey's phrase,[103] is losing ground.

In this context, we must make a methodological point. On the one hand we have identified tools that are used recurrently, and thus patterns

---

[101] See Chapter 4.   [102] See Chapters 6 and 15.   [103] See Chapter 6.

of COIN or insurgencies. On the other, it has become abundantly clear from the examination of our 'small-n' sample of case studies that the complexity of each case rules out utterly any prediction of further cases (n+1). One can make some limited predictions on how individual societies will behave in the near future, given their own track records and the evolution of larger trends around them. However, hypothesis testing of a primitive kind (whenever we find this independent variable X then this dependent variable Y will be Z) and monocausal explanations are entirely inappropriate in so complex an area of enquiry. For example, while the US proclivity to resort to the use of fire power at a distance, e.g. in bombing ISIL or using drones in Afghanistan, is in keeping with past US proclivities, the atrocities committed by American soldiers in Abu Graib Prison in Afghanistan were not predictable. While there is an inner logic as to why the German military involvement in Afghanistan was so extremely pussy-footed and why the accidental killing of civilians in an air strike on the Kunduz River in 2009 ordered by a German officer became a scandal that put Germany's entire participation in ISAF at risk, it could not have been predicted nor from previous German behaviour in the Second World War (see Chapter 7), nor from the behaviour of other militaries. Both examples were unintended deviations from stated policy and strategy, one at worst emanating from an organisational sub-culture out of tune with the over-all values of the country, the other an error of misinformed judgement. This is not to deny that both incidents had major strategic and policy repercussions, and ultimately influence how a supposed 'national style' is perceived by others, but how a nation is seen is not necessarily how it is.

Have All Sides Become More Humane?

So far, we can go along with the American psychologist Stephen Pinker's argument that Western powers – at any rate Britain, France, Italy, Spain, not to mention the former European neutral states with their enduring proclivity to see all involvement in war as evil, and perhaps even America – have become 'nicer', more humane.[104] This would also be confirmed by the total transformation of the German approach, which went from utter excesses of brutality in the first half of the twentieth century, culminating in the conduct of COIN on the eastern and southern fronts of the Second World War, to a total absten- tion from engaging in any military operations, only very gradually

---

[104] S. Pinker, *The Better Angels of Our Nature: Why Violence Has Declined* (New York: Viking Books, 2011).

transmuted in recent years into hesitant co-operation in UN-sanctioned multilateral interventions. It would also explain, however, not just how, but why, democracies often lose small wars.[105]

Thus our chapters on China and Russia show that this far from being a universal phenomenon, which in large part falsifies Pinker's findings. At best what can be said is that Russia and China in recent years have not faced insurgencies on the scale witnessed up to the 1950s, but the older patterns of brutality, on a much larger scale than practised by other powers, still seem to hold.[106]

Indeed, there have been cases in which extreme violence, cruelty and repression led to long-term success for COIN forces, from the brutal Roman repression of the Iceni revolt in 60 CE, to the two-pronged approach of violence against the adversaries and wooing of the neutral and conservative population applied by the Greek government in the Greek Civil War,[107] but also by the victorious insurgents, as one should call them, of General Francisco Franco and his Fascist movement in Spain. There seems to be a clear correlation between extremely authoritarian regimes and such approaches. It goes well beyond the scope of this book to comment on the success of such measures, but it is difficult to think of cases where extreme repression did not lead to mass trauma that would come to haunt later generations, as even the cases of Greece and Spain illustrate.

More generally, while Liberal Democracies with a commitment to human rights clearly do have difficulties 'winning' small wars in the sense of eradicating insurgent movements and lastingly pacifying the country under a stable, law-abiding government, we cannot think of examples where extreme repression has been the ticket for long-term pacification either, unless we count in total extermination, the genocide of whole native tribes. Nor does brutality bode well for the establishment, in the long term, for post-bellum good-neighbourly relations between secessionists and the state that previously exercised authority over them. It may be the way (or even reluctant choice) of that culture to wage war, but it does not follow that it is the way to lasting pacification – if that is what the state aims for, and not a continuous conflict, to justify its own powers in a state of perpetual emergency.[108]

---

[105] G. Merom, *How Democracies Lose Small Wars: State, Society, and the Failures of France in Algeria, Israel in Lebanon, and the United States in Vietnam* (Cambridge: Cambridge University Press, 2003).

[106] See Chapters 4 and 5.   [107] See Chapter 13.

[108] A process called 'securitization' by the Copenhagen school of International Relations, see Barry Buzan, Ole Wæver and Jaap de Wilde: *Security: A New Framework for Analysis* (Boulder: Lynne Rienner, 1998).

By contrast, but probably due to their ability to signal a perpetual state of emergency (and 'revolution'), a number of insurgent movements have managed to establish themselves and cling to power over decades, despite (in part) resorting to extremely brutal practises. These would include the Soviet Communists, Mao's Communist Party, the North Korean Communists and the Kim dynasty, the Vietnamese Communist Party, and Franco's Fascists, curiously themselves all born out of rebellions against an existent regime. Most of these regimes have long fallen, washed away by the tide of globalisation. It is questionable whether similar authoritarian regimes with brutally repressive past and present tendencies will be able to hold out against a tide of information about how others live spreading through the cybersphere, however much they have tried to contain them. There lies hope, then, in the convergence of cultures which globalisation may in part bring. Such hope lay initially in the 'Arab Spring', a tide of unprecedented insurgencies aimed against authoritarian regimes in a number of Arab countries, facilitated by old and new media.

But the 'Arab Spring' has given way to an 'Islamist Winter' with the resurgence of religious extremism, especially, if not only, in the Middle East.[109] Nor is there much evidence that insurgency movements have become humanely respectful of human rights the world over, as a glance at the Taliban in Afghanistan, ISIS in Iraq, the Lord's Resistance Army in Uganda, or the various factions contesting the central government in Libya or South Sudan shows. We must dampen our expectations by remembering just how capable even advanced civilisations are of turning their backs on reason and progress, and towards more credulous, emotion-, dogma- and superstition-driven world views. The resilience of habits and rules excused by reference to religions, and their immunity to arguments of practicality, health, not to mention human rights, should serve as a warning: different approaches to violence and the value of the individual human being, and his or her essential rights, persist. This is hardly a feature of 'national' style, more a 'clash of civilisations'. It contains the danger that the initially more humane side gradually lowers its standards, becoming more and more like that which it tries to combat, or thinks it can pull up the drawbridge of its indefensible cloud cuckoo castle, be it the EU or *Fortress America* (not to mention, post-Brexit Britain).

---

[109] Articles by Hussain Abdul Hussain, David Schenker, and Michael J. Totten: 'Arab Spring or Islamist Winter?', *World Affairs* (Jan/Feb. 2012). See Chapter 14.

Index